HARPER'S UNIVERSITY

THE BEGINNINGS

THE UNIVERSITY OF CHICAGO

HARPER'S UNIVERSITY
The Beginnings

by Richard J. Storr

Drawings by Virgil Burnett

CHICAGO AND LONDON

THE UNIVERSITY OF CHICAGO PRESS

Library of Congress Catalog Card Number: 66-13890

The University of Chicago Press, Chicago & London
The University of Toronto Press, Toronto 5, Canada

© 1966 by the University of Chicago. All rights reserved
Published 1966. Printed in the United States of America

Designed by John B. Goetz

To the Memory of Harold H. Swift

Preface

A university is no man's possession. Physically a school may be the investment of a proprietor, and it may sometimes be identified with its master because it expresses his thought and will; but a university is something more than an exalted school. The University of Chicago belonged neither to its Founder nor to its first President. Yet precisely because the Founder refused categorically to treat the University as if it were his property, the President could attempt on his part to make his ideal university a reality. Out of his work there arose a tradition that the University of Chicago was in some sense his. Although the ideal was not wholly realized and the tradition lacks complete reliability, the fact remains that in the actual University, distinct from both the institution projected and the work of the first President remembered, the life of a man and the affairs of a university did fuse. But how and to what effect? The early history of the University may throw a light across the possibilities of academic life, upon a portion of American history, and also into a corner of human nature.

It is impossible for the author of a book such as this to make full acknowledgment of the assistance he has received. In conversation or through the pages of the literature on higher education in the United States, innumerable persons have provided facts and ideas which have influenced the writing of this book.

The responsibility for defects in the combined effect of these contributions is of course entirely mine. I stand in particular debt to the Trustees and officers of the University of Chicago for granting me unrestricted access to the papers of the University on the sole understanding in regard to their use that I should draw upon them to write a book covering significant aspects of the history of the University. The terms of the license could not have been more generous, or more stimulating: they were prepared in 1952 by Lawrence A. Kimpton, then Chancellor of the University, and the late R. Wendell Harrison, Vice President and Dean of Faculties, in consultation with the late Harold H. Swift of the Board of Trustees. I am also deeply grateful to Mr. David Rockefeller and to Mr. Joseph W. Ernst, archivist in the office of the Rockefeller family and its associates. That office possesses documents that are indispensable to an understanding of the early history of the University. The collaborative effort which made the establishment of the University possible found its reflection in the opportunity offered me to make copious use of the papers in Chicago and New York.

Some essential letters and memoranda by persons who served the University in academic and administrative posts are available because members of their several families have placed collections of personal papers beside the official records in the University archives. The papers of two members of the original faculty appeared most opportunely: I refer to the papers of Ernest D. Burton, Professor of New Testament Literature and Exegesis and third President of the University, presented by his daughter, Miss Margaret Burton, and the papers of John Ulric Nef, Professor of Chemistry, presented by his son, Professor John U. Nef. More recently, the scrapbooks and correspondence of Amos Alonzo Stagg have been given to the University. (Other collections of papers are listed in the introductory paragraph to *Notes,* with a key to abbreviated titles.)

A number of colleagues have given me their assistance. It was fortunate that Professor William T. Hutchinson read a large portion of the manuscript as it was originally being given shape; his masterly criticism has had much to do with determining the proportions of the whole. Mr. Emery T. Filbey and Dean R. Wendell Harrison measured the manuscript against their knowledge of the University and their experience in conducting its affairs; and Mr. Robert Rosenthal, Curator of Special Collections and University archivist, and the members of his staff will, I trust, see the evidence of their help everywhere in this book. For freedom from administrative cares I am indebted to my colleagues Walter

Johnson and William H. McNeill, Chairmen of the Department of History during the period when this book was being written; to Chauncy D. Harris and D. Gale Johnson, Deans of the Division of the Social Sciences; and to Edward H. Levi, Provost of the University. Miss Marie Moe, Assistant to the Dean, and the secretaries of the Department of History smoothed away many practical difficulties. Over a period of years, research assistants have given me invaluable help in the day-to-day routine of research and have also provided me with a running commentary upon the import of that research. My assistants have been James S. Counelis, Marianne Drott, Judith Binyon Farnell, Victor C. Ferkiss, Karl Gunther, Vincent G. Harding, Robert L. Jetter, George M. Joseph, Vera Laska, John O. Liebert, William W. McGrew, Earl G. Medlinsky, Ruth F. Necheles, William R. Savage, Selwyn K. Troen, William R. Usellis, and Anne Wilson Vanderhoof. Mrs. Mary E. Lottmann, an alumna of the University, acted as an assistant when research was just beginning. Owing more to the quality of their help than to their long service, Miss Necheles and Mr. Medlinsky gave me assistance for which thanks in print are even less adequate than they usually are. Miss Drott and Mr. Troen helped greatly in the penultimate tasks of getting the manuscript ready for the University Press. Mrs. Jean F. Block has also given me indispensable assistance. The attention which my wife has paid to the final preparation of the manuscript is but the most recent of the contributions which she has made to the writing of this book and which perhaps only the wives and families of scholars can fully appreciate. My thanks to my wife, without whose help this book would never have been written: the words have become a seeming formula only because they have long expressed most simply the simple truth.

R. J. S.

April 1966

Contents

xi

Contents

 Illustrations

List of Illustrations

Introduction

Like Oxford in its valley, Cambridge near the fens, and Harvard just above tidal waters, the University of Chicago is built upon low ground, the inshore bottom of the glacial lake that became Lake Michigan. Here the Sunday gardener, digging in his backyard, will turn up sand if he does not handle his spade gently. The surface of the land is broken only by the railroad elevation that lies like a perforated dike between the University and the lake to the east. A garland of morainal hills to the west and south lies out of sight: beyond is the prairie. Just the names of streets, Stony Island and Blue Island, remind one of the southern knolls where the lake receded, leaving marshland, before the beginning of settlement; and to the north, the view is cut off by industrial haze and the jagged silhouettes of the Loop. So the University stands where the eminences have been the works of man—smokestacks; office buildings; apartment houses; church spires; for the summer of 1893, the Ferris Wheel; and for the rest of time, by warrant of the "Alma Mater," the towers of the University.

> The City White hath fled the earth,
> But where the azure waters lie,
> A nobler city hath its birth,
> The City Gray that ne'er shall die.

Although the greenery of the neighborhood relieves the eye grown tired of watching soot increase that grayness, and the occasional cawing of crows calls back memory to vacations in the country, nature seems very far away. Yet even as the author of the "Alma Mater" called the University a city, he slipped into the metaphor of living things. A university had been born rather than constructed, and in the course of its history it was to escape death rather than the disintegration that levels deserted cities.

But the words of an academic hymn are no guarantee against mortality: the history of a university may well be an obituary. Although (obviously) the University of Chicago did not die, the early condition of its material health worried its officers and friends as much as its academic achievements gratified them. The young University—in myth, a golden boy—would have lacked daily nourishment if the founder, John D. Rockefeller, had not served also as foster parent; and the stripling might well have collapsed under the strain of over-exertion if the first President of the University, William Rainey Harper, had forced its growth much faster than he did. Rockefeller and Harper, with scores of other persons, made—and might have unmade—the University; it owed its being and development to the processes of human rather than natural history. It *grew* only metaphorically, under the hands of men and women who sought to create an institution, as the Chicago architects did a new form of building, by conscious exercise of man's capacity for design. Working often in concert but also in the presence of great options and sometimes at cross-purposes, the creators of the University resorted constantly to negotiation. It was the particular tool of their métier. As Frederick T. Gates, another organizer of the University, recalled years after the founding, the conferring that preceded it was conducted mainly by letter because Rockefeller, Harper, Gates, and their associates lived in widely separated places. The correspondence was voluminous, "from the point of view of the historian . . . a most fortunate circumstance"; and it was notably frank. Consequently—here Gates anticipated the experience of the fortunate historian—it is possible to trace not only the events that led up to the founding of the University but "even the progress of thought in those who had to do with it." And a like record survives for the administration of President Harper. Reconstructing twenty years of conference, with the circumstances in which it took place, we see an institution coming to have—the imagery of nature is inescapable—a life of its own.

PART ONE

THE FOUNDING

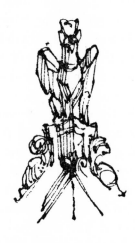

In the Beginning:
The Phoenix

In heraldry, that heirloom of the age when universities were new, the University of Chicago is represented by a phoenix. The University was founded nearly a generation after the Chicago Fire and has never burned in a fire of its own, as have Swarthmore, Wellesley, William and Mary, and how many other colleges; but it did rise from ashes—the intangible debris of a gutted dream. In 1857, an institution bearing the same name as the present University began preparatory instruction and shortly thereafter became a college. Its auspices were Baptist, but its government and sources of support were not exclusively denominational. In 1858, Stephen A. Douglas deeded the University ten acres of land to the west of Cottage Grove Avenue and a little north of Thirty-fifth Street, where construction of a building, designed somewhat in the style of the Water Tower, had already begun.* The University immediately borrowed $25,000 against its property and subsequently secured other large loans until in 1876 its debts were funded in a $150,000 five-year trust deed (or mortgage), given to a creditor, an insurance company, at 8 per cent interest, payable semiannually. All interest or principal not paid on schedule was to bear 10 per cent interest. Because the University was unable to extinguish its indebtedness, which increased as unpaid interest accumulated, the trust deed

* The site of the campus was close to the plot, just west of the Illinois Central tracks, where the Douglas monument now stands.

was foreclosed, after prolonged litigation, and instruction stopped in 1886. "We can say for the Baptists of America," wrote the editor of the denominational paper in Chicago, "that they will never again try to build up a great institution of learning upon borrowed money." And again: "Anything is better than to borrow money, whatever the exigency, . . . in a way to imperil the trust."[1]

The University had indeed jeopardized its trust—and consequently any hope of becoming great—by anticipating greatness. In court, the governors of the University were caught between disparate fidelities, one to their cause and the other to contract. They virtually asked for leave to step back from an intolerable present and to remake the financial history of the University. Acknowledging an obligation in equity to return the money actually received plus interest charges at 6 per cent (or a total sum of approximately $156,000 as against nearly $300,000 awarded the insurance company under the terms of the trust deed), the Trustees fought settlement by foreclosure. Presumably with the sole intention of forcing the insurance company to accept a negotiated settlement, the lawyers for the University argued that it had exceeded its powers when it gave the trust deed: it was therefore an invalid contract. When the court ruled that the insurance company did have a full claim against the University under the instrument, the University was left entirely vulnerable. The attorneys for the company saw naked repudiation, the more outrageous because of its particular authorship:

This institution professes to stand for the great Baptist church of America! An ordinary uncircumcised sinner who expects, in the next world, the *quantum meruit* of his deserts, would not dare do such a thing. It is reserved for the elect, the predestinate, the foreordained, to borrow other people's money . . . and then repudiate the debt, and still to believe *that such election will not be contested.*[2]

That charge was the terrible interest on defeat. It was overwhelming, the *Chicago Daily News* asserted; but the shock to morale was even more disastrous. "It looks now as though the university had lost not only its property but its character."[3] The thrust went to the quick. In a general convention, the Baptists of Chicago disavowed any disposition to criticize the management of the University or to impeach its integrity of purpose but then declared: "We deem it due to ourselves to say that we utterly deprecate anything that savors of repudiation, and greatly regret that any action should ever have been taken that should have ever seemed to give color to such suspicion."[4]

Its existence accentuated the humiliation of the fall of the University, making it appear indeed a fall from grace; but the legal tactics of a last desperate defense had not alone compromised the educational interests of the Baptists in Chicago. The building plans of the University had been pretentious, the pseudo-Gothic hall being the academic counterpart of a plunger's extravagant house, his folly; and the financial arrangements devised to support those plans had been inherently speculative, however noble in purpose. The foreclosure of the trust deed seems but the predictable end of a prodigal life—the last act of a gaslit melodrama about a debtor's ruin or, more profoundly, a tragedy of harsh but just retribution. The very appropriation of "university" seems a sign of *hubris,* hardly mitigated, in light of available resources, by the desire of the University to attract Ph.D. candidates.[5] Yet the usage was conventional in the United States. Inflated nomenclature and shaky financing were inseparable from the enterprise that has characterized American education. Its general progress has required willingness to take risks; and how, except by hindsight, is the heel-and-toe pace of bold but sound management to be distinguished in particular instances from needlessly cautious shuffling or running out of control? After the event, it was easy to see that the old University of Chicago had moved dangerously fast; for it did trip and break its neck— and was booed for committing a foul. Before the foreclosure, however, a supporter of the University might well have said, yes, we are taking serious risks, but daring is a virtue. The second University of Chicago would test that proposition.

In 1885 and just after, a few Baptist laymen, several ministers of Chicago churches, the editor of the denominational paper, and officers of the Baptist seminary in suburban Morgan Park attempted to salvage the old University and to vindicate its record. The standard engine of meetings, exhortations, resolutions, and solicitations was put in motion; but the Baptist community hardly stirred. Its lethargy bore witness to a loss of confidence that made a mockery of rhetoric and nullified the practical initiative of the denominational leaders. Presently a party among them gave up thought of resuscitating the old University and began to advocate a new departure. A college would be built on a site free of old associations, perhaps away from the city. (Long since, the Methodists had founded Northwestern University in Evanston, and the Presbyterians had founded Lake Forest University in the suburb of that name.) On October 1, 1886, three prominent Baptists approached the Blue Island Land and Building Company, which owned land in Morgan Park and was improving the property for residential use. In a classic pattern of town

5

development—and perhaps because the owner had once been a Baptist—the company sought to encourage the promoters of the college by offering twenty acres of land and other assets on condition that they secure $100,000 toward endowment and erect a building and open the school not later than September, 1888. (The deadline was to be extended.) The offer helped to inspire more organizing and planning, but very little money came in sight. With a few exceptions, the laity remained passive, and one by one, the leaders, lacking a following at home, looked beyond the city for help.[6]

The most persevering advocate of the new cause was Thomas Wakefield Goodspeed, one of the three who had turned to the Blue Island Company. A man of deep loyalties, Goodspeed had studied for three years at the old University before training for the ministry at the Baptist seminary in Rochester, New York. He returned to Chicago just as the city was recovering from the Great Fire. In 1873, he became a trustee of the Morgan Park seminary, which was in such bad condition financially that the chairman of the board thought it should be closed. After finding money in his own congregation, Goodspeed was asked by his fellow trustees to become a fund-raiser—only temporarily, they said; and he left his church, but to remain permanently in the service of higher education. As agent of the seminary, he had been exploring the financial resources of the Chicago Baptist community for ten years at the time the old University closed.[7] In January, 1887, Goodspeed broached a program for what would now be called the development of the prospective college. His premise was quickly put but full of implicit history: "We cannot afford a failure." The Baptists were greatly discouraged, he wrote, by the destruction of the old University, but if a friend would put $50,000 or $100,000 into endowment, they would rally. The initial gift could be doubled, and the University would be vigorous, self-supporting, growing from the outset. Once it had been put on its feet with ample grounds—Goodspeed had the land offer in mind—two buildings, a library, and endowment, it would never perish. Money would come to the University, students would multiply, new departments would be added; and the University would speedily grow into the greatest of Baptist institutions. As a matter of fundamental principle, debt was to be avoided; and every dollar secured should be invested until the University had a broad basis of productive funds to build on.[8] Goodspeed, the fund-raiser and projector of a new University, was addressing John D. Rockefeller.

CHAPTER I

"These Terrible Truths"

At one end of Hutchinson Hall, until lately the Commons of the University of Chicago, hangs a portrait by Eastman Johnson of John D. Rockefeller. Were the subject unidentified, the picture might be labeled "Portrait of a Gentleman with His Mail": a lean-faced but not emaciated man with a slightly drooping mustache has just looked up from his reading. The gaze is serious but not inquisitive, cool but not forbidding, reserved but not awesome—above all, it is direct. So Rockefeller must have sat in New York as he pondered letters from Chicago; and so he must have appeared to his callers—courteous, ready to listen, initially non-committal, and always self-possessed. In 1887, Rockefeller was in his late forties. He had already established both an extraordinary fortune, derived largely from Standard Oil, and the habit of charitable giving; but he had not entered philanthropy upon the grand scale. Unlike Leland Stanford, he had not lost a son bearing his name and paternal hopes; and unlike Ezra Cornell, he did not seek a second vocation in the daily supervision of university-building. Although he was not, as Thorstein Veblen later intimated, "of the untutored sort,"[1] he had not attended either a college or a university and so had neither an alma mater to assist nor any reason to feel personally indebted to higher education. Over generations, many men of wealth and philanthropic intentions had chosen to act by last will and testament—as Johns Hopkins did to conspicuous effect. Yet Rockefeller was a devout Baptist, and he was prepared to listen while his co-religionists discussed plans for immediate action.

John D. Rockefeller was a man of conscience who strove to be both a good churchman and a good businessman. If he observed any incompatibility between the implications of "good" in religion and in business, he gave no sign of it. His good works would not be undertaken in expiation of sin, as the Social Gospel would define it, but rather in response to the imperatives of his orthodox faith, specifically to that of Christian stewardship. The Baptist manual current during Rockefeller's youth declared it an error to consider the relinquishment of property a free gift that entitled the giver to credit in his account with God. Man's bounties were, strictly speaking, the Lord's, who committed them to human *trust,* with obligations not only of gratitude but also of *service.* Every righteous man was obliged to ask himself: "How MUCH *do I owe to my Lord?*" The answer required "the most impartial and prayerful investigation."[2]

Rockefeller approached his Christian duty much as he conducted business. Part of its essence was economy—not penny-pinching but precise adjustment of means to ends. A dollar or a great investment received equal respect as wealth to be accounted for; each represented either an exact quantum of accomplishment or so much potential lost. The commitment of either to a particular purpose had to be preceded by rigorous, objective scrutiny of potential merit. Large projects required correspondingly large aggregates of capital but justified neither carelessness nor waste in the disposition of the parts, however small. In the Rockefeller office at 26 Broadway, the princely gesture, made without calculation of costs, received no applause and sentimentality had no voice. Yet refusal to act impulsively and the habit of attending to detail obviously did not preclude enterprise of virtually imperial scope. To create Standard Oil, Rockefeller had to devise and carry forward grand strategies, and he had to delegate an enormous amount of responsibility. What he sought was a combination of large plans and the men capable of putting them into effect in fields where he himself could not exercise expert judgment. Comparably, great philanthropy would be designed not to palliate special cases of distress but remove its general causes. It would require the services of highly talented executives, men who would be more the colleagues than the legmen of the donor. Business as Rockefeller knew it also possessed a capacity for indefinite growth, under alert and adaptable management. So, too, philanthropy would seek out those opportunities which, once seized, created fresh opportunity. Rockefeller practiced a kind of pragmatism, although the exponents of the formal doctrine might not have recognized him as the embodiment of their principles. Before taking a step forward, he explored the ground ahead, and if it appeared to be sound, he moved decisively. Before taking another step, he would appraise whatever had been accomplished, and, if it seemed productive, he would look ahead again; if not, he shifted course. In short, he was a man of vision but not of visions. Hypothetical situations did not interest him, but he was alert to the possibilities of the present and the foreseeable future.[3]

Here was the first question: how was a Baptist businessman to diagnose the ills of his time and make a choice between cures? Traditionally the Baptist community was highly decentralized, having neither priestly hierarchy nor synod to give direction to good works. At the time of Rockefeller's birth there had indeed been many individual churches that resisted the growth of any kind of national Baptist organization; and throughout his life there existed some tension between the ideal of independent churches and the practical need for general agencies to manage activities which extended beyond the limits of single congregations. All the same, the Baptists had created several national societies for the promotion and management of particular interests. One of these was the American Home Mission Society, concerned largely with spreading the Baptist faith in the West and among Negroes, Indians, and foreign-language groups. Although the Society spent most of its funds in the work of preaching and church-building, it also helped to subsidize struggling educational institutions, particularly colleges. For in the eighties the denomination had no agency charged principally with the care of its educational interests. In 1868 an educational commission had been instituted, but it was allowed to perish.[4] By default, responsibility for the colleges fell into the hands of the Home Mission Society.

In 1887, the corresponding secretary (i.e., chief executive officer), Henry Morehouse, inserted three foresighted paragraphs in his annual report. There was a feeling prevalent in the West as in the East, Morehouse wrote, that each Christian denomination should have its own educational institutions. Some denominations had recently organized societies which made it possible to plan for a vast region. The Baptists had no such organization and no comprehensive plan; the establishment of schools was left solely to individual action. Perhaps the owner of a town site would offer land for a campus and a few thousand

9

dollars would be pledged for buildings, a high-sounding name would be decided upon, trustees selected, resolutions passed by some local Baptist association, and thereafter the institution would be said to have claims upon the denomination. Without endowment and with small tuition fees, the school could be maintained only by contributions from churches, most of which were feeble and largely dependent upon the Home Mission Society for the support of their pastors. The result was obvious. Again and again these educational enterprises had made such drafts upon mission churches as to retard their progress toward self-support; and the Society became indirectly the financial helper of these institutions. Sometimes an agent would be appointed; and his urgent appeals would divert funds from missionary work. And not uncommonly, after a few years of painful struggling, the institution ceased to be. Early death or lingering misery was the usual lot of institutions prematurely started with but a small and feeble constituency to nourish them. Was it not time for the denomination to have a defined policy and better methods in matters of such importance as the establishment of denominational schools in the West? Should the Home Mission Society continue to act as the general educational society of the American Baptists in the western fields? Was there not need for an organization whose attention should be given to these affairs —an organization to advise what should be done, when, where, and how it should be done, and to render needful assistance in doing it?[5]

At the annual meeting of the Society in 1887, Morehouse offered several resolutions calling for the appointment of a committee to consider the advisability of forming an American Baptist Education Society. If it seemed desirable to effect its organization, the committee would issue a call for the purpose and prepare a constitution. Although the plan was not universally popular, most notably among eastern Baptists, the resolutions were adopted. The committee called for a national educational convention, to be held in connection with the anniversaries (or annual meetings) of the established Baptist societies. After Morehouse had marshaled forces to support the movement, the convention launched the American Baptist Education Society in May, 1888.[6] Morehouse believed that there were great things to be accomplished by the Baptists in educational work before the end of the century—things to be done in a manner to arouse the entire denomination to a sense of its obligation and to increase its self-respect and its power for good from the Atlantic to the Pacific.[7]

Morehouse immediately recruited Frederick T. Gates to serve as corresponding secretary of the newly formed society. Gates, then in his mid-thirties, was a graduate of the Rochester Seminary. While there, Gates had been a member of Morehouse's congregation and had conferred with him about entering the ministry. Lately pastor of a Minneapolis church, Gates had succeeded in raising an endowment of $50,000 for a Baptist secondary school in Minnesota. Like Morehouse, Gates was by nature a man of affairs, endowed with sweeping imagination, business acumen of the first order, and a keen eye for facts. Impatient with pointless speechmaking, he possessed a gift for energetic speech. He repeatedly probed generalities for the truth embedded in sentimentality, and sliced away fat to get at the sinew of real policy.[8]

The Chicago proposal was but one of many that American Baptists generated within the field to which Gates was charged to bring order. The span of business of the Society was very wide in point of geography, educational levels, and finance, e.g., the Society granted $1,200 outright to a college in East Tennessee; pledged $5,000 to another college in California on condition that it raise $15,000; decided that still another college, in Iowa, ought to become an academy; and gave attention to a proposal for a $20,000,000 university to be located in New York and open only to college graduates.[9] (The last project was the obsessive dream of Augustus H. Strong, distinguished in his denomination as a theologian and as president of the Rochester Seminary. Strong was also personally acquainted with John D. Rockefeller: in 1889, Charles A. Strong, son of the one man, and Bessie Rockefeller, a daughter of the other, became husband and wife.)

Although Chicago had no special claim upon the resources of the Society, the city immediately attracted Gates's attention. From the time that he accepted office, he may have thought of a great Chicago institution, with feeder academies in nearby states; within his first month of service, he decided that the Society was more urgently needed and had better prospects in Chicago than anywhere else.[10] The speed with which Gates turned his eyes toward Chicago suggests that he may have been prompted. Perhaps Morehouse anticipated Rockefeller support of a college in Chicago; but Rockefeller did not immediately contribute to the Society and, when he did, gave no indication that a particular community should be favored. Yet Chicago itself was an obtrusive fact. According to the census taken just two years after Gates became interested in Chicago, the city had more than trebled in size in two decades and had become the second largest in the United States: the sheer presence of the rising city in the West partly explains the founding of the University.[11]

Entering into Chicago affairs at a time when a committee was being organized to make provisional arrangements for a new college, Gates chose to move quietly: "I am figuring underground. . . ."[12] Although the attitude of Goodspeed, G. W. Northrup, president of the Morgan Park seminary, and Justin A. Smith, editor of the Baptist *Standard,* favorably impressed Gates, he found unsatisfactory the general morale of the Chicago Baptists. The response to a circular, he discovered, did not represent the moneyed men; and the atmosphere of a conference including both ministers and laymen left much to be desired. Members of the conference spoke with a disappointing lack of seriousness and did not exhibit that sort of feeling out of which amid difficulty great things are carried to successful issue. "Besides this," Gates later wrote, "I felt constantly that there was a lack of perfect frankness. One could not be sure that the whole truth was being spoken. One felt that there might be slumbering volcanoes there. I did not observe any tendency to get right down to business and expose the bed rock facts."[13] After private conversations, Gates concluded that men of means among Baptists in and around Chicago were exceedingly distrustful of any attempt to found a college. Some of them said that they would give large sums if the institution could start with a million or so: what was involved in the Morgan Park proposition neither appealed to their pride nor furnished them with the security they demanded. Gates knew that Goodspeed and others had approached Rockefeller, who had declined to take the initiative but had encouraged the hope, Gates believed, that he would do something worthy when he was satisfied that Chicago was behind the effort. Having seen something of "the inside workings," Gates was less hopeful than he had been originally. Gates saw but one path to success, that leading to Rockefeller, but he did not appeal immediately to New York.[14] Morehouse advised Gates to wait until it became evident that two ministerial solicitors were failing to raise funds and that Goodspeed could not persuade Rockefeller to lead off with a large contribution. Then Gates could take a prominent part in the enterprise. Gates himself was diffident but willing to stand ready to act if the Chicago men saw fit to commit the project to the Society.[15]

By the end of July, the way was clear for the Society to take the initiative if it wished. Fearing that a public failure would be irreparably disastrous, Gates sought assurance of success prior to any open commitment by the Society. He planned to conduct "a thorough and prolonged canvass, without a syllable of publicity," among more than one hundred Baptists in Chicago before the Society met to consider adopting the Chicago project and making it national.[16] Gates was certain that quiet persuasion would produce far greater results than a loud proclamation of the project: the latter, thought Gates, would be like flashing powder in the open air instead of shooting to kill.

Gates spoke privately of the Chicago project as the most resistless in appeal of any in years. Since the Chicago men had possessed neither the leisure nor the data to study the question on its merits, Gates believed the case had never been stated with a tithe of what was in it; their failure with Rockefeller and others, including some of the wealthiest Baptists in Chicago, was not conclusive. Gates intended to be "exceedingly cautious," but he was willing to adopt the Chicago project as his primary business and push it through to a happy or a bitter end. The goal for the first year would be $500,000—secured against mortgage—for a university of Chicago to be presented to the denomination in 1889.[17] In succeeding years, the Society would seek to establish a large number of preparatory academies in the West. There was one caution: the Society would not accept the project without the assurance that the Baptists of Chicago would act.[18]

As soon as Goodspeed supplied him with a list of wealthy prospects together with the amount that each ought to give, Gates planned to take hold of the "big end" first, in the hope that the $125,000 necessary to meet the Morgan Park conditions might be raised from about a dozen men. The less affluent were expected to give two or three times their usual donations, once the wealthiest had shown their confidence. For a moment, Gates was tempted to inform Rockefeller of his plans but decided against an immediate approach to New York.[19] Morehouse agreed, saying he was sure that *writing* Rockefeller would accomplish nothing; when Gates could make a good showing of what had been done in and around Chicago, he would gain Rockefeller's confidence and generous support.[20] During the canvass, as it proved, Gates discovered that his expectations had been unrealistic. Although the men less able to give were willing to do their share, the few wealthy Baptists held off.[21]

Having decided to concentrate his efforts for a time in Chicago, Gates felt that to launch new projects elsewhere would be unwise; but before he could report decisive results in Chicago, he did look at Augustus Strong's plan for a great, graduate university in New York. In Gates's opinion, the Baptists were neither prepared educationally for such an institution nor so much hurt by the absence of "supplemental" (i.e., graduate) studies as by deficiencies at the level of the academy and college—deficiencies that obliged a large number of bright but immature men to seek education in non-Baptist institutions. The Strong scheme, Gates believed, would practically destroy the theological seminaries, perhaps to replace them with something much better but in the face of bitter opposition. Even so, Gates was attracted by certain features of the university proposed by Strong, notably its distinctly Christian character and its limitation of admissions to college graduates. Gates suggested that the institution should be not merely a local university but a complete educational system, graded from the home upward, symmetrical in its extension and broad enough to cover the whole land: a Baptist university with its head in New York and its corporate parts extended over the whole land (presumably including a college in Chicago). A scheme so vast, so continental, so orderly, so comprehensive, so detailed would capture the imagination of a Rockefeller.[22] But Morehouse was not captivated. He feared that the Society might lose its integrity by absorption into the university, that Strong wanted the Society to "play tender to his engine." Yet the matter might be put into shape to appeal to Rockefeller: Gates should master the facts to touch him where he had not been touched before.[23]

Gates inquired not only into the facts of Baptist sentiment in Chicago but also into the state of Baptist education in the West and thus pitched his thought between the grandiose planning that Strong's proposal inspired and the negotiation of local affairs in Chicago which offered little promise of yielding a persuasive case for outside support. Looking across the West, Gates searched for precise information and principles upon which policy might be based. His findings were first laid before the Baptist ministers of Chicago on October 15, 1888. Gates had concluded that all American colleges relied chiefly upon local patronage, e.g., 79 per cent of the students at both Brown and Denison lived within one hundred miles of their college. Institutions of learning created the demand for the higher culture which they supplied; and the area of their power, unless they occupied a commanding location, was comparatively circumscribed. Within the West to the Rocky Mountains, the Baptists had eleven institutions of learning which gave instruction in all or nearly all of the branches usually taught in the colleges. The value of the property of these institutions was $831,670; and the total enrolment as of 1887 was 1,257 students. In the same period, the Congregationalists had eight colleges, with property worth $1,743,000, and 1,639 students. As the number of Congregationalists in the West was only 145,000 as against 373,000 Baptists, the Congregationalists had more than five times as much academic property per member as the

Baptists, and in proportion to their membership had nearly four times as many students. The Methodists had twenty-one colleges with $5,303,916 worth of property and 5,652 students—more than six times as much property as the Baptists had and nearly five times as many students.

The geographical coverage by Baptist colleges in the West was no more satisfactory than their resources and enrolments. A circle with a radius of fifty miles drawn around Kalamazoo College encompassed the homes of all but three of its collegiate students; that area was about one-seventh of Michigan. Franklin College drew 70 per cent of its students from one-fourth of Indiana. Shurtleff College, on the western edge of Illinois, received only four Illinois students living outside a half-circle embracing one-fourteenth of the state, and only three students from Missouri. William Jewell College, in western Missouri, derived 70 per cent of its students from one-third of the state and only two from Kansas. These four colleges were the oldest, best known, and largest Baptist institutions in the West and offered nearly all of the collegiate work sponsored by the denomination.

Defining "areas of attractive influence" as those from which colleges derived seven-eighths of their students, Gates found that only one-fifth of the Baptists of the West lived within the area of a Baptist college; conversely, four-fifths of the Baptists lived beyond the horizon of any of the Baptist colleges and received no educational impulse from them. If facilities were provided, the Baptists might educate more than 6,000 instead of 1,257 students. Gates estimated the annual loss to be nearly 5,000 students. (Gates did not say—and perhaps did not stop to consider—that 5,000 places in college would provide for only 1,250 students in each class, given a four-year curriculum.) Gates believed that a majority of the young Baptists were probably not seeking advanced instruction of any kind, while a large minority, numbering perhaps 1,500 and including the ablest and most promising Baptist youth, were attending either the schools of other denominations or what he spoke of as State Higher Schools of Irreligion, a "loss in Christian effectiveness which God only can measure." In addition, the fraction of the Baptist population that existing colleges reached would become smaller every year as the population moved west.

Only six of the eleven Baptist colleges in the West had endowments, a total of $469,000, or an average of $78,156. In comparison, the University of Rochester and Madison University (shortly to be renamed Colgate University) each had about half a million, and Brown had almost a million. The average salary of professors in western Baptist colleges was $1,015. The size of faculties was so limited by poverty that the variety of work necessarily placed on each professor forbade special skill in any department, and the absence of preparatory schools made it necessary for all the Baptist institutions to do their own preparatory work. It should not surprise the Baptists, Gates said, if the classrooms of the western colleges failed to exhibit the range of scholarship, accuracy, and contagious enthusiasm which characterize first-rate work.

Of the 1,257 students in the West, only 285 were enrolled in regular college classes. Ninety-six were women and so could not be included in any comparison with the eastern colleges, which were not coeducational. Of the 189 young men, only 110 were pursuing the full classical course—a number smaller than that of the male classical students at Colby. And 46 per cent of the students in western colleges dropped out before reaching the senior class. In 1887, the nine western colleges from which Gates had gathered relevant figures graduated a total of 21 male classical students. Of these nine were studying for the ministry, one for every 600 western Baptist churches.

If the colleges were young, Gates continued, and if they were planted in strategic educational positions in eleven of the most important and commanding western cities, the Baptists could look forward to a great educational future. But the colleges were neither young nor well-located. That fact, rather than any supposed apathy to education among Baptists or niggardliness in educational giving, was the chief reason for the comparative failure of the denomination. With the possible exception of Des Moines University, the Baptist colleges had been fixed in small towns, surrounded by an impecunious population, far removed from the centers of western life and means, and lying out of the sight and interest of wealthy churchmen. The sources of revenue and endowment were limited to the scanty means of local friends within the narrow field of college influence. The colleges had never been able to unlock the wealth of the cities and drew not half a dozen students from the larger towns. Yet, if growth continued at the rate then current, the West was destined to hold twice as many Baptists as the East and to be the seat of American power.

The first and most important remedy for Baptist needs was to found a great college, ultimately to be a university, in Chicago—

an institution with an endowment of several millions, with buildings, library and other appliances equal to any on the continent; an institution commanding the services of the ablest specialists in every department, giving the highest classical as well as scientific culture, and aiming to counteract the western tendency to a merely superficial and utilitarian education; an institution wholly under Baptist control as a chartered right, loyal to Christ and his church, employing none but Christians in any department of instruction; a school not only evangelical but evangelistic, seeking to bring every student into surrender to Jesus Christ as Lord.[24]

Such an institution should be located in Chicago, Gates argued, because the city was the social, financial, literary, and religious eminence in the West. Chicago was its heart—"the fountain of western life." It was quickly and cheaply accessible: all roads led to Chicago, all cities, all rural homes, faced it. Such an institution, so located, would attract Baptist youth who otherwise would matriculate in state universities or in the colleges of other denominations. The institution would immediately give stimulus and inspiration to all of the Baptist preparatory schools; and even before its foundations were laid and its walls reared, the mere assurance of such an enterprise would lift up the heads of all Baptist colleges and clothe them with renewed vigor and larger influence. No other imaginable work in education would "at once remove so many difficulties, restore so many disaffections, reduce to harmony and order so many chaotic elements, meet needs so wide . . . and so immediate, or confer so large a boon on the cause of Christ in the west." A new university well founded in Chicago would be a lever long enough and strong enough, with the blessing of God, to raise all Baptist interests to a higher plane and multiply the Christian effectiveness of the Baptist church. So Gates ended his case.[25]

The Chicago ministers who heard him were astounded, confounded, dumbfounded, amazed, bewildered, overwhelmed—as Gates reported to Morehouse.

It was these terrible truths about western education, every one pointing to the necessity of a great University at Chicago and that at once, that slew the brethren. The truth has never before been told, but I told it for once without reproach of course and mingled with praise for the heroism and self abnegation of our western educators. I am greatly encouraged believing that a great victory has been won in Chicago from which we shall reap substantial and lasting fruits.[26]

As soon as Gates delivered his paper, Goodspeed asked permission to send it beyond the ministerial circle: "The way has opened today most unexpectedly for me to make I believe effective private use of the facts to advance the cause we have at heart. The paper stirred my heart. I want it to stir another. . . ."[27] Rockefeller had just talked at length with President James M. Taylor, of Vassar College, and with William Rainey Harper, professor at Yale, who was well acquainted with Goodspeed and had written him euphorically of the meeting. Gates's terrible truths about Baptist education in the West might be relayed to Rockefeller through Harper's good and indeed conspicuously energetic offices.

CHAPTER II

A College
for the Metropolis
of the West

Unlike James M. Taylor—or Gates and Goodspeed and, traditionally, most college presidents and many college professors—William Rainey Harper did not enter academic affairs from the ministry: by training and vocation he was a university professor. Harper was born at New Concord, Ohio, in 1856, a year— as it happened—when Americans who sought to create some counterpart of European universities were extraordinarily optimistic. The great American university was not then founded; but long before Harper had graduated from Muskingum College, Yale had instituted the first successful Ph.D. program in the United States. Graduate instruction was being established and the work of the university professor explored while Harper was growing up. He himself entered Yale as a graduate student in 1873, and having written a comparative study of the prepositions in Latin, Greek, Sanskrit, and Gothic, received his doctorate, at the age of eighteen, in 1875—one year before the Johns Hopkins University opened as an institution devoted primarily to graduate studies. In 1875, after having become Doctor Harper—and having turned nineteen— Harper married Ella Paul, daughter of the president of Muskingum, and also assumed responsibility for an educational institution as principal of Masonic College in Macon, Tennessee. According to Thomas W. Goodspeed, who years later became Harper's biographer, it was then that Harper discovered himself:

"He found that he could teach what he knew, in a way that awakened and interested his students and gave delight to himself."[1]

Had Harper been slightly less precocious he would have left Yale just as a set of Hopkins fellowships were drawing young scholars to Baltimore; and had Harper gone to Baltimore he might never have come into the Baptist orbit. Of Scotch-Irish ancestry, he had grown up in Presbyterian surroundings, and did not join the Baptist denomination until after he had begun to serve, in 1876, on the faculty of a Baptist college, Denison University. In 1879, Harper moved to the Baptist seminary in Morgan Park to teach Hebrew, a language to which his mind was ever after to return. His initial writing dealt with the linguistic elements of Hebrew, but his studies pulled him toward the problems and the controversies of the higher criticism. While still a very young man, he became one of the leading Baptist students of the Old Testament. For Christians of his persuasion it was surpassed in relevance to faith and morals only by the New Testament that completed divine revelation. Harper did not doubt that the Bible was indeed holy—uniquely so among books; but he believed, to the perturbation of Augustus H. Strong of the Rochester Seminary, that the words of the Bible, as distinct from the Word of God revealed through the Bible, had been established in the course of a long evolutionary process by men who had not escaped history. The authors of the Old Testament had been divinely inspired, but each spoke in the linguistic, cultural, and religious context of his own time. Critical scholarship would assist the reader of the Bible to find the immutable meaning of God's Will through understanding of its historical expression. Harper was convinced that such Bible study would yield, not skepticism, but a deeper and more nearly universal piety. To the advancement of Hebraic studies he brought not only learned insight and a gift for teaching but also a combination of energy, initiative, and executive ability that enabled him to develop a battery of correspondence and summer-school courses. In 1883, he began to teach during the summer at Chautauqua, where he also became an administrative officer. In 1886, he was asked to salvage the Chicago college that had been called a university; instead he accepted a chair at Yale where his duties included the instruction of graduate students. He had opted for a career in which Chicago, without a university, could have no part; but he kept in touch with the men and the educational interests of the Baptist community in the West.[2]

From New Haven, Harper traveled regularly to Poughkeepsie to give a course on the Bible at Vassar. At the time when Harper met Rockefeller and

Taylor there, Rockefeller's position in the denomination was difficult and perhaps nearly intolerable; for he lived amidst a confusion of supplications without benefit of either the advice or the protection of a professional staff. He was himself obliged to explore the minds of co-religionists experienced in education. Would Washington, D.C., he asked Taylor, be the best place for a university if one were to be founded? The query was pointed because President James C. Welling of Columbian University (now George Washington University) was seeking to realize the even-then old dream of a great university in the national capital. Rockefeller was not clear in his own mind, he indicated, whether aid should be granted for the upbuilding of a large university or for the establishment of colleges. Taylor answered that the smaller colleges of the country were doing more for the denomination than a great institution could do and argued for the necessity of a strong institution in Chicago. Rockefeller seemed to be inclined, Taylor thought, to accept his view of the colleges in general and of Chicago in particular. Taken in conjunction with Taylor's remarks, agreement pointed toward a college rather than a great university in Chicago. Harper gained a different impression of Rockefeller's thought while spending almost thirteen hours in his company on the same week end. Rockefeller was exasperated by the attitude of the Chicago men, apart from that of Goodspeed and George W. Northrup, president of the seminary, but displayed great interest in the Education Society and, to Harper's surprise, talked at length of establishing a great university at Chicago instead of New York. As soon as he saw how the matter struck Rockefeller, Harper lost no opportunity to encourage that interest. He came away confident that the money Rockefeller had proposed to spend in New York (as Harper thought) might be diverted to Chicago.[3]

But as yet Rockefeller had not committed himself to either a college or a university for Chicago. Harper's reading of Rockefeller's thoughts may reveal more about his own nature than about Rockefeller's intentions. Perhaps that week end of conversation was important less as an occasion for Harper to persuade Rockefeller than as an opportunity for Rockefeller to take the measure of Harper's persuasiveness. Nothing in Rockefeller's subsequent actions indicates that the uncertainty that he described in his initial question had been swept away by Harper's words. Rockefeller was not mastered; but he was sufficiently impressed by the prospect in Chicago, by Harper, or by both, to meet Harper again in Poughkeepsie.[4]

In the interval, Gates was uneasy, but Morehouse advised him to do nothing until Rockefeller had had time to read his speech to the Chicago clergy. Even as

Morehouse wrote, the transmission of that paper from Goodspeed to Harper and from Harper to Rockefeller was taking place. It must have been in Rockefeller's hands by the first of November. Although Rockefeller probably had not read the paper when, less than a week later, he and Harper met, Harper gave Rockefeller its gist and came away with the conviction that Rockefeller was practically committed to the Chicago project.[5] "It is absolutely certain that the thing is to be done; it is now only a question as to what scale."[6] The financial and academic dimensions of the projected institution did indeed have to be worked out.

Possibly Rockefeller had a great university in mind, but initially his intentions were revealed to the Chicago men through the refracting prism of Harper's mind. It was Harper who wrote of a great plan calling for a college and university at Chicago, other colleges in the West, and a theological seminary of high grade in New York.[7] Rockefeller himself wanted at once to seek advice from the three Baptist professors who held positions at Cornell and also requested that Goodspeed come to New York.[8] Apropos of that visit, Harper spoke of clinching the Chicago matter more firmly; but Rockefeller made no final and definitive statement. Instead, he asked Goodspeed for his inmost thoughts about the form and dimensions of the Chicago project, so that Goodspeed ceased to be merely a suppliant and became an adviser. He recommended that Rockefeller propose to give outright $1,500,000 and to join in further effort to build the institution when $500,000 had been raised from others. For every $100,000 secured from others, Rockefeller would contribute another $200,000, until a total of $4,000,000 had been reached. Rockefeller's gift—more than three million—was to be paid in ten annual instalments, and the offer was to continue in force for ten years. The program was designed not only to make certain the attainment of the goal but also to secure the largest possible sum from the denomination. To collect that much in ten years, Goodspeed said frankly, would be an almost impossible task which could be completed only under the inspiration of a Rockefeller offer and the pressure of its conditions. If the matching gifts of $200,000 seemed too large, the figure might be reduced to $100,000.[9]

If Goodspeed suggested this alternative out of fear that Rockefeller would find the original proposal too steep, he was acting upon a sound premonition; for Rockefeller did draw back. Harper reported an impression that Rockefeller found the Goodspeed program "a little too much out of proportion," but to Goodspeed Rockefeller himself wrote that he was not prepared to name anything like the sum in Goodspeed's letter.[10] Even so, Rockefeller invited Goodspeed to lunch at his office.[11] Goodspeed's return to Chicago prevented him from accepting the invitation, but he did take it as evidence that Rockefeller was willing to hear more about fund-raising. Goodspeed's next proposal called for an initial gift of $1,000,000 from Rockefeller and matching gifts of $200,000 for every $100,000 secured elsewhere, Rockefeller moneys to be used only for endowment. Goodspeed was not at all sanguine in his hopes that the Baptists would subscribe so much money and took care to caution Rockefeller against expecting too much. Many men with large faith and no experience would say that the money could be raised in twelve months; but Goodspeed, being a man of much experience—if also of large faith—could not ignore such sobering facts as the size of the Brown University endowment, which in more than a century had not reached $1,000,000. "Experience has taught me not to indulge in too large hopes." (Strange thing to write to a prospective donor! Goodspeed, who referred explicitly to the ruin of the old University by great expectations, obviously felt that he was morally bound to write as he did.) Perhaps because he had doubts about the Baptists' readiness to make large pledges, Goodspeed was convinced that Rockefeller's first million should be given unconditionally, to provide from the outset a solid foundation for the enterprise. It would be worth everything to have confidence awakened.[12]

Harper thought that Goodspeed had made a mistake in lowering the size of the initial gift from $1,500,000 to $1,000,000: "You ought not to have lowered the amount. He [Rockefeller] is ready to pledge a million and a half to begin on, and there ought to be no diminution of this amount."[13] Also, six rather than ten years should be the term of the drive. That conflict of judgments could easily have been explained at the time by the differing impressions which the two men may well have had of Rockefeller's reaction to Goodspeed's original proposition. Yet the disagreement between Harper and Goodspeed went beyond the particular case. Through the years to come, Goodspeed's expectations of assistance from the Rockefeller fortune were no less great than Harper's, but Goodspeed's hopes moved at a tempo set by patience. Long after Harper's death, Goodspeed believed that more might have been received from the Founder than was given had Harper not jumped ahead more rapidly than conservative finances warranted.[14] Neither man, however, was inflexible in disagreement. Goodspeed insisted that it would be foolish and criminal to assume more than there was any probability of accomplishing but readily admitted that Harper should hold to the original figure for an initial gift if Rockefeller was amenable.[15] And Harper presently softened his criticism: "I am anxious to see him do a big thing and am therefore impatient in consideration of anything that is small."[16] The temperamental grounds for some imperfection of sympathies remained but did not produce a rupture.

Goodspeed devised no less than four optional plans, all but one of which embodied his conviction that Rockefeller's first gift should be unconditional. He favored a plan that called for Rockefeller to give $3,000,000 to endowment in six or ten annual instalments and for others to raise $1,000,000 in six or more years for land, buildings, libraries, scientific apparatus, and "all the necessary external equipment of a first class University."[17] Although that plan would probably seem one-sided to Rockefeller, it was not really so because it would force the supporters of the University to raise $1,000,000. The plan would not only have the greatest power of appeal but would put prospective donors under the greatest pressure. Goodspeed thought primarily of the Baptists, but he did reach out in his imagination to every public-spirited man in the city, regardless of denomination.[18] Such thinking was far from being new in the eighties, but it was decidedly prophetic. The pursuit of the wealth lying in the hands of Chicago's richest businessmen, most of whom were not Baptists and some of whom were not Christians, would lead Goodspeed of the University of Chicago to people to whom a fund-raiser for a Baptist seminary had no access.

After seeing Goodspeed's first proposition, Rockefeller had been anxious to have the matter discussed impersonally, to have the members of the denomination express themselves and commit themselves to a university, to give those who opposed the Chicago scheme an opportunity to present their objections, and to avoid the alienation of Augustus H. Strong, who continued to advocate the founding of a great university in New York.[19] Through the early winter of 1888, Rockefeller gave no indication that his mind had changed. Strong's attitude was particularly worrisome to the Chicago group. His importunity chilled Rockefeller; but even a Strong powerless to do good in New York might have sufficient influence to do harm in Chicago. He had never set his face against the founding of a *college* there, but true to the plan upon which he had set his dearest hopes, Strong insisted that Chicago was decidedly not the place for a university, by which he meant a graduate institution. A university established in Chicago—"a mongrel institution," of necessity provincial and sectional rather than national and international—would not attract college graduates for years. In the meantime, its founders would have the strongest temptation to add a

23

collegiate department and so the institution would cease to belong to the category of universities proper.[20]

Strong's sentiments touched many nerves. Harper never beat the drum for "the great American university," separate from and above all colleges, perhaps because his own experience in New Haven had given him an opportunity to appreciate the capacity of a college for growth; but he did share with Strong the conviction that the denomination should aim at the creation of a university. For a time, Harper may have been attracted by Strong's plan—certainly Strong courted his support; but Harper had fixed his eyes on the West: "I believe most thoroughly," wrote Harper to Gates, "that the best place for a Baptist University, in the highest sense of the term, is in the city of Chicago. . . ."[21] What he had in mind was a system of higher education resembling a big business. "Why should not this university erected at Chicago," Harper asked Rockefeller, "include as an organic part of it besides the theological seminary also various colleges throughout the West? . . . And let it be a university made up of a score of colleges with a large degree of uniformity in their management; in other words, an educational trust."[22] As Goodspeed fully realized, a great western university would threaten Strong's plans. Strong understood that the ideal of his heart was to be built in Chicago instead of New York—or so Goodspeed read Strong's mind. To persuade him to consent to that transformation and to convince him of its wisdom would be impossible, and the attempt would only precipitate a conflict that by all means should be avoided. "You must tell him," Goodspeed wrote to Harper, "that if you conveyed the impression that his great University was to be built in Chicago, it was a mistake . . . that we have in mind a very different sort of institution . . . ," such an institution as Strong approved of for Chicago. "The *great University* consisting of post graduate departments only is not what we have in mind." What the Chicago men did want was a college—to begin with. If a college grew into something more, no one could blame Chicago.[23] But that emphasis disturbed Harper, who refused to take the consequences—which he dreaded—of talking only about a college. "I am sorry to say," Harper responded to Goodspeed,

that I can hardly agree with you and the other brethren in reference to the policy to be pursued in the matter. I hardly think it is legitimate, for if the thing you are wanting at Chicago is only a college, I have been working upon a wrong tack, and as surely as you convince Dr. Strong that this is the case, he will react on Mr. R., and the result will be that a college is all that we shall get. This would be very sad indeed, for it is not a college, but a university, that is wanted. I can hardly think that any but a straightforward, definite line of action will be successful.[24]

Harper was willing to write Strong in the vein Goodspeed had suggested, although Harper still believed that what was wanted was "a university of the highest character, having also a college. . . ."[25]

Goodspeed responded that Harper ought not to offer an opinion so clearly opposed to his own. He believed that Harper himself did not want what Goodspeed understood to be the kind of university Strong advocated, one consisting of postgraduate departments only, to cost from twenty-five to fifty million, and to be the crown of the American educational system, far above and beyond Johns Hopkins, Harvard, and Yale. "We want a first-class College with certain graduate departments, a western Yale. A University in the American sense, but not according to Strong's understanding of that word."[26] To tell Strong that the university he had in mind was to be transferred to Chicago would be to deceive him and to arouse his active hostility. Indeed, it did not seem to Goodspeed that Rockefeller intended to build the New York university in Chicago. The Chicago institution should not be talked of as it might sometime be, "but as it is to be *now* in its inception, the best thing Baptists now have, a western Yale, but not the most advanced & magnificent University in America."[27] (The repetition of Yale's name need not be dismissed as flattery for Harper, a Yale PH.D. and professor: to Goodspeed, Yale may well have represented a concrete standard and process of growth.)

When Goodspeed wrote to Gates, he was even more emphatic in his disavowal of any intention to create a great *national* Baptist university in Chicago. Strong's foreboding was "all wrong, an utter misconception." The Chicago institution was not designed to take the place of the Great University—"cannot come into competition with that, but is something wholly different."[28] Goodspeed's ambition for the Chicago project was conspicuously regional. Goodspeed was content to speak only of the West: "This is a big country & any locality that puts on airs & assumes to be the center of the whole country, & talks about its institutions being *National* will have every one jumping on it. A University for the West, for the *Northwest,* is big enough for us."[29] Yet perhaps Goodspeed did anticipate that success in Chicago might hurt Strong's project. "Our thought," Northrup later said about his and Goodspeed's intentions, "was to make a flank movement and not a direct issue with Strong, believing that if the Chicago enterprise was taken in hand it would grow to such dimensions that the New York Scheme would never be heard of again."[30]

Seeing the wisdom of dropping any suggestion of "national" aspirations from discussion of the Chicago project, Harper suppressed his own, larger hope. Even before Goodspeed had spoken of a university for the West, Harper had intimated that the institution could have no better name than the University of the West.[31] Writing to Strong, Harper described the university he had in mind for Chicago as one "in the ordinary sense of that term."[32] To Rockefeller, he wrote that "this idea of a college *now*, perhaps a university later" was most excellent.[33]

Gates, too, followed suit. When Harper had originally talked of a graduate university for Chicago, Gates acknowledged that Chicago was a better place than the East for a university with an endowment of four to ten million dollars:

. . . the post graduate business is rather overdone in the east, and is likely to take on far more extensive proportions very soon. So with professional schools. The educational growth in the east will be almost wholly in the line of provision for post graduate studies and professional schools while in the west the field is practically open for preemption.[34]

But Gates displayed no interest in the use of Society funds to finance graduate work anywhere; he was immediately concerned with the elevation and rational organization of undergraduate instruction and of feeder academies. "I would suggest that Mr. Rockefeller proceed now on the basis of a very high grade college [in Chicago] with not less than two or three millions of money." The college, with an academy near it, would meet the most immediate and pressing needs of the Baptists. Even with a university in view, the different schools could probably be founded and developed at intervals and as opportunity offered rather than all together at the start. Later, appeals could be made to Rockefeller with much more definiteness and certitude arising from more careful study.[35] Thus by mid-January, 1889, Gates, Goodspeed, and Harper had arrived by different ways at a common position.* And Rockefeller told Harper, ". . . I have not really needed a University to absorb my surplus." He added: "Of late I had rather come to feel that if Chicago could get a College, and leave the question of a University until a later date, . . . that this would be more likely to be accomplished."[36]

But still the subjunctive! Morehouse believed that Rockefeller was waiting for

---

* By February, 1889, George W. Northrup's faith in the project reached what he called a vanishing minimum: "We began with a University, then dropped to a College and now Dr. [Justin A.] Smith is working away at Mr. [George C.] Walker to induce him to start an academy. If he fails I propose to make one last effort with the view of establishing a Baptist kindergarten at Chicago" (George W. Northrup to Harper, February 26, 1889 [COFHA, Box I, Folder 6]).

the right man to be found for the presidency of the institution: "He takes great stock in men." Specifically, he would commit himself if Harper would.[37] Gates shared that same view. When, at the end of 1888, Strong attacked Harper's religious orthodoxy, Gates feared that Strong's inquisition would serve, with other reasons, to deter Harper from wishing to come to Chicago.* "I am strongly impressed," Gates wrote Harper, "with the idea that our matter hinges at last on your acceptance of the presidency."[38] When Yale offered Harper an extraordinary appointment, including two chairs held at a salary and a half, an assistant, leave for travel in Europe at full salary, and a cash advance, Gates and Goodspeed, who was desperate, urged Harper to consult Rockefeller. At first Harper was hesitant but agreed to pay Rockefeller a visit.[39] Rockefeller advised Harper against binding himself to his professorship for more than three—or at most five—years but did not promise a competitive offer on behalf of a new Yale.[40] Rockefeller was plainly interested in Harper but was not ready to commit himself to Chicago in order to insure that Harper would be immediately available for the Presidency. Soon after, Harper accepted the enhanced appointment at New Haven.

In January, 1889, even Morehouse, who had consistently advised Gates not to press Rockefeller, came to feel that uncertainty was dangerous. Trying to ride two horses, the Education Society might fall between them, should the land company withdraw its Morgan Park offer and Rockefeller fail to act.[41] In the same month, however, Rockefeller asked: "Cannot Mr. Gates write?"[42] Within a fortnight, Gates presented what he characterized as a bold and revolutionary plan—which he thought wise to outline only to Rockefeller. Three existing colleges in the West were to be moved to nearby cities; several so-called colleges or universities were to be made into academies; one "university" was to be strengthened on condition that it took the name of a college; and the eventual creation of two new colleges and of more feeder academies was to be contemplated. The Baptists would have colleges in the six chief centers of wealth and population in the West—Indianapolis, St. Louis, Kansas City, Des Moines, Omaha, and Minneapolis–St. Paul—with a cordon of academies around each. The Society would assist in the necessary removals, but local wealth and interest would be relied upon to take care of future development. That difficult, "even . . . dangerous," work was to be accomplished by the planting of a great and overshadowing

---

* Gates declared his own belief in the liberty of private judgment, said that heresy-hunting was at best an unpopular and risky business and could rarely be vindicated, and remarked that Rockefeller could scarcely repress the suspicion that Strong's motives were far other than zeal for truth (Gates to Harper, January 5, 1889).

college in Chicago. It would bring the existing colleges into subordination by drawing off their most promising students to Chicago. Impossible dreams of dominance and empire would be nipped in the bud, and the colleges would become tractable; they would grasp any proffered aid which promised permanence and self-protection, even at the cost of removal, and the selfish voices of village interests would be overborne. A powerful institution in Chicago would stimulate the six cities to invite the changes Gates had in mind. He believed that the plan could be carried out because of "the almost resistless power of organization, kindly, tactfully but undeviatingly devoted to chosen ends, an organization controlling varied resources and using them, an organization careful at every point not to antagonize public sentiment and to mould it in advance of its action." The policy should be followed step by step but never divulged as a whole, and institutions should be dealt with seriatim in order to prevent combinations of resistance. When the desired changes had been effected and the interests of western education were secured, the question of a university in Chicago—Gates emphasized "university"—would invite renewed attention.[43]

At last Gates met Rockefeller face to face. Rockefeller remained non-committal but asked a great many questions and seemed pleased with the plan outlined by Gates. "In parting with me," Gates wrote, "he said that his mind worked slowly in these matters, but he was glad to have had this opportunity for extended conversation, and closed by saying 'I think we are in the way of progress.' "[44] He meant, Gates thought, to help in carrying out the scheme of western educational development.[45] In December, 1888, the Board of the Society had taken the first step toward adoption of the Chicago project by declaring that "a thoroughly equipped Baptist institution of learning in Chicago" was an immediate and imperative necessity. The Board also directed Gates to use every means in his power to bring it about.[46] Specific details were left undecided. Although free to negotiate, Gates had no plan to offer Rockefeller in the name of the Society. His desire to hear the voice of the denomination remained unsatisfied but for a general fiat that left all practical questions unanswered. Nor had the Board taken a position on the highly charged issue of whether the institution should be a university or a college which might ultimately become a university. What were the limits of wise expenditure where so much invited limitless expansion? And what of the claims elsewhere? These were Gates's queries as he considered the project and the fierce competition for the attention and support of the Society.[47] Gates proposed that it appoint a committee to study Chicago and prepare a plan on the scope, costs, and site of an institution that might be presented to Rockefeller as the will of the denomination: "We believe," Harper wrote of Rockefeller, "that he is ready to take hold but that he wants something more definite than has yet been presented, and at the same time something that will relieve him of all responsibility."[48]

Asked if creation of a committee would embarrass him—in which case it would be dropped immediately—Rockefeller not only gave his approval but volunteered that, in the event he made a gift for a Chicago college, he would prefer to do so through the Society.[49] Contrary to the expectation of some that Chicago Baptists might feel that the project was being taken out of their hands, they also gave their hearty approval. Goodspeed felt that for the first time the project was on the right track.[50]

The committee included two professors (E. Benjamin Andrews of Cornell, Harper of Yale), a college president (James M. Taylor of Vassar), two seminary presidents (Alvah Hovey of Newton and H. G. Weston of Crozer), two pastors (Samuel W. Duncan and J. F. Elder), a businessman (Charles L. Colby), and the secretary of the Home Mission Society (Henry L. Morehouse).[51] Two of these men, Harper and Morehouse, had taken part in the development of the Chicago project; but neither was so involved that his advice would be attacked on grounds of personal interest. (Gates's attitude toward self-seeking in the committee would presumably have been the same as his principle on the composition of the Board itself: "We must keep every man off our board who has personal affiliations or we shall be checkmated at every turn.")[52] As a group, the committee represented years of experience in academic affairs.

Before the committee met, Gates solicited advice from sixty men in Chicago and the West whose names were suggested principally by Goodspeed.[53] The Chicago men first thought of sending an agent but instead presented a statement written by Goodspeed and discussed by the ministers and laymen. Although their opinions differed in regard to co-education and the location of the institution—George C. Walker, sponsor of the land company offer, and one other person favored a suburb—the paper was signed by a clear majority of the persons who had been consulted and was approved by the faculty of the Morgan Park seminary. It expressed a desire that the seminary and the University should be connected organically. "One institution, one interest, one great & united constituency would seem to be the wise & successful policy," Goodspeed wrote.[54] The Baptists had regained confidence and were finding unity of purpose.

Meeting in New York on April 12, 1889, the committee worked from ten in the morning until six in the evening to produce a report which followed closely the recommendations of the Chicago group.[55] Gates's larger strategy of pressure and incentives was not reflected in the clauses of the report. Its preamble touched upon much the same ground that Gates had explored publicly with the Chicago ministry: again, the central location and importance of Chicago as the inland metropolis of the country, the weakness of Baptist higher education in the Northwest and the total absence of a Baptist college in the Chicago area, the consequent loss of young Baptists who sought education under other auspices, and the chance which the establishment of an institution would give the Baptists "to lay hold of & influence mightily the intellectual, social & religious life of the entire West."[56]

The committee recommended that the Education Society at once take steps toward the founding of "a well equipped *College,* leaving any desirable further development to the natural growth of time."[57] The "college-now" formula would be presented officially to the denomination. The privileges of the institution were to be extended to men and women on equal terms. The endowment required to support the salaries of the President, professors, and other officers would be $1,040,000, the total cost of the institution, including a preparatory school, being $1,815,000. The Society would pay in approximately two-thirds of that amount over a period of four years, and Chicago and the West would be expected to provide the remainder. The committee thought it essential that the college should be placed within the city limits and proposed the establishment of a preparatory school in some locality other than the college site—a veiled but still recognizable suggestion that a gift of land in the suburbs would still serve education. When Walker agreed that an academy instead of a college might be built on the land offered in Morgan Park, the anomaly of a University of Chicago rising beyond the city limits ceased to be a possibility. Yet at the time the committee met, the supporters of the Chicago project had received no other substantial offer in support of a college, wherever located. Goodspeed was moved to say privately: "Anything will be better than the present paralyzing uncertainty. . . ."[58] And Harper: "Whether Mr. R will come down now is the question."[59]

The answer came at the time of the May anniversaries, the annual conventions of the Baptist national societies that gave the denomination opportunity to act as one brotherhood despite its lack of synod or council. Voting on the report of the committee, the Educational Society would speak, as nearly as a single body could, with the voice of the Baptists. Just a week before the meeting, Rockefeller invited Gates to call with any new and interesting suggestions he might have to offer.[60] As Gates recalled the event years afterward, he met Rockefeller in New York on Sunday afternoon, May 12, and again the next day. Gates told Rockefeller that action had to be taken or the movement would lose momentum; and Rockefeller consented to commit himself. At first he proposed to give $400,000 toward a million; but Gates answered that the remainder could not be raised: Rockefeller would have to give $600,000 in order to turn the balance toward success. Rockefeller then offered $500,000, and Gates declined to take even that, insisting that nothing but a generously preponderant subscription would do. The two men came to agreement after breakfast on Monday as they walked to and fro in front of Rockefeller's New York home on Fifty-fourth Street just off Fifth Avenue. Gates was to remember it as a delicious May morning. Rockefeller promised $600,000 for the endowment fund for a college in Chicago on condition that an additional $400,000 be raised elsewhere for land and buildings.[61]

The Chicago men had been hoping for a Rockefeller pledge for about three years, from the time of the collapse of the old University. Their correspondence, reporting the apparent ebb and flow of Rockefeller's reactions, leaves an impression of a man who was indeed slow to make up his mind. Rockefeller had been perplexed in his attempt to discover the wisest use to which his wealth could be put in response to the demands of religion. Yet the month (exactly) between the formulation of a definite program by a representative Baptist group and Rockefeller's acceptance of that program was not a long period of labor before the birth of a major philanthropy. Given concrete advice that could be taken as the voice of the denomination, Rockefeller moved very quickly: foundation officers could hardly act upon applications more speedily. It has been supposed by some commentators that Harper exercised an irresistible influence over Rockefeller. Yet it was Gates who assisted Rockefeller most directly in making his decision to back the Chicago project. Of all the men with whom Rockefeller came into contact as he entered the world of major philanthropy, Gates was the one Rockefeller found most compatible. Before the year was out, Rockefeller had begun to forward begging letters to him for investigation, saying, "I am disposed more and more to give only through organized agencies."[62] Gates shortly became Rockefeller's lieutenant, to expand enormously the work of organized philanthropy that began in the Education Society.

In making his pledge, Rockefeller stipulated that his intention was not to be revealed until the Board had resolved to raise $1,000,000 immediately for such a college as the committee had recommended. In effect, the Board was to commit itself to a financial campaign on the merits of the cause alone. Yet as a student of human nature Rockefeller may have anticipated that members of the Board would try to second-guess him; secrecy was no defense against the possibility that they would gamble on the chance that he had already committed himself. The committee had been created to bring Rockefeller's thought to a focus; and each Board member could put whatever interpretation he pleased upon Gates's submission of resolutions which were based upon the committee's recommendations except for the price tag. Harper had recently seen Rockfeller, again in Poughkeepsie, and understood that Rockefeller was largely satisfied with the report of the committee; the resolutions themselves contained a clue to Rockefeller's intentions—of the $1,000,000 to be raised, $600,000 was to go toward endowment.[63] If Rockefeller had reason to expect adoption of the resolutions, why did he keep the Board in doubt about his state of mind until it had acted? By insisting that the Board of the Education Society should approve the plan as its own spontaneous act, Rockefeller made certain that the paternity of the new institution was clearly established. The college in Chicago was to belong to the Baptist denomination and not to a single Baptist who happened to be very rich. By his willingness to listen, Rockefeller had encouraged his brethren to produce a scheme acceptable to the denomination; and by his reticence during negotiations, he determined the location of initiative and responsibility, which were not to lie, for a moment, in his hands but in duly constituted, educational bodies—first the Education Society and then a Board of Trustees to which the Society would give way. Scrupulous discrimination between the sources of wealth and responsibility for the power it gave would be the major premise of the government of the University.

The Board passed the resolutions. The general meeting of the Society applauded a motion indorsing the action and then burst into a tumultuous cheer at Gates's announcement of the Rockefeller gift.[64] But when the jubilation quieted and the singing of the Doxology came to an end, where precisely did the Chicago project stand? For what could its supporters reasonably hope, and to what were they committed?

32

As secretary of the Education Society and as negotiator of the Rockefeller gift, Gates assumed the responsibility of a canvass to raise $400,000. Gates had himself discovered that Chicago did not contain many Baptists who were at once wealthy and predisposed to give to a college. No sum like $400,000 had ever been produced for the old University or promised for a new University of Chicago. It was for Gates to discover if the "generously preponderant" Rockefeller gift would in fact loosen purse strings. Were the campaign to fail, Rockefeller would have every right to withdraw his support from Chicago forever. He had made it clear to anyone who was willing to listen that he took no responsibility for the ultimate success of the University of Chicago, even as a college. And yet Gates was not pessimistic over the outcome of the difficulties that he anticipated: "This thing is going to succeed. . . . Dr. Goodspeed's is the only voice I have heard that is fearful."[65]

Goodspeed was decidedly disturbed by the conditional character of the pledge.[66] From the beginnings of discussion over what form Rockefeller support should take, Goodspeed's prime strategy for raising funds in Chicago presupposed an outright Rockefeller gift to guarantee other subscribers against disappointment and to put the pressure of obligation upon western Baptists. The goal of $1,000,000 fell far short of the sums that Goodspeed and Harper had discussed: if the University of Chicago was to be a western Yale in wealth, it would have to possess at least five times as much as it had been pledged. With a million dollars, the University of Chicago might achieve much as a college; but it could neither hope for distinction among universities nor expect to attract professors who had tasted the delights of university as well as college life. The projected institution would fulfil the terms of Rockefeller's pledge and of the commitments of the Society by becoming no more than a college. Any reference to the possibility that it might develop into the great American university was conspicuous by its absence.

After the anniversaries, one man who had advocated Washington, D.C., as the site of "our National University" asked Gates: "Why do they still persist in talking about the Chicago *University?*"[67] Augustus Strong came away from the anniversaries expecting that the Society would create another special committee to hear the case for New York. "I assure you," he wrote Gates, "that we are determined to be heard."[68] After consultation with Rockefeller, Gates promptly killed that idea; but the denomination did not designate the University of Chicago as heir to the New York plan.[69] For the failure of others to recognize the college as a great university in embryo its friends were themselves responsible. They had disavowed any intention of seeking deliberately to create a graduate institution: if natural growth produced a university, well and good. The will to strive upward that makes university-building a cause did not show itself in the words of the men who floated the college for Chicago—except in the suppressed opinions of William Rainey Harper.

CHAPTER III

Financing a College
and Founding
a University

The Education Society had one year from the date June 1, 1890, to meet the terms of Rockefeller's pledge. The task of organizing a campaign for $400,000 fell jointly, by virtue of office, to Gates and, by virtue of loyalty and experience, to Goodspeed. At first Goodspeed hoped that the canvass could be conducted by volunteers, primarily by the ministers of the western churches.[1] That method, which followed the classic Baptist pattern of local action, would enable the Society to draw upon an indefinitely wide (although not very deep) pool of resources without constructing a special fund-raising apparatus. "If the movement falls into good hands I have great hope of large success," Goodspeed remarked on the second day of the campaign, but added, "there is as yet no concert...."[2] However premature, the observation was pertinent, perhaps more so than Goodspeed then realized. The identification of the University with the denomination at large would be complete only if the Baptists achieved sufficient unity to fulfil Rockefeller's conditions.

In the first two months of the drive, the Chicago Baptists gave emphatic support to the cause by subscribing $200,000, or one-half the required total.[3] Local confidence had been restored and the shame of 1886 wiped away. But the pledges from the city, like the returns in an election, came in much more quickly than the subscriptions from outlying areas. The country, as Goodspeed called the Baptists' constituency outside Chicago, was slow to respond, appearing to be quite willing to allow the city to assume the lion's share of responsibility for the enterprise: "We find that we must raise our money here in Chicago."[4] Although the subscription form simply described the proposed institution as a college *in* Chicago, western Baptists may have substituted the preposition *of* as they thought about the project. A college of Chicago was not The University of the West, and the existing colleges, none of them rich, remained in need of support. Both Gates and Goodspeed argued against the idea that the new institution would be primarily local rather than regional, but the contributions made by the states west of Chicago (excluding Illinois) did not indicate that widespread enthusiasm had been aroused. Measured by numbers of subscriptions on record, the support of the University outside Chicago (which yielded about 560 pledges) lay not in the West or even the Midwest but preponderantly in Illinois, with about 510 pledges, and in a block of three states north and west, Wisconsin, Iowa, and Minnesota, which provided 81, 69, and 42 subscriptions, respectively.* Kansas gave $1,846; Missouri, $1,695; and Nebraska, $1,335—or in each instance less than $400 per annum for the five-year period during which payments were to be made. Several of the states east of Illinois provided much larger amounts than the western states, but the numbers of subscribers were small. Contributions from the South and the states beyond the Continental Divide were small in amount as well as in number. A few Baptists pledged at least $10,000 each, and over 900 pledged less than $50. Because a large portion of the contributions fell between $5 and $50, the University must have interested many Baptists of moderate income. The contributions by churches as such may conceal the widow's mite. The total number of subscriptions was 1,440, of which some (although probably a small minority) were made by non-Baptists. If the subscriptions of churches covered as many pledges as were identified with individual givers, the members of the denomination who supported the University probably numbered somewhat more than 2,500. Even a constituency of that size would account for less than 1 per cent of the Baptist population of the West, according to Gates's estimate of 1888. Concert was indeed not achieved.[5]

The cause had the hearty support of the editor of the *Standard,* Justin A. Smith.† Yet as neither the printed word nor volunteer effort sufficed to drive

---

* The subscriptions from the four states included 22 from churches, through which an unknown number of persons lent support to the University.

† A reader of the *Standard* wrote Goodspeed: "I have been much interested in your 'notes on the new College' . . . and want to do something for the cause. I have a good many goods but

the campaign forward, it became, first and last, a labor of direct solicitation by the organizers. Their experiences as fund-raisers determined the outcome of the campaign—and also what people and what interests would support the University in the future. Gates moved to Chicago to make his chief duty fulfilment of the commitment of the Society; and Goodspeed transferred his services from the Morgan Park seminary to the Society. Working amicably and tirelessly as a team, the two "secretaries" wrote publicity material, organized drives, notably one among alumni of the old University, prepared lists of prospective donors, and persisted in the endless task of making calls. The rhythm of their life was a quick march from door to door:

At 5 P.M. Gates and I [Goodspeed] met the Committee of the Alumni. . . . Thursday we saw A. A. Munger, the richest of the old alumni. . . . The day was stormy and we could not find the men we wanted and came home early. . . .

We have not had a specially encouraging week in our work, owing to the difficulty of finding the men we wanted to see.

Tuesday we saw two or three wealthy men without encouragement.

Any day now the door may open wide among the businessmen and yet we may not get it unlocked until January.

We have about 30 more letters to wealthy laymen to write and then we begin the work of personal solicitation again.

We meet some reverses but also many encouragements. . . . We are universally well received and even welcomed in business offices of millionaires. . . .

Every day we have found men who encourage us to come and see them again. . . .

I [Gates] went back alone and got three subscriptions of $1,000 each from men who had said no.

The only cloud in the horizon is the great strike threatened for this week, which may bring all business to a standstill. . . .[6]

While the campaign was dragging in the "country," Gates and Goodspeed found hope in the reception granted them by "the big outside men"—wealthy Chicagoans who were not Baptists.[7] Even before the campaign began, Goodspeed anticipated an appeal to local pride and public spirit and planned a committee of businessmen to work among their colleagues in Chicago and else-

---

not much money so have concluded to make you the following offer, I have a Stock of Carriages . . . and among them is a two seated Extension Top Surry made by Studebaker Bros of South Bend Ind, it is a fine job and I will crate and deliver it . . . and will donate the proceeds to the New College . . ." (Frank G. Warren to Goodspeed, May 6, 1890).

where: F. E. Hinckley, perhaps the richest Baptist in Chicago, believed that the wealthy men of the city would help the University if it secured their confidence and awakened their enthusiasm.[8] As autumn gave way to winter, it became apparent that the University had to find its money at home: "There seems to be a general disposition East & West," Goodspeed wrote Harper, "to compel us to do the whole thing here in Chicago."[9] The largest hope of the campaign lay in wealthy non-Baptists, in the absence of strong support from Baptists at large.[10] "I have never understood until lately the utter lack of cohesion in the Baptist denomination." That disillusionment, reported by Gates to Morehouse in November, marked a profound shift of expectations.[11]

Originally the canvassers had no entrée into the non-Baptist (and vastly richer) part of the Chicago business community. They were advised to approach Charles L. Hutchinson, who had stepped by virtue of family into a position that he could otherwise have attained—and did brilliantly maintain—by his own ability. He had diversified business interests but centered his attention upon the Corn Exchange Bank, founded by his father, of which he was president. Since the bank did business with members of the Board of Trade (or grain exchange), Hutchinson worked in the closest possible touch with the economic life of Chicago. He had never attended college, was engaged in business before he reached his majority, and began at twenty-one to use capital of his own. Having lost some of his money in speculation, he promptly became a conservative investor and remained so the rest of his life.

Hutchinson was indeed a capitalist but not the incarnation of Economic Man. The closer type was the Christian Gentleman—devout, wealthy, public spirited —the evangelical peer, humanized by an abiding taste for the arts. Hutchinson was simultaneously the superintendent of a Universalist Sunday School and president of the Art Institute, which he helped to found. Having inquired anxiously if the University cause had anything to do in any way with the old institution and being assured that it did not, Hutchinson gave the new movement his full support. He immediately subscribed to the campaign and arranged to have the University case presented to the Commercial Club, whose members stood at the center of Chicago business. He also consented to serve as a Trustee of the University and recommended for membership on the Board Martin A. Ryerson, a close friend whose situation and interests were very like his own. Gates and Goodspeed used Hutchinson's name with every man they approached; and they succeeded in securing pledges, some from Hutchinson's near-neighbors on Prairie Avenue, then a fashionable street.[12] As if in one step, the campaigners moved into the midst of a society that possessed both power and cohesiveness. Hutchinson had opened the way to an alliance between the University and those economic leaders of Chicago who made its cultural advancement a second vocation. The University would become the beneficiary—and a rallying point—of an elite determined to save Chicago from its own materialism.

As the campaign was carried to non-Baptists, the religious implications of the University movement were at once remembered and broadened. When Marshall Field promised the University land in the erstwhile suburb of Hyde Park—a gift which finally put an end to argument over the site of the institution—Gates wrote Rockefeller:

This is by far the largest thing Mr. Field has ever done, and the influence on his own character can not fail to be of great value. His wife is an ardent and devoted Christian, we learn, and will be a powerful reinforcement for good. We think a few appreciative words from yourself of his interest in this enterprise would be prized by him more than any other reward, and would be besides a personal blessing and means of grace to him. I opened the whole subject by proposing that he "unite" himself with you in this matter "in a large way."[13]

Rockefeller did write of the delight and honor he felt on being joined by Field, "in this good partnership relation, which I hope may prove a blessing to the present and future generations."[14] In point of religion, the partnership was neither indiscriminately latitudinarian nor narrowly discriminatory. When one powerful busnessman indicated that his interest in the University would depend upon its "catholicity of spirit," Rockefeller warned Gates to be careful. Rockefeller approved of that spirit but did not know the particular construction that the prospective donor might place upon "catholicity," or whether, indeed, he was "a Christian man at all." The University should keep clear of any promises which might tie its hands: "The question of money may not be so important a factor later on as that freedom which we always want to have in the administration of the proposed university."[15]

The practice of the canvassers was consistent with Rockefeller's use of "Christian" as a descriptive adjective and not as a limiting noun. Although the project was designed to serve the cause of Christian men, the subscription-book remained open nevertheless to men who were not Christians. In particular,

German-Jews gave their support to the campaign through the Standard Club, an organization to which a number of well-to-do men belonged. When Eli B. Felsenthal, a graduate of the old University, began to represent Chicago Jewry on the Board of the new University, he brought alliance with another community of Chicago men possessing great wealth and the will to use it in the interest of culture; and when Rabbi Emil G. Hirsch, appointed to the chair of Rabbinical Literature and Philosophy, joined Christian proponents of the higher criticism in the faculty, reformed Judaism and reformed Protestantism met as friends in Hyde Park.[16]

Thanks to the merger of interests, the Education Society met its deadline with a little time to spare.* At the end of the campaign, when its success was assured, denominational enthusiasm reasserted itself dramatically. At the May anniversaries of 1890, the members of the Society interrupted Goodspeed's report on subscriptions to announce small gifts or pledges in the names of places from Maine to California, from Dublin to Bangkok, from Nova Scotia to Burma—and for the Tama Indians of Iowa, "my persecuted brethren of Siberia," and finally "the Isle of Guernsey and my mother."[17] So, in sentiment, the members of the Society identified themselves with the University and the University with the world. Yet the moment was one of token victory for the denomination as such. While the outcome of the campaign was in doubt, a scattering of churches and some individuals, with the membership of the Chicago region, had contributed very heavily—so heavily that by far the larger part of the required $400,000 came from Baptist sources; but the Baptists of the United States had not then united in material support of the new institution. Within less than a year, E. Nelson Blake, a leader among Baptist laymen and a supporter of the project, was to defend himself for declaring that the institution was not a "Baptist university": "I say that the denomination lost the opportunity to make it such...."[18] Baptist sentiment in the large constituted an opinion to be consulted, not a voice to be obeyed. The Baptist faith, moving individual men and women, gave the world a university that the denomination never owned—a benefaction that was profoundly true to the spirit of independence in the Baptist movement.

* More than four hundred of the pledges—more than one-fourth of the whole—were never paid in full. The loss can be blamed, at least in part, upon the depression of 1893, which occurred during the term of the subscriptions. (Payments on pledges are recorded in the subscription book of the campaign of 1889-90, University of Chicago Archives.)

The University of Chicago was incorporated on September 10, 1890, under articles signed first by John D. Rockefeller.* In conformity with the resolutions upon which the Rockefeller pledge and the matching subscriptions were premised, the Articles of Incorporation stipulated that at all times (and forever) two-thirds of the twenty-one Trustees constituting the Board as well as the President of the University should be members of Baptist churches.[19] Otherwise, no test or particular religious profession was to be required in the University, i.e., for admission or for election to any professorship or other post in the corporation, its departments, or "institutions of learning."[20] The phrase was not plural by chance. The corporation was enabled to conduct a multiplicity of agencies, including one or more academies or preparatory schools (in Chicago and elsewhere); manual-training schools in connection with such preparatory departments; one or more colleges; and a university in which all branches of higher learning might be taught—"literature, law, medicine, music, technology, the various branches of science, both abstract and applied, the cultivation of the fine arts, and all other branches of professional or technical education which may properly be included within the purpose and objects of a University."† The grant of power plainly went far beyond the need of the well-equipped college envisaged in the resolutions of the Education Society and gave ample space for the "natural growth of time" that its special committee had contemplated.

As the assets of the University were being transferred from the Education Society to the new corporation, Gates explained the precise terms upon which such further development might take place:

It has never been the purpose of the society to seek to limit the institution to the work of a college. It has been hoped and believed that a good college located in this city would naturally and inevitably develop into a great university. . . . But from the first, it has been believed that the enlargement would be effected naturally by the inherent life of the institution and would by no means require the fostering care of the Society. The Society undertook only so much as seemed indispensable for it to do; that was, to found a college on a solid basis. It is for a college pure and simple therefore, that

* The incorporators were John D. Rockefeller, E. Nelson Blake, Marshall Field, Francis E. Hinckley, Frederick T. Gates, and Thomas W. Goodspeed. Although Rockefeller was recognized by the University as its founder on seal and letterhead, he himself did not formally associate his name with the University except as an incorporator. In law, the new University was completely distinct from the old University. The still existing Board of the old University relinquished the name, "The University of Chicago," for use by the new corporation. (See the Articles of Incorporation in "An Historical Sketch," PR 1892–1902, pp. 503–5, with explanatory notes.)

† Opportunities in all departments of higher education were to be furnished to "persons of both sexes on equal terms"—the exact language of the resolutions.

the funds have been subscribed. Mr. Rockefeller made his pledge "Toward an endowment fund for a college to be established in Chicago." The other subscriptions are likewise limited. They can properly be used only for a college. For this purpose alone the appeal has been made throughout the canvass. We have announced that other departments of instruction, if founded, would be supported by other funds.[21]

So it was that the Board was bound to work only in the interest of a college, "pure and simple," so long as it used funds derived from Rockefeller's pledge and the first canvass. In the beginning, that was the sole charge of the Board. As if to perpetuate the spirit as well as the letter of the farewell injunction, the Board employed Goodspeed as its financial secretary. In this capacity, and later as Secretary of the Board, he presided over the collection of the original subscriptions; more important, he embodied fidelity to the principles of conservative finance and evolutionary growth.

Legally, responsibility for leading the University out of the limbo of intentions, immediate or ultimate, lay entirely in the hands of the Trustees, who constituted—after nomination of charter members—a wholly self-perpetuating body, answerable in no way to the Baptist denomination at large and obligated to the Education Society only under the terms of that original effort to finance a college. One of the resolutions upon which the campaign had been based called for the reversion of real estate to the Society in the event that the Trustees ever mortgaged it: the lesson of the old University again.*

Gates seems to have taken the initiative in the selection of the Board of Trustees, watching for suitable men during the canvass. The Executive Board of the Society approved nominations, as did subscribers representing more than $900,-000 of the fund collected.[22] The original twenty-one members were Joseph M. Bailey, E. Nelson Blake, Charles C. Bowen, Elmer L. Corthell, Eli B. Felsenthal, Edward Goodman, William Rainey Harper, Francis E. Hinckley, Charles L. Hutchinson, Herman H. Kohlsaat, Andrew McLeish, John W. Midgley, Charles W. Needham, Alonzo K. Parker, Ferdinand W. Peck, George A. Pillsbury, Henry A. Rust, Martin A. Ryerson, Daniel L. Shorey, Frederick A. Smith, and George C. Walker. The first President of the Board was E. Nelson Blake, who was succeeded in office by Martin A. Ryerson before the University opened its doors. Although Felsenthal was the only Trustee representing a specific group of donors, in a broad sense the members represented all the important interests that made the University financially possible, save the most

---

* Invoking an "obligation of honor," the Society asked the new University to adopt the alumni of the old ("Report by Rev. F. T. Gates," *Standard*, XXXVII, No. 46 [July 17, 1890], 1).

important—Rockefeller himself. More than half of the Trustees had each pledged at least $1,000, and many much more. Four had served on the Board of the sponsoring Society. Goodman was a proprietor of the *Standard,* which had been the campaigners' voice among Baptists of the Chicago region. More than half of the Trustees either were (or had been) major officers of banks, railroads, or other large-scale business enterprises or were associated with the management of capital as directors of corporations or possessors of fortunes. Peck and Walker as well as Hutchinson and Ryerson were sons of wealthy men: Chicago was not then so young that its riches were all new and its rich men all self-made.

The bar and the bench together provided five Trustees, and engineering and the academic world one Trustee apiece. At least nine of the Trustees had been educated formally beyond the level of the high school or academy; and one, Harper, was a ph.d. and professional scholar. Another, Shorey, a lawyer by profession, was scholarly in the classic sense, being well-versed in Greek and Latin literature. (His son—Paul Shorey—was to devote his life to classical humanism.) Through the affiliations of its Trustees, the University was associated with a number of cultural and social institutions—the Art Institute; the Public Library; the Auditorium Association; the Chicago Literary Club; and the Chicago, Standard, and Union League clubs.

The University was similarly connected with several religious bodies, Baptist, Unitarian, Universalist, and Jewish; but except in the instance of one church, the connecting link was lay rather than clerical. Alonzo K. Parker was the sole minister among the Trustees, and he was the last to be selected.[23] Looking at the penultimate list of nominations, which did not include Parker's name, Harper had found it strange to see a board without a single minister on it.[24] What he was witnessing was one episode in the displacement of the clergy by laymen, often of business, in the government of higher education. Elsewhere, as at Yale in Harper's time, the process was gradual.[25] In Chicago, ministerial influence was abruptly discredited by the catastrophe of 1886. Afterward, the attitude of some pastors had not favorably impressed Rockefeller and Gates, and the pastors' role in the campaign was subordinate. One ministerial veteran of the University movement might have become a positive embarrassment to the campaign by insisting that the new University occupy the site of the old, had Gates and Goodspeed not passed him by.[26] Was Goodspeed thinking of the ministers emotionally involved in the fall of the old University and the rise of the new when he remarked: "The Board is . . . a capable body of *business men.* . . . There will not be a man who has any personal ends to serve"?[27] Gates de-

43

scribed the Board as a new bottle for new wine. Several years later, he would remind Goodspeed that they had promised donors that "the old management would not be retained in the new institution; that first class business men would be substituted on the Board, instead of ministers, and that every possible guard would be thrown around the institution so that the mistakes of the past would be avoided."[28]

Inevitably, John D. Rockefeller had been nominated for a place on the Board when the roster of Trustees was drafted; but he neither accepted service himself nor designated a lieutenant. As a result the founder of the University did not have a voice in its government as it was put under way. A shakedown cruise had already revealed the possibilities of the vessel and the hazards of its course when Gates became a member of the Board in 1896 as a representative of the Founder—to be joined by John D. Rockefeller, Jr., in 1898. After the campaign, Rockefeller remained, as of old, a careful listener intent upon fixing responsibility for the use of his money in duly constituted independent bodies. In 1892, Gates explained at Rockefeller's behest:

While he is of course closely interested in the conduct of the institution, he ... would prefer in general not to take an active part in the counsels of the management. He prefers to rest the whole weight of the management on the shoulders of the proper officers. Donors can be certain that their gifts will be preserved and made continuously and largely useful, after their own voices can no longer be heard, only in so far as they see wisdom and skill in the management, quite independently of themselves, now. No management can gain skill except as it exercises its functions independently, with the privilege of making errors and the authority to correct them. The only way to assure a wise management during the whole future of the institution, is to ... keep the board at all times up to the highest point of skill and efficiency.[29]

The very form of that statement, putting Rockefeller in the third person, exhibits his intended relation to the University.

In a kind of dialectical synthesis that gave form to the early University, Rockefeller's absence from government was the antithesis of Harper's presence. Even as men, Harper and Rockefeller were opposites in many respects; Harper was pudgy in physique, scholarly in tastes, ebullient in temperament, and conspicuously outgoing in manner. Had Rockefeller and Harper not in fact collaborated, it would be easy to overlook their common qualities (piety, for one) and suppose that they were destined to be antagonists. Had Rockefeller not kept his distance, they might well have become so; and the University as it is would have been impossible. Simply as a Trustee, Harper had a share of responsibility for the character of the University which was no larger than that of twenty other men. As one of its first acts, however, the Board created a committee to work upon the organization of the University, and Harper became a member. Simultaneously the Board in effect connected the question of scale with the choice of a man to manage the University from day to day by charging the committee to nominate the head of the institution. It required no elaborate canvass of presidential talent to bring the attention of the Trustees to William Rainey Harper.[30]

His colleagues were reaching out toward a man, not a blueprint of university development. Well before the campaign began, Harper had advocated the foundation of a university "in the highest sense"; but he had also acquiesced in the decision to distinguish between the Chicago project and Strong's plan for a university. As the campaign was closing, he did give thought in New Haven to great university problems—as one of Goodspeed's relatives reported.[31] Yet prior to his election, Harper did not publish his views on academic education, as Charles W. Eliot had done before his election as president of Harvard. Harper's program was indeed more nearly determined by the terms upon which he accepted office than was his election by his academic politics.

Harper was far from being a committed candidate. On the contrary, he had already refused a college presidency in Chicago. He was a scholar whose studies as he conceived them meant the salvation of souls, and a professor whose university had extended itself to give him every advantage. Timothy Dwight, the president of Yale, said bluntly that Harper could not leave his post with honor.[32] A Yale colleague, George T. Ladd, asked Harper:

What do you really want to do as your life-work? Hold the perfectly unique position for the cultivation of your own scholarly character and influence, and that of others, —in O.[ld] T.[estament] lines? or, give up this, and become a business colleague of a few wealthy men, in founding another "University"? Don't for a moment flatter yourself, my dear fellow, that you can do both things. You can't. You have immense vigor, and versatility; you can make yourself a power in one of these lines, but not in both.[33]

Those inverted commas around University alone suffice to reveal the writer's mind. Without accepting "not in both" categorically, Harper put the issue, not in terms of what he wanted, but rather in the morally tough language that his Scotch-Irish ancestors would have recognized as necessary. A man's calling was of God. The great question before Harper was whether or not he could continue his lifework as a biblical specialist and do the work which the University of Chicago would demand: "... if not, whether I am justified in giving up the life-work."[34] The matter was with Harper night and day: "I cannot throw it off; if I would, others will not permit me. It is becoming the torment of my life."[35]

Harper may have exaggerated his personal anxieties as he did the expectations of enterprises that engaged his attention. Yet his was the real predicament of the scholar with a talent for organizing the work of other scholars—and, for Harper, scholarship had that meaning beyond earthly concerns. His standing in the world enabled him to ask much of Chicago; his position before his God required him to accept no less than he would give up.

Competing against Yale for his conscience, Harper's fellow Baptists of course refused to let him rest with arguments for the status quo; and one, the president of Crozer Seminary, Henry G. Weston, even denied his right to make his own decision: "Men must submit to the judgment of their brethren."[36] When Harper inquired whether the cause of true Bible study was not higher than that of the denomination, he was told by a Crozer professor that the answer, intrinsically, was *yes* but that circumstances might make the lower duty more pressing: "If one of our graduates who is a physician as well as a preacher finds insufficient medical men in his village during a dangerous epidemic, would it not be monstrous for him to refuse to do the indispensable lower office because he had given himself exclusively to the higher?"[37] Attacking on a different line, Justin A. Smith, the editor of the *Standard,* asked whether Harper could afford to make his lifework of a specialty—a description of his studies that Harper could not reject. Smith wrote:

God has endowed you with that power to grasp the essentials of large organizations and that power also of executive direction which are needed in those positions which comprehend many lines of work, and combine many agencies. At the head of our new university, you will have an outlook over a field of educational service that is practically limitless. You can do much of what you are now doing and vastly more....[38]

Gates, too, construed Harper's election as a divine call to a place of greater power but also argued that, in Chicago, Harper would enhance rather than diminish his chosen work:

This [is] the path of usefulness, and so of happiness, I mean the highest and largest usefulness and happiness, and so the path to be chosen at any personal cost.... I believe it will afford you a coigne of vantage from which you may by wise use of your opportunities achieve *more* in scholarship, *more* in elucidation of the Bible, *more* in reaching the hearts of men than [from] your present position in Yale....[39]

46

In effect, Gates passed by the idea of a college, pure and simple, to present Harper with the image of an institution that would be more for him than the western Yale envisaged by Goodspeed. A university—without inverted commas —would satisfy the terms dictated by the moral problem confronting Harper; but *was* the new institution to be a university?

And could it actually be one? Harper was quick to force the issue of scale by questioning the likelihood that what ought to be done in Chicago and what the denomination and the world expected could be accomplished with the money in hand. "There must in some way be an assurance of an additional million. . . ," Harper wrote Goodspeed on July 31, 1890. "If Mr. R. is dead in earnest, possibly the case will not be so difficult as we may think."[40] Within a week, Rockefeller himself wrote Harper, in words that Gates later described as perhaps the most pregnant ever uttered on the history of the University: "I cannot conceive of a position where you can do the world more good; and I confidently expect we will add funds, from time to time, to those already pledged, to place it [the University] upon the most favored basis financially."[41] Responding to that intimation of Rockefeller's purpose, Harper recommended that the formula of gradualism be drastically revised:

The denomination and indeed the whole country are expecting the University of Chicago to be from the very beginning an institution of the highest rank and character. Already it is talked of in connection with Yale, Harvard, Princeton, Johns Hopkins, the University of Michigan, and Cornell. No one expects that it will be in any respect lower in grade and equipment than the average of the institutions to which I have referred, and yet with the money pledged I cannot understand how the expectations can be fulfilled. Naturally we ought to be willing to begin small and to grow, but in these days when things are done so rapidly and with the example of Johns Hopkins before our eyes, it seems a great pity to wait for growth when we might be born full-fledged.[42]

Harper had returned to the hope that he had suppressed to conciliate President Strong.

Within six weeks Rockefeller pledged $1,000,000 outright for the support of theological and graduate studies at the University. No matching gift would be required. In accord with Rockefeller's intention, the lion's share—$800,000— was allocated to graduate work.[43] Rockefeller's action was the outcome of a conversation that had taken place on Sunday, August 17, when Harper met Gates in Morgan Park. They spent the afternoon out of doors. Harper had of course lived in Morgan Park, and a child of his was buried there. The two men visited the grave; and that afternoon Harper was in a tender, fruitful mood. According to Gates's recollection, Harper was making a momentous decision.[44] What he actually said remains in doubt. Unquestionably, as the future would show, the meeting marked the turning of a corner in the history of the University; but it also produced a chain of uncertainties and misunderstandings. The meeting and its aftermath were critical not only because of their particular results but also because they foreshadowed a pattern of ambiguity in the management of University affairs. Other meetings during the years of Harper's administration would also leave question marks.

As Gates and Harper talked they both possessed knowledge of Rockefeller's intimation that he might well add to his original pledge; and while walking about the suburb, as Gates and Rockefeller had walked in New York before Rockefeller agreed to support a college, Gates and Harper probably discussed a program for immediate organization of a university.[45] As Gates remembered their plan, the seminary would be moved to Hyde Park to become an organic part of the University. The old buildings in Morgan Park would house a University academy. Instruction in Hebrew and Old Testament criticism would be transferred to a University department, with Harper as head professor. Rockefeller would give a million dollars as an unconditional gift for the seminary and graduate work; and Harper would visit Rockefeller to accept the Presidency.[46] Under the terms of the plan, Harper would have the double role that his Yale colleague had said that even Harper could not play; he would resolve the issue of scholarship *vs.* administration by living two lives.[47] Such a plan for the organization and financing of the University and also for Harper's duty did presently go into effect; but was Harper's acceptance of the Presidency the condition *sine qua non* of the arrangement, and did he explicitly agree to serve the University if the other terms of the plan were fulfilled?

It is a fact that Harper visited Rockefeller at the time the gift was made— again, what Harper said is not recorded, but immediately after the meeting in Morgan Park, Gates reported that Harper was strongly inclined toward Chicago.[48] Harper himself asked for and was granted six months in which to answer when he was formally elected President in September, 1890—as if Harper and the Trustees understood that he had an option.[49] If Rockefeller had the same thought, his gift must be considered a bid against Yale rather than a payment in fulfilment of an agreement with Harper. Conceivably Rockefeller thought his gift would be overwhelming if Harper could be made to feel that, without saying yes categorically, he had given Rockefeller reason to expect his acceptance. It need not be supposed, however, that either man sought to coerce the other: Harper had his reasons of conscience for hesitating to accept the Presidency, and Rockefeller may only have believed that, as Harper's mind was divided, an outright gift for theological and graduate studies would be not only the decisive weight in the balance but also a welcome answer to Harper's doubts.[50] Yet in the interim before his formal answer was due, Harper sometimes acted as if he believed himself to be already in charge of the University.

Harper's behavior was markedly ambivalent. He began to frame the "official bulletins" that would announce the proposed organization of the University. (The first bulletin, published in January, 1891, contained the statement that it was expected that Harper's "decision as to the acceptance" of the Presidency would be made known in the spring.[51] How would subsequent bulletins have dealt with a decisive *no* from the nominee?) Harper also opened discussion of another extension of the University beyond the terms of the original subscriptions and against the spirit of the limited purposes to which the Education Society had been committed during the campaign. Harper proposed that Columbian University in Washington, D.C., a sometime candidate for Rockefeller support in its own name, be united with the University of Chicago. "I feel now," Harper wrote Morehouse in November, 1890, "that if this cannot be carried through, I do not care to go to Chicago."[52] The remark indicated the other aspect of Harper's activity. He labored for the University as if he were still not wholly a part of it. It may have been a similar display of *yes, but* that Gates observed during his meeting with Harper in Morgan Park. When Harper had a promising enterprise in hand, the effect of his presence was pure affirmation; words reflecting anxieties or reservations might pass unheard. Perhaps in August, 1890, Gates understood that Harper had not said *yes* explicitly, and later may have deliberately chosen to believe that Harper had committed himself absolutely; or perhaps Harper's words and his manner that Sunday contradicted each other, and the manner may have made the more lasting impression. Frequently, in every circumstance, it would be the memory of the men who dealt with Harper that he had agreed with their plans.

In the winter of 1890–91, Harper again and again expressed second thoughts about the prospective, and double, post as President and professor. In particular he called attention to the differences between his view of the Bible and that of other Baptists, and he asked if he was suitable for the Presidency and would be free as a professor. His misgivings were not invented for the occasion: about two years earlier, he had said: "I do not believe that, with Strong upon my back,

—for he is going on with his persecutions,—I am the man to head the institution. . . ."[53] He was, Gates thought, worn out physically and correspondingly nervous: "He . . . is morbid on the question of his own supposed heresy."[54] Goodspeed, too, noticed that Harper apparently felt compelled to announce at once any point of possible religious difference which he chanced to discover.[55] In September, 1890, he discussed his religious views with members of the seminary at Morgan Park and was found to be sound on essentials, but he remained uneasy. In November, he consulted Goodspeed and in December, Northrup. In January, Gates reminded Harper that he himself had once spoken of the way in which Jesus had tempered his teachings to the unreadiness of his hearers. Such candor as Harper wanted was the subtle temptation of the evil one—a temptation especially strong to open, generous natures like Harper's: "I see it [that temptation] leading to nothing but disaster, disaster to your influence, and injury to thousands and thousands of worthy people."[56] When Gates wrote those words, Harper had already appealed directly to Rockefeller, proposing that he select three or four men—Morehouse's name was mentioned—to hear the exact facts of Harper's position. He would then know whether he should have the privilege of teaching his views and, in case that privilege was denied him, whether under the circumstances his acceptance would be wise for the University and for himself. His views could be taught at Yale, he remarked, not only without condemnation but with the constant and hearty encouragement of the president and the theological faculty. Harper had returned to the issue of Chicago *vs.* Yale. He said himself that he might be morbid; certainly he failed to reconcile the possibility that he might accept office in Chicago despite some limitation on his freedom with the flat assertion, made at one point in his statement, that he could not consent to accept a position in which the privilege of teaching as he had would be denied him.[57]

Characteristically, instead of answering directly Rockefeller handed the case to Henry Morehouse who, after several weeks, wrote Harper a letter which Rockefeller approved and in which his approval was mentioned but from which Harper could glean no single sentence to be taken either as an ultimatum or as a categorical promise from the Founder of the University. Harper could answer the argument without challenging the man. Morehouse's response was adroit, as Harper was aware. Harper had already committed himself to the University, said Morehouse, and could not honorably append a further condition which had not been discussed when Rockefeller made his $1,000,000 gift. "The responsibility of non-acceptance now would be tremendous, while the responsibility of acceptance even in view of the suggested possibilities of the case, may be left in the hands of Him whose grace and guidance we all seek."[58] In other words: if you persevere in making your understanding of the Bible an issue, you are setting your own judgment against Providence. Because Morehouse treated Harper's acceptance as a foregone conclusion, he dealt with the question of Harper's freedom as a hypothetical case to be left to the logic of events. "It would seem wiser for you, if necessary, to forego the exercise of some right in the way of dogmatic teaching . . . , than to insist upon it at any cost, and in case it were not granted, involve the enterprise in unspeakable embarrassment by your withdrawal." Morehouse also declared that Rockefeller had neither time nor inclination to decide theological questions and to assume the responsibility for saying what Harper should teach—especially when that responsibility rested elsewhere.[59] This attitude was presumably a major premise of the pragmatic logic that Morehouse invoked: Rockefeller would not interefere.

When Harper accepted the office that may seem in retrospect to have been inevitably his, he realized that Morehouse and Rockefeller had not committed themselves explicitly to the principle of freedom; but he felt that they had not tied him too closely. Without demanding further explication of Rockefeller's position—indeed Harper remarked on the wonderfully fine shape in which Morehouse and Rockefeller had put the situation—he stated that he accepted the Chicago offer with the understanding that the platform was broad and free and that everyone had known beforehand what his position would be: ". . . I am free to do in the way of teaching what, under all the circumstances, seems to me wise."[60] This declaration expressed a view which influenced Harper's whole administration: the teacher was expected to exercise discretion, but he was not to be coerced into following the promptings of a mind and heart not his own.

The life of the University of Chicago as a college pure and simple was short. Although its first growth toward university stature owed nothing to the natural processes that had originally been expected to produce expansion, this growth had not violated conservative principle, financial or otherwise. The history of Harper's personal affairs in Chicago did begin with indebtedness because he borrowed $9,000 from the University in order to return money that Yale had advanced him against salary—and Harper remained in debt to the University for more than ten years.[61] The University, however, had not mortgaged the future to buy an extravagant present; the Rockefeller gift was assured wealth. Academically, the initial purpose of the University had been supplemented rather than scrapped; the commitment to build a college remained. Although the attempt to create undergraduate and graduate programs simultaneously did not accord with the history of older American institutions, it had precedent in the experience of Johns Hopkins, which was never without a college. The University had only about two-thirds as much money, on hand or in pledges, but was under no obligation to its donors to enter into rivalry with Johns Hopkins or any other institution. In Harper's eyes, the image of a great university shimmered in the air over the unprepossessing land that the Trustees received from the Education Society; but the terms of gifts specified only a college, a divinity school, and the beginnings of advanced study. Much more might be expected of the future of the University, but only what was planned and perhaps a modest enlargement of graduate work could be demanded of the funds actually committed to the University. Yet it *had* secured William Rainey Harper. Although there is no need to suppose, as folklore suggests, that in 1890 Harper embarked on a career of calculated and insatiable exploitation and every reason to believe that he entered his double appointment with a divided mind, the fact remains that he was an immensely energetic and highly strung young man. He had already had the heady experience of quickening the growth of the University and had begun to elaborate designs that would far outreach the resources at his command.

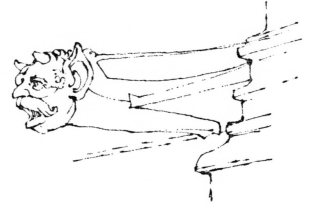

PART TWO

THE PLAN,
THE PEOPLE,
AND THE POLITY

A University among Universities

The University of Chicago was the lengthened shadow—or the projected radiance—of many men and women; but the initial work of refining the meaning of such words as "college" and "university," of adapting or inventing devices for instruction and investigation and of adjusting the parts of the University to make an architectonic whole—the work of creating the first plan fell largely to one man, its scholar-president. Once Harper was encouraged by Rockefeller's second gift to look beyond the limits of a college, the machinery of his imagination whirled. While he was traveling away from Chicago on a trip in September, 1890, the whole plan, he said, outlined itself in his mind: "It is 'bran splinter new' . . . and yet as solid as the ancient hills."[1] Harper predicted that the plan would revolutionize college and university work in the United States.

Although Harper may have planned the University in the physical seclusion of Pullman accommodations, moving across not so ancient farm country toward the eastern hills, intellectually he did not work within a closed cell. Experimentalism was in the air, and a number of innovations had already made headway against academic tradition. Charles W. Eliot had been a president-reformer for more than twenty years; he had written about the New Education before Harper graduated from college. Andrew D. White had already resigned the presidency of Cornell University, where he had sought to break new ground.

55

Johns Hopkins University, with Daniel G. Gilman at its head, had demonstrated the merits of a predominantly graduate program—and may have passed the high point of its early career.[2] G. Stanley Hall and his colleagues at Clark University had departed all but completely from the custom of offering undergraduate instruction; and at Stanford University, David Starr Jordan was about to set up a new model of higher education. In the Midwest, the state universities of Michigan and Wisconsin were moving forward aggressively. Yale had long since introduced the advanced studies from which Professor Harper had not finally withdrawn when he first planned the University of Chicago. It was novel as well as new; but the nature of its blueprint, and of its faculty and government, would reflect the fact that the University of Chicago did not stand alone as a university.

CHAPTER IV

The Old Testament
and the
New University

While he was planning the University of Chicago, William Rainey Harper borrowed designs freely, but he did not simply piece together an institution from the experiments of other men. Like a gifted artist working within the limits of an established style, he combined existing motifs with something from personal experience to create his own idea of a university. Yet Newman's phrase must be used guardedly. Harper's mind was powerful, but it was not speculative: Harper was a theologian only in the limited sense that he taught students of divinity. As a scholar he did not build a systematic philosophy of God, man, or truth; and as a university president he did not deduce the elements of the institution placed under his care from an idea or formal theory about the universe and the ways men must seek to understand it. Rather, his manner of working was inductive, a word which he used constantly. His plan was a mosaic, the bits of which were cemented into a pattern by a generalization derived from a single case, his own life as an investigator and teacher of the Bible. The one address by Harper, *The University and Democracy,* that may be considered a systematic treatment of a philosophy for higher education is organized around an analogy drawn from biblical society. The university was the prophet, priest, and sage of democracy. Although Harper spoke of the reference as a digression, it actually provided the rubrics of his analysis: ". . . the thoughts and the forms of thought of the ancient Hebrews have made deep impressions on my mind."[1]

Harper and the men about him had perforce examined the position of the scholar as he devoted himself to the highest and most controversial interests of Man. Their findings, published piecemeal in a journal, *The Old and New Testament Student,* over which Harper presided, virtually constituted a commentary upon the issues of academic life. The major premise of biblical scholarship was that God had unmistakably set his approval upon *"the search for His truth."* Harper never doubted that an absolute, divine truth did exist—and thus he was not a "modern man" if adherence to relativism be the test; but he saw nothing sinister or subversive in uninhibited research per se. Free inquiry did not necessarily require or produce a Faustian fall from grace.[2]

"The charge is made," ran an editorial in *The Old and New Testament Student,*

that a critical study of the Scriptures leads too often to a mere multiplication of doubt, and to the unsettling of the grounds of religious faith. One is told that it is hard enough at the best to hold unswervingly to the true path, to clear the mind of skepticism, and to receive in child-like faith the *credenda* of revelation. To gratify an idle curiosity by digging beneath the foundations is only to undermine them. Suppose we grant that the immediate result of criticism is an increase of doubt, that traditional conceptions to which the heart clings as to cherished heirlooms are ruthlessly shaken or overturned, and that the destruction of familiar and venerable beliefs, even in making room for the larger and better, is always painful and distressing. Nevertheless is it not the universal law that the increase of knowledge works increase of sorrow, at least for the time being, or until it has become possible to readjust ourselves to the new aspect of truth? Intellectual progress begins in questioning, and questioning begets doubt. It is harmful only when it stops at doubt. Outside the sphere of direct revelation it is unquestionable that every higher truth, or every enlarged conception of its relations, has been reached only by cutting a passage through opposing doubts to the sunlit heights beyond. It is the perpetual conflict with ignorance, error, and superstition; and conflict means suffering, but it means victory too. No man holds truth intelligently who holds it merely because he has been told to hold it in this form or that. A really intelligent grasp of truth, even of traditional truth, if we please, is possible to him only who has carefully examined and tested it, who has resolutely battled his way past skepticism, and who, when challenged, can give a valid reason for the faith that is in him. Criticism does not undermine the foundations. In the end it serves to reveal their impregnable solidity and strength. The soul of man is so constituted that it craves the larger knowledge even at the cost of present pain.[3]

Where enthusiasm for a pet view might lead a man astray, even dogged and obstreperous conservatism might render service. In the face of opposition, new truth would have to separate itself from false accretions:

The proclaimer of strange doctrines usually gets about what he deserves in the way of hard knocks. But what cares he? He knows that he has seen something that is real, and . . . still that real thing shall come forth unharmed, nay rather, better fitted to take its place in God's universe of enduring reality.[4]

Facts constituted the starting point of constructive thought. The search for facts should be specialized. The student of a difficult language and a complicated literature knows from experience that the grubbing, of which the general scholar may be contemptuous, has its essential uses; for the difference between the true and false generalization lies in the trustworthiness of the facts embraced and in the completeness with which they are grasped. The specialist and the specialist alone is their source. In pursuit of them he has to have freedom: "Let him uncover as many facts there as possible. We want the facts."[5] Yet the ultimate end of scholarship will not be served until the specialist's findings are brought together in understanding of the Bible as a whole. That is the sole end of studying words and sentences.

The calling of Bible study demanded of its followers an unending evangelical effort to enlarge the number of men capable of reading the Bible intelligently until the boundaries of humanity itself were reached.

Has not the day come when scholarship and the results of scholarly work shall no longer be kept apart and away from the masses? There are scholars who disdain to speak or to write in any other than a technical way; who feel that they are casting pearls before swine, if they make a statement which may be understood by others than those working in their own specialty. Is not this idea becoming antiquated? Is the popular presentation of scientific truth at all inconsistent with a real appreciation of that truth? . . . There has been a growing disposition to break down the wall which stands between knowledge and ignorance, between the few and the many. The contempt of the few for the ignorance of the many has not been greater than the distrust on the part of the many, of the knowledge of the few. But the breach is diminishing and let us hope that the best men in the ranks of scholarship will begin to feel, as they have never felt, the responsibility which rests upon them in this matter. Of him to whom much is given, much also is expected.[6]

In *The University and Democracy,* Harper was to say that the motto of the true university would be: "Service for mankind wherever mankind is, whether within scholastic walls or without those walls and in the world at large."[7] He went out to the world himself, with syllabus and the Word.*

* *The Old and New Testament Student* observed that it was not a fact of experience that the truth would prevail, however it was presented. A teacher might do everything in his power to win the student's acceptance of his opinions, he might simply lay an unclassified list of all opinions before his students without giving them any principles in accordance with which their own

The plan of the University, announced in its *Official Bulletin, No. 1,* called for both intra- and extramural programs or for virtually a union of scholarship and the academic counterpart of evangelism. The institution was to have three parts: the University Proper—the conventional academic division, University Extension Work, and University Publication Work. The University Proper would consist of preparatory academies, organized by the University or affiliated with it; four undergraduate colleges, of Liberal Arts, Science, Literature, and Practical Arts; affiliated colleges; a non-professional graduate school; and schools of divinity, law, medicine, engineering, pedagogy, fine arts, and music. Many of these elements fitted into a scheme adumbrated by the earlier history of the University project. The Articles of Incorporation empowered the Trustees to manage preparatory academies; and the plan which Gates and Harper devised in August, 1890, provided for the use of the Morgan Park Seminary buildings for a preparatory school. In effect, the *Bulletin* brought the program into accord with Gates's vision of academies clustered about centrally located colleges. Undergraduate instruction was required of the University itself by the terms of the initial pledges. The affiliation of colleges with the University had been foreshadowed by Morehouse's concern over the lack of central planning in Baptist higher education, by Gates's strategy for improving it in the Midwest, and by Harper's idea of an educational trust. Provision for some graduate studies and transformation of the seminary into a divinity school followed necessarily from the settlement that brought Rockefeller's second gift and (finally) Harper himself to the University. The other professional schools had not been much discussed before publication of the *Bulletin* but may have been subsumed under the rubric of natural growth. Such schools had long since been associated with American "universities," as the Rush Medical College had been with the old University of Chicago. The professional schools other than the

---

opinions might be formed, or he might help the student to decide for himself by arranging all the important facts of a case according to examined principles. The last method was preferred. The model of the teacher was Jesus, who did not, the *Student* said, announce that commonly accepted views were wholly false but rather accommodated himself to circumstances—as Gates reminded Harper. The *Student* distinguished between the matters at stake in Bible teaching and those of purely human science. The scientific man followed truth wherever it led him without much concern for the results that would follow from acceptance of his views; observing the results of shipwrecked faith, the Bible teacher—if he had sympathy and insight as well as learning—would hesitate long before taking a position opposed to accepted views or seeming to weaken the fundamentals commonly believed. Harper was a critic but by temperament no devotee of iconoclasm in matters of faith (*Old and New Testament Student,* XII [May, 1891], 258–60; VIII [October, 1888], 43; XIV [May, 1892], 260).

seminary were to be established as soon as the funds of the University permitted.[8]

University Extension had already been imported into the United States from Great Britain but had not figured in the earlier debate over the character of the University: instruction off-campus was apparently introduced into the plan on Harper's initiative. The division was to include (1) regular courses of lectures delivered in and about Chicago, "in accordance with the best developed plans of University-Extension" (on the British model?); (2) evening courses in college and university subjects also offered in and about the city for men and women kept away from regular courses by their jobs; (3) correspondence courses for students, in all parts of the country, who were unable to go to college the year round; (4) special courses in a scientific study of the Bible in its original languages and in translation; and (5) library extension (or the provision of books) in connection with the Extension courses.[9]

University publication work had been under way elsewhere in the United States but, like Extension, first appeared as part of the University program in the *Official Bulletin, No. 1*. Even then, the division was not designated a "university press," although it was designed partly to print and publish books "prepared" or edited by University instructors. Its other, somewhat miscellaneous, duties were to print and publish official University documents; to provide the same service in regard to special papers, journals, or scientific reviews, also prepared or edited by University instructors; to collect (by exchange) papers, journals, reviews, and books similar to those published by the University; and to deal in books for the students, professors, and the library.[10]

That tripartite design for a University plainly bore the personal stamp of a teaching investigator, an educator of the public at large, and a writing editor. The general regulations of the University were similarly marked. An unresting practitioner of summer instruction, Harper planned an academic year nearly as long as the calendar year. The University would be open four quarters, beginning, respectively, on the first day of October, January, April, and July; an interval of a week would separate one quarter from the next. The vacations of individual faculty members were to be so arranged that a working force should always be on hand. The standard annual load of teaching would be three quarters, or thirty-six weeks of lecturing, ten to twelve hours a week.* The instructor might accumulate credit for vacations, e.g., by serving four quarters for

* It was presently announced that the number of students in each course or section thereof would be limited to thirty (*Official Bulletin, No. 2*, revised edition [April, 1891], p. 13).

three years, and thus becoming entitled to twelve months of vacation on full salary. Also, he might vary the distribution of his load by teaching only six hours a week for two quarters instead of twelve hours a week for one quarter. By teaching more than the required amount, he could increase either his salary or his credit toward a vacation. Each quarter was to be divided into two equal "terms" of six weeks, the period which would fix the length of all courses. (The same subject might be continued through two or more terms.) Each course would be classified either as a Major, calling for ten to twelve hours of classroom work each week—an instructor's full load in any given term—or as a Minor, with four to six hours required.

The corps of lecturers and teachers was to be divided into twelve classes: Scholar, Fellow, Lecturer, Reader, Docent, Tutor, Instructor, Assistant Professor, Associate Professor, Non-Resident Professor, Professor, and Head Professor. The *Bulletin* implied that each head professor was to govern a department until his retirement from the Faculty, and this in fact was the rule after the University opened. He was to supervise the entire work of his department in general, prepare all entrance examination papers and approve all course examinations prepared by other instructors, arrange course offerings from quarter to quarter, examine all theses offered in the department, determine the textbooks to be used, edit any appropriate papers or journals, conduct a club or seminar, consult with the librarian about needed books and periodicals, consult with the President on appointments of instructors, and countersign the course certificates in the department. He was expected to consult with instructors about courses and textbooks; but of departmental democracy there was no other hint. Alone among department members, including professors, the head professor had explicitly defined powers.

In each of the larger jurisdictions, the academies, colleges, and schools of the University, the officers of instruction would constitute a Faculty, which was to meet at least once a month. The several faculties might meet together when there was no special reason for separate meetings. A University Council was also to hold monthly meetings to consider matters relating to general interests of the University or designated by Trustees as the proper work of the Council. Its decisions would be carried into effect only with the President's approval. The Council was to be composed of the President, the deans of the academies, colleges, and schools, one elected representative from each of the Faculties, and certain executive officers, i.e., the University Examiner, the University Recorder, the University Registrar, the University-Extension Secretary, and the University Librarian. These administrators, as well as the President, were to teach.[11]

The organization of the student's work reflected Harper's idea of intellectual economy and the demand that he made upon his own students, that they should immerse their minds in Hebrew studies. Normally the student would take one Major and one Minor each term, which meant a concentration of two-thirds of his study time upon one subject. Up to half of his work might be done in the University Extension division; and residence might begin at the opening of any quarter. Upon completion of six Majors and six Minors, the student would be advanced in class standing, and he might presently receive a Bachelor's, Master's, or Doctor's degree on recommendation of the appropriate Faculty body. No honorary degrees were to be conferred by the University. This regulation, the last to appear in the *Official Bulletin, No. 1,* was printed in italics: the University was concerned academically with nothing but work, unceasing work.[12]

The plan of the University, as it was first announced and subsequently amplified, was covered by a filigree of details. As indicated by Harper's jottings to himself in a series of red memorandum books, he had a passion for extended enumeration. The *Official Bulletin, No. 1,* ended with a list of twenty-six advantages possessed by the plan, the first being that it would secure concentration on the part of the student and the last, that it would provide "for the administration of the institution in accordance with a truly American and a truly University spirit."[13] Harper's mode of expression almost belongs in the literary genre of the imaginary land minutely described. He fell painfully short of a Dean Swift in vivacity of phrase, but he had some of the satirist's magic in the use of particulars. Moving from feature to feature of the plan, the reader forgets that it is a prospectus and not an account of an existing institution. There stands a university, possessing factitious reality in the manner of a *trompe-l'œil.*

Harper's lists give an effect of indiscriminate emphasis, even of idiosyncracy. Greater stimulation of original investigation appears as an advantage of the plan just before a reference to the possibility of a course in bookkeeping and stenography. Yet the objects before Harper's mind as he considered the uses of the plan were at once widely and deeply significant, e.g., accommodation of the impecunious, acceleration of the able, elevation of standards, and the encouragement of "an independent feeling on the part of all men who share in the advantages of the University."[14] The administrative gimmicks sprang from a mind that had its own simplicity.

Long after Harper's death, an observer of the University described it in Dickensian language which is as appropriate to the original plan as to the mature institution. The University, he said, had "a completeness—a kind of universal dovetailedness with regard to place and time—a sort of general oneness."[15] The unity of Harper's conception lay in his dedication to the discovery and dissemination of truth for the good of Man. In its essence, the plan was a statement of intention: the University was to be a great series of experiments in human enlightenment. The core of the apparatus would be a body of teaching investigators like Harper himself. They would be encircled by audiences: the students on the University campus, the students and faculties of other institutions to be brought into the orbit of the University by affiliation, the scattered company of aspiring students who lived away from learned institutions, and the reading public at large. Listeners in each circle were to be reached in a manner suited to their situation and by methods so flexible that nobody would be excluded because he did not fit into a conventional pattern of study. Presently Harper would remark upon the vastness of the field for experiment in education; if only those who experimented would be quick to discard what was wrong, education had nothing to fear: "No one can fail to see that our institutions of learning are as much trammelled by traditions embodying ideas which have been dead for decades, as the church is trammelled by dogmas of which the real meaning has been forgotten."[16]

When Harper was composing the plan, he felt that it had so many new elements in it that he would be surprised if he had not made some serious mistakes.[17] Publication of a precise blueprint might itself have proved to be a colossal mistake, making the whole project seem an illusion, if Harper had refused to lead the institution he planned. When the University had been open but three months, he said that doubtless definiteness of plan appeared premature but that it had already shown it had power to move men to action.[18] For the years after he had accepted office, the published expectations of the University assuredly left him no excuse to rest. And once committed to the University himself, he took it for granted that others shared his dedication to the task of making the projected institution an actuality.

CHAPTER V

Negotiations

Having openly committed itself to a large plan before a public already accustomed to the display of academic enterprise, the University set about to procure the physical resources and faculty of a great university in an academic community already competitive. The actual rate and direction of the growth of the University beyond the limits of a college had yet to be determined in a series of critical negotiations. Rockefeller's second gift—$1,000,000 for theological and graduate education—sufficed to inspire Harper but not to underwrite his ambitions for the University and the public expectations that they in turn inspired.

When Goodspeed received word of the gift, he was overjoyed. "It is a glorious thing you have accomplished," he wrote to Harper.[1] But in less than a week he was moved to tell Harper that such a union of the University and the seminary as would complete the endowment of the latter would defeat Harper's plans. Too much, Goodspeed intimated, was being expected of a million dollars, and the division of Rockefeller's second gift was not in fact easily arranged. From the beginning of his incumbency, Harper could never spend money as freely as he wished. Finding that Harper was troubled, Goodspeed urged him to be content at the start with a seed and to let it develop instead of beginning with the "biggest thing in the world."[2] Goodspeed's "very conservative" estimate that the University would have an income of $75,000 for the first school year was intended to hearten the President: ". . . you will have all the money you need."[3]

Writing in a similar vein, Martin A. Ryerson offered Harper whatever consolation he could find in thinking of the possibilities before the University, "even though they make our financial means look smaller every day."[4]

For Harper, the pleasure of discovering those possibilities failed to offset the pain of finding how short a distance the resources of the University would stretch. Goodspeed's prediction was irrelevant as long as Harper's impatience at seeing opportunity missed exceeded the satisfaction to be derived in balancing accounts. Presently Goodspeed felt that cautionary words were required:

While I am ambitious for the University that it shall have the best of everything, I am most anxious that we shall go forward carefully, avoid debts, as we have from the beginning promised to do, by a wise business management commend the work to the business public & to the man who has done the most for it. . . . You know it is a favorite idea of yours that a great University is simply a great business.[5]

"It is impossible," Goodspeed wrote again a few days later,

to overstate the importance of our keeping our heads *financially* clear up above water. I think it will go far to keep your stock away up above par with the Board if they find you co-operating with them in making for the University the cleanest kind of a financial record. If we can do this especially during the next five years it will be worth other millions to us with J. D. R. who as you know is a careful business man & will look with great favor on a like carefulness in us.[6]

The thought of securing other millions from the Founder by a display of carefulness in finance was to stay with Goodspeed through the years.[7]

The men of the University had reason to worry about the Founder's attitude. As Gates reported, anxiety over Chicago was making Rockefeller ill: he had begun to fear that Chicago was not doing its part. Although he wanted to keep in sympathy with the work, he was much troubled lest more was expected of him than he was prepared to perform. Gates tried to cheer him up by reciting a long list of encouraging signs from Chicago, but also wrote Harper of Rockefeller: ". . . we must be very considerate of him. . . . We must not press him for money." Gates added:

I hope you will be able to repress every tendency to larger things than are really necessary for a respectable opening. Leave room for growth. We are just setting up housekeeping and the public will not expect everything at first. Nobody expects a full-fledged University at the start. Will it not be wiser to begin too small than too big?[8]

Later, Gates spelled out that advice. The very outside limit of expenditures for the first year should fall considerably within accurate estimates of income. ". . . I need not argue with you," Gates wrote Harper, that it would be folly unspeakable for any institution to start out on a permanent plan of expenditure in excess of a just estimate of income. The friends of the University will not consent for a moment to any plan of subscription for current expenses. That is, in my opinion, the certain road to ruin. Every dollar that can be raised at all should go into buildings, equipment and endowment. Nothing would more certainly and immediately cripple the institution, scare off its friends and bring it into disrepute than subscriptions for deficiencies and current expenses.[9]

As Gates was to recall, he and Goodspeed viewed Harper's early plan for instruction with alarm. They sought to impress their views upon the Board, Gates (with the greatest solemnity) reporting Rockefeller's objection to the incurring of debt and his determination neither to pay debts nor to assist with the current expenses.[10] In August, 1891, E. Nelson Blake, first President of the Board, noted to his disappointment that some of the Baptist subscribers had not yet paid anything: "We have laid out too magnificent plans."[11] While the retirement of Blake from the Presidency of the Board was under discussion, Goodspeed backed Ryerson as the man to head the corporation. With Ryerson as President of the Board, Hutchinson as Treasurer, and Ferdinand W. Peck as Chairman of the Finance Committee, the University would have in responsible financial positions "three of the leading young business men of the city. . ." and would have a pull on the wealth of Chicago that it could not get in any other way. "Those three men can raise more money than any other three men in Chicago."[12] Their presence in positions of responsibility would emphasize the liberal spirit of the institution. (Some ministers protested to Alonzo K. Parker, the only ministerial Trustee, against what they thought would be giving control of the Board to a non-Baptist; but Parker was himself pleased with what he had seen of Ryerson.)[13]

Money did begin to come in. A "splendid liberality" quite refuted the pessimism felt by Gates when the Trustees had decided on the purchase of enough land to create, with the land Marshall Field had donated, a campus covering four city blocks.[14] Toward the end of 1891, the University launched a million-dollar drive for buildings to be erected before the end of the first academic year. It was Harper's hope to get this support from "outside parties," by which he presumably meant persons who were neither Baptist subscribers nor non-Baptists already committed to the University.[15] The acquisition of the Berlin library, an important collection of scholarly books purchased in Germany, had a happy moral effect upon this canvass. In February, 1892, Sidney A. Kent of Chicago gave $150,000 for a chemical laboratory; and Marshall Field offered the University $100,000 if a million was secured in sixty days—a limit which was soon extended. Toward the end of the campaign, Goodspeed was despondent, but Harper predicted that the University would get a good deal of money beyond the million. Gates, standing at a distance from the campaign itself, was inclined to share some of Goodspeed's feeling. Then a syndicate, led by Hutchinson, guaranteed to cover any shortage.[16]

In mid-February, Hutchinson chatted with Harper by letter from the Nile: Egypt was a land of *bukra*—or tomorrow—and the modern Arab was born, lived, and died begging baksheesh—or alms. Hutchinson might have added that the words were applicable to Harper's life, although not precisely in the sense known to the fellahin. To bring the future into the present, Harper was obliged to beg: the end justified and necessitated the means, which he accepted, he insisted, to his own distaste. Somewhat later, after having visited Abu Simbel, Hutchinson spoke of Egypt and the University together: "This is a marvellous land. Its monuments are overwhelming. We must build well at the new university if we hope to leave as enduring evidences of our work behind. This we shall do however in spirit if not in stone."[17] After the early months of 1892, the new University could expect to build in stone and also to escape the particular fate of its predecessor; but building funds, however large and quickly come by, did not cover current expenses. The most critical item among them was the academic payroll, the size of which would be fixed by the number of Faculty appointments and by the salary levels.

The composition and quality of the Faculty would go far toward determining the spirit of the University. At its opening, the University did not have a complete Faculty: the first *Official Bulletin* of January, 1891, specified that the University Proper was to consist initially of an undergraduate department, a "nonprofessional" graduate school, and a divinity school, the establishment of other professional schools being left to the future.[18] Looking back after a decade upon the organization of the University, Harper was to intimate that some thought was given to the immediate creation of a Department of Technology, but it did not seem wise at the time to lay too much emphasis upon the practical side of education. "No one could fail to see that sooner or later in an environment like that of Chicago the practical side would be sufficiently cared for."[19] The original Faculty was to be devoted principally to instruction and research in the arts and sciences, or to what is sometimes called "pure" scholarship and science. Harper himself used the adjective.

Even a Faculty prepared to cover the arts and sciences alone would be a numerous company; for academic learning had already become specialized in the United States. The omnibus chairs—or settees—of the old-fashioned colleges were obsolete. To staff each of the recognized departments with one man or woman in each of the several grades that Harper envisaged in his original plan, a university would have to recruit staff members by the dozen. Patronage of disciplines which were not already fully recognized would increase the size of the Faculty. Clark University, which had just opened when Harper began to gather together a Faculty, did not try to do justice to all of the arts and sciences but rather concentrated its resources upon a few departments, notably the sciences. (Johns Hopkins University had originally offered graduate instruction by but five full professors—in Greek, mathematics, biology, chemistry, and physics: one of Harper's correspondents told him that the founders of Johns Hopkins had been advised, ". . . get a great mathematician and a famous Hellenist, and the rest will come.")[20] For the University of Chicago, Harper approached men and women in a large number of the disciplines, old and new, and at the outset created small cadres of the Faculty called for by his grand design.

Harper's success as a builder of a Faculty was spectacular but not easy, for the academic world in which Harper moved was neither impoverished nor unappreciative of professorial talent. From his own experience at Yale, Harper must have learned how far existing institutions would go to hold a first-class professor. (In 1893, Frank K. Sanders, one of Harper's associates at Yale, remarked to him that no university could possibly be made to dominate the whole country— the University of Chicago could not do so even with billions to spend.)[21] Moreover, Stanford University was also recruiting academic talent. "I find that we are likely to cross each other's path more than once in the selection of our faculty," President David Starr Jordan wrote Harper.[22] He was warned by the economist, Richard T. Ely, that "it requires a much larger capital to start a great university than it did fifteen years ago. If the Johns Hopkins were starting out to-day with its original endowment, it could not duplicate the work which it has done. We started at a peculiarly favorable time, when in our field there was very little competition. . . ."[23]

A Faculty of first-rate scholars proved indeed to be expensive. The men and women Harper sought were not so unworldly that they were indifferent to the dollar value put upon their services. Professional loyalty and pride fortified whatever self-interest each of them consulted: the person who accepted less in salary than the importance of university instruction warranted and the dignity of the academic calling required would let down the profession. The University might have searched primarily for promising but relatively untried and available young scholars and scientists; but Harper attempted to create a Faculty led by men of established reputation, which meant that he had to move the least mobile members of the academic world. If he succeeded, the University would have unsurpassed prestige from the day it opened; if he failed, the *Official Bulletins* might seem but the gaudy scraps of a punctured balloon.*

The University was not without weapons in the competition for talent. Harper's persuasiveness was to become legendary. Alice Freeman Palmer, who had lately resigned as president of Wellesley, wrote Harper: "If you would see people enough, you could make them do anything."[24] Even as Professor Harry P. Judson of the University of Minnesota drew back from an offer which had been made to him, he admitted that for a time he had been a convert to Harper's eloquence: "I allowed my enthusiasm to run away with my judgment."[25] (Eventually, Judson did join Harper's original Faculty—and stayed on to become Harper's immediate successor in the Presidency, where he would not often let enthusiasm run free.) Harper refused to hear the word *no,* and he had the greatest faith in negotiation, in which he was remarkably patient and inventive.

In the spring of 1891, Harper approached Ernest D. Burton of the Newton Theological Institution, who was to become Head Professor of New Testament Literature and Exegesis—and Judson's successor in the Presidency. Burton asked a number of questions about an appointment but was not wholly satisfied with Harper's answers, partly because there were no specific promises of increases in salary. An initial salary of $3,000 Burton thought inadequate; the professor who accepted that sum would be hampered. "This is perhaps one of the details which you would prefer to have left to the future. But it seems to me that it had better be fixed to begin with." In June, Burton was still non-committal, and Harper apparently allowed negotiations to lapse for the time being. In December he asked for an interview, which Burton granted. Burton promised to reach a decision within a week, but later wrote to ask for more time. He was still undecided in March, 1892, when President Hovey of Newton Seminary wrote to Burton, in not very cryptic language, of the "larger and congenial sphere of influence" Burton would have if Hovey resigned his presidential office,

---

* At Johns Hopkins University, President Daniel C. Gilman had employed the strategy of appointing promising young men to professorships, but not as a matter of free choice. He sought at first to attract men already distinguished (see Hugh Hawkins, *Pioneer: A History of the Johns Hopkins University, 1874–1889* [Ithaca: Cornell University Press, 1960], pp. 38 ff.). Gilman's success with the alternative was brilliant, but he had not given such hostages to potentially unfriendly opinion as Harper did from the moment *Official Bulletin, No. 1,* was published.

which he said he would do if Burton agreed to stay at Newton. (Perhaps it was with thoughts of leading the seminary that Burton began to draft a financial appeal to a now unidentified donor. Did Burton hope that Rockefeller would help Newton as he had Morgan Park?) Almost exactly a year after the opening of his negotiations with Harper, Burton declined the Chicago offer. Harper answered by wire: "Your telegram was a source of surprise and great disappointment to me. I appreciate of course that you are the only person to decide this matter, but I hope it is not finally decided, and beg that you will let me have one more chance before I am obliged to give up. What in the world do you expect us to do?" Despite some forebodings about the religious atmosphere of the University, Burton did specify terms, and Harper accepted them: "The whole thing is settled."[26]

It was characteristic of Harper's negotiations that Burton was promised an increase of salary effective within two years. Harper did not hesitate to pledge the future in the interest of immediately securing what he wanted. "You invite me to come to Chicago for the sake of a prospect . . . [and] to be candid, the *prospect* is absolutely all that has interested me in your proposition"; "Before I can say yes or no, I need to be informed precisely what I am asked to do, and also how much is implied by your phrase about 'promotion in the immediate future' "; "I said sincerely . . . that the appointment pleased me . . . because of what the work is in itself, and because of what you have intimated in reference to the future."[27] These are the responses that Harper's advances called forth. But how far did Harper's intimations carry him into moral commitments which exceeded the actual capabilities of the University?

Undoubtedly Harper's faith in the future was inspiring. His conviction that a great possibility lay ahead made Chicago seem a new dispensation. One of Harper's correspondents wrote, "I am interested in any plan for starting an institution unshackled by vicious yet time-honored usage."[28] And others caught fire with enthusiasm for things that ought to happen in scholarship and science:

President Albion W. Small of Colby College: Sociology is really, though not ostensibly, an attempt to organize a *Novum Organum* of all the sciences that contribute to an understanding of life. The task is so prodigious that very few men conceive it in its entirety. . . . Our Chicago scheme is the first on this continent to provide for Social Science a chance to be fundamental & comprehensive.[29]

Professor Charles O. Whitman of Clark University: The time has now come when we must recognize and live up to the necessity for greater organic unity among kindred sciences. It is not enough today that an investigator have the means to carry out his own researches. He must have colleagues around him who will take care of the more important special branches so that something like a whole can be represented by the associate workers. We are now forced to specialize, and the only corrective for the dangers of specialization is combination and co-ordination. That is the path of progress in the future.[30]

Professor John U. Nef of Clark University: I am really convinced that it will be possible to develop a school of Chemistry at Chicago comparable with the best in Germany. That is my great ambition and to that aim and object I am willing to devote all the strength and enthusiasm that I possess. There is not the slightest reason why this country should not develop men who love chemistry for its own sake and who will be willing to sacrifice much for it....[31]

Miss Marion Talbot of Wellesley College: I would suggest the establishment of a "department of public health." I am encouraged to do this by Prof. [George H.] Palmer's assurance that the Univ. of C. is to do pioneer and unique work along advanced lines in addition to its other functions. Such a department has recently been organized in some of the foreign universities but there is as yet in this country no large opportunity for work in this field....[32]

But great expectations, however persuasively and persistently exhibited, were not enough to win the University a Faculty. The situation before Harper was well described by the reflections of Professor George H. Palmer. Writing to Professor J. Laurence Laughlin of Cornell, he remarked:

If half a dozen men like you and [Professor William G.] Hale, who are recognized throughout the country as masters in your departments, will go, Chicago will be as distinct a power in the country as Harvard or Yale.... A group of men freshly selected, who had confidence in one another, and who were all alive for conquering the ignorance of the country, could make a tremendous impression.

But that is where my doubt lies. If only a few persons of this high University grade go, they will be powerless. ... But I would not advise anybody to risk himself there, unless he had a suitable number of associates who shared his own higher ideas and were determined to fight for them....[33]

It might well have struck Harper that he was caught in a vicious circle. Professors worth appointing would wait until the University proved that it had a faculty worth joining.* Harper had worked for many months on the organization of the University when, in the winter of 1891–92, Laughlin and Hale ac-

---

* The case was not unique. In 1876, while Gilman was organizing Johns Hopkins University, he had exclaimed: "We can't have a great University without great teachers; & great teachers won't come to us till we have a great University!" (Daniel C. Gilman to C. F. B. Bancroft, February 7, 1876, quoted in Hawkins, *Pioneer*, p. 42).

cepted head professorships. These men were the first to join the Faculty at that level and consented to come to Chicago only after a drastic change of policy in regard to salaries. Although it might have seemed to the world that Harper had limitless resources behind him, in the beginning he could not make remarkably large offers, even to prospective head professors. Hale did not allow the University to forget the possible consequences of that fact:

Hale to Harper, September 10, 1891: You said to me that you felt sure that the salaries would be raised before long. How much more valuable the higher salaries would be now, when you are endeavoring to get men to go to you! Your plan is to get the best men that can be found. Chicago trustees must be capable, as business men, of seeing that the best persons in any art are not easily to be dislodged from places where they have taken root.

Hale to Harper, October 29, 1891: So great a University as you desire yours to be should offer an adequate salary, sufficient to induce able men to leave places they have become attached to. . . . Believe me, I am not thinking only of a possible interest of my own. I am thinking of the good of the University of Chicago, and of education in America.

Hale to Charles L. Hutchinson, November 14, 1891: I believe that the University has it in its power to command a great future. But it must start with a body of teachers and investigators whose names will place it in the front rank from the beginning. What is done now, for good or ill, cannot be undone in twenty years. You will hardly succeed at all upon a $5,000 scale. You will be sure of a moderate success at $6,000. But you will not, at that salary, be able to move a single full professor, or assistant professor with a full professorship before him, from Yale or Harvard. But this would simply mean that you were content to start in the second rank, in the hope that in another generation you might reach the first.

Hale to Hutchinson, November 25, 1891: No absolutely new thing remains for the University of Chicago to do, in order to be great from the outset, except to get together a faculty of the first order. . . . If you had already age, an assured endowment, and a faculty of the first rank, then you would find excellent men to come at $6,000. But something more is wanted now. The thing you could do is so admirable that I cannot reconcile myself to its not being done.

Hale to Harper, December 26, 1891: I am deeply interested in your plans and believe that the University of Chicago has a great future before it, if certain things are done. One of these things is the recognition of the value to the University of the services of the men whom you select, a value founded on long years of training and successful labor. If your Board of Trustees does not recognize this, then I do not believe that the University will win a distinguished success. If they do recognize it, then that recognition will show itself in the actual estimate set upon a professor's work. . . . I do not believe you will command success, if your Trustees cannot take a large view of University policy. And they can take it more easily now than after they have got started. I think we shall be of service to you by making [them make] their attitude known now.[34]

As far as Hale himself was concerned, attitude was all important: "If I judge that the policy of the Trustees, *as far as their convictions go,* will be against a $7,000 scale . . . then I shall telegraph you merely to hand in my declination. I don't want a salary unwillingly paid."[35] As Hale declared his intention to Harper on the day after Christmas in 1891, he made plans to join Ryerson and Hutchinson on the train at Syracuse as they traveled to New York. Hale wanted to take the measure of the Trustees at first hand; but the illness of his son, threatened by diphtheria, kept him in Ithaca. Laughlin, however, did meet Ryerson and Hutchinson in New York; and after talking with Laughlin, the two Trustees wired Harper. Meeting in Chicago on December 29, the Board of Trustees increased the salary of head professors from $6,000 to $7,000, and voted for the appointment of both Laughlin and Hale at that level.[36] Hutchinson declared, "I have no fears to the future of the University;" and Hale was jubilant:

I cannot tell you how great an impulse I believe you have given, not only to the University of Chicago, but to the status of the professional body throughout the country, by bringing your trustees to the last step taken. They must also be enlightened men, to have been persuaded to the step.

We shall come with the greatest hope and cheer. You can hardly imagine the difference that last thousand made. And you will be able, if not now (though I think now), at least very soon, to command any man whom you want to have come. . . .[37]

Hale's optimism was excessive. He thought it vital that Harper should break into Harvard or Johns Hopkins—"And I think that . . . it will give greater éclat to break into the former"; but Harper failed to breach the senior faculty of either institution.[38] William I. Knapp, Street Professor of Modern Languages at Yale, did follow Harper to Chicago, in disgruntlement over what Knapp thought to be the unjust, not to say outrageous, distribution of Yale appointments between modern and classical languages; and two professors from Clark University, Albert A. Michelson and Charles O. Whitman, came to Chicago with a number of other men of lower rank—almost half of the Clark faculty.[39] Clark was then short of funds; and a number of men there, who happened to constitute a large segment of a very small faculty, were discontented with the administration—as Knapp was at Yale; they were ready to listen to a president on a raid for talent. The sensational and, for Clark, terrible effect of Harper's enterprise testifies no less to the vulnerability of that university than to the seductiveness of Harper's offers. What President G. Stanley Hall described as the hegira from Worcester may explain but does not justify the impression still conveyed by academic folklore that Harper carried everything before him.*

The difficulties which Harper encountered in the eastern universities were offset by his success elsewhere. He secured Hermann von Holst from the University of Freiburg as head professor of history, and he persuaded Thomas C. Chamberlin and Albion W. Small to leave presidential chairs—at Wisconsin and Colby—to become head professor of geology and head professor of sociology, respectively. (The recruitment of two presidents for senior posts indicates the attractiveness of a university professorship and throws light on Harper's own unwillingness to relinquish his Yale post to take a *college* presidency. Harper's colleagues were men of his own kind, not only in ambition but in experience as academic governors: the Faculty, including the fellows, and the administration contained nine persons who at some time had been seminary, college, or university presidents.)

Von Holst, Chamberlin, and Small, with Knapp, Michelson, Whitman, Laughlin, Hale, Burton, and Harper himself constituted the core of the Arts, Literature, and Science faculty as head professors: the University was indeed headed by authentic leaders of the several disciplines.† Gifted men and women appeared in the lower ranks of the faculty down through the level of the fellows, among whom were several PH.D.'s, including Thorstein Veblen. The members of the Faculty were distributed between the Divinity School, University Extension, and the departments of the Arts, Literature, and Science, to which the great majority were assigned.‡ During the first year, the Faculty con-

* One joke of the time ran: Caller (at the door of eastern college professor)—Is Dr. Sanskrit in? Servant—He is, sir; but he is engaged. Caller—Engaged! Great Caesar! Is that Chicago University going to get him too? (Quoted from the *Chicago Tribune* in the *University of Chicago Weekly*, I, 2 [October, 1892], 7). The fact is that Harper did not usually encounter sentiment in favor of secession among eastern *university* professors.

† Galusha Anderson, Eri B. Hulbert, and George W. Northrup moved from the seminary at Morgan Park to become head professors in the Divinity faculty, where Harper and Burton also held appointments (*Register*, 1892–93 [Chicago: University of Chicago Press, 1893], p. 136).

‡ At the end of the first year, following partition of biology, the departments of the Arts, Literature, and Science were: Philosophy (with Apologetics and Christian Ethics and later Psychology and Pedagogy); Political Economy; Political Science; History; Social Science (Sociology) and Anthropology; Comparative Religion; Semitic Languages and Literatures; Biblical and Patristic Greek; Sanskrit and Indo-European Philology; Greek Language and Literature; Latin Language and Literature; Romance Literature and Philology; Germanic Languages and Literatures; English Language, Literature, and Rhetoric; Biblical Literature in English; Mathematics; Astronomy; Physics; Chemistry; Geology; Botany; Zoölogy and Palæontology; Anatomy and Histology; Physiology; Neurology; Elocution; and Physical Culture (*Register*, 1892–93 [Chicago: University of Chicago Press, 1893], p. v).

tained 147 regular members including docents, fellows, and so forth, as the statutes stipulated, or 77 members in the now conventional faculty ranks of instructor and above. At those levels, the members of the departments of the humanities, by the present system of classification, constituted about half of the Faculty of Arts, Literature, and Science; and the biological and physical scientists with the mathematicians about a third, the social scientists making up the remainder. Yet that division is arbitrary: in the broad meaning of the humanities that embraces much of history (for example), the Faculty members, in the greater part, were humanistically inclined in their work. The seventy-seven instructors and professors of the several grades had studied at more than fifty colleges, universities, technological institutes, and other institutions of higher learning scattered over two continents, from Naples and Stockholm to Waterville, Maine, and Berkeley, California. By the measure of earned degrees granted to members of the Faculty, Yale was much more strongly represented, by sixteen, than any other institution; in that sense, the University did become a western Yale. Harvard had granted eight; the University of Michigan seven; the Morgan Park seminary (officially the Baptist Union Theological Seminary) seven; and Johns Hopkins five. Leipzig had also granted five—a fact that might appear to indicate a point of equilibrium between the pull of Germany and the effort to create an American equivalent of advanced study abroad. According to the count of all ph.d. degrees held by faculty members, the balance had already shifted to the American side. The number of German ph.d.'s was fourteen and of the American twenty-one or possibly twenty-two. (The nature of one ph.d. is in doubt.) Of those American degrees, Yale had granted nine.

The thirteen head professors, who were in the most powerful position ex officio to influence the academic life of the University, held five (or six) earned ph.d.'s, of which two were German. European modes of education and investigation had become known to a significant fraction of the professoriate at first hand; but the greater number of such models as the degrees of Faculty members represented lay at a shorter distance to the East. What memories and aspirations, as well as what frustrations, the getting of degrees had yielded can only be guessed at.[40]

The distinction of the Faculty did not lie wholly in the quality of men and women who conducted the more conventionally academic programs. Harper secured Richard G. Moulton, one of the most successful Extension teachers of England, to lecture in the Extension division of the University; and he brought

Amos Alonzo Stagg to establish a Department of Physical Culture within the pale of the Faculty. But Harper failed in an attempt to secure Frederick T. Gates as "University Inspector" in charge of relating the University to other institutions—the affiliation program: "This is a delicate and yet a most important work. It is just the thing you can do to perfection."[41] Gates was indeed a gifted and experienced practitioner of institutional diplomacy, but he preferred to assist the University without accepting a portfolio—a decision which reveals his mastery of the art. His usefulness to the University would depend upon his freedom to serve as an inspector not of other institutions but of the University itself. Harper also failed to find a person capable of providing brilliant leadership to the library. Melvil Dewey, inventor of the decimal system of book classification bearing his name, was inspired by a visit in Chicago to generate a set of suggestions only a little less sweeping and no less enthusiatically phrased than Harper's ideas; but the University would not meet Dewey's terms. He wanted a commission and a salary commensurate with the scope of his great dream, according to which, one suspects, Dewey and Harper would have been more nearly alternatives to each other than likely colleagues.[42] (Harper never did find a first-class university librarian—and this perhaps was his greatest and most puzzling failure as an academic organizer.)

The men and women who joined Harper in Chicago brought with them ardent attachments to a number of causes and movements. Stagg indeed personified the ideal of collegiate athletics as a moral force. Albion W. Small and Charles R. Henderson, who became the University Chaplain, represented sociological study as an instrument of Christian social reform. Alice Freeman Palmer and her assistant, Marion Talbot, had been deeply involved in the crusade on behalf of the education and rights of women. Harper, Ernest D. Burton, and others were committed to a reformation of Protestantism through scholarship. Ten years after the University opened, George E. Vincent, sometime fellow of the first year who had become Dean of the Junior Colleges, echoed a remark by Harper concerning tradition at the University, that from the outset the Faculty was itself a complex of traditions. Vincent explained that the men and women who were brought together from the East and West and from overseas embodied divers customs, habits, and ideals: "Conflict between these forces was inevitable. The sons of Harvard praised the ways of Cambridge; the men from New Haven had much to say of the Yale spirit; the Hopkins doctors and the Germans were keen for research; the men of the Middle West were a bit impatient with what they deemed the conservatism of the East."[43] The devotion which the several Faculty members felt for their own, specialized disciplines or departments was sometimes divisive. Yet the ideal of inquiry and the cognate idea of academic service as a high profession enjoyed wide support within the Faculty. Its members were not usually inclined to talk, as had an earlier generation, of the great American university; but they had learned by heart the lesson taught by their predecessors. The academic way was itself a cause.

The professoriate was an incalculably valuable asset academically, but one which the University could ill afford financially. True, estimates of expendable funds rose slightly. Assuming a return of between 5 and 6 per cent on $1,400,-000 (the sum of the two Rockefeller gifts for the support of the University exclusive of the Divinity School), Gates estimated that income from investment would be about $75,000. Adding $40,000 from tuitions—which, he felt, was too high—Gates found that the University would have $115,000. For safety's sake, he dropped the figure to $105,000. That, he intimated, should be the limit of commitments for the first year: "An endowment of $1,400,000 will not run a $3,000,000 institution. . . ."[44] But until all instalments of the Rockefeller subscriptions had been paid in, the University would not in fact have even $1,400,000. Of this Gates was fully aware; for he asked Harper explicitly if he would be willing to have Rockefeller commit himself to pay interest on the whole amount of his pledges on condition that the Treasurer of the University should forward a quarterly certificate showing that interest payments had met expenditures. Gates also implied that the Founder might immediately fulfil his pledges: "What encouragement would Mr. R. have to pay up fully now in order to avoid appeals for current expenses, if the schedule [of expenditures] is considerably beyond any just estimate of income even if all were paid up?"[45]

Harper was entirely willing to accept Gates's proposition and indeed asserted that he had never in any way proposed to spend more than income—that he had proposed from the beginning and at Rockefeller's own suggestion to make an appeal for a special fund to carry the University over the first three years, unless sufficient income from endowment were secured. He did not want Gates or anyone else to think that he had ever deliberately planned to carry the University into debt. That he had, Harper added, was the implication of Gates's remarks. Harper had planned on a larger income because he felt that the University should secure funds in addition to the Rockefeller gifts.[46] (Such expectations were not fatuous. The University learned that it would receive a large segment of the estate of William B. Ogden, long a leading resident of Chicago who for years had presided over the Board of the old University. The terms of a gift were arranged after much negotiation, and the Board authorized establishment of the Ogden (Graduate) School of Science in 1891. The first payment on the Ogden Fund was not made, however, until October, 1893, or until the expenses for salary of the members of the Ogden Scientific Faculty had already been incurred. The hopes of the University were justified but not in time to help during the academic year of 1892–93.)[47] Gates also contemplated the possibility of a larger endowment. He wanted the University to get more money as fast as it could, although he believed that ". . . enlargement should be built on the rock of funds on hand, not on the sands of hope."[48] The Board was similarly conservative. At approximately the same time that it authorized Harper to offer as much as $7,000 to head professors, it voted a ceiling of $100,000 for the academic payroll for the first year. (That sum exceeded income as then estimated by $25,000; but members of the Board pledged themselves to provide that amount.) When Gates visited Chicago in January, 1892, he was pleased to find that the Board was determined that there must be no debt.[49] On the other hand, Gates was appalled at the inadequacy of the provisions in sight for the work "thrust upon" the institution for the first year.[50] The predicament of the University was not of its own making; it was not the product of mistakes by the Board but rather of the load of instruction the University would have to bear. "The problem is no longer how to get students, but how to provide for them."[51] It was quite impossible, Gates said, to meet the diversified needs of seven hundred postgraduate and undergraduate students on a salary list of $100,000. Half again that amount was needed for Faculty alone, and negotiations then in progress would more than use up an added $50,000.

Gates's acceptance of that prediction was a key to his advice to Rockefeller. Far from condemning Harper for opening such negotiations, Gates noted that Harper did not dare to close with Faculty men then ready to come to Chicago until funds were in sight to pay them. Nor could Harper dally: "He is in much trouble." Gates sought to assist him by quickly recommending that Rockefeller provide either $2,000,000 or the income of such a sum, the principal to be pledged. The income of half of that sum (or $50,000) should be used for more academic salaries and the income of the remainder for the Divinity School, books, apparatus, and various necessary expenses. Although the last three items represented temporary expenses, Gates asked for principal to provide for them. The pledge was required to meet the certain demands of the first year and would remove the difficulties in the way of securing some men the University wanted. The pledge would also give an immense impulse in regard to buildings; it would remove a crushing load from Harper; it would enable the University to open in some degree commensurate with public expectation; it would justify the brave men who had consented to come to Chicago on faith; and it would enormously facilitate the affiliation of other institutions and so lift up the whole educational system. Gates assured the Founder that the funds (or income thereof) might safely be placed in the hands of the Trustees and urged that a pledge should not be held up until the opening of the University: "... the men cannot be secured unless we know *now* that there will be funds to pay them." As if he realized that the request was extraordinary, Gates concluded:

... in justification of Harper, Northrup, Goodspeed and all of us, let me say that none of us dreamed at the first of the magnitude of the opportunities, the promise, the occasion. It has grown on our wondering eyes month by month. ... I stand in awe of this thing. God is in it in a most wonderful way. It is a miracle. No such body of *Christian as such* men has ever before been gathered together in any University faculty on this planet. So Harper declares. Think of the significance of that. Harper, Goodspeed and myself, as we look into the great future of this land and consider what seems certainly to be the great part God is raising up this institution to fill, uncover our heads and walk very softly before the Lord.[52]

By making such a report to Rockefeller, Gates became a party to drastic revision of University finances. He came, he saw, and he was conquered—but by what? In part, perhaps, by Harper's enthusiasm; but Harper had conjured up neither the men whom the pledge would support nor the students whose needs gave Gates such anxiety. Gates did not relay Harper's recommendations without question; on the contrary, he wrangled up and down on every point of the salary matter before the figure of $1,000,000 was reached as a compromise. Harper had insisted that much more was absolutely demanded.[53] Gates reacted, not to a man but to the implications of an unforeseen situation, one full of promise and bearing the mark of Providence. For better or worse, Gates lost the moment when Harper might have been forced, if ever, to hold expenditures within the limits fixed by the first Rockefeller gift in support of a college and the second which was supposed to make possible expansion into graduate studies. Had Gates wanted to hold the University in check until the fruitfulness of these gifts was fully apparent, Gates should have refused to recommend a third gift.

Rockefeller himself did ask some hard questions. Gates discussed the finances of the University with nine Trustees as well as with Harper and Goodspeed and then submitted a revised proposal. Would Rockefeller make two gifts of

$1,000,000 for endowment, one outright, the other to be matched by a third million from others for buildings and equipment?[54] The Founder of a college and then a university responded by giving $1,000,000, the income of which would be payable as of December 1, 1891—as Gates had suggested—for current expenses; but Rockefeller was unwilling to appear before the University again as the giver of a conditional pledge.[55]

Harper did not drop the case for another million. Noting that the University stood side by side with Harvard and Yale in the estimation of the world, he argued—to Gates—that it was sometimes more difficult to maintain a reputation than to achieve it. And in Harper's mind the very size of the University had become a reason for increasing its resources: "With a crowd of students and a large corps of professors, the patience and good nature of everybody will be taxed to the utmost. A harder task rests upon my shoulder than to raise the million dollars, namely to keep all in close contact with each other and to weld them into a homogeneous influence. Nothing could possibly help me in this tremendous task so much as another gift on the day of opening."[56] The present was an immense opportunity: the men of the city had done a great thing in raising their last million—"and we ought not to let the matter grow cold."[57] The University should use the momentum which it had already picked up in the city to pull ahead of its financial difficulties. Gates had gained the impression that Rockefeller did not plan to give the University more funds, if at all, until the machine had been put successfully into working operation.[58] All the same, Gates did visit Rockefeller and made an urgent appeal for the University; yet when it opened in October, 1892, Rockefeller had not acted.

Before the end of November, Harper had entered the winter of his discontent. To Gates, Harper confided the thought that Gates had made a mistake in urging him to give up his work in New Haven.[59] Soon Harper was saying, "I do not believe that I am the man to do the work which is necessary to be done here, under all the circumstances. If there were any honorable way of pulling out, I should pull out within twenty-four hours. I am not discouraged; I simply detest the work. I am sick and tired of the whole business."[60]

One of Harper's frustrations was perhaps typical of many. Since Marshall Field had contributed largely toward the building fund, it was appropriate for the University to name a building after him; but, except for a laboratory, it was impossible to find a building to bear Field's name, and a laboratory could not be built for as little as $100,000, the amount of the gift. Yet both Field and C. O. Whitman, whose department would use the laboratory, had been promised a building worth $150,000. Harper insisted that the (inflated) promise had to be fulfilled whatever the consequences.[61] Gates was blunt: ". . . you ought not to have promised Field that building. Indeed you ought not."[62] And in November, 1892, salaries could not be increased in any department.[63] Harper's exuberance was bearing bitter fruit. Then, in December, Rockefeller promised the University another million. The income was to be used largely to support the existing Faculty. Before the formal letter of gift was dispatched, Gates asked Harper for a guaranty that no more than $20,000 would be used for new instruction.[64] Hopes for expansion were not to override consolidation of the gains already made.

Pushing up the salary levels of head professors had helped to create a striking discrepancy between the highest and the lowest salaries paid by the University. Some professors received as little as half, or even less, of the $7,000 which head professors received; and not all of them received that. Instructors were paid about one-sixth or one-fifth as much. The patience and good nature of which Harper spoke would be heavily taxed in the event of financial crisis and delays in salary increases. Harper was himself successful in recruiting Faculty members from Clark because of its shortage of funds, which forced President Hall to deal—as he said—Jesuitically with his faculty.[65] At Chicago, Harper was obliged at least once to exploit his power to inspire confidence:

. . . In the making out of the budget [Harper wrote Charles L. Hutchinson in 1894] . . . a deal of time has been spent in conferring with the various departments concerning the reappointments for the next year. I wish you could have been in the office during some of the days. We are, of course, carrying a good many people at a rate which is just above that of starvation. Naturally enough these good people feel that they earn more and deserve more. It has been my function during these days to persuade these people that they are advancing the cause of science and serving the University. I have succeeded in most cases in showing them the utter absurdity of being mercenary; the sublimity of self-sacrifice. I endeavor to send them away from the interview feeling that it is a high privilege which we grant them. . . .[66]

When the time came for Ernest D. Burton's salary to be increased according to the terms upon which he had agreed to come to Chicago, his claim could not easily be met, with the result that the relations between Burton and Harper were severely strained. Burton thought that Harper had given a personal guaranty. When he discovered that such was not Harper's understanding, he refrained from pressing Harper to pay out of his own pocket; but Burton did announce his readiness to accept the odium of seeming to exact his pound of flesh, presumably from the University. As late as 1897, when Harper and Burton were again negotiating, Harper remarked that he was happy to say Burton would never know the cost of the transaction. Pain of spirit was part of the price the University paid for its Faculty.[67]

Even before the University opened, one scientist, Clarence L. Herrick, resigned a professorship of biology with the conviction that Harper had acted in bad faith. Like so many others, Herrick had spread an elaborate plan before Harper in the course of negotiations and apparently accepted an appointment with the impression that he had established a pre-emptive right to what would today be called the interdisciplinary area where neurological and psychological studies meet. There is no surviving evidence that Harper promised Herrick exclusive control of these studies, but neither is there evidence that Herrick was forewarned of any possible necessity to adjust his work to the interests of other men. Harper had not then discovered the scientists at Clark University. While Herrick was in Germany preparing for his work at the University, he learned, without benefit of official notice, that Charles A. Strong, a psychologist at Clark, had been appointed by the University of Chicago. Somewhat later, and just as casually, the appointment of Henry H. Donaldson, assistant professor of neurology at Clark, also came to Herrick's attention. Perhaps Harper assumed that the new appointments did not jeopardize Herrick's plans, perhaps he decided that those plans would have to be curtailed, or perhaps he simply was too busy to think through the implications of the possibly overlapping commitments he had made; without question, Harper alienated Herrick, who resigned from the Faculty an embittered man.[68]

In the case of the economist Edward W. Bemis, Harper's methods produced public indignation as well as personal distress. Harper wanted the new institutional or "historical" school of economic thought to be represented in the University, and Richard T. Ely, an acknowledged master of the school and Bemis' mentor, proved to be unattainable. Instead, Harper offered Bemis an associate professorship, which carried tenure, in University Extension. Bemis was an advocate of reform and a critic of monopolistic business but not a militant polemicist. At the time Bemis was appointed, Harper knew both that Laughlin, the head professor of political economy, was not prepared to receive Bemis as a regular member of that department and that Bemis considered teaching in Extension only a way station on the road to departmental membership. Harper indulged in the hope that as time passed an essentially makeshift arrangement would yield an accommodation: Bemis was to teach on campus one quarter of each year, and Laughlin consented to Bemis' offering one course in political economy during the spring quarter of 1892–93.[69] Laughlin did not promise—and Harper did not demand assurances—that Bemis would eventually be brought more fully into the work of the department. The situation would become difficult if Laughlin withdrew his marginal recognition of Bemis' competence as an economist; the situation would be impossible if Bemis could not attract a large following in Extension, where ability to extend the audience of the University was an ingredient of competence.

Yet how many students was enough? In his first year (or two quarters) of service as a lecturer, Bemis stood second from the top among six members of the Extension faculty then lecturing, in the number of courses taught; but the average attendance at Bemis' courses was the second smallest. Charles Zueblin, a sociologist who resembled Bemis in point of view and interests, taught only five courses while Bemis taught thirteen, and in the first quarter the two men addressed classes that were not very different in numbers; but in the second quarter Zueblin attracted classes that were more than twice as large as those of Bemis. In the first quarter of the second year, Zueblin taught six courses with an average attendance of 132, Bemis only one course with an attendance of 75 students, the smallest average. By that statistical calculation, Bemis never addressed more than 100 people at one time. Nathaniel Butler, the only other associate professor in Extension, never had an audience of less than 104 and in one quarter had classes of almost 200. Richard G. Moulton, famous as a lecturer—and the only full professor in the division—always lectured to more than 250 people.[70] In January, 1894, Harper wrote Bemis that his work in Extension that year had been largely a failure, that the doors seemed to be closing in the University Proper—Laughlin did refuse to receive Bemis—and that he could do better in another institution. Harper's tone was friendly; the implication of his words is plain. Harper had decided that Bemis' appointment had to be brought to an end.[71] Perhaps, as Walter Metzger suggests in *The Development of Academic Freedom in the United States,* a quiet or conservative Bemis would have kept his post: Harper's motives lie beyond conclusive probing.[72] Quite possibly Harper, who as President was sensitive to public opinion, gave particular attention to evidence of the impact of Bemis' work; Bemis spoke his mind when he thought the emperor was wearing no clothes. Quite possibly also Harper believed that a Bemis heard no more widely as a lecturer than the record indicated had indeed failed and would only become an academic remittance man if his appointment continued. Even so, should Harper have arranged for Bemis to be tried by his peers in Extension on open charges of incompetence? A verdict for Bemis would have left him still blocked in the career-line he had hoped for; and a finding of incompetence would have led to public dismissal. But would the academic world understand that Bemis' merits as an economist and as a teacher in the ordinary classroom had not been at issue? It was doubtless Harper's intention that Bemis and the University should part amicably without giving start to public questioning. Perhaps that hope arose in some part from fear that the University might be hurt by the light; humanity demanded that Bemis should not be.

Bemis neither protested Harper's decision loudly nor resigned quietly. Instead of dropping Bemis' name from the budget for 1894–95, the Trustees assigned the appropriation for his teaching on campus to Social Science (i.e., Sociology) and allowed Bemis to continue lecturing in Extension.[73] Bemis was thus a member of the faculty during the Pullman strike of 1894. When he publicly questioned the justice of the railroads' case, it could be inferred from his remarks that the railroads had not come to court with clean hands to obtain an injunction against the strikers. Harper was pounced upon everywhere. Much annoyed, he wrote Bemis to propose that he speak very carefully while he remained in the University.[74] The letter was unfriendly in tone but toothless in bite if it was meant to be threatening rather than merely remonstrating; Bemis already had reason to know that his stay in the University would be temporary. Before July, 1895, Harper and Bemis agreed that Bemis might lecture in Extension until July, 1896; that he should receive fees for such lecturing but no fixed salary after the summer of 1895; and that he should resign not later than July 1, 1896.[75] At about the time when that date was put to the end of Bemis' appointment, public interest in his situation became thoroughly aroused. In a Convocation statement of October 1, 1895, Harper denied publicly and flatly that there had ever been an occasion for condemning the utterances of any professor and that any donor had ever sought to control the teaching of professors in Political Economy, History, Political Science, or Sociology. Harper did not, however, speak explicitly of Bemis' dismissal.[76] In October, Bemis declared publicly that he was being dropped because of his opinions; the University answered that the reason was incompetence.[77] The issue was joined and the Bemis Case had been created. A suspicion that the University had persecuted Bemis came to overshadow the possibility that Bemis might have had no case, except to claim—which he did not—that the University had been irresponsible in giving him tenure and so promising him a future in a post perhaps wrong for him. The University could not extricate itself from an ill-conceived commitment without jeopardizing its reputation as a free institution.

CHAPTER VI

Academic Polity:
The President
and the Professors

The University of Chicago formally opened with a simple ceremony on October 1, 1892. It is tempting to think of the moment as the rising of a curtain upon a tableau. "The days of dreaming are passed," Harper wrote on the next day, "and now real action begins."[1]

Yet members of the Faculty had bestirred themselves long since. Almost from the appointment of the first head professors, they worked to modify the plans that Harper had begun to make before anyone—even Harper himself—had consented to teach and study at the University. When Harper remarked a decade later that the charm of the University was that each man was allowed to pick his own way according to his own ideals, Harper did justice to but half of the force that the Faculty constituted.[2]

The Faculty was built upon the aspirations of its several members; but upon entering the service of the University, the professors sought to pick a way for it as well as for themselves. Members of the first Faculty worked as true colleagues of the President. They acknowledged the peculiar importance of Harper's position and qualities, but they refused to be merely passive beneficiaries of presidential enterprise. This relationship of President and professors was the essence of academic polity at the University. According to the *Nation*, the Faculty came to life none too soon:

86

At Chicago it seems to us that far too much has been settled in advance by the president and trustees without the possibility of consultation with the faculties. The circumstances, of course, were exceptional; the University had to be organized in some fashion before there could be any faculties to consult. But was it necessary to elaborate the educational plan in such detail? And is the dictatorship of the president, necessary as it may be in such a formative period, to be prolonged after the University is fairly in operation, or is a constitutional era to be inaugurated?[3]

Perhaps it was such criticism that prompted Harper to observe when the University had been at work but a short time that from the beginning there had been a definiteness of plan which doubtless had appeared premature.[4] The foundations of constitutionalism had already been laid when the Faculty first met. The *Official Bulletin, No. 1,* had described a "University Council" to be composed of administrative officers and single, elected representatives of the colleges and schools, each of which was to have its own Faculty; but the first head professors were not content to wait for the organization of the Council to discover what the powers of the Faculty would be. Less than six weeks after Hale and Laughlin had been appointed (with the opening of the University more than half a year in the future), and while the two professors were still in Ithaca, they fell into disagreement with Harper over University policy. The issue was instruction by correspondence, in which Harper had had much experience and put great faith. Since Melvil Dewey, secretary of the New York Regents and one of the men who refused a post at the University, had just attempted to organize a state-wide system of University Extension, Hale and Laughlin may have been particularly touchy about such an innovation.[5] Their objection was too strong to be turned back by soft words.

Hale to Harper: You wrote "I am somewhat surprised, I must confess, to see how seriously you took the differences of opinion between us." Your surprise is itself surprising, for it shows how easily you expected, after Laughlin and I had accepted to persuade us to join in a system of work the bare proposal of which, at any earlier time, would have led us to decline your call without a moment's hesitation.... Your assumption that the persuasion might properly come after the acceptance was an error....

It was a matter of the greatest grief to him, Hale continued, that Harper's plans, which showed an entirely different conception of the work of the University than that which Hale held, should not have been made known to him until the sixth in the series of interviews he had had with Harper. Up to that time, Hale wrote, everything had pointed in a different direction. (In fact, Harper's plan was in print.) "There were some points of difference between us, but they were not fundamental, and I was willing to experiment." Hale had ardently shared Harper's ideas about the advanced work of the University, but Harper had not hinted at the conception of developing the University, graduate school and all, into an institution in which half of the work at any period, the beginning, the middle, or the end, might be carried on by correspondence. Indeed, Hale believed that the conception had been virtually ruled out. "The situation is a deplorable one on both sides. . . . You devoutly and conscientiously cherish certain conceptions, we devoutly and conscientiously cherish the exact opposite." Would Harper come to Ithaca?[6]

Harper responded by wire but apparently did not promise to join Hale and Laughlin immediately in the East. Hale answered:

I should have been reassured if you had said that you would come at once, but as it is, I am afraid that you don't realize how deep the difficulty lies. It is not a question whether Laughlin and I like or dislike a particular project of yours. There are, and will be, other men whose opinions also should weigh. It is a question of the *method of settlement*. I have never so fully realized . . . how little a man knows, in going into the University of Chicago, what the method of settling questions is to be. When a man accepts an invitation to Harvard, or Yale, or Cornell, he knows what he is coming to. But precisely this part of University administration has not been arranged for at Chicago. I don't want to force my opinions upon anyone, least of all a President. But I want a definite way arranged, by which discussion shall lead to joint action, and also by which nothing that is seriously objected to by anyone shall be put before the country as even the temporary policy of the University, until the University has got to work and ample and long discussion has been brought to bear upon every proposed new feature.

Even as he wrote this, Hale took sharp exception to the way in which Harper's mind was running in regard to the affiliation of the University with schools and colleges. "I could not at once see all the bearings of so complicated a scheme, nor could anyone." Affiliation was but one of a great number of developments involving fundamental principles: "We absolutely must have an interview. . . ." There ought not to be a single day of delay: "We signified that we should accept the call of the University of Chicago, but that was under impressions which have since proved not to correspond with the facts, and we cannot sign the formal documents unless you can devise some working solution. And we have reached almost the last moment, for our resignations from Cornell are soon to be acted upon by the full Board of Trustees." So close did Hale come to issuing an ultimatum.[7]

Harper did go to Ithaca—he could hardly do anything else. Laughlin was later to recall long and serious conferences about the fundamental organization of the University:

> I can remember distinctly when, sitting in Professor Hale's house with him and President Harper, I said, "We have been deciding here very large questions of University policy. It is not right that these far-reaching conclusions should be arrived at on the judgment of two or three professors in consultation with the President. These matters ought to go properly to a body composed of the heads of all the departments of the University, and their opinions should be decisive in forming the University organization with which we should begin work." I remember clearly how the President, sitting at the end of a sofa, looked up at me and in a flash said "That's right. It should be the Senate." And the Senate was born then and there.

A body of that name had been established at Cornell in 1889, possibly because the faculty may have felt that the first president took too much upon himself. The fresh memories of Cornell men may again have worked to influence the University of Chicago.[8] The Senate was to be the supreme legislative body in the realm of academic affairs.

When Laughlin came to feel, shortly after the University opened, that the Faculty was restive, he argued vehemently against the settlement of educational questions by interview:

> It opens the way for scheming and intriguing and personal pressure, while, if brought in a dignified and frank manner into the senate for full discussion, personal elements disappear, and the subject is treated on its merits as a part of a broad University policy. To use an illustration, it is the difference between absolutism and constitutional government; the former is weakness, the latter is strength.

. . . .

> Men are at their best only when they feel that they are trusted and honored. If any system, no matter how good, has been created, and then applied to a set of intelligent men of character and independence, such as scholars must necessarily be, and that system is not adopted by them on grounds of their own belief in it and conviction that it is the best, then, being called upon to administer a system not in accordance with their convictions, they will feel that they have not been trusted in being called in to help shape the policy, and the inevitable consequence is either listless feebleness or friction. Unless the system is one which grows out of their united convictions and scholarly purposes, and is the expression of their development, no man will feel content, but on the contrary will always be restless. No salary or money can to a scholar make up for the want of adjustment between his scholarly ideals and his environment....

. . . .

> Healthy strength in our University life can only come by stimulating frank and free discussion of all these questions, and accepting those things on which we can all jointly unite; that kind of unity is strength.[9]

A president, Laughlin added, could rarely go farther than he could carry his Faculty.

Laughlin returned to the same subject in 1894 when Harper failed to consult the Senate before proposing to the Trustees—as he did—that his presidential duties be divided between himself and E. Benjamin Andrews, whom Harper hoped to attract to the University from the presidency of Brown. Laughlin attacked the proposed arrangement:

Being not a mere matter of executive appointments, it has affected the whole educational system here; for so I regard it. And yet you never laid this before the Senate until it had been acted upon by the Trustees. You distrusted us; & inevitably we distrust the whole plan. It is now a plan in which we were not consulted, placed upon us from the outside, & it is none of ours; consequently it will be regardedly [*sic*] critically, exciting antagonisms, & cannot have our loyal support. As a friend of President Andrews, you have made a difficult future for him; & also you have lost hold on our enthusiasm for the University. You have done it, consciously or unconsciously, on the Napoleonic plan. It is yours not ours; & yet you expect us to act as if it were ours.[10]

It was the old question of constitutional methods, ". . . as old as Magna Charta & human nature." Several members of the Senate protested jointly against the prospect of diarchy, and Harper shelved the proposal.*

The creation of the Senate, however, did not enfranchise the entire Faculty; the Senate consisted only of head professors. (They were called heads of departments from the academic year 1898–99 on.) The *Nation* remarked:

In Columbia, which has not commonly been regarded as a radical institution, the central organ of the professors . . . consists of delegates from the several faculties; and

* Like Laughlin, Thomas C. Chamberlin was worried over the impact of the incident on the constitution of the University but saw danger signals in a different quarter:

"I believe that the specific questions that relate to the presidency fall wholly within the province of the President and the Board of Trustees, and that the President and the Board are entirely free to use their discretion in advising with the Faculty, or any part or member of it, relative to such questions. I believe that an efficient administration of the University requires that this province and this discretion shall remain untrammeled and inviolate. While, in general, as free consultation with the Faculty as the nature of the case may render discreet is doubtless wise, such consultation is to be regarded as a discretionary extension of function and not as a privilege to be claimed by the Faculty or any part of it, much less as an obligation to be insisted upon. . . .

"I respectfully urge that, whatever action you may take on the ground of personal comity, nothing shall be done that shall recognize a vested function or privilege inconsistent with the free performance of the presidential function and with the untrammeled exercise of those discretions which are so inseparable from an efficient administration of the University." Chamberlin had himself known the presidential function, at the University of Wisconsin (Chamberlin to Harper, Jan. 12, 1894).

in the election of these delegates the junior and assistant professors have the same voice as their seniors. It is certainly surprising to discover that a more conservative, not to say reactionary, policy has been adopted at Chicago.[11]

The general representative assembly described in the *Official Bulletin, No. 1,* was not in fact organized; and the Senate did possess power to veto the actions of other bodies. Yet government was not left wholly to the small circle of head professors. A body known as the Faculty of Arts, Literature, and Science was called together as soon as the University opened and constituted something like a general faculty as most appointments lay in departments classified under those rubrics. It seems to have been taken for granted that the Faculty possessed some initiative. In theory, the Faculty had charge of Faculties for the Graduate School of Arts and Literature, the Ogden (Graduate) School of Science, the University (later Senior) Colleges, and the Academic (Junior) Colleges.[12] But these bodies failed to emerge immediately from limbo.

In January, 1893, on recommendation of the Faculty of Arts, Literature, and Science, the Board of Trustees authorized the establishment of four administrative (but not legislative) boards within the Faculty for the two graduate schools and the two sets of colleges.[13] Soon four more administrative boards were organized to conduct the business of the libraries, laboratories, and museums; physical culture and athletics; the University Press; and affiliations. Supreme responsibility for administration was placed in the University Council which had the same name but not the same function as the general faculty described in the first *Bulletin*. The new Council was composed of the deans and other administrative officers of the University.[14] Thus, administration was formally separated from legislation; but the actual administrator was frequently a Faculty member wearing another hat. Then in November, 1895, the Faculty of Arts, Literature, and Science recommended, and the Trustees presently voted, that four Faculties should replace the four boards for the graduate schools and colleges. The Senior College Faculty was composed of departmental representatives, one for each department instructing Senior College students; but each of the other Faculties consisted of all instructors appointed for a term of more than a year to do work—in the language of the statutes—in connection with that Faculty.[15] The franchise was broad. Yet the voting population of the University was split up; the Faculty of Arts, Literature, and Science was abolished as the new Faculties came into being. The scientist directing the research of graduate students might have no place in which to vote his opinion of the college curriculum, and the humanist teaching undergraduates could be equally voiceless when what had once been called "strictly University work" come up for debate.[16]

The younger members of the Faculty, Harry P. Judson later recalled, had not been apt to feel entirely free in the expression of their views; also, in the meetings of the more general Faculty, policies relating to one school or college might often be carried by votes of persons not directly concerned.[17] A desire was felt to fix a more definite responsibility upon the instructors in particular fields of educational work and to differentiate the problems that presented themselves.[18] Under the new system, particular cases were brought before a picked body of men and women, each of whom was familiar with the disposition of similar cases in the past. As a result, one observer said, decisions were usually wise.[19] Yet the reorganization of the Faculty produced, the same observer said, a "detached system of legislation" which operated as if, for instance, the Academic Colleges had no vital connection with the University Colleges or the graduate schools. The members of the Faculty felt that they did not have a share in the settlement of all-University questions; they had responsibility without power. Robert Herrick, one of the younger members of the Faculty, thought that Harper was following the principle of divide-and-rule. "It is the worst move since the University was started and will damage the scholarship of the place irremediably."[20] Herrick's prediction proved erroneous; but for years the suspicion, or conviction, that Harper had the instincts of a political boss tinctured the feelings of some Faculty members.

After 1896, some functions of a general faculty were performed by a body called the Congregation. It embraced the administrators and Faculty members of the rank of instructor and above; ph.d.'s of the University; some other alumni; and the officers of affiliated institutions when elected by the Congregation. (In 1896, the year when it was instituted, Harper wondered how the holders of doctorates in particular might be kept closely connected to the University.)[21] The Congregation had no power to legislate but did make recommendations to ruling bodies of the University and had the right to review their actions. The reasons for actions of which the Congregation disapproved had to be reported to it promptly. (Originally, Harper anticipated that no regulation would go into effect until approved by the Congregation.)[22]

Although University officers may have outnumbered outsiders in attendance —in one instance at least four to one—the decisions of the Congregation were supposed to express a sentiment more general than that of any Faculty or

Faculties. The Congregation constituted a forum for the ventilation of important issues, e.g.:

That the University should establish a course leading to the Bachelor's degree in which Latin is not required (1897).

That the University should seek closer and more vital relations with the secondary schools (1897).

That more courses of instruction in the Junior Colleges should be given by older members of the Faculty (1899).

That immediate steps should be taken for forming a plan for the retirement of professors on pensions (1899).

That the present seminar policy in the University of Chicago is not satisfactory (1899).

That the examination system of the University stands in need of revision (1902).[23]

Formal briefs on each side of such propositions as these were prepared by members of the Congregation, usually by academic or administrative officers of the University Proper, and published in the printed record of University affairs. The public opinion of the University was to be expressed, in no off-hand way, by an unusually comprehensive assembly.

When the Faculty of Arts, Literature, and Science had been divided up into separate Faculties, Martin Ryerson was troubled by what he thought was a tendency away from simplicity toward elaborate organization.[24] No doubt, the form of government was complex, but the actual conduct of University affairs had a single, unmistakable point of focus. Although Harper tried more than once to divide the Presidency along the lines of the Roman consulate, he was never allowed to divest himself of year-round responsibility for the state of the University. His position as a ruler was more nearly feudal than Roman.

The shires of the realm were the departments, which Harper had brought into being but could claim in no other sense as his creatures. Harper's eye looked everywhere, but his glance was not an irresistible command. The individual departments possessed great autonomy because of the formal status and personal force of the head professors and because of the prestige belonging to academic disciplines which the departments represented. At the University, departmentalism originally took its simplest, most atomistic form. The departments were not organized into divisions; and in the humanities and social sciences—anachronistic groupings—even intellectually related departments did not constitute schools such as that of Political Science, including history, etc., at Columbia. When political economy and sociology both laid claim to instruction in statistics, no divisional dean was there to arbitrate: the case came to Harper in the form of irate letters from Laughlin and Small.[25] The scientific departments were parts of the Ogden School, as beneficiaries of a single donation; but when geology and zoölogy fell into dispute over the location of paleontology, Harper sat in conference and heard the conflicting arguments in person—somewhat to his bewilderment.[26]

The department devoted to one branch of learning, as distinct from the professorship, was not an ancient form of academic organization in the United States when the University of Chicago was founded. During the nineteenth century, departmentalism was indeed a product of the same general movement toward academic reform that produced the University itself. Yet departmentalism had become common when Harper began to gather together a faculty, and apparently he did not consider any alternative to convention. The *Official Bulletin, No. 1,* described the University without explicitly designating the departments as units of government, but only, it would appear, because their organization was taken for granted. Specialized study was a matter of principle with Harper; and in practice departmental organization allowed a necessary delegation of authority while the manifold work of framing the University was under way.

By 1896, Harper had the most serious misgivings. The different departments were organized for convenience of administration, Harper then argued; but in most instances sharp lines of separation could not possibly be drawn. The work of one department fitted into that of another and was necessary to proper understanding of work in the other. Hence the closest correlation of subjects was necessary if the student's work was to be conducted to the best possible advantage. "In this line little or no progress has been made in most of our institutions. Nowhere is there better opportunity for forward movement." A movement *against* the tendency to separate departments more distinctly should be encouraged.

The work of the student in the future will not be cut off into departments; on the contrary it will be the study of problems which will lead him into and through many departments of study. The need of correlation does not receive from most of us the appreciation which it deserves. Our work as an institution will secure that unity of purpose, and that unity of result which are in the highest sense desirable only in proportion as each department works in the interest, not merely of itself, but also of its sister departments.[27]

94

Harper did not demand immediate action, certainly not the amalgamation of departments as distinct from the integration of studies; but he did not forget the drawbacks of departmentalism.

In 1898, Harper attacked more sharply: "In these days . . . the distinction between Botany and Zoölogy, between Latin and Greek, between Political Science, Political Economy and History, is a distinction which is purely artificial. . . . The time will come when these so-called distinctions of departments will disappear. . . ." The separation of departments had been too greatly emphasized by some of their heads; and certain divisions of work had been isolated from other, closely related divisions because no sufficient effort had been made by the heads of related departments to work out the plans of instruction together. The result had been a duplication that was wasteful of both energy and money.

It is exceedingly important for the best interests of the University that this growing evil be corrected and to this end the officers of certain groups of departments will be requested to meet and take such steps as the difficulties in the situation demand. An arrangement of work which is formal and which had been introduced merely for the sake of convenience must not be permitted to interfere with the best interests of students or of instructors or of the University at large.[28]

The evil appeared to be greatest in the departments of science: "here positive injury may be done the student. . . ."*

In 1898, a committee of the Congregation discussed the organization of the related departments into conferences or groups for the purpose of co-ordinating courses. Groups did appear in 1899; but, except for some joint action in regard to PH.D. requirements, their duties were confined to correlation of more or less parallel courses and routine administration, including revision of announcements to avoid conflicts in hours among departments. The departments of the social sciences gave some thought to library problems, which arose from one of the most conspicuous results of departmental organization, the physical division into distinct libraries of a large part of the University collection of books. The institution of groups did not cut very deep into the autonomy of

---

* C. O. Whitman, head of the Department of Zoölogy, had not been indifferent to the danger. In 1896, at the laying of the cornerstone for the building of his department, he had said: "The tendency to differentiate into separate departments must be so guided as to ensure organic unity. That is a paramount consideration, *and our greatest* cause for rejoicing is, not so much for what our departments gain individually as for what they gain as parts of a more perfect unity. The supreme importance of this unity becomes manifest when we reflect that our sciences bear to one another the relation of root, trunk, and branches of a tree" (*Record*, I, No. 18 [July 31, 1896], 290).

the departments. When the classics conference produced a set of joint PH.D. regulations, the head of the Greek Department, Paul Shorey, went his own, formidably individualistic way. And it was perhaps waving a red flag before most of the social scientists to label their group, as Harper did, "Historical."[29]

The idea of the department as a discipline was essential to Harper's conception of academic freedom: in that connection departmentalism was the stuff of which constitutional government was made. As a scholar with advanced views in a field where the struggle between orthodoxy and heterodoxy was sharp, Harper had himself been under attack; he knew at first hand the need of the inquiring mind for protection. The investigator of the Bible was not to be condemned as long as his thinking proceeded from facts and according to the recognized methods of biblical criticism. As a master-craftsman, the scholar had the freedom of his discipline; and, more broadly, membership in a university conferred liberty—or a liberty—upon the professor, much as the franchise of a medieval town made the citizen a freeman. At the same time, membership obliged its beneficiary to cherish the interests of the corporation.

In 1895, when the Bemis case was yet to be argued publicly, Harper declared that care should be taken not to confound personal privilege (one's freedom as a citizen?) with official duty, not to mistake popular pleading for scientific thought. He added that, when such confusion arose, ". . . the time has come for us to forfeit our positions as officers in The University, because we have mistaken the purpose for which we were appointed and because we have forgotten that to serve The University we must employ scientific methods and do scientific work."[30] Harper did not say that he had passed judgment against Bemis under that principle or as President he would ever *demand* the forfeit. He may have meant to preach a homily.* In 1900, after almost ten years in office, Harper spelled out the practical details of his thought. It was the privilege of the University ("of course") to drop a member of the Faculty, appointed for two, three, or four years, who exercised his right in such a way as to do himself and the institution serious injury. But if an officer on a permanent appointment abused his privilege as a professor, the University had to suffer. It was proper that it should suffer; for that only followed directly and inevitably from

---

* In 1903, Harper cautioned Jerome H. Raymond, associate professor of sociology, in regard to some of Raymond's utterances in Extension lectures. They stirred up strife. Raymond protested; and Harper answered: "My letter was intended to raise the question with you as to the employment of your own judgment; it was not intended to direct you as to what you should say or not say" (Raymond to Harper, Dec. 15, 1903; Harper to Raymond, Dec. 17, 1903. University of Chicago Archives).

lack of foresight and wisdom in the original appointment. The injury to the University would be far less serious than that done by a request for a resignation; for, Harper said, in his positive case for academic freedom: "The greatest single element necessary for the cultivation of the academic spirit is the feeling of security from interference. It is only those who have this feeling that are able to do work which in the highest sense will be beneficial to humanity."[31] Before the publication of this statement, which was first given orally, Hale urged Harper to say that every professor is a citizen and that every citizen is bound to form an opinion on national issues and privileged to try bringing others to it: that, Hale said, was really the vital issue.[32] Harper may have thought that this point was covered by a reference that he made to the professor's absolute right to express his opinion, but if so he did not emphasize it. What primarily concerned him was *academic* privilege as such—the freedom that the professor enjoyed as a citizen of his own narrower community, the freedom that was the *sine qua non* of discovering and teaching the truth. He staked the liberty of the University on the worth of its particular disciplines.

All the Faculty members remained subject to dismissal—in the language of the statutes—"for inadequate performance of duty or for misconduct" or, in Harper's words, for incompetence or for immorality. The professor would be removed for immorality when he had been guilty, as Harper said, "in the opinion of those in authority . . ."; and presumably the professor would be found incompetent by the same court.[33] Legally, the authority to appoint and to dismiss belonged to the Board of Trustees; but the exercise of authority was delegated in fact to the President of the University, William Rainey Harper.*

---

* Although the decision to dismiss Edward W. Bemis was apparently Harper's, the Trustees did discuss whether the University should make a public statement. Everyone agreed, the Secretary of the Board, Thomas W. Goodspeed, reported to a Trustee in New York: ". . . that where a professor leaves under pressure the University will not state the reasons. It ill becomes a great University to force an unfortunate teacher out and then assail him. A professor who has failed here may succeed elsewhere, and we will not lay a straw in his way." Goodspeed indicated, however, that some members of the Board thought it a mistake to make no official statement. The Trustee, Francis E. Hinckley, had written from a Wall Street address: "I have no doubt but that Bemis has said some hard things and many truths about the gas trust, and with that we have nothing to do; we have no apology to make either for or to the gas trust, it is able to take care of itself, but I do object to the University being responsible for the sins of the gas trust, or that it should be put in a position even by implication of defending the trust. With intelligent people there is no force in the statement, that because the gas company gets its supply of oil from the Standard Co. that Rockefeller demanded the removal of Bemis; yet there are plenty of silly fools who believe it" (Goodspeed to Hinckley, Aug. 27, 1895 [SBL, B, 209]; Hinckley to Goodspeed, Aug. 24, 1895 [TWG: Correspondence re history of the University]).

Indeed John D. Rockefeller had no legal power to concern himself with the opinions of

He governed in the presence of the Faculty. Its influence was strikingly demonstrated in Laughlin's disapproval of Edward W. Bemis and in the same professor's support of Thorstein Veblen, whose views differed radically from Laughlin's and whose private life may have begun to exhibit the unconventionality that marked it later. During the national controversy over imperialism, the Congregation produced a statement that formulated the opinions held by the University community insofar as it spoke with one voice. Harper reported

---

faculty members and did not do so informally. His attitude is reflected in a letter written by Frederick T. Gates in 1896, when the establishment of a theological journal was being discussed: "I think Mr. Rockefeller has no objection at all to the *Divinity* School, as distinguished from the University, taking the leading part in the publication and editing of such a journal as you suggest. Indeed, he would hardly have the right to interpose objections even if he had them. The Divinity School is controlled by a Board of Trustees who were elected by an incorporated association which may fairly be said to represent the Baptist denomination as a whole. The Divinity School is responsible directly to the denomination at large for its conduct, and dependent upon the denomination for its support. The Divinity School existed before Mr. Rockefeller had contributed anything to it, and his contributions to the Divinity School have been of comparatively minor importance and would entitle him to no greater voice than that of many others. He does not feel in any wise responsible for the Divinity School or its teachings. On the contrary, the denomination is in every sense responsible, and the Divinity School is itself responsible directly to the denomination.

"The University on the other hand, is in a peculiar sense the creation of Mr. Rockefeller himself. He has given nearly all its permanent funds and he has received many letters from every part of the country complaining of the attitude which the University has seemed to take regarding the Bible, holding him responsible for what is a real or fancied injury to religion. He prefers that the denomination shall settle its own theological affairs. He founded in Chicago a secular institution of learning. He had no thought of the institution entering the theological arena. He would prefer that the great power and prestige, financial and moral, of the University should not be thrown into the theological scale on either side. The sphere of theology should be relegated to the Divinity School and the denomination may hold the Divinity School responsible.

"For these reasons, he has preferred that the proposed journal, if it is to be launched, should be launched exclusively under the auspices and, so far as is necessary, supported by the funds of the Divinity School. In this way, the responsibility for the proposed journal will fall where it justly belongs" (Gates to Harper, Mar. 17, 1896).

The just placement of responsibility for the University was Rockefeller's abiding concern. On one occasion when a professor, Hermann von Holst, expressed an unpopular opinion, Gates did intervene to the extent of saying that Von Holst's views coincided with the best thought in New York; and on another occasion, he asked whether Harper could afford to appear in the magazine that was publishing Thomas W. Lawson's articles on "Frenzied Finance" (Gates to Harper, Dec. 23, 1895; Gates to Harper, Nov. 9, 1904). From time to time, Rockefeller's office forwarded complaints it received about Faculty members; but the traffic was light and the covering notes non-committal. Once Gates directly answered a protest against the reported remarks of the anthropologist Frederick Starr: "I do not know whether he is really a professor in the University or not. . . . Of course I do not believe a word of the stuff this man is said to have uttered—I do not believe it any more than you believe it. It is trying to us all to hear other people make light of and deny in toto the truth which we profoundly believe and hold

the action of the Congregation with his implied approbation. Discussion began in the Congregation when Thomas C. Chamberlin presented a set of resolutions which virtually coupled a declaration on the principle of academic freedom with an admonition that professors should have scrupulous regard for the good standing of the University. Laughlin was disturbed that it should be known that such a matter was open to discussion; and his colleagues toned down the objectionable part of the resolutions. The revised version stated that the principle of complete freedom of speech on all subjects had been regarded as fundamental from the beginning and could not be called into question in the present or future; that it was desirable to have it clearly understood that the University did not appear as a disputant on either side of any public question and the utterances which any professor might make on a public issue were to be regarded as solely his own opinions.[34] Belief in freedom and solicitude for the institution were coupled together. In 1923, Herrick, who was not a conformist, wrote: ". . . in the thirty years of my connection with the University of Chicago I cannot recall a single instance where in the slightest degree I have ever felt any restraint upon my thoughts, words or actions and above all in my teaching, except the very necessary restraint imposed by oneself as a member of a social institution functioning in a community."[35]

Harper felt keenly a need for the University to become a society. As a human being, he was gregarious; as a Baptist, he belonged to a religious denomination which had been made to feel its solidarity; as a student and professor at Yale, he had beheld a prime example of a close-knit academic community; and as a university president he greeted his Faculty, at its first meeting, with the words: "The question before us is how to become one in spirit, though not necessarily in opinions."[36] The greatest danger confronting the University, he was presently to recall, did not lie in the securing of funds or of students, but in the

dear, but I reflect also that it must be pretty trying to other people who do not believe at all as we do, to hear us announce with great confidence things which they profoundly disbelieve, and I do not know of any way in the world by which we can arrive at the truth except by letting everybody speak out what he believes to be the truth within the limits of public morality. And it seems to me that there is no place on earth where this liberty of utterance should be so carefully guarded and cherished as in an institution of learning which at least pretends to be a place of impartial research. The fact that such an institution is founded by private money or denominational money seems to me to make no sort of difference and must not be allowed to interfere in the smallest degree with this freedom of inquiry, freedom of opinion, and freedom of utterance. Indeed, it seems to me to be one of the chief glories of the Christian religion and of the Baptist Church that it frankly dares to found precisely such an institution" (Gates to H. C. Mabie, inclosed in a letter from Gates to Harper, June 17, 1905).

heterogeneity of the Faculty: would its members work together harmoniously and with one spirit?[37] At its opening, the University lacked the physical amenities which nurtured *esprit de corps* in the ancient colleges, but a makeshift way of life—soon with the Fair grounds next door—was found bracing. Organized in 1893, the Quadrangle Club brought together the members of the Faculty and other persons who valued what the University represented. At the beginning of the second year, Harper reflected upon the impact that the University had already had upon the lives of its members.

In the process of settlement under ordinary circumstances there comes first the breaking of the old relationship, then the seemingly temporary acceptance of the new; for however sharp the separation may have been, there is at first, in spite of one's self, a feeling that it is only for a period, and that sooner or later the old relationships will be taken on again. After this experience it is frequently one's privilege to go back and come in contact with the old, and to his surprise he finds it not that which since the separation from it he has imagined it to be, but the same old relationship which after careful consideration had been exchanged for the new. The two thus brought into contact are now better understood. The limitations of the old in contrast with the greater freedom of the new are appreciated, and one comes back to the new with a feeling of greater satisfaction. In fact, he is for the first time, since the separation from the old, coming home; for at the first coming it was not home. This, I am persuaded, has been the experience of many of the members of our University, instructors and students. A year ago we came together, strangers to the situation and to each other. We lived together and worked together during the year, our minds continually going back to that which we had left; for as yet the new situation could scarcely be said to have become permanent. We separated at the end of the scholastic year to go away for the season, and now we have come together again. This time under circumstances very different from those which attended our first meeting a year ago. We have come home.[38]

During the first year, Harper had doubted sometimes that the "experiment of bringing together so large a number of strong men" would succeed; but in the middle of the second year, as he later recollected, he witnessed the birth of a spirit of unity unhoped for: "The Saturday morning on which this new spirit first manifested itself in its fulness may be regarded as the date of the spiritual birth of the institution."[39] No spectacular event of record occurred at the time of which Harper spoke, and the substance of his memory remains unknown; perhaps its significance was subjective. Harper talked to the Senate about the appointment of E. Benjamin Andrews as co-President (in the opinion of some Senate members) on a Friday in the middle of the year; and it may be supposed that on the following day the objecting senators besieged his office.

Was Harper referring in his recollections to a backhanded vote of confidence from men who personified the autonomy of the departments?

Had a dual presidency been instituted, the University would not have had the particular cohesiveness that it did, for Harper's administration was bound together less by chains of command than by personal ties. Even as Laughlin launched one of his protests against the neglect of the Senate, he wrote Harper:

It may, perhaps, be improper for me to say these things to you as President, but you have honored me with your friendship, and if you will permit me to speak as a friend, I am sure you will understand that what I say is based [partly] . . . on personal affection for you. . . .[40]

A sense of Harper's personality supported the regime just as great blocks of concrete supported the whirling intricacy of the Ferris Wheel. On occasion, Harper sought to separate his personal and official attitudes vis-à-vis his colleagues; but, hearing Harper speak, they might wonder which voice he was using. Asked to attend a Convocation sermon, a dean once wrote Harper: "It is rather difficult to sharply distinguish between our University duties, which we are bound to see are carried out on sound general principles, and a desire to be personally obliging to yourself."[41]

The informal constitution of the University was the accumulation of agreements into which Harper had injected his enthusiasm when he negotiated with prospective colleagues—What do you want?—and when he dealt with them at the University, not infrequently in review of original commitments he had made—Won't you see us through? Confidence in his executive capacity, in the plenitude of his energies, and in his honesty constituted the foundation of polity; and correspondingly, erosion of confidence in Harper threatened the essential strength of the University. If the contents of Harper's correspondence files reflect the concerns of the Faculty, frustration of hope was far more serious than fear of repression. Some criticism took the form of friendly remonstrance, some of passionate yet loyal protest; but other criticisms went further. Despite Harper's ability to gain and hold the support of other men— call his gift charm, magnetism, or charisma—Harper did not succeed in preventing the bitter alienation of some erstwhile colleagues. Years after Harper's death, William C. Wilkinson, sometime professor in the Department of English, sent Albion W. Small these lines:

> A man of parts, a man therewith of—what?
> Assuredly of boundless push and—"pull,"
> And of devices shrewd innumerable.

"Devices may be shrewd, while scrupulous not."
Oh, yea, but his were scrupulous to a dot;
   He no device would practice without full
   Frank answer from it to the question, You'll
Quite satisfy the point of honor? Blot
   On my escutcheon I could nowise bear.
What is my point of honor? *To succeed.*
   The stain of but one failure I should wear
Forever like a wound that still must bleed.
   Let truth, let justice, of themselves take care,
My point of honor must have all my heed.

Small was outraged at the "monstrous" insinuation that Wilkinson's "indictment" was a judicious estimate of Harper's character; but Small added: "Anyone who knew him [Harper] fairly well and did not know that some of the temptations of his qualities lurked in the direction you [Wilkinson] indicate would be mentally or morally blind. I told him so more than once. . . ."[42]

Harper not only received but also heard criticism. It was of the essence in the history of the University that Harper was a man capable of viewing his behavior through the eyes of other men. When Harper described the place of an academic president, he spoke little of formal duties and much of the human relationships—or of their ambiguities—and of the costs paid by a governor in the coin of human feeling. Of his office, Harper wrote:

The president of a university who succeeds at times in concealing his real thought concerning this man or that subject is politely called a diplomat. Is it diplomacy, or is it lying? or may a more euphemistic phrase be found to describe the policy which must characterize his dealing with all classes of men, if he is to remain a college president?

A closer study of the case, and the examination of specific instances will furnish evidence that the professor who thought he had been promised promotion or an increase of salary, made petition to this effect, was received courteously, and mistook courteous treatment for a business pledge. The student, it will be found, forgot that the president was his judge. A judge is silent until sentence is to be pronounced. The student mistook that silence for acquiescence in his own statement. It is easy enough to imagine that the person to whom one talks has in his mind the thought of the speaker. The next step is easier still, actually to believe that the listener has approved the words of the speaker, or perhaps that he has spoken them.

Possible it is, to be sure, that the president in expressing his desire that such and such a thing should be, sometimes makes a statement that is open to stronger interpretation than he intended. It would be strange if he did not occasionally consent to a proposition which, upon later consideration, might appear to be impracticable; or which, however urgently he might present it to the powers that be, would fail to secure their approval. Does he likewise sometimes forget? Unquestionably; for he is human. Does he sometimes really undertake to do the impossible? Surely; and he discovers this fact to his cost. In all these cases, from the point of view of the other man, he is, in the language of the street, a liar. And yet, I dare say, he still supposes himself worthy of the confidence of his fellow creatures.

. . . .

It is contended, with some show of plausibility, that the modern college president is, first and last, a "boss." Does he not have almost unlimited power? May he not exercise this power at his own pleasure? Does he not set up and pull down? Can he not brow-beat and threaten? Is not the life of every professor in his hands? Does he not make and break careers? Is not the administration of a college or university in these times an example of one man power? It is so maintained, and we must confess there are some facts which seem to favor this contention.

. . . .

A close study of the situation will show that when all has been said, the limitations of the college president, even when he has the greatest freedom of action, are very great. In all business matters he is the servant of the trustees or corporation; and his views will prevail in that body only in so far as they approve themselves to their good judgment. In educational policy he must be in accord with his colleagues. If he cannot persuade them to adopt his views, he must go with them. It is absurd to suppose that any president, however strong or wilful he may be, can force a faculty, made up of great leaders of thought, to do his will. The president, if he has the power of veto, may stand in the way of progress, but he cannot secure forward movement except with the co-operation of those with whom he is associated. If there is one institution in which the president has too much power, there are ten in which he has too little.

The office of the college president is an office of service. Everything good or bad which connects itself with service is associated with this office. True service everywhere involves suffering for others. In no other profession, not even in that of the minister of the Gospel, is vicarious suffering more common. But one cannot be suffering for another unless he suffer also with that other. A fundamental characteristic of the president must be a sympathetic nature. He is doomed to failure unless he is able to place himself in the position of others with whom and for whom he has been called to work. In the truest sense the position is a representative one. He does many things, not of his own choice, but because he represents his colleagues. He may not do this or that thing according to his own pleasure, or his own sense of what is proper. The decision to do or not to do must rest largely upon the possible effect, helpful or harmful, to the institution of which he is head. In short, he is the slave of his environment, and must submit to the drudgery and, as well, the misery of that slavery.

And besides, another feeling which gradually grows upon the occupant of the presidential chair is that of great loneliness; the feeling of separation from all his fellows. At certain times he realizes that in all truth he *is* alone; for those who ordinarily are close to him, seem to be, and in fact are far away. On occasions of this kind courage is needed; strength, of a peculiar character. An ordinary man, and after all the college president is an ordinary man, cannot thus be cut off from his associates and fail to experience the sorrow of such separation. The college presidency means the giving up of many things, and, not least among these, one's most intimate friendships. Moreover, this feeling of separation, of isolation, increases with each recurring year, and in spite of the most vigorous effort, it comes to be a thing of permanence. This is inevitable, and it is as sad as it is inevitable.

While it happens that the words as well as the actions of the president are misunderstood by those about him; even by those of his colleagues who stand nearest to him, he is indeed fortunate, if a worse thing does not come,—the wilful effort to misrepresent him. He cannot exercise the functions of his office honestly without disturbing at times some even of those whom he believes to be his friends. And when this happens, these friends, perhaps unconsciously, will cease to find back of his actions the motives which he himself entertains. It is sometimes pitiful to see how easily men will misunderstand each other, and how complacently the misrepresentations of another's thought are spread from mouth to mouth.

. . . .

There come likewise times of great depression when one contemplates in all its details the bigness of the task which lies before him. In many instances this bigness becomes overwhelming, because of the exciting nature of the demands made, together with the number and magnitude of the difficulties involved. So numerous are the affairs of a great university; so heavy are they, in the responsibility which they impose; so delicate and difficult, in the diplomacy which their conduct requires; so arduous, in the actual time required for their management; so heart engrossing and mind disturbing, that there is demanded for their adequate supervision a man possessing the physical strength of a giant, and with this, an intellectual capacity and a moral courage of the most determined character. One, indeed, possessed of strength, feels himself weak, when he is brought face to face with all that is demanded; and one becomes sick at heart when he contemplates how much additional strength is needed to enable him to fulfil his duties as his conscience tells him they should be fulfilled.

Besides all this, there is found in moments of greatest encouragement a feeling of utter dissatisfaction with one's own work. To what definite thing can the president point, and say—this is my work? Does he not find his highest function in helping others to do the things which he himself would like to do? Yet he must stand aside and see others take up this very work which in his heart he would desire to handle. The head of an institution is not himself permitted to finish a piece of work. It is his business to find ways and means by which others may be helped to do their work. Some presidents never learn this difficult art, the art of letting others do things which one wishes himself to do. And for this reason not a few men fail to fill satisfactorily the office of president. There are two common maxims which if quoted in a form exactly the opposite of that in which they are in vogue, must regulate the work of the chief officer of a university if that work is to be successful. The first of these is this: *One should never himself do what he can in any way find someone else to do.* It is fair to presume that, with a single exception, there is no function of the presidential office that cannot better be performed by one or another member of the staff, than by the president himself. I mean by this, that for each particular function there can be found a man who has the peculiar ability to do that service better than the president can do it. The one function which may not be included in this statement is the selection and nomination of new members of the staff. Further, *the president should never do to-day what by any possible means he can postpone until to-morrow.* Premature action is the source of many more mistakes than procrastination. No decision should ever be reached, or at all events announced, until the latest possible moment has arrived; for how many are the instances in which new evidence has been introduced when, alas, it has been found too late to make use of it.

But there is also a bright side to this picture. How can one fail to find great satisfaction in a work which brings him into close association with life confessedly higher and more ideal than ordinary life? If in any environment idealism reigns supreme, it is in that of the University. There one works for and with young manhood and womanhood; and nothing in all the world is more inspiring than work in such association. It is the period in human life of greatest inspiration, of most intense enjoyment and of loftiest aspiration. The sadness of life is for the most part a thing of the future. Ambition is the keynote; and affection is in its best and purest mood. The life of a university officer is in many respects the most ideal that exists. The minister meets everywhere sorrow and sickness and death. The lawyer struggles against dishonesty, dissipation and fraud. The physician is almost wholly occupied with want and pain and suffering. With the college professor and the college president it is essentially different. They have to deal with all that is uplifting in life, with the constructive and not the destructive forces of life. The satisfaction which this brings no man can describe.[43]

"I am sure your face shows some trouble," Laughlin observed two days before the University opened. He had just offered to serve as Harper's confidant: "... you must not shut yourself up."[44] Five years later, Harper would write that the life of a university president was a tremendous struggle—"and the question is asked again and again, is it worth while."[45] The world watched a prodigy; but Harper, watching the official, asked what he was doing. An impressionable university was led by a man who felt impelled to explain himself.

Organizers and Trustees

Thomas W. Goodspeed

Frederick T. Gates

Charles L. Hutchinson

George C. Walker

John D. Rockefeller, Jr.

Martin A. Ryerson

In April, 1891, Thomas W. Goodspeed wrote William Rainey Harper: "The idea of Mr. R[Ryerson] & Mr. H[Hutchinson] is & it agrees with my own view perfectly to draw out on paper the entire plan at the start with the locations of buildings fixed & then build it building by building as we are able" (Goodspeed to Harper, April 14, 1891). That policy was adopted: Ryerson had in fact already sketched out the locations of buildings. The Trustees voted in the same month to ask for plans from six architectural firms, including that of Louis Sullivan. The architect chosen was Henry Ives Cobb, one of the designers of the (now-razed) Chicago Opera House.

In this "study," drawn in 1893, the campus is viewed from the southeast, with residential Foster Hall in the near corner of the picture. Lexington (now University) Avenue is at the bottom, 59th Street to the left. The buildings near Foster Hall were designated the Women's Quadrangle, those in the upper left the Graduate Quadrangle, and those in the two corners at the right, the Undergraduate Quadrangles. Somewhat more than half of the land here covered by buildings is actually occupied by buildings of different design or has not been built upon. Rough brick halfway up the side of the Walker Museum has still to be knocked out to make way for a bridge to a larger museum building, standing in this picture just to the south (the viewer's left) of the archway on Lexington Avenue. The most imposing of the other buildings never constructed are the Gymnasium on the other side of the archway, the Chapel behind it, the octagonal Biological Lecture Hall to the right, and the towered University Hall and Library at the back.

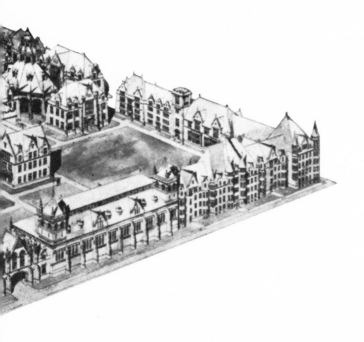

Henry Ives Cobb

Actuality

The land donated by Marshall Field in 1890 was a plot of ten acres lying east of Ellis Avenue and north of 57th Street, including part of the land now named Stagg Field. While holding the assets of the prospective University, the American Baptist Education Society bought more land from Field. The Society turned over three city blocks of land to the Trustees of the University after it had been incorporated. Charles L. Hutchinson argued that the University would be hampered in the future if it did not own still more land, and he had support in the Board; but some of the Trustees believed that expansion of the site was not to be justified financially. In April, 1891, the Board voted to buy a fourth city block from Field, partly on credit. The original gift and the purchases put the University—after some exchange of land parcels—into possession of a rectangle of land two blocks wide on each side and adjacent to 59th Street, or the Midway. The Chicago City Council vacated the streets and alleys. A low, wooded ridge and a water-filled depression in the southwestern part of the site offered no serious impediment to the arrangement of buildings in the regular quadrangles that gave the University one of its nicknames.

THE SITE OF THE UNIVERSITY

THE UNIVERSITY UNDER CONSTRUCTION DURING THE WINTER OF 1892–93

The point of view in this picture is roughly that of the architect's sketch of the completed University. Cobb Hall, donated by Silas B. Cobb, the first building to be completed, is to the left, the unroofed Kent Chemical Laboratory to the right of center, and the foundation of the Walker Museum to the extreme right. The Trustees originally thought of building the University in granite, but finding it too expensive, they chose what is known to quarrymen as blue Bedford stone. As seen by other eyes, its color justified poetic references to the "City Gray." A black and white photograph fails to show the effect of the sheet-copper work which ornamented the roof of Cobb Hall and the other buildings designed by Henry I. Cobb. This architectural embroidery turned light green as the tile-red roofs darkened to approach maroon.

THE FACULTY ROOM AWAITING ITS MEMBERS

Creating a Faculty

The First Two Head Professors

WILLIAM G. HALE

J. LAURENCE LAUGHLIN

HARRY P. JUDSON

ERNEST D. BURTON

ALBION W. SMALL

THOMAS C. CHAMBERLIN

GEORGE W. NORTHRUP

JOHN DEWEY

Faculty Members Who Bore the Title of Head Professor or Professor and Head of Department during the Harper Administration

GALUSHA ANDERSON, Homiletics
JAMES R. ANGELL, Psychology
LEWELLYS F. BARKER, Anatomy
CARL D. BUCK, Sanskrit and Indo-European Comparative Philology
ERNEST D. BURTON, New Testament Literature and Exegesis
THOMAS C. CHAMBERLIN, Geology
JOHN M. COULTER, Botany
HENRY H. DONALDSON, Neurology
JOHN DEWEY, Philosophy
WILLIAM G. HALE, Latin
WILLIAM RAINEY HARPER, Semitic Languages and Literatures
LUDVIG HEKTOEN, Pathology and Bacteriology
CHARLES R. HENDERSON, Ecclesiastical Sociology
HERMANN E. VON HOLST, History
ERI B. HULBERT, Church History

JOHN FRANKLIN JAMESON, History
EDWARD JUDSON, Homiletics
HARRY P. JUDSON, Political Science
WILLIAM I. KNAPP, Romance Languages and Literatures
J. LAURENCE LAUGHLIN, Political Economy
JACQUES LOEB, Physiology
JOHN M. MANLY, English
ALBERT A. MICHELSON, Physics
ELIAKIM H. MOORE, Mathematics
RICHARD G. MOULTON, Literature (in English)
JOHN U. NEF, Chemistry
GEORGE W. NORTHRUP, Systematic Theology
ROLLIN D. SALISBURY, Geography
PAUL SHOREY, Greek
ALBION W. SMALL, Sociology
GEORGE N. I. STEWART, Physiology
JAMES H. TUFTS, Philosophy

CHARLES O. WHITMAN, Zoölogy

Designers of Student Life

MYRA REYNOLDS   DEAN MARION TALBOT   ELIZABETH WALLACE
                        Heads of Houses

CHARLES R. HENDERSON   AMOS ALONZO STAGG
University Chaplain   *Director of the Division of Physical Culture*

The Quadrangles, 1893

The University of Chicago campus viewed in 1893 from the Ferris Wheel at the World's Columbian Exposition. There is no knowing how many future students saw the University for the first time as they were lifted up above the Midway in the cars of the Ferris Wheel. The observer is looking north toward the city, where clouds—or retouching—give a false impression of hills. In the foreground, planted trees have not entirely replaced the natural scrub, and standing water remains. Cobb Hall is on the left, Kent and Ryerson laboratories in the center, Walker Museum in middle right, and Foster Hall at the extreme right.

MEMBERS OF THE LION'S HEAD

THE QUADRANGLERS

The Lion's Head and the Quadranglers were undergraduate clubs. Quadranglers is still in existence. In 1895, the members of Lion's Head were Harry Delmont Abells, Henry Magee Adkinson, James Scott Brown, Forest Grant, Carr Baker Neel, Fred Day Nichols, and Joseph Edward Raycroft. Members of Quadranglers were Theodosia Kane, Ethel Keen, Jennette Kennedy, Anna J. McClintock, Elizabeth Messick, and Edna Stanton.

The last photograph in the first issue of The University of Chicago Yearbook, *Cap and Gown,* 1895

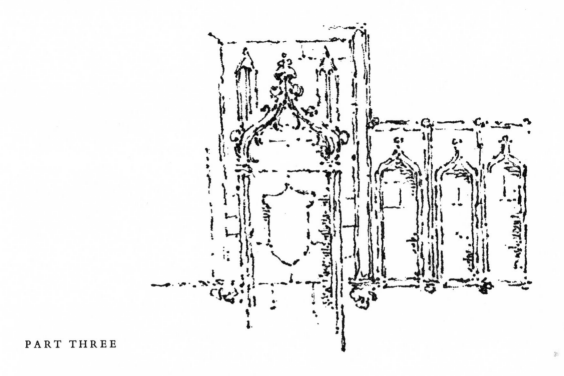

PART THREE

THE ACADEMIC WAY:
THE FIRST TEN YEARS

The Student Body

Inevitably, the students constituted the last group to join the University before the opening; it would be the students, turned alumni, who finally completed the University as an enduring coalition. During the first year, somewhat less than 750 students appeared in the Quadrangles: the records of enrolment differ slightly. Nearly one-third of the student body was undergraduate and one-fourth graduate, in Arts, Literature, and Science. In the latter group, the scientists were outnumbered by a ratio of just less than three to one. The remainder of the students were distributed between the Divinity School and a catchall, unclassified students. No one segment of the student body promised to dominate the life of the University by sheer weight of numbers. A little more than a quarter of the whole student body consisted of women— enough to indicate that coeducation would not be an empty principle. Of the students who entered the University from secondary schools, slightly more came from public high schools than from private academies: more than one- third of the undergraduates had attended college elsewhere. The graduate programs received students from 95 institutions, the largest single contingent, fourteen students, coming from Wellesley College.[1]

Almost three-quarters of the students came from homes in Chicago and the Middle West. About one in seven lived in the northern and middle states of the East, where more than one-third of the students had had some previous education. (Was the University pulling some young Midwesterners back into their own region for advanced education?) The strength of the tie that the University had with the Northeast must be attributed partly to causes which were not lasting, namely, the withdrawal of students from eastern universities to follow their professors West and the paucity of facilities in the East for the graduate education of women. Less than 3 per cent of the students came from the southern Atlantic region, from the central South, or from the West. Twenty students came from Canada, and a total of a dozen from other foreign countries.[2]

Since the University did not ask the students their religious affiliation and kept little detailed information on other aspects of their background, the religious, racial, and the socioeconomic composition of the first body of students can only be guessed at from evidence for other years, which often yields no more than fragmentary impressions. In any university, everyone knows at a glance what the typical student is; but no one may think to count how many students run true to type. If a survey made informally in 1903 offers a fair sample of the religious affiliations of the students—and there is no reason to suppose that the general impression given by the findings is misleading—the Baptists constituted the most numerous but hardly dominant minority in a student body that was strongly but not exclusively Protestant. Of 119 students (in a graduating class of 142) who indicated the religion they professed, 24 were Baptists, 19 Presbyterians, 15 Episcopalians, 13 Congregationalists, and 13 Methodists. The next group in order was composed of Jewish students, of whom there were 10 in the class. There were also 8 Roman Catholics. Other denominations were represented in smaller numbers, and one student was listed as an Independent.[3]

Officially, the University drew no color line and did admit some Negro students. In 1901, five students of about thirty-five hundred were Negroes. At the same time, Harper noted that very few Negro students appeared at the University. On one occasion of record, Harper empowered an informal recruiting agent in Texas "... to get rid of anyone who may be obnoxious to you" and said that the University was reluctant to admit Negroes.[4] (Harper obviously desired to attract white students from the South, where the Baptist denomination was strong. A summer migration from Texas was conspicuously large, but the appeal of the University in the South was not strong enough to yield a large number of southern students in other seasons. Statistics do not bear out Harper's statement of 1899 that "southern sentiment is turning largely in our favor.")[5]

Apparently the University only drew minorities of its students from either gravely deprived or highly privileged families. The former could look with as much or more hope to the state universities and land-grant colleges and the latter with great expectations to the East. "We suffer the disadvantage," an officer commented in 1903, "of being so near and so familiar as not to arouse the same kind of sentimental interest in boys that some of the eastern universities do."[6] At its opening, however, the University may possibly have possessed the charm of novelty for students who could afford to choose a college; unquestionably it did attract students who had to work their way—and it organized a board to administer student employment.[7] Scholarships and fellowships regularly carried an obligation to render service to the University. A large proportion of the students from Chicago may indeed have belonged to families of working people: so Harper observed in a decennial report on his administration.[8] Yet those students probably constituted far less than half of the whole student body. A dean calculated percentages for the occupations pursued by parents of graduating seniors in one class: 40 per cent were in business; 14 per cent in the trades; 11 per cent in farming; and 5 per cent of unknown occupation; the remainder were in the professions and government. He had no figures for comparison, but the dean felt confident that in an eastern college the proportion of students whose parents were in the professions of ministry, law, teaching, and medicine would have been much larger than among Chicago students.[9] Somewhat later, Dean Marion Talbot noted a difference in the backgrounds of the men and women, the men coming from a lower financial level.[10]

In his decennial report Harper undertook to sketch a portrait of the student body. Perhaps he worked in the light of his own standards, seeing what he hoped for in the reality presented to him; perhaps also hope and reality had much the same face. Harper wrote:

It has been a subject of general comment that the chief characteristics of the student body have been steadiness, sturdiness, strength, strong individuality, high ideals, and clear purpose. . . . The student constituency does not perhaps equal in outward polish that of one of the larger institutions of the East, but in ability to organize work, in skill of adaptation of means to ends, in determination of purpose to win, in readiness to make sacrifice for the sake of intellectual advancement, no body of students ever gathered together in this country, or in any other country, has shown itself superior to the student body of the University of Chicago.[11]

There is no knowing exactly what of that character the student brought to the University and what it imparted. Undoubtedly the process of converting Harper's grand scheme into a way of life was determined by the reciprocal action of the influences exerted by the students as they presented themselves and of the efforts made by the University to provide for them academically and socially.

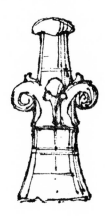

CHAPTER VII

The Approaches
to Academe

Like the plant designed for the University, its academic program consisted of compartments; but unlike the physical site, that program lay in terraces. The University marked off one more level than many institutions. Before students had appeared in the Quadrangles, the University drew a line between what were originally called the Academic Colleges, later Junior Colleges, and the University or Senior Colleges, that is, between the lower and upper halves of the conventional four-year college. The Academic Colleges looked back toward the drill of the preparatory academy, the University College forward to university work.[1] The students were permitted by the regulations to move upward only by defined pathways. The outskirts of the University were broad, but the summit of academe was not easily reached. Having a place in the Quadrangles was, in a double sense, a matter of degree.

UNCLASSIFIED STUDENTS

The "unclassified students" stood farthest from the academic center. The presence of students so designated did not result from a desire on the part of the University to maintain instruction upon the Quadrangles as a treasury of knowledge upon which Everyman might draw at will. The obligation of a university to serve the people was not construed to mean that the public should be welcomed in departmental courses, as distinct from the offerings in University Extension. It was never supposed that men and women who wanted to take a course on campus simply to learn something would constitute a regular part of the student population, existing, as it were, by right of curiosity alone. The *Official Bulletin, No. 2,* of April, 1891, announced that students not candidates for a degree might be admitted to courses but stipulated that such students should show good reason for not entering one of the regular classes.[2] To that provision, which was but one of several, the statutes added others, including the requirement that the student must be not less than twenty-one years of age and must enter the University to do advanced work. Admission of unclassified students was explicitly described as a privilege which would be terminated by the faculty in individual cases if the best use was not made of the privilege.[3] Thus the University recognized the needs of persons who did not fall into the conventional categories and provided for them as exceptions to the rule. Such students occupied the anomalous position of stateless persons in a world of nations. What they shared within the Quadrangles was not a substantive program of their own but a negative condition, the lack of a recognized place in the hierarchy of degree programs.

About one-third of the unclassified students (in one seemingly typical year) expected to become regular students; another third consisted of persons, usually teachers, who had some definite object in view; and the remaining third was a miscellany—women from faculty families or the neighborhood, an occasional young lawyer or physician, and "... young women who get some real or fancied help in artistic, club, or social life."[4] Many of the students who planned to seek a degree refused to declare their intentions in order to avoid the need of satisfying admissions requirements promptly or of meeting certain undergraduate requirements, whether curricular or extracurricular (e.g., physical education).[5]

The numbers of unclassified students were far from negligible. In the autumn of 1892, they numbered seventy-three—or about 10 per cent of the whole student body. Through the spring of 1898, the proportion never fell below that per cent, and once, in the summer of 1894, rose to 28 per cent. The percentage may have dropped in later years—statistics on unclassified students were not regularly published after 1898–99; but in 1902–04 the absolute number of students was nearly equal to that in 1898–99. The unclassified students were most numerous in the summer quarter when battalions of teachers attended the University. Women usually outnumbered men by a wide margin, sometimes by a ratio of two to one.[6]

The spread in the chonological age of the students was wide; but the unclassified students in much the largest single age group were from twenty-two to twenty-five years old.[7] The University was seemingly most attractive to young people—particularly the young woman who had taught school a few years—who had not been able to enter college directly from secondary school but had not lost the ambition to go to college. In educational and geographical background, the unclassified students were notably diversified: in 1897–98, they came from 286 schools, and in 1898–99, from thirty-seven states or territories, the District of Columbia, and several foreign countries.[8]

The students did markedly different amounts of work. Over one year (for which a summary of studies is available) from 12 to 24 per cent of the students took only one major from quarter to quarter; from 16 to 30 per cent took two majors; from 45 to 64 per cent took three majors (or a normal amount of work); and from 2 to 9 per cent took four majors. More than nine-tenths of the work of these students was done in undergraduate courses and one-half in courses at the Junior College level.[9] Much of the work was not in fact advanced.

It was commonly remarked, a dean reported in 1897–98, that the list of unclassified students contained some of the very best and some of the poorest students in the University. A small number were "undoubtedly undesirable." Requirement of full work, the dean said, would quickly remove all those who did not regard their University connection as a serious interest. Also, many summer students cared rather to browse than to "work severely" on assigned tasks. Yet the proportion of delinquents in classwork was, the dean found, considerably smaller among the unclassified students than for the Junior Colleges. "No menace has been felt from them [the unclassified students] for scholarship among us."[10] A number of the unclassified students eventually moved on into regular work, e.g., 46 in 1896–97 and 37 in the following year; hence a pool of unclassified students was a valuable feeder for the college degree programs—more valuable numerically for the years mentioned than all of the affiliated schools combined.[11]

Fundamental policy in regard to unclassified students remained unchanged during the Harper administration; most of the changes in detail were apparently designed to enforce that policy and to secure the fulfilment of its implicit major premise, namely that the unclassified students should be assimilated into the body of regular students. In 1896, the University insisted that students would not be accepted to work in the elementary subjects only (that is, they could not take beginning French unless they also took advanced work in some other subject).[12] In 1897, they were required to pass the specific entrance examinations of the departments in which they desired to study.[13] Thus a demand for what amounted to partial matriculation was instituted. An exemption was allowed teachers who had graduated from accepted high schools and who for two years had taught the subject in which they proposed to do advanced work. "It seems to me," the dean of unclassified students said, "that the university has [a duty] ... to encourage our old friends, the teachers, who come for exact training for their work, who are proud of their University connection, who come year after year, who are carrying higher standards of scholarship throughout the Middle West, and who send us their students from high schools and academies. . . ."[14]

In 1897, unclassified students were required to take work in physical education if they had as many as five credits toward admission to a degree program. "We succeed," the dean wrote in 1897, "when we bring these students fully into the spirit of companionship of the general student body, making them an integral part of the family of scholars in whom the University is to find its success and support."[15] As of 1897, a student was permitted "to classify"—the verb acquired an intransitive meaning—if his credits toward admission and for work done in the University equaled the *amount* of work required for admission, without regard to subject matter studied.[16] The next year it was ruled that the University, not the student, was to decide whether or not he was to stand unclassified: "If he can be classified, it is to be done."[17]

The dean argued that all students who could do so should be urged and even compelled to take the full college course: ". . . these students are not prevailingly advanced and prepared to specialize, but still need the disciplines leading to scholarly maturity."[18] Yet the principles governing the acceptance of unclassified students could be summed up, the dean said, in *maturity* and *earnestness*. The University was confronted by a disparity between the seasoning that comes with growing up and the development required of the college student in particular. A new dean remarked in the next year—did he intend an Irish bull? —that the problem of the unclassified students was their classification. In many respects they were like graduate students and unlike undergraduates, from whom they differed in age and other ways, and yet they were treated like Junior College students, the least mature of the undergraduates. The unclassified students had perhaps a year or two to spend in special study at the University to fit them for better work or a better position in their profession (i.e., teaching); if they took the required studies of the Junior Colleges and made up some entrance conditions, they got but little of that special work. Perhaps they failed to recognize the value of general training in comparison with the special instruction they sought. But they could not afford the regular course. "What can be done for these students? It is difficult to say. They are so unlike that they must be treated individually on their own merits as special cases."[19] That was the rub. The University sought to feed the hungry for whom there was little or no place in conventional education; but it declined to become Liberty Hall. In the eyes of the University, the case of the unmatriculated student *per se* was inherently special.

The problem of the unclassified was not pushed nearer to a solution. The announcement of work for such students remained what it had been since the publication of the *Official Bulletin, No. 2,* a pendent to the plan for the Junior College students (i.e., freshmen and sophomores). Originally they themselves had only a tenuous claim to a place in the Quadrangles.

THE JUNIOR COLLEGE STUDENTS

At the first meeting of the Faculty of Arts, Literature, and Science, Harper expressed the hope that the work of the lower colleges might be removed from the campus. That statement but echoed the *Official Bulletin, No. 2,* proposing that such work should be accomplished largely through affiliated colleges: "This will permit the University in Chicago to devote its energies mainly to the University Colleges and to strictly University work."[20] If the Faculty had made the fulfilment of Harper's expectations its chief business in regard to undergraduate studies, the University would have worked a revolution. Anything resembling the old-fashioned four-year college program would have disappeared from the Quadrangles. In October, 1892, however, the less mature students were there to be dealt with, and the professors did not choose to follow Harper's lead.

More than five months before the University opened, Harry Pratt Judson asked Harper if it was worthwhile to attempt to maintain the distinction between the Academic and University Colleges: "I am convinced that the line of demarcation will be quite soon a very dubious line."[21] Laughlin found much force in the question when it was brought to his attention, apparently by Harper.[22] When the Faculty of Arts, Literature, and Science set to work after the opening of the University, it virtually tabled drastic reorganization of undergraduate education as it turned to a more pressing matter. Before the end of the first quarter of the first academic year, Dean Alice Freeman Palmer was writing Harper of "this puzzling business" of arranging courses. "I am thankful," she wrote, "that you have talked frankly with Mr. Chamberlin about the Science complications. Nothing could be more foolish from their [the scientists'] point of view than the present arrangement, and the reform should come from them."[23] For years "science complications" were to pre-empt hours of the Faculty's time as the scientists proposed reform measures.

During October, 1892, the month in which the University opened, Chamberlin argued (unsuccessfully) in the Senate that the subjects required in the course of the Academic College of science should be mathematics, science, history and political economy, and language, and that Latin and advanced French should be alternatives to each other (i.e., that Latin should not be singled out, as it was, in the prescription of studies).[24] In January, 1893, Chamberlin proposed that for admission to the University eight science majors should be expected of all candidates. If the total demands made of candidates would be made too great by simply adding these majors, some might be presented as alternatives to certain other subjects in each group of admission subjects. (The *Official Bulletin, No. 2,* had specified six groups, of which only three contained science.) The sets of alternatives which Chamberlin had in mind were to be established for each group separately according to its primary design. The proposal was embodied in a resolution moved by Chamberlin in the Senate in January, 1893, and referred in February to the Faculty of Arts, Literature, and Science.[25] There Chamberlin received a request to report a statement of the specific groups of subjects which served the purpose he had in mind. The plan which he presented allowed many choices. Before the Faculty had acted upon this proposal, Hale moved to substitute a set of six groups which differed only at a few points from the existing requirements and offered no alternatives. Paul Shorey, Hale's fellow classicist, wrote Harper: "There is no logic in establishing alternatives within the groups, when the groups themselves are alternatives."[26] Shorey thought that Chamberlin utterly disbelieved in classical education.* After these plans had been submitted to the faculty by individual members, a committee on admissions presented a third plan which was adopted with slight amendment.[27]

The third plan established a common currency of credit for secondary-school work. It was understood to contain thirteen "units," each being equal to three majors in the academies run by the University—which in fact meant Morgan

---

* Shorey's letter throws light upon the way University business was conducted. Shorey said that he was sorry Harper was displeased with the tone of Shorey's remarks at a faculty meeting and that he was glad that "you have frankly told me so." Shorey added that long speeches only confused questions before the faculty and made intelligent debate impossible. "They can be met only by the pre-emptory presentation of a narrow issue" (Shorey to Harper, Feb. 13, 1893).

Park Academy alone. A major, the standard unit of academic credit at the University, called originally for eight to ten hours of classroom work for a term of six weeks and, as of 1895–96, for half that much work carried through a quarter or two terms. In either case, a major represented a third of a student's work each quarter. Thus a student in residence from October to June—for three quarters or the ordinary academic year—would earn nine majors. The University had sufficient regard for convention to require four times that much work for a Bachelor's degree; hence the planning of a curriculum was, in mechanical terms, the choosing of thirty-six majors.[28] A student was to be admitted to the lower colleges of the University upon passing examinations in any thirteen of twenty-two specified units in Latin, English and history, Greek, French, German, mathematics, and the sciences, provided he offered one unit in English and two in mathematics. Although he was not absolutely required to distribute his thirteen units in any particular way, he was "strongly advised" to arrange his preparatory study in accord with one of three programs pointing toward the degrees of A.B., Ph.B., or S.B., i.e., to follow a defined path leading to the degree of his choice.[29] Notably prospective scientists were expected to present no less than two years of Latin; other applicants should have four.

As of 1893–94, the recommendation of particular studies gave way to quasi-requirements; and as of 1896–97, some of them were made explicitly unconditional.[30] Concurrently the list of subjects carrying credit toward admission, without regard to particular programs, was lengthened.[31] The University was at once tightening up the process of full collegiate matriculation and giving more generous recognition to the work of the secondary schools. Instruction in some but not all of the recommended or required subjects—one-third in 1898—was offered at the University so that the student lacking credit could partly make up deficiencies in the classrooms of the University.[32] To this extent the University provided the student a remedy for limited opportunity or bad advice given him in academy or high school.

The *Annual Register* after 1893–94 specified how much Junior College work the student would have to do in continuation of his earlier studies. Originally, the *Register* called for three majors of Latin in all of the programs. The totals of required studies allowed the student time for no more than three "elective" majors (or the equivalent of a year's study in one subject) that might be used for work of the student's own choosing or in making up deficiencies.[33]

In the course of time, the details of the system of admissions and prescribed degree requirements were changed again and again. Not only was prescription extended and the list of possible admissions units enlarged but the value of a "unit" was recomputed, the number of required admissions units was increased, and under certain circumstances acceptance of secondary-school credits by certification was substituted for examination; yet the essential scheme proved durable.[34]

Almost as soon as the plan was devised, Harper used a metaphor that was to become a commonplace. In a memorandum book dated 1893, he advised himself to make the Academic College a clearing-house to broaden and balance up the courses.[35] In high school and as an underclassman, had the student acquired credit for the learning that a liberally educated man in his field could be expected to have as a foundation for specialized studies? In its fully developed form, the clearing-house system was based upon the equivalence of credits for a subject as studied in preparatory school and as studied in college.[36] (A year of secondary study was sometimes equated with two, not three, majors of college work.) Customarily, the equivalence was manifested in the publication of tables—for each of the Bachelor's degrees—in which recommended admissions units and prescribed college majors were consolidated. The whole set amounted to a battery of six-year programs for study below the Senior Colleges. The student seeking a particular Bachelor's degree was presented with two lists. One indicated the preparatory studies for which units of credit toward admission would be granted and the other the studies he was obliged to complete before entering upon the studies of his last two years of undergraduate education in a Senior College. By meeting the terms of the first list, the student could acquire an entrance visa into the Junior Colleges and by meeting the terms of the second, he could secure his exit visa. While the program was in effect, it was ruled that a student might enter the Senior College with twelve rather than eighteen majors of Junior College work; but it was still required that recommended studies not actually pursued in secondary school should be made up. By using a twofold standard, the University sought to reconcile the great heterogeneity in college preparatory work in the West and the principle of prescribed general education. As the dean of the Junior Colleges observed in 1897–98, the history of admissions requirements showed the effort to assimilate the ideal scheme with which the University started with the environment in which it was placed and at the same time to maintain the high standard which it had inherited from the older universities in the East.[37]

The clearing-house system was an ingenious piece of machinery, but it did not automatically resolve such issues as Chamberlin raised in 1892–93. It was one thing to speak in the abstract of general culture and a fair balance of subjects, as Chamberlin did, and quite another to establish viable curriculums that satisfied the concrete specifications of the several departments. As substantial masses of subject matter were pressed both into the entrance recommendations or requirements and into the collegiate programs, some students were heavily burdened; indeed those who did not (or perhaps could not) follow the lists very closely in secondary-school studies were not likely to have any real choice of electives in the Junior College. Providing relief meant not only adjusting the total sums of credit required but also reducing the amounts of study in particular subjects held dear by one or another of the departments. The requirements for the s.b. degree caused the most trouble. The candidate who had only two years of Latin on entering the University was obliged to study Latin in college, which meant that he might be able to take only three majors of science instead of the six deemed desirable for s.b. candidates and required of students with four years of Latin at matriculation. The number of students in that situation was not small: in 1901, nearly half of the scientists in the Junior College had taken only two years of Latin in school.[38] The student with just that much Latin and many deficiencies in recommended or required subjects, no matter how well supplied otherwise with credits toward admission, would need more than eighteen majors of work, or more than two years of study, in the Junior College. And when two years of Latin was made a requirement for matriculation, the door of the College was shut to a class of students described by Small as those ". . . who have no idea of going to college until late in the High School course, who therefore do not care for Latin, but who have good stuff in them, and at graduation from the High School are as able to do good work in some directions as the classically trained boys are in others. . . ."[39]

In 1896, eight members of the Senate objected emphatically to the grave defects that experience, they said, had developed in the course for the s.b. degree. Its enrolment was small in comparison with that of the two other courses and with the percentage of scientific students in the graduate school and in other institutions: in the Junior College in February, 1896, there were only fifty-six candidates for the s.b. degree (18.3 per cent of total enrolment). The senators believed that the grade of work in the University had suffered from a curse, a lowering of average quality in s.b. candidates; ". . . for scantness of patronage naturally leads to less rigor in weeding out unsatisfactory students. . . ."[40] Actual attendance departed from what might fairly have been anticipated from the sources of supply immediately at hand. Less than 1 per cent of over 1,400 students graduated from Chicago high schools in a two-year period were s.b. candidates in the Junior College; and about 35 per cent, by the senators' reckoning, were shut out by the technicalities of the system of admissions: "These technicalities discriminate against modern science and modern language in favor of ancient languages."[41] The University thus lost a large part of the best material available for the course. The requirements themselves were open to grave objection because they were ill-adapted to subsequent work and because they were unbalanced. It was impossible, under an apportionment of time unfavorable to the sciences, not only for the several departments of science to do their individual work satisfactorily but also to combine departmental offerings in "a strong, continuous, wisely co-ordinated scientific curriculum. . . ." The rub, as the senators explained it, was that in the preparation for and in the content of a course called scientific, the study of "raiment" such as language was twice as important as the study of scientific substance.[42]

This statement spelled out the science complications of which Dean Palmer had spoken. As the senators' words suggest, Dean Palmer might as well have spoken of the Latin question. Although many subjects of study were involved in the intricate manipulations by which the University sought to make the clearing-house work, Latin was most often the bone of contention. Proposals for reducing the amount of Latin required of the scientists were put forward in one Faculty body or another and in one formulation or another—frequently through Chamberlin's agency—for a decade after the opening of the University. There is perhaps an understandable edginess in the recommendation of a Junior College committee, in 1902, that the University should maintain, for a period of a few years, a system which prospective students might count on with certainty.[43]

The debate over Latin struck different persons in different ways. For Whitman, head professor of zoölogy, argument over Latin year after year became a bore: in 1898, he washed his hands of the matter.[44] For the senators, including Chamberlin, who wrote the protest of 1896, the question arose partly out of the impracticability of developing a strong scientific curriculum and constituency under prevailing conditions. Professors viewing the debate in that light might or might not find Latin absolutely valuable in education: the desideratum was an arrangement of studies in which the ordinary pattern of work of a secondary school would not become handicaps for the scientifically gifted. Practical interest was closely related to a belief that science and other modern studies were victims of discrimination: the statement of 1896 obviously reflected that view.

Latin provided a narrow issue, in Shorey's phrase, in terms of which the protagonists of both the old and the new learning could express a general sense of grievance. Discussing the location of buildings with Harper in 1902, Hale wrote:

In the struggle going on in the educational world today, the great issue is whether the ancient literatures and disciplines shall be regarded as superseded, and shall be put into an inferior position. I ask only a position of equality. But this means that there should be a separate classical building, as generously equipped as possible, *and that it should be one of the buildings upon the great main quadrangle, facing the two great buildings of science.*[45]

Like possession of a building, the control of three majors for study, alternatively, of Latin or science, may have been sought after as a symbol of the recognition due one's subject. The ultimate conflict was that over the place of humanism and science in the education of students who had too little time to study everything.

The poles of feeling in the Faculty were represented by the opinions of Charles W. Eliot held by Hale and Chamberlin, who frequently acted, respectively, as spokesmen for and against required Latin. "It is really a pity," Hale wrote Marion Talbot, "that so much greatness should have been wasted in President Eliot. I am inclined to think the final judgment upon his life will be that he has done the cause of education harm, in spite of the frequent ways in which his courage and free speech have done it good."[46] To Eliot himself, Chamberlin expressed his interest in Eliot's reconsideration of entrance requirements: "I am in the most hearty sympathy with your advanced attitude, to which I am sure the educational world generally will come at an early date."[47] Directed against local targets, the feelings of the two professors produced some random sniping. Once, when Chamberlin was explaining delay in his geological research, he remarked to Harper: "I hope, however, to get on better now as I have religiously promised myself to squander less time on impossible living fossils and devote more to those who were good enough to die in their appropriate historical periods."[48] On his side, Hale wrote, when recommending a fellow Latinist as the prospective author of newspaper articles on the University: "He would be inclined to do justice to every department, and would have the literary skill required. It would be hard to find any one in the scientific departments who had the latter."[49]

Two cultures were in conflict; but the front did not lie along a clearly defined line between scientists and humanists. According to a poll of the Ogden School of Science taken in 1899–1900, exactly one-half of the members voting (or nineteen of thirty-eight) answered without qualification that some Latin should be required for admission to the s.b. course. The balance shifted away from Latin, but only by eighteen unqualified votes against sixteen, when the members of the school were asked whether additional Latin should be required in college. The proposition was put subject to a proviso that the student with less than three and one-half units of science on entry into the University would be guaranteed the use of electives for scientific study. Thus some members who voted for required Latin may have meant to say that Latin ought, if possible, to be retained. One member did vote to require additional Latin without the possibility of abatement. Another member commented: "I think that scholars should be gentlemen. I think that all gentlemen should know English, Latin, Mathematics, History, their Specialty."[50] And one ballot carried the declaration: "I believe that Latin is a valuable subject . . . [but] do not believe that it is more important than most other subjects presented for entrance work, and I am opposed to making it more prominent by legislation than its merits demand."[51]

Although Latin's pre-eminence was disputed, its claim to a place in the education of scientists was not invariably disallowed. (Albion W. Small once remarked to Harper that lack of harmony among the scientists was a tremendous tactical advantage for the classical majority.)[52] Opinion was also divided outside of the scientific Faculty. Four of the eight senators who signed the statement of 1896 taught neither the biological nor the physical sciences. Yet it is notable that one of the signers was Eliakim H. Moore, head of Mathematics, which obviously contributed directly to the education of scientists; another was Small, whose field, as he defined it, was the science of society; and still another was John Dewey, who within five months would advocate reorganization of pedagogical study after the pattern of scientific investigation and would explain the need for a "laboratory" school. (Without referring specifically to local conditions, Dewey called attention to a state of affairs that helped to produce the debate over the place of Latin: "The accumulation of knowledge has become so great that the educational system is disintegrating through the wedges of new studies continually introduced."[53] Dewey added: "It is as nearly certain as any educational expectation may be that if the increased demands, as regards number of languages, range of literary study, of history, and of the physical and biological sciences are to be met, even halfway, in the college and high school, the response must proceed from changing the methods in the lower grades, and by beginning work along these lines in the primary school—yes, and in the kindergarten."[54] The Faculty did not begin its ordering of education so early in the life of the student.

In 1896, sentiment in the whole Faculty of Arts, Science, and Literature was indicated by the vote on a motion made by Chamberlin. What he had in mind ". . . involved the entire removal of Latin from the s.b. course."[55] Of the non-scientists, five voted for the motion and twenty-four against it; and of the scientists, seven voted for and eleven against the motion.[56] After the dissolution of the Faculty into smaller bodies, the professoriate was not polled as a single body. The majority in the Junior College Faculty, which had primary jurisdiction over required Latin, favored the status quo until 1902. Until then, the position of the College differed sufficiently from the wishes of the Ogden School to create a situation in which the Senate was obliged to arbitrate as the body superior to both the College and Ogden School Faculties. In the Senate itself, opinion was split almost in half. Indeed, in 1896, a motion to experiment with an s.b. course without college Latin, parallel to the existing course, was lost on a tie vote.[57] In 1900, the introduction of substitutes for that Latin was adopted with a most meager majority, twelve votes to eleven, with two senators not voting.[58] The result plainly outraged Hale, who immediately moved that neither mathematics, nor Latin, nor science be required for admission to the University— the Senate should be consistent in its absurdity. Presumably taking Hale's motion seriously, Chamberlin also made a motion to the effect that Latin was not equivalent to the group of scientific subjects but merely one of a group of languages—again the contention that Latin should not have a distinctive place— and that allowing substitutions for Latin should not be regarded as a precedent for like action in regard to a group, "since it [Latin] is not itself a group."[59] Chamberlin was relentless in making the point. (A committee, chaired by Judson, to which the motions were referred, reported against Hale's motion and recommended no action on the other.)[60] The will of the Senate was declared to the Junior College Faculty, where the question of substitutions was virtually reopened and where in 1902, after the passage of almost two years, Harper called upon Judson to review the matter, as if the College—was it deliberately?—had half forgotten the vote of the Senate in 1900.[61]

Harper's own attitude toward the requirement of Latin at once shaped and reflected its history in the University. The presence of the requirement, without possibility of abatement, in all of the programs at the time of opening must be attributed largely to Harper's original planning. It was Small's view, expressed to Harper, that: "Of course everybody understands that so long as you are opposed to any concession a majority of the Faculty in its favor will be impossible, and they know too that even if it could pass the Senate the Trustees would vote as you advised."[62] Yet Harper did not identify his program dramatically with the defense of Latin. In 1899, he called attention to the fact that the members of the scientific departments and of the Senate were almost equally divided in regard to required Latin in college; and he also gave evidence of how evenly the arguments for and against the status quo were balanced in his own judgment; both sides in the controversy were right, and both sides were wrong. With the "conservatives," Harper believed in "... binding the student closely to the past and all that is bound up in the past"; for—Harper argued in substance —to reach maturity a human being had to recapitulate the evolution of the human race both culturally and biologically. "Any system of education ... which will permit the student to begin at the end (for to begin with science is to begin at the end) does the student a distinct injury." The dislodgment of the humanities would ultimately prove hurtful to the best interest of science itself. With the "radicals," Harper believed that Latin as ordinarily studied by the uninterested student did not bring him into touch with the institutions and literature of the past: "The great majority of students who pass through this routine fail to gain any conception whatever of what Rome or Greece represents in the ancient world and in the modern." And it was very doubtful whether two or three years of Latin really served any satisfactory purpose in furnishing an understanding of English or the ability to use it; witness the number of college graduates with Latin and Greek who had utterly failed to secure any skill in English. Then Harper proposed that a number of courses in the history, institutions, and (perhaps) the literature of the past should be substituted for courses in Latin.[63]

Retrospectively, this "intermediate policy" appears to have constituted an effort on Harper's part to ground the emotional charges that had been induced by years of debate. A distinction drawn between the importance of humanism and the actual impact that Latin sometimes has upon education did not subvert Latin study in principle but left in grave doubt the justification of continued strife over but three majors. In 1900, Harper voted with the Senate majority— a majority by one vote—for establishing alternatives to college Latin, as he had suggested.

In 1902, when substitution was put into actual practice, certain secondary-school studies, e.g., advanced German or French, were allowed to replace the latter two years of secondary-school Latin, which had been the equivalent, for scientists, of college Latin. Thus alternatives to it were created; college Latin was still required of students who had studied Latin for only two years before entering the University and had not earned credit for the specified substitutes.[64]

The concrete changes wrought in the curriculum during years of involvement in debate over admissions and degree requirements had less significance for the University as an institution than that involvement itself. Once discussion about these requirements began, the University never gave serious thought to Harper's iconoclastic idea of removing instruction of underclassmen—and the students themselves—from the University campus. Although three institutional devices, the separate Junior College Faculty, a quasi-degree—Associate in Arts, Literature, or Science—granted for completion of Junior College work, and the coordination of that work with preparatory study, served as monuments to Harper's belief that the education of underclassmen was distinct from true University work, the University did not differ greatly from older institutions in point of essential conformity to the tradition of the four-year college. The University observed a difference between the first and second halves of the undergraduate program, but so did Yale.

The impact of a full undergraduate population needing instruction became evident soon after the opening of the University. In 1894, John U. Nef, who had come to Chicago with the migration from Clark University, inquired of its president, G. Stanley Hall, if he could return there. (Hall answered that he felt Nef was the best chemist in the country but was obliged to say, "I do not *at present* see any possibility of appointing a single new man. . . .)[65] Nef was dissatisfied in Chicago partly because his department had been asked by the Junior College Faculty to offer a general course for non-scientists.[66] To a man intent upon advanced instruction and research, that request must have seemed a straw blown by an ominous gust of wind. Yet, for non-scientists and scientists alike, instruction in the elementary branches of knowledge was a logical solution to the problem of deficiencies. The University was pulled two ways, first by its dedication to higher studies and second by a desire to supply the wants of Junior College students. As the University became deeply engaged in the education of underclassmen, it felt the stresses created by the characteristically American conjunction of collegiate and higher learning.

In 1893 Harper conceded that the time had not come in America to separate the college from the university: ". . . the line between the two has not yet been clearly drawn."[67] Of necessity, he became a college as well as a university president, but he persisted in his hope of separation. In 1894 he said that the junior year should be "the real university entrance";[68] in 1896, that the high schools should become the colleges of the future: "I believe that this is their destiny";[69] in 1902, that "Junior College work must go off the central Quadrangles."[70] Possibly when he made the last assertion Harper meant removal of only a block or so; but, in his decennial report of about the same time, he stated that as early as possible the work of the freshman and sophomore years should be added to that of the Morgan Park Academy.[71] The proposal looked straight back to Harper's early planning. In the same report, he also noted that from the beginning freshman and sophomore work had been sharply distinguished from that of the junior and senior classes, "so-called."[72] Desire to split college and university apart along the line not clearly drawn in America still moved in his mind.

CHAPTER VIII

The Higher Teaching:
The Senior Colleges
and the Beginnings
of Professional Education

Study within the Senior Colleges meant no deviation from plan; and that study, in its pristine state, engendered no controversy similar to that aroused by the program of the Junior Colleges. The presence of upperclassmen did not hang upon the students' pre-emption of a place as squatters. It was taken for granted from the beginning that Senior College work was not preparatory and that Senior College students would have much freedom of choice between courses. Within certain broad limits, the control of programs that they followed lay in their own hands; as a result, a multitude of decisions by students rather than debate by Faculty members gave shape to education in the Senior Colleges.

The initial experience of the University did not produce a notable alteration of the plan of studies presented in the *Official Bulletin, No. 2,* save in nomenclature and in the enumeration of the disciplines in which instruction was offered. (*Department* replaced *school* in the designation of those disciplines, the list was reduced as hope gave way to reality, and the ambivalent phrase *University College* went out of use along with *Academic College.*) At the opening of the University and for five years thereafter, only three general regulations governed the selection of courses by a Senior College student: (1) he might not select more than nine majors (or half of his work for two years) from any single department;* (2) he might not select his courses during any three consecutive quarters from more than four departments; and (3) he was to select at least one-third of his work from one or more departments in a group specified in accord with the degree sought, namely all of the departments except those of natural and physical sciences, for the A.B. degree; the same group of departments in the humanities and social sciences except Greek language and literature, but including Latin language and literature, for the PH.B.; and the departments of science for the S.B. degree.[1] (Mathematics alone belonged to all of the groups.) Specific regulations, which were promulgated seriatim while the system was in operation, obliged the student to devote some time to physical education and to take two courses in history and philosophy; but these requirements were plainly exceptions to a rule of electives. Almost two-thirds of the student's time was left unassigned to even the most broadly defined fields.

The first and the second of the general regulations were calculated to effect what has been known elsewhere as distribution and concentration. According to the third regulation, the University presumably expected that the student might—and usually would—study one subject (or one set of related subjects) continuously through the two years of Senior College work. Taking one course of the three studied each quarter from the same department for six consecutive quarters would result in the student doing one-third of his work in a single department. The strict letter of the regulations did not prevent the student from spending the greater part of his time within a group of departments not associated with his degree: a candidate for the A.B. degree, if he wished, could take more courses in the natural and physical sciences than in the humanities and the social sciences, and the S.B. candidate, if he wished, could specialize in Semitics. But apparently such anomalies were not expected to occur often enough to be made a subject of legislation. What the one-third rule prohibited was so much disparity between degrees sought and subjects studied that there would be little distinction between the degrees offered.

In 1898, the executive committee of the Congregation recommended consideration of a proposal to abolish the three degrees and to replace them with

* In the *Official Bulletin, No. 2,* and originally in the *Annual Register,* the limitation was phrased in terms of majors and minors taken during any period of thirty-six weeks, i.e., during any three consecutive quarters—which could constitute a conventional year of study. Whether calculated by periods of three quarters or over a two-year interval, the amount of work that a student might do in a single department was not to be more than the total amount of work he did elsewhere (see the *Official Bulletin, No. 2,* p. 19).

certification (apparently without the award of any degree); and in 1900, the Congregation debated the proposition that it was advisable to substitute one degree, the A.B., for the three.[2] Speaking for the proposal, John Dewey stated that the PH.B. and the S.B. originally had been introduced as concessions or necessary evils and the stigma survived. He also urged that, since two-thirds of the Senior College work was common in all courses, different degrees did not represent characteristic and important differences in the work done by the students.[3] When the proposition was referred to the Junior and Senior Faculties and to the Senate, each of these bodies rejected it, as did Harper. "My mind," he wrote Hale, "is not at all in doubt on this question, nor has it ever been. . . . I see no way to grant the scientists their liberty and at the same time allow them to use the A.B. degree. It seems to me that if it is necessary to yield at any point it is better to yield in allowing them a little larger liberty on the S.B. degree [presumably, to ease the Latin requirement]. We must, however, hold the A.B. sacred."[4]

The University could have given each of the degrees a more sharply defined identity if it had associated the A.B. with study of the oldest disciplines, the S.B. with study of the natural and physical sciences, and the PH.B. with study of modern languages and the social sciences—rather than with study in departments carved out of the A.B. group. Perhaps, however, the meaning of the sacred A.B. would have been impaired by the symmetrical partitioning of learning at the level of undergraduate studies. The American A.B. had represented the holder's introduction to all disciplines deemed worthy of a place in the college as well as to the classical tradition. Whether work toward any degree possessed greater coherence than the regulations required or was as scattered as they—or the stretching of them—would allow depended upon the judgment of the students. During the four quarters of 1898 (which Benjamin S. Terry, dean of the Senior Colleges, thought a representative year), the maximum number of departments in which elections were made by any one student was thirteen, and the minimum three. The average number of departments in which a student took courses was slightly over eight. About 20 per cent of the students selected courses from ten or more departments, but only 10 per cent elected courses in ten or more departments not closely related to each other. At the other extreme, 12 per cent of the students selected courses in less than five departments. Most of these were actually graduate students from other colleges who had matriculated in the Senior Colleges in order to secure a Bachelor's degree from Chicago. Only 2 per cent of the students who were strictly undergraduate worked in less than five departments. More than four-fifths of the students took at least one year's elective work (three quarters) in a single department; and 93 per cent took that much work in closely related departments. The statistics moved Terry to conclude that the University did not need to adopt the "group system"—the required clustering of courses—which had been advocated as a check on the students' allegedly unwise use of electives. About 75 per cent of the students selected their courses in groups: "... and yet this is not specialization, for the central theme is supplemented by other electives ranging from over six to ten departments. This is certainly a satisfactory showing." The dean was equally pleased when he looked beyond statistics:

...the Senior College is slowly evolving its own distinct idea. While, on the one hand, it is bound neither by tradition nor precedent to any hard and fast lines of policy, its spirit is yet conservative; it has shown no disposition to cater to new educational fads. It has more than once set its seal of disapprobation upon attempts to introduce purely technical subjects among its courses; it has steadily discouraged "specializing" among its students; it has steadily encouraged the extension of those subjects which lay hold of the sources of human life and action, and develop the wider sympathies of the student.[5]

Terry attributed the evolving of that idea to a process of attrition. Had he been describing the College during the whole of the first decade, he would have been obliged to speak of concretion as well. In that period, some parts of the original scheme for the Senior College were worn away (or simply dropped) and some programs not contemplated in 1892 were added to the plan of the College. Indeed, in the same year that provided Terry's statistics, the University announced a program that took into account the student's prospective calling: he might take a PH.B. in the "College of Commerce and Politics."[6] Earlier, the statement in the *Official Bulletin, No. 1,* that the University Proper would include a "College of Practical Arts" had been echoed in the first *Annual Register,* where the curriculum of the College was described (in the present tense) as one arranged "with immediate reference to the practical departments of engineering and business life"—but where also a footnote indicated that the College would not be opened during the year 1893–94.[7] The same announcement of a delay in the opening of the College appeared for the next three years, with successive advancement of the date, and then all reference to the College disappeared.

In 1895, while the College subsisted only on paper, Harper asserted in a

Convocation address that the development of university life over twenty-five years had been most markedly characterized by ". . . the adaptation of methods and training to the practical problems of the age in which we live."[8] The University would be derelict in the performance of its duty if it did not enter the fields opened up by modern civilization: "The times are asking not merely for men to harness electricity and sound, but for men to guide us in complex economic and social duties."[9] And, not long after the College of Practical Arts was mentioned for the last time, Harper privately jotted down a scheme for a large number of Senior Colleges offering programs in the professions and fine arts—to be organized "as early as convenient."[10] (Harper thought of the colleges as being the counterparts of the whole groups of departments associated with the three degrees: a student should do at least one-third of his work, but not more than one-half, in a single college.)[11]

Harper did not seek to defend the existing Senior College as if it were an ivory tower; he was committed to the eventual establishment of an education that prepared students for practical life. A broadly utilitarian intention, however, carried neither a guaranty that such education would be financed nor specific prescription of the ways in which it could be kept from becoming illiberal. Later, when Harper expressed his belief that general training could be secured in a curriculum made up partly of subjects closely related to a calling, he added: "Everything depends upon the spirit with which the work is conducted. . . ."[12] A university generated the necessary, saving spirit; but it could not be introduced into education for the callings just by promulgating the university idea. Specific proposals for the redemption of practical education raised highly debatable questions of academic practice.

In the winter before the University opened, it had seemed that the estate of the late Joseph Reynolds would be devoted largely to the creation of a technical school affiliated with the University. Frederick T. Gates reported to Rockefeller: "A few weeks will close the matter. . . . We can do all our work in applied sciences through this school. It will be the greatest thing of the kind in the world. . . ."[13] Reynolds had been deeply interested in water transport, as proprietor of the Diamond Jo line on the upper Mississippi, and had also invested in railroads: a technical school would have been perhaps the obvious memorial; but the weeks passed into years and it was not built. The vision of "a great school, or schools," of engineering was again presented to the University in the first quarter of the first academic year by Elmer L. Corthell, a Brown alumnus, a civil engineer who had supervised railroad and bridge construction in the United States and abroad, who was also a Trustee of the University.[14] In 1891 he had traveled in Europe to study six universities and technical schools in order to gather ideas for a school of engineering to be connected with the University.[15] In the second academic year, Harper declared that the time had come for the organization of technological instruction, the purely scientific having already been provided.[16] And in the same year Corthell asked the question that, left unanswered, would controvert Harper's initial advocacy of instruction in engineering; "Now! . . . Where is the money to come from?"[17]

Harper's solution was characteristic. When the University was unable to create entirely new facilities out of its own resources, he contemplated the annexation of an existing institution: time and time again, in many projects, Harper sought to bring such an auxiliary engine into operation. In 1896 the University turned toward the Chicago Manual Training (High) School, an independent institution devoted to the education of boys through shopwork as well as academic instruction. It was neither a vocational school nor a school of elementary technology but did emphasize the practical arts. By absorbing it, the University would acquire important assets, including a fund of $50,000, which the University was willing to maintain intact as an endowment for technological work. The University proposed that the institution be reorganized, with the appointment of University Board members as its Trustees, to become the nucleus of a school of technology. Legally it would remain a separate body but academically it would become a part of the University.[18] In May, 1897, formal arrangements for consolidation on these lines were completed and carried into effect; but agreement on the future of the school had not been reached. Following some discussion of the step with Rockefeller's lieutenant, Harper acted on the premise that consolidation was acceptable in New York; but Gates in fact utterly disapproved of the plan. As he interpreted its terms, they did not unquestionably protect the power of the University to act freely: the Trustees might find presently that the law obliged them to maintain the school in its original state. The argument that the original Trustees of the school had agreed to a change in its character and that the University was thoroughly protected against entangling alliances did not satisfy Gates, for he had acquired a profound skepticism when it came to the reactions of men in sight of money. He opened his mind to Harper:

I have had so much experience with persons who are disposed to take every advantage of rich corporations that I have great fear that before you get through with it you will find the Chicago Manual Training School a thorn in your side. Perhaps our own experience has made me unduly cautious about putting a possible club in the hands of evilly disposed persons. If you could be here in this office [John D. Rockefeller's] and see the exhibitions of human meanness, and even dishonor, among otherwise respectable men when they come to negotiate with Mr. Rockefeller's wealth, you would appreciate better than you can now how this perhaps unnatural caution has arisen.[19]

Seek the very best legal advice, Gates concluded, before changing the school. And so it remained a secondary school and became neither a thorn to wound the University nor a school of technology to amplify it.

Another effort to establish technological instruction revolved around the prospect of an alliance. In 1894, Harper had expressed the hope that the Boston experience—i.e., the conducting of such education at the Massachusetts Institute of Technology, outside of a university—would not be duplicated in Chicago.[20] At the turn of the century, as if to forestall that eventuality, he worked over a period of several years to arrange an affiliation between the University and the Armour Institute of Technology, which, with the support of Philip D. Armour, offered instruction in the elements of engineering. The gist of the several plans put forward was that the institute and the University should join in technological work, the lower studies being maintained by the institute, as it was, and higher studies being inaugurated at the University or in close proximity to it.[21] A school situated near the University, one proposal stated, would have ". . . the advantage of the university atmosphere; and this, as educators know, is something invaluable."[22] The contemplated end was an equivalent of M.I.T., connected with the University and financed by Armour.[23] If affiliation was not arranged, one argument ran, a duplication uneconomical for the city would occur because the University would be compelled to undertake engineering work in order to complete itself.[24] Although Armour and the trustees of the institute considered affiliation with the University as early as 1897, they had not reached agreement with the University by 1901, when Armour died.[25] In spite of its situation in a city owing much of its vitality to technology, the University did not succeed in establishing a program of instruction in engineering during the first decade of Harper's administration. However much the service that the University intended to render may have been needed, it was not demanded effectually.

Preparation for business, another conspicuous source of the strength of Chicago, did become possible at the University—as the *Announcements* of 1897–98 for the next year indicated—primarily because of the initiative displayed by the University. The new College was projected *toward* the community of businessmen rather than called forth by them. Unlike technology, business activity was directly interesting to a department within the University, political economy. If on one hand it had been wholly oriented by its head, Laughlin, toward abstract speculation, pursuit of its intellectual interest would not have carried the department toward education designed to prepare students for practical careers. On the other hand, deep involvement in the then new institutional analysis, which Bemis was appointed to represent (in the University but outside of the department), could well have separated the department and the business community; for the new economics leaned heavily toward criticism of the institutions customary in the community. When Bemis addressed a *tu quoque* argument to the railroads at the time of the Pullman strike, Laughlin was distinctly annoyed, particularly because he was just then seeking to interest the railroads in the University. This activity was but part of an effort that he made to secure business a place as a profession.

Laughlin was both a member of the classical school and a sometime businessman—the president of an insurance company—who had not been alienated from business when he accepted academic appointment. After Laughlin's death, Wesley C. Mitchell, who took his degree in the department, described Laughlin as a man who "cordially approved the business life."[26] When he came to Chicago, there was only one American institution, the Wharton School of the University of Pennsylvania, at which a student could prepare directly for that life under university auspices. Elsewhere, the formal introduction of the young to business was left to a miscellany of institutions, including the "business college," the commercial courses of high schools, and instruction by mail.[27] "Considering the actual work of the world," Laughlin once wrote, "the means of preparation for it are sadly out of joint."[28] Certain professions in the past had obtained recognition and munificent endowments without being carefully weighed against the whole need of society. "The country now has well-supported schools for the training of men in war, medicine, law, and technology; but it is quite within the truth to maintain that no one of these interests has as much influence upon the actual work and welfare of the people as those connected with railways alone, to say nothing of the wider field of trade and industry."[29] The powerful and ambitious youth of the land who were drawn to the exploitation of its new resources had little inducement to come to the universities; and if college and graduate schools continued to be confined largely to preparing advanced teachers, the universities would become more and more detached from the world around them.[30] That appraisal of the place occupied in academic life by the preparation of teachers aroused in Laughlin such a sense of injustice done as some of his colleagues (but not Laughlin) felt when they contemplated the traditional pre-eminence of the classics; and it was directly related to the claim implicit in his proposals that education for business could be as liberal as existing instruction. The advanced work of the graduate schools in literature, arts, and science had become, without question, Laughlin argued, practically a training course for professional teachers; ". . . and the undergraduate work has been very largely influenced thereby. . . ."[31] The obvious question was raised, as Laughlin pointed out, ". . . whether, apart from training investigators, the present endowments of our universities are not applied out of all proportion to one traditional profession to the neglect of the others as much or more important to the life of the nation."[32]

Laughlin contemplated an education for business that would teach men "to think in the affairs of their profession," that would not tell a man "how to perform a task today without at the same time teaching him, by a training in fundamental principles, how to think out a new and better method if a new adjustment shall be needed tomorrow."[33] The idea reached beyond business alone. In the implications of his thought, Laughlin was contending for acceptance of management or administration as a liberal art; and after a change in name, the institution which was founded under his initial inspiration was known as the College of Commerce and Administration. In retrospect it appears that the second term was used, not to designate a distinct subject to be taught in addition to commerce but to indicate that aspect of commerce which made it worthy of academic study. The same warrant covered other subjects. In name, the College was never that of commerce alone; and in plan, prospective or actual, it from time to time embraced preparation not only for journalism as well as business but also for diplomacy and social service. It was as if the University—after groping for words—sought to redefine the old idea of life spent in the public service (or politics, most broadly considered) in terms of specific professions for which men might be directly prepared. Education for business was but a partial response to the needs of a society becoming increasingly complex. The word "administration" carried such connotations; it left open and somewhat vague the future of education for public affairs.

The members of the Faculty did not quickly agree upon the precise organization and scope of the institution that became the College of Commerce and

Administration. In 1894, Laughlin presented the Senate with a plan for a "School of Commerce and Industrial Science." His explanation of the institution implied that it would be comparable to schools of medicine and law, hence apparently the choice of *school;* but the program that Laughlin proposed somewhat resembled that of a Junior and a Senior College combined. The curriculum extended over four years and included general subjects not derived from commerce or industry, i.e., French and German, mathematics, "English Writing," psychology, and history.[34] By vote of the Senate, the name of the projected school was altered to read "of Commercial and Political Science," the latter term giving way presently to "Politics." The school itself was designated "a distinct college co-ordinate with the three colleges now existing."[35] In 1895, Laughlin moved that it be entitled a *school,* as if that usage had been questioned and Laughlin wished to confirm the similarity of the institution to the schools for the established professions. The motion was lost; and a special committee, consisting of Laughlin, Judson, and Small, was appointed to report upon the name of the institution. It recommended "College," and the word came into official use with the obvious implication that the program of the new institution would be comparable not to that of a professional school but rather to the three undergraduate curriculums.[36]

In the source of its offerings, the new College did resemble the old; the curriculum was a mosaic of subjects controlled individually by the several departments. The College, as a college, possessed no head empowered to preside over the construction of a program independent of the courses that the departments saw fit to offer; and the Faculty was an assemblage of department members. In 1898, when announcement of the College was being prepared, Rollin D. Salisbury, professor of geographic geology, attacked the establishment of the College as a mistake for reasons that stemmed precisely from the fact that the courses did not constitute an addition to existing offerings. "I should not object," Salisbury wrote Harper, "to a college which should do what this purports to do; but my objection is based in part upon what seem to me its unjust claims; that is, it does not seem to me to do the thing which its name indicates that it will do."[37] Calling attention to a statement that a student coming to the College would find courses of the same character as those pursued by other students, Salisbury asserted: "This is true, and is just the mischief of the scheme. The courses are of the same character as other students may take, and do not especially prepare for commerce or politics, or any other particular thing."[38] (A reference to journalism especially disturbed

Salisbury: "If journalists give the matter any attention whatever, you may be sure they will ridicule any course here outlined [in an *Announcement*] as a preparation for journalism, in any other sense than any college course is a preparation.")[39]

In the same year, Charles Zueblin, associate professor of sociology, detected another weakness, as he believed, in the program of the College. It was hardly possible that the different departments would fill in gaps if responsibility were to be purely departmental: "There must be a unity to the College which it at present lacks."[40] In short, it needed a director. (Zueblin made the recommendation with the defects of departmentalism explicitly in mind. He referred to a lack of adequate co-operation among the departments of political economy, political science, history, and sociology; and he intimated, guardedly, that the horizontal, i.e., departmental, organization of the University caused considerable dissatisfaction.)[41]

In 1900, Laughlin himself became exercised over the relation of the College to the departments and protested to Harper against the confusion of jurisdictions. He disclaimed thinking that the work of the College should be a part of that in political economy any more than a medical school should be a part of the department of biology. (Laughlin apparently thought that eventuality most improbable: today, the medical school of the University is in the Division of Biological Sciences.) But, Laughlin argued, if courses in the medical school were offered to undergraduates in biology, the department supervised the courses falling within that subject. It had always been Laughlin's understanding of his duty and position that, if economic work was offered in any nominal division such as a college, that work should be organized under one department, his own. Laughlin believed, however, that the control of the policy and the adoption of courses in the College could not possibly go to his department or to any single department. Policy should be determined by a proper Faculty, of which the heads of the departments affected should be members. But how was such unity as Zueblin found wanting to be attained? Laughlin did not specify any mechanism, other than a Faculty, by which the multiplicity of authorities possessed by the departments might be directed to a single purpose. He disapproved of direction by a committee, which then obtained. Laughlin's criticism went beyond the immediate case to general polity: ". . . it [the committee] is too much after the fashion in our University, which takes away from the men immediately concerned the right and duty to share in shaping the work they are carrying on."[42] It left them uninformed as to policy and made them listless and unambitious; it was a way to kill their enthusiasm and spontaneous desire to help.

In 1901, Harper told his administrative secretary, Francis W. Shepardson, of his uneasiness about the slow way in which the work of the College of Commerce and Administration was progressing.[43] Shepardson answered that he had been thinking and talking about making what he called a *practicable curriculum* that would appeal to students. "I do not believe," he said, "in rushing into print as was done before with an unworkable scheme, which confuses students."[44] And he added that he did not think Laughlin would be *practical*. That perhaps unintentionally ironic judgment may not have been entirely fair to Laughlin, who had long been denied a test of his ideas in their mint state. Yet there was historical truth in Shepardson's words. The College had been announced prematurely in 1898. Its purpose had not been sufficiently clarified nor had its organization been perfected. As a going institution, the College occupied an ambiguous and unsatisfactory position. In 1902, referring to the College confusedly as a School, the Senate appointed a committee to consider its reorganization. Although it was presently allowed a deanship, an office common to professional schools and lacking in the several colleges in arts, literature, and science, the Senate again balked at giving the enterprise the formal status of a professional school. In amendment of the report submitted by its committee, the Senate approved the phrase "technical college."[45] The qualifying adjective was consistent neither with Terry's general conception of the Senior College nor with Laughlin's particular intention in regard to slighted callings; and the term was applied to only one college. It was a square peg but was not discarded: the history of the professional School of Business hangs upon Laughlin's much amended proposal.

The movement into education for administration, especially of business, swung the undergraduate program from the latitudinarianism of the original regulations. Requirements in the College of Commerce and Administration reduced the student's freedom of choice by introducing many prescriptions. In 1898, the announced program in the College was divided into three parts— (1) courses in the "group" (undefined) in which a student's main work was to be done, (2) work selected from "courses specified" (but not actually indicated), and (3) electives from the departments of political economy, political science, history, and sociology and anthropology.[46] In 1899, this inchoate scheme was displaced by the requirement of nine majors, or half of the student's work, in that many subjects, namely, political economy, economic history, public finance, constitutional law, international law, common law, recent American history, Europe in the nineteenth century, and the sociological conception of society or its equivalent. Selection of the other half of the student's program was subject to the approval of the directing committee of the College.[47] Reaching toward professional education, the University thrust itself away from the elective system.

In the same year, the requirements for all three degrees were adjusted to enable students to take a premedical course. The one-third rule was modified for A.B. and PH.B. candidates who were registered for premedical work: only four of the student's eighteen majors were to be taken in the departments— all non-scientific—associated with the degrees.[48] Presumably the scientists did not need special relief. Soon it was announced that an S.B. candidate who had completed the work of the Junior College of Science or transferred into the University with an equivalent record was permitted to take the first two years of work in medicine as the third and fourth years of his Bachelor's course. But he must also take three required courses in history and philosophy in an extra quarter or as extra work during three quarters. Candidates for the A.B. and PH.B. degrees might take from one to one and a half years of the medical program.[49] Perhaps to forestall a charge of vocationalism, the University stated that the first two years of work in medicine consisted ". . . almost entirely of courses in pure science." The same point was made within the bosom of the Faculty.[50]

The premedical program resulted from a critical decision. When Harper first discussed the need for a school of technology in 1894, he also spoke of medicine and law, about which, he said, he was asked every day, ". . . and some days many times."[51] Publicly, Harper's answer was to declare himself against speedy action along the then conventional lines, the direction of which was largely determined by a tradition of proprietary schools. Harper argued that the country had enough medical and law schools conducted without endowment and managed for the pecuniary or professional profit of those in charge. Instead of duplicating that work, "whether of high or of low character," the University should adopt the better policy of patiently waiting until broad-minded humanitarians should see an opportunity to do something of which the world would be proud.[52]

The establishment of a law school did not immediately become a practical issue; but the question of participation in medical education was put to Harper repeatedly and in concrete form. When he spoke in 1894, the University had already been asked to consider association with two existing schools, and privately Harper had been in correspondence with Dr. E. Fletcher Ingals, a prominent laryngologist, who was a professor and registrar at Rush Medical College. Its professors constituted its board of trustees, according to the custom that had arisen from organizing medicine around proprietorship. Founded in 1837, Rush was, for Chicago, an old school. Rush commanded the loyalty of several extremely able doctors, who combined practice and teaching with an interest in the science of medicine; and it also had access to the clinical facilities of the Presbyterian Hospital. Rush was in debt; but of the existing colleges, none could have seemed more promising academically to Harper. Rush was affiliated with Lake Forest University, but not so tightly as to preclude negotiations with the University of Chicago. On one hand, Harper had been advised not to consider the overtures of existing colleges: ". . . seductive propositions," a doctor wrote, "were made to the Johns Hopkins University and resisted. Had they not been, she would not be in the vanguard of medical education in America."[53] George S. Goodspeed, who had been intimately associated with Harper at Yale, argued that it would be a good deal better to build up a *new* medical department than ". . . to hitch on some older institution with its traditions and its fossil professors." Better no medical department for the time being than a sort of hanger-on, a source of contention or a bulwark against progress of every sort.[54] Goodspeed's remarks did scant justice to the Rush faculty, but they did touch the issue involved in consolidation. Should the University move into new fields immediately by following that path, at the risk of losing its freedom of action; or should it wait until it could find its own way, at the price of being but part of a university in the interim? Gates opposed union with Rush.[55] Yet Ingals displayed pertinacity and enthusiasm the equal of Harper's own.[56] Through union, Ingals saw hope of elevating education in conjunction with medical research:

Think of the millions who have been saved by Jenner's thirty years of experimentation, of the hundreds by Pasteur's laboratory researches, of the thousands by the antiseptic surgery which has developed along this line, and of our escape from cholera which would never have happened but for the researches of the past ten years. Think also of the terrible diseases which still devastate our homes which may be prevented when we know a little more, of diphtheria, of scarlet fever and consumption. . . .[57]

No conceivable work would be so beneficial as that of a great and thorough medical school equipped for original research. For years Ingals held firmly to the conviction that Rush and the University should join forces in that cause.

When in 1896 it seemed probable to Ingals that Rockefeller would sometime endow a medical department, Ingals did not think exclusively of Rush as the prospective beneficiary but was moved to declare: "Of course I still believe that it would be a waste of money to try to establish a new clinical center. . . ."[58]

Although the University did not move, Ingals made an impression on Harper. In March, 1897, Ingals suggested that Harper speak in Convocation of an endowment that would furnish "the very best facilities for those who wish to become superior physicians and for those who will devote their time to original research in methods of preventing and curing diseases";[59] and at Convocation in April, Harper did say that the greatest single work remaining to be done for the cause of education in the city and in connection with the University was a medical endowment large enough to provide (among other things) for ". . . facilities of investigation and research which may be used by those who devote their time to the study of methods for prevention of disease as well as of the cure of disease."[60] Looking ahead, Ingals had written Harper of the health and lives of "our children & grandchildren"; and Harper spoke of the benefits to be enjoyed by "our children and our children's children through all the generations."[61] The amplified echo of Ingal's phrase presumably emanated from some agreement with his thought. Harper had spoken advisedly, it would seem, of a work to be done *in connection* with the University in order to leave a door open to some arrangement short of union. (In June, 1897, Harper heard another voice speaking of medicine; Gates wrote: "I am just now reading the recent book on the practice of medicine by the head of the Johns Hopkins Medical School [William Osler, actually physician-in-chief of the hospital], and have scarcely ever read anything more intensely interesting.")[62] By the early winter of 1897, Ingals was arguing privately for affiliation and again gave Harper advice about the line that he should take, an indication that Ingals believed Harper to be sympathetic.[63]

The University did not give Rush official encouragement until December, 1897, when representatives of the college proposed affiliation in place of union.[64] Negotiations then moved rapidly, although initially Ryerson was cool toward affiliation.[65] The conditions set by the Trustees of the University were substantial. In its government, Rush was to break entirely away from the tradition of proprietary medicine. The teaching, practicing doctors were to be replaced as Trustees by men who were satisfactory to the University Trustees, were "interested in education," and had no pecuniary interest in the earnings of the school —in short, the control of Rush was to undergo the same change of hands, to government by laymen, as had occurred when the Board of the old University gave way to the Board of the new. In addition, Rush was to pay off all the debts that had encumbered it; and the reorganized Board would pledge itself to raise admissions requirements to two years of college work by 1902.[66] The doctors accepted these terms although they did not receive assurance that Rush would ultimately become the medical school of the University. Although Harper spoke privately—and perhaps but loosely—of the association to be effected as "union," the Trustees of the University neither announced that union might sometime occur nor stipulated that it never would.[67]

The representatives of the Founder did not tolerate this silence. Gates had not been consulted at length before affiliation was voted, and indeed he objected to the whole proposal: "I see nothing whatever to be gained in affiliation with Rush Medical College, possibly something to be lost."[68] Harper thought the trouble was that Rockefeller believed in homeopathic medicine and was ". . . somewhat disturbed concerning the Allopathic tendency indicated in the proposed alliance."[69] This explanation was correct in regard to the negative reasons for Gates's hostility to affiliation but did not go to the heart of a positive idea in Gates's mind. He agreed that Rockefeller desired the University to enter into no relationship with allopathic institutions; but Gates also thought that the issue of affiliation involved something other than a choice between doctrines over which doctors had long fought. Gates wrote Goodspeed, marking the passage so that its importance would be appreciated and its significance absorbed:

I have no doubt that Mr. Rockefeller would favor an institution that was neither allopath or homeopath but simply scientific in its investigation of medical science. That is the ideal. For that the University should wait and reserve the great weight of its influence, authority, and prestige instead of bestowing the same gratuitously on Rush Medical College. Such an institution would have to be endowed and would be run on a far higher principle than the principle of Rush College or any other of the ordinary institutions.

What might be lost was an opportunity to attempt fulfilment of the ideal, with Rockefeller's support. How much Gates knew of Rush in particular he did not explain; but he asked to know exactly what the University had promised. "I believe," he said, "that the vote of the Board . . . was a very serious blunder in the history of the University of Chicago."[70]

Goodspeed was greatly disturbed by Gates's letter. The arrangement was an affiliation pure and simple—somewhat later he described it as ordinary; no promises of any sort whatever had been made; and there were no written agreements that Gates had not been sent. The future action of the University would be absolutely unhampered. Referring to the marked sentences in Gates's letter, Goodspeed said, "... we assent cordially, warmly, unanimously."[71]

In response to Goodspeed's attempt to give reassuring explanations, Gates denied that the affiliation of Rush was ordinary: it was the more objectionable because it lacked the distinct written terms of ordinary affiliation. Two great institutions of learning should never take action involving general co-operation without recording what that co-operation meant. The situation was rendered yet more grave by the fact that the conditions set for the affiliation involved great risks that entitled Rush to claim corresponding benefits from the University. Insofar as Rockefeller's fears were concerned, it meant nothing to say that either the University or the College might withdraw at any time. Once Rush had fulfilled the terms of affiliation, could the University withdraw without doing the College serious injury?

The whole effect and tendency of this movement will be to make Rush ultimately the medical department of the University of Chicago as against that far higher and better conception, which has been one of the dreams of my own mind at least, of a medical college in this country conducted by the University of Chicago, magnificently endowed, devoted primarily to investigation, making practice itself an incident of investigation and taking as its students only the choicest spirits, quite irrespective of the question of funds.[72]

It did not satisfy Gates that, when Harper announced the affiliation, he said it was important to note that the University remained without a medical school of its own. Harper also said, "Whether Rush Medical School will ever become the Medical School of the University, time will show."[73] Gates's comment: "Exactly." Goodspeed's response was to ask why the affiliation with Rush might not be made simply a step toward the realization of Gates's dream. Goodspeed deeply regretted that any step had been taken without consultation; but the step had been taken and the University could not retrace it without dishonor. Having defended at length the decision of the University, he reached the extremity of frustration: "What then shall we do? You must now assist us in finding a way out of the difficulty into which we have been brought. I beg of you to give this your most earnest thought and send us your suggestions."[74]

At a conference in New York—for the difficulty was taken there—Harper and the Founder's representatives composed an amendment to the original plan for a Rush affiliation. It was agreed that affiliation was not intended to encourage

Rush to believe that it might become the medical school of the University, and it was the distinct purpose of the University to establish such a medical school when funds were available.[75] When Rush Medical College met the conditions fixed for affiliation, the University gained an opportunity to influence medical education; but at best the University saved its place at the center of Gates's dream—if saved that place was—by asking Gates to salvage a plan that left him cold.

CHAPTER IX

The Higher Teaching
and the
Higher Degrees

"William Rainey Harper, PH.D., D.D. . . . .": so begins the roster of University officers presented in the first *Register*.[1] The University frequently broke with custom, but it never departed from the convention of identifying a scholar by reference to his higher degrees, and it organized the higher teaching around the requirements for these degrees. To that extent, the forms in which the higher learning took shape at the University were traditional. In the laws of England, from which the institutional structure of American higher education had been derived, possession of the power to grant degrees distinguished a university from a college, where an incorporated community of scholars might conduct the pursuit of learning as effectively as a university; and college fellows provided far more actual instruction than Oxford and Cambridge professors. In the light of that precedent, it is more to be wondered at that American universities were teaching institutions than that they marked a scholar's progress toward the higher learning by awarding degrees.

In America, the powers of the university and the work of the college had been consolidated under the pressure of colonial conditions to produce a university-college, a type distinct from either the English university or the English college —and from the university college, a term used later in England and in the United States. The fusion of university and college did not efface the idea of the degree; rather, the work of institutions devoted to the higher learning became so closely identified with the combined processes of teaching undergraduates and of awarding the A.B. that the idea of advancing scholarship *per se* became attenuated. A college excluding candidates for the Bachelor's degree, an American counterpart of All Souls College, would have been incomprehensible; and the word *institute* came into use when, about 1900, the collegial principle was applied to the organization of research. It had not flourished in the American colleges; and proficiency could not be inferred from a professor's possession of an A.M., a D.D., or an LL.D. degree. Those old forms of the doctorate had long since become honorific; and the A.M. was, by custom, conferred upon any A.B. who sought one after blamelessly following a liberal calling for three years. (When the University of Chicago was founded, a belief that the A.M. should be earned by formal study had gained much ground; but vestiges of the old practice were still visible at Yale.)

At mid-century, degrees did not inevitably figure in the plans of men who attempted to establish universities informed with the ideal of inquiry. In 1856, by happenstance the year of Harper's birth, Benjamin Peirce, professor of mathematics at Harvard and an unresting academic reformer, failed to mention degrees when he devised a scheme for the foundation of a university that would concentrate all the powerful minds of the country in conjunction with a library, observatory, collections, and laboratories for "the elucidation, illustration, and investigation of every species of knowledge."[2] Peirce's mind worked somewhat idiosyncratically, but his silence in regard to the once distinctive power of a university did not offend the prominent scientists who constituted his circle, the self-styled Lazzaroni. In comparison with their thinking on the nature of the great American university, the *Official Bulletin, No. 1,* and the *Official Bulletin, No. 4,* on the graduate schools of the University, seem profoundly conservative. Between the sixth and the last decades of the nineteenth century, graduate study in the arts and sciences was established in the United States; and it was oriented toward attainment of the originally German PH.D., beyond the Anglo-American A.M. degree. As opportunity to acquire the degrees was offered to American scholars, so presently possession of advanced degrees was required of American professors; in that sense supply created demand. Yale regularly awarded the PH.D. after 1861; and fifteen years later, Johns Hopkins began its career as the model of the university that was essentially a community of productive scholars and a nursery of PH.D.'s. Such a university fostered research and also enforced standards for the pursuit of the higher learning by classifying the pursuers.

Insistence that they earn degrees through advanced study was a means to the doubly academic end of the university. By 1891 the way of reform that higher education had entered upon led not away from the granting of degrees but toward their identification with demanding labors within a university. Harper and many of his colleagues knew that path as their own; and they had not found it intolerably dusty. The University attempted to balance the equation of graduate studies and degree requirements by its emphatic declaration that *"no honorary degrees will be conferred. . . ."* The degrees of LL.D. and D.D. would be granted "for work done."[3]

Those degrees with the A.M., PH.D., and M.D. were the first to be announced, in 1891.[4] The doctorates in divinity and medicine immediately dropped out of sight. Although the Divinity School contained a graduate division designed primarily for the instruction of college graduates, it at first awarded only a *Bachelor* of divinity degree. Advanced degrees were offered by the School, but they were the A.M. and the PH.D. already available in the departments of the arts, literature, and science. After affiliation with Rush Medical College, the University participated in the professional education of prospective physicians but did not award the M.D. The earned LL.D. survived on paper until 1897, when the requirements were published for the last time with what had become by then a standing comment: "Candidates . . . *will not be received* until further notice."[5] In 1892, the degree had lost its specific connection with legal studies and had acquired metaphilosophical status: candidates were to be PH.D.'s, study three years in residence at the University, present a printed thesis, and pass a final examination.[6]

Perhaps the LL.D. was designed to afford recognition of the studies pursued by persons who entered the University, as did four holders of fellowships in 1892, after already having received PH.D. degrees. Had the University devoted its resources to the enlargement of this group from year to year and had it (conceivably) organized an institute of post-doctoral studies, it would have added another story to the structure of higher education, just as older universities had built the graduate school upon the college. Had the University at the same time carried out Harper's plan for the transfer of freshmen and sophomores to outlying institutions, it would have so elevated the limits of its population that the graduate student, in the commonplace meaning of the term, would have stood at the middle rather than at the highest of the three levels into which studies were divided. When, in 1899, the University did confer an LL.D., the recipient was the President of the United States, William McKinley, a man ". . . who, at the time of gravest crisis, when the weal not only of this Republic, but of foreign states, was put in deepest peril, and the path of wisdom lay dark before the people, served each highest interest, and . . . out of confusion brought a happy ending. . . ."[7] The tradition of awarding honorary degrees had been received into the Quadrangles; indeed, the University had tacitly acknowledged that such degrees had meaning by recording Harper's possession of a D.D. degree.

THE MASTER'S DEGREE

The A.M. had a continuous but troubled history as an earned degree and as the matrix of other degrees. Before the Faculty began to act in 1892, the prospective program at the level of the A.M. was partitioned by institution of the S.M. and PH.M. degrees co-ordinate with the old degree.[8] The tripartite division of post-graduate studies, under the same rubrics that were employed in the under-graduate programs, was virtually adopted by the Faculty when it voted, in June of the first academic year, that the Master's degree should be "assimilated" to the Bachelor's degree.[9] The *Register* published in the first academic year exactly repeated the requirements presented earlier in the *Official Bulletin, No. 4*: to qualify for A.M., S.M., or PH.M., the candidate had to (1) complete the corres-ponding Bachelor's course, (2) spend at least one year of resident study at the University in pursuance of an accepted course of study, (3) present a satisfactory thesis, and (4) pass a special final examination upon the work of the year.[10] This basic scheme long remained unchanged, but it invited explication. What did a Master's degree mean as a mark of learning? That the University believed a Master's should represent some measure of specialization in subject matter was implied by the offering of three degrees. Had the degree continued to stand for a level of liberal learning in general, the A.M. alone would have sufficed. The same belief presumably accounts for the statement, of 1893–94, that the degree was granted in a minimum of one year to candidates who, as undergraduates, had reached "a considerable degree of advancement in their chosen field."[11] In 1895, the University stipulated that at least two-thirds of the necessary year of study should be spent in a single department. (Each department decided which of its offerings carried credit toward the degree.) These regulations suggest that a Master's represented an extension and intensification of specialized study in college; but the University did not say so explicitly. Plainly, the degree was not meant for students who were what had once been called "resident graduates," persons who hung on after graduation, doing essentially undergraduate work that they had not done before taking a Bachelor's degree. Judson was to say that another Bachelor's was the appropriate degree for students who studied to round out their college education.[12] Was specialized, graduate study toward a Master's degree intended to deepen the candidate's liberal learning by enabling him to get to the bottom of some scholarly topic? Did award of the degree in that sense mark the end of the recipient's liberal education, thus being terminal? Or was the degree to represent something added to liberal education—either an amount of learning or some aptitude developed? In the earlier years of the Harper administration, the nearest approach to a concrete definition specified only what the degree did *not* mean. Beginning in 1893–94, the *Register* carried a notice that attainment of the degree, while bearing witness to ability and scholarship, "does not necessarily imply the possession of the power to conduct original research."[13]

In January, 1895, or nearly two years after Master's requirements had been announced in the *Official Bulletin, No. 4,* the dean of the graduate schools, Harry P. Judson, asked the graduate school boards what constituted candidacy for a second degree.[14] The boards discussed the question at length but gave Judson no help; in February, board members asked the Senate, seemingly with the emphasis of the much perplexed: may a graduate student holding *any* Bachelor's degree and devoting himself to *any* department of study be a candidate for *any* Master's degree?[15] The Senate answered elliptically: yes, provided the student has fulfilled the requirements of the University for the corresponding Bachelor's degree.[16] The boards' question had arisen from the particular case of a Princeton B.A. who had studied paleontology at the University for a year: was he qualified to take either an A.M. or an S.M. degree? The Senate ruling meant that a student in that situation could take the S.M. if he had studied enough science for the S.B. as an undergraduate.[17] What was to be watched, in the case of any given student, according to the requirement of correspondence, was his undergraduate preparation and not necessarily the Bachelor's degree he had taken: under University regulations, it was possible that a student might complete the work for more than one Bachelor's degree.

The replacement of differentiated degrees by a single Master's was debated two months after the Senate gave its answer to the boards. In June, 1894, they decided upon the appointment of a committee to consider the requirements for the Master's degree. When it reported in January, 1895, Small moved the resolution, as a substitute for a recommendation of the committee, "That it is the sense of this Board [the combined graduate school boards] that only one Master's degree be conferred; (viz.: Master of Arts!)."[18] By implication: either the degrees did not, or an ideal Master's degree should not, stand for significant differences in studies, according to subject matter. After lengthy discussion, the motion was tabled until the next meeting, where Chamberlin offered a substitute for Small's substitute. (The parliamentary history of degrees was notably complex.) Chamberlin proposed that rules for the degree should be formulated in accord with three principles: (1) the degree should be given for graduate work done at the University of Chicago solely, except insofar as similar work done at equivalent institutions should be accepted; (2) the amount of that work should be such as of itself to justify the granting of the degree; and (3) either one degree should be given for all such graduate work or else the degree given should be such as to indicate specifically the major nature of the work done.[19] The force of the first two principles, taken together, was that a Master's degree should stand for a quantum of advanced study sufficiently large to merit recognition. (Chamberlin believed that two years of residence rather than one should be required.)[20] The third principle, actually a choice between two, was seemingly designed to force the issue of the specialized Master's degree: the University ought either to grant it without reference to broad distinctions or it should announce the specialty of the holder, presumably by departments. Have the courage of some conviction: be explicit or silent about specialization. The first two principles were adopted provisionally on the day they were presented. The third was amended by excision of the latter half, to leave the principle of one degree, but was not put to a vote. It was discussed a second day and voted down on a third. Then Chamberlin's whole substitute was voted down. Small's substitute was also defeated.

The committee report, indorsing three variants of the Master's degree but amended to conform to the Senate ruling on candidacy, was adopted as a recommendation to the Faculty of Arts, Literature, and Science.[21] There Small moved that the ruling should be replaced by the statement: "The University grants as a second degree the degree of Master of Arts only."[22] The amendment carried; but, at a special meeting of the Faculty, Chamberlin moved successfully for reconsideration of that vote.[23] Although he had been ready to consider the granting of a single Master's degree, he presumably could not stomach restoration of the A.M. as *the* Master's degree. Perhaps to forestall argument over invidious distinctions, the Faculty did not put Small's exact proposition to a second vote but rather, at still another meeting, voted differentially on three plans, in none of which was the A.M. singled out. The plans were: (1) the existing system with three degrees; (2) a single Master's degree, "title to be fixed later"; and (3) two degrees, in arts and philosophy, with philosophy absorbing the existing s.m. That compromise received no support when the vote was taken; and the existing plan was overwhelmingly preferred to the granting of a single Master's degree. After thus reversing its original vote on Small's proposal, the Faculty adopted the Senate ruling as it had been phrased by the committee of the graduate school boards. The somewhat clarified status quo had been confirmed.[24]

In the academic year 1898–99, the nature of the Master's degree was again examined, but on new premises. The University in effect consulted its own experience, which yielded a definition not to be found in the announced purposes of the University or in its disavowal in regard to the meaning of the degree. As dean of the graduate schools, Judson reported that the existing regulations called for the same kind of specialization that was required for the ph.d. degree: "Thus the Master's degree is a Doctor's degree of less magnitude." Graduate degrees were available only to students who wished to pursue a specialty "in the highest sense" and were able to devote at least one year to the work.[25] That fact left Judson unsatisfied; he pointed out that students often wished to supplement, and not just round out, their baccalaureate course by graduate work not confined to one or two departments. These students were not seeking specialization; their study was "culture work" of a high order, worthy of recognition. They were in effect unclassified graduate students: the force of the participle was presumably appreciated by Judson's colleagues. Judson urged that the Master's degree be made available to such students. It might well be treated as "a culture degree—a thing not now provided in the Graduate Schools." Specialization would still be recognized—if of one grade by the Master's degree in its existing forms, if of the highest grade by the ph.d. degree.[26]

Judson was not alone in his concern. In October, 1898, the Congregation referred to committee a request that the graduate Faculty discuss the advisability of abolishing the requirement of a thesis for the Master's degree.[27] (A Faculty, or more accurately, two Faculties, had replaced the graduate school boards.) Simultaneously, Harper suggested that the graduate Faculties consider the regulations on the a.m.[28] The Faculties responded by creating a committee, so that two were on the field at once. Since the Congregation could only advise, the initiative in legislation lay with the committee of the Faculties. After what must have been much deliberation, or prolonged inactivity, it reported in February, 1901. The committee found that existing requirements were based upon the idea of the Master's degree as a stage in preparation for the ph.d. degree. There was, however, another legitimate conception: the degree might stand for a certain amount of graduate work without narrow specialization and might properly be conferred upon students not expecting to go on to the doctorate, "who do not perhaps possess the training or ability to pursue original investigations."[29] (In brief, the formula that had originally been appended to all Master's degrees might be used to separate two classes of candidates, as it were, horizontally. Vertical division of the generic Master's degree into the A.M., PH.M., and S.M. was not at issue; reinstitution of a single degree, connoting no specialization, was apparently a lost cause.) The committee concluded by presenting the possibility of offering students two paths to a Master's degree, one with and one without a thesis requirement.

The Faculties accepted both conceptions of the Master's degree. The student was either to do at least seven majors of graduate work in one department and write a dissertation, or to do at least nine majors of graduate work, distributed among no more than three departments, without writing a dissertation.[30] On the recommendation of the dean, the Faculties ruled that a candidate could not, under the latter plan, do more than six majors of work in any one group of related departments, for instance, in philosophy and education.[31] The rule, which was nearly the reverse of the old requirement—at least six majors in one department—was presumably calculated to prevent students from reverting to a once mandatory concentration.[32] Work toward the degree under the new dispensation should not become simply a way for would-be "specialists" to dodge the thesis requirement. The word belongs to the time. The two kinds of degrees were designated "specialist" and "non-specialist"—a verbal dichotomy that still left the Master's degree hanging, although only partly, upon a negative.[33]

THE DOCTORATE

In contrast to the Master's degree in arts, philosophy, and science, the earned doctorate took a simple form and possessed a single meaning that was explicitly qualitative. Less than a month after the University opened, the Senate approved what was to become an enduring policy of the University: "The degree of Doctor of Philosophy is given, not on the basis of the completion of a certain amount of time spent upon a specified programme, but as the recognition and the mark of high attainments and ability in the candidate's chosen province, shown first by the production of a thesis evincing the power of independent investigation and forming an actual contribution to existing knowledge, and secondly by the passing of examinations covering the general field of the candidate's sub-jects. . . ."[34] Burton put the matter most succinctly: "Quantity of work is not the essential thing."[35]

The gist of the ph.d. requirements was a demand for research. As early as 1890, Carl D. Buck, a Yale ph.d., who later rose to the headship of the Department of Sanskrit and Indo-European Comparative Philology, expressed the hope that the degree of ph.d. would be made very difficult at Chicago: "In every case the thesis required should be a real contribution to the subject and worthy of being published and so given to the world for judgment."[36] Von Holst, a Heidelberg ph.d. and head of History, did honor to the same view, on the principle that the exception proves the rule, when he recommended that a particular thesis be accepted although, as he said, it neither revealed any important fact previously unknown or shed new light on the events in question.[37] "There should be no doubt . . . ," Small asserted, "that, beginning with registration in the Graduate Schools, research, and research only, should be the standard of requirement."[38]

The first and the last issues of the *Register* of the Harper era announced substantially the same ph.d. program. In addition to submitting a satisfactory thesis and passing a final examination, every candidate was required to possess a Bachelor's degree; to have a command of French and German—and English; and to pursue his studies systematically for three years, of which no more than one could be devoted to courses taken *in absentia*.[39]

Specification of particular studies was left to the departments, which severally determined to what extent the studies associated with the degree were prescribed quantitatively, subject to the overarching rule of quality. A contrast between the a.m. and ph.d. requirements in history is illuminating. The specification of requirements for the a.m. begins: "For the Master's degree at least one year's work in the Graduate School shall be submitted for examination." Such work should consist of nine majors (the normal load for a conventional academic year) or the equivalent nine "'double minors." The criterion is decidedly quantitative. The comparable passage on the ph.d. reads: "The candidate for the Doctor's degree in History will be expected to pass an examination upon the entire field of history . . . ," the main stress falling upon the subdivision, ancient, medieval, or modern, where the topic of the thesis lay.[40] The department said nothing about majors of work or about courses except in regard to the candidate's undergraduate preparation. In turn, the Department of Sociology and Anthropology, which remarked that the city of Chicago was one of the most complete social laboratories in the world, announced that thirty-six minors (i.e., two years of study) taken within or under the direction of the department were required of its ph.d. candidates.[41] Thus the formulation of concrete work for a ph.d. varied between departments.

But for the recognition given a limited amount of work done away from campus, the University program did not represent a new departure for American graduate schools. Indeed, the phrasing of the general statement on the ph.d. echoed a passage in the register of Cornell University, and it was Hale, lately arrived from Ithaca, who introduced that statement in the Senate. At the University, the highest teaching was dedicated, as if by acclamation, to an ideal that had already been given clear-cut form and had not lost its freshness.

A question of altering the essential form of the doctoral program arose only from the stubborn issue of Latin. When the University opened, candidates for the ph.d. degree were required to have completed a Bachelor's course, "including an amount of Latin equivalent to that required for the Bachelor's degree in the University of Chicago."[42] In March, 1893, it was proposed that this clause be replaced by another simply requiring completion of a Bachelor's course at some institution of good standing. William G. Hale, head professor of Latin, then introduced and withdrew a counterproposal, calling for the minimum amounts of Latin and science in any required course at the University, and Judson moved that the old regulation be continued but with the phrase "including an amount of Latin" struck out.[43] The motion carried, and the requirement read that candidates were to have completed a Bachelor's course, "equivalent to that required for the Bachelor's degree in the University of Chicago."[44] (Apparently it did not occur to Judson and his colleagues that by excision they had produced a sentence which did not express their obvious intention, that is, that candidates should have a Chicago Bachelor's degree or the equivalent.)

Judson's amendment removed specific mention of a controversial topic from the regulations but did not effect their force. As of 1893, all of the University programs for the Bachelor's degree called for college Latin; hence all ph.d. candidates were required, by implication, to have had Latin. In April, 1894, Hale moved in the Senate that the degree Doctor of Science (which the Statutes mentioned) should be awarded to a student whom the board of the Ogden Graduate School of Science had recommended as a ph.d. candidate although the student lacked the Latin required for a Bachelor's degree. The motion was debated, apparently on grounds of principle, and then withdrawn, whereupon Hale proposed—and the Senate agreed—that the case in hand be considered by itself and that formulation of requirements for the s.d. degree be taken up at a later time. The student was then admitted to candidacy for the ph.d. as an exceptional case, by a vote of four to three.[45]

In May, presumably to prepare the way for the pending debate in the Senate, Harper called the attention of the graduate school boards to the fact that the Statutes recognized the s.d. degree but that no provision had been made to grant it. The boards voted that a committee be appointed "to consider the advisability of indicating the requirements for the degree. . . ."[46] On November 3, the Senate made the formulation of requirements for the s.d. and ph.d. the special order for its next meeting and asked for a report from the administrative board of the Ogden School. On December 1, the Senate again discussed the substantive question. The gist of the recommendations before the house was that the ph.d. should be the only doctorate offered by the University and that the s.d. should be erased from the Statutes. After discussion, the Senate put off a decision by again voting that the matter be made the special order of a subsequent meeting. On January 5, 1895, Hale proposed, as a substitute for the recommendations under debate, that the degree of s.d., provided for the Statutes, be so interpreted as to bear the same relation to the s.b. as the ph.d. bore to the a.b. or ph.b. Hale had the support of four other senators, but he needed the votes of six. The substitute was lost, and a motion for the ph.d. as the sole doctorate was carried six to five.[47] Rejection of the s.d. left the would-be ph.d. without much Latin at a disadvantage but not friendless. The attack upon Latin in the s.b. program (and so in effect upon the Latin required of ph.d. candidates) was getting under way in 1895.

When debate over the s.d. had barely begun, Whitman wrote Harper:

I am decidedly opposed to multiplying degrees. The argument for *differentiating* degrees to correspond with special lines of work is self-refuting—for it is based on the idea that the degree is given for the *kind* of work rather than the *quality,* and that leads, if consistently carried out, to as many degrees as there are distinct lines of original work. To me, the degree of ph.d. means a mark of scholarship and ability to do ORIGINAL work of a *scientific* order in any line whatsoever. So far as I know, this is the general view.[48]

Whitman's impression may have been closer to the truth within the departments of the arts, literature, and science than the narrowness of the Senate vote on the s.d. suggests. Two of the five senators who voted for the split doctorate were members of the Divinity School Faculty. If Whitman's appraisal of sentiment was accurate, it is not surprising that the University declined to award more than one doctorate. By the same token, however, the refusal of the Faculty to accept the proposed consolidation of the Bachelor's and Master's degrees requires explanation: why one degree at the top of the curriculum and three at each level below? Why *E Pluribus Unum* and not *Unitas Scientiae* all the way? At the level of the college, custom warranted a policy that convenience indicated. By partitioning the degree, as other institutions had done, the University saved itself the pain of a struggle over a single program. The rule of correspondence between first and second degrees carried the uneasy peace of to-each-his-own into the vaguely defined region between baccalaureate and doctoral studies. There, as in the college, the humanist, social scientist, and natural scientist could each claim for his students a degree that the others might even disdain for theirs. Hale and Chamberlin sorely tried each other's patience, but they would doubtless have collided explosively—and to what damage to the University?—if a single Bachelor's or Master's degree had been instituted. At the level of doctoral studies, agreement upon the award of one degree was as necessary to the preservation of peace as partition of degrees was elsewhere. The professors revered the ph.d. as the symbol of the highest ideal regardless of their disciplines. When Hale proposed that the s.d. was the appropriate sequel to the s.b., he did not follow to its conclusion the logic of correspondence. The price of consistency would have been the divorce of the ph.d. from the arts course. Conversely, when the Senate divided on the motion to award the s.d., all of the scientists voted *nay*.

The University refused to deviate from the received tradition of the ph.d. even when innovation would have served the interests of persons in the Faculty. In 1898, when it was proposed that the degree might be conferred on assistant professors and associate professors as a special class of candidate, the graduate Faculties determined that the University should have only one set of requirements for the degree.[49] In the next year, the Senate tabled a more comprehensive proposition, presented by Burton, Chamberlin, and Small, that any Bachelor might acquire a ph.d. degree by three or more years of purely investigative and scientific work in the field of his profession or by two years of professional work and two of investigation: "Let the prerequisites [for receiving the honor of the degree] be solely the demonstration of intellectual power and the ability to investigate." The Senate was not ready to carry the degree toward that ultima Thule of qualitative definition—or along the way, as the senators may have thought, that the a.m. had once taken when it had ceased to be an earned degree. The propositions were never taken from the table.[50]

From day to day, research meant whatever the departments severally inter-preted it to mean as they regulated the actual work of students in seminar or laboratory. Each department representing a discipline had its own intellectual valence, fixed by tradition, opportunity, and the immediate interests of the pro-fessors. Latin studies, directed by Hale, tended to be syntactical—hence a thesis upon the participle in Plautus, Petronius, and Apuleius—while the investigation of Greek literature was inclined under Shorey's influence toward literary and philosophical topics.[51] Sociology reflected hopes that Small entertained for social reformation and for social science in the large; political economy, as personified by Laughlin, followed other lights. German scholarship was not universally emulated. Apropos of Von Holst's appointment, Judson registered his objection to the neglect of will and personality and of popular needs in the German uni-versities: "Of course there was a time when German notions were a valuable leaven in America—German enthusiasm for pure knowledge and careful spe-cialization. But I think that that day has about gone. We have learned the Ger-man lesson—quite too thoroughly. . . . I should be hopelessly out of accord with a fragment of the German empire transplanted to Chicago."[52] Hale and Chamberlin, both native Americans, were often out of accord; obviously they did not possess identical ideas of what culture was required by the United States. Yet did research, as a method of thinking—and a way of life—supply a stress powerful and pervasive enough to render the departments but parts of one great, self-sustained ramp lifting teaching and learning higher? In 1905, Small wrote:

The prime duty of everyone connected with our graduate schools is daily to renew the vow of allegiance to research ideals. . . . There is more glory for a graduate school in stimulating one mind to a genuinely critical attitude toward conventional ideas than in graduating countless contented repeaters of commonplace formulas. The first commandment with promise for graduate schools is: Remember the research ideal, to keep it holy![53]

Perhaps Small did not quite mean to say that research was literally a sacred office; but it was an austere calling, promising revelation and inspiring its own kind of passion. In differing—but were they discordant?—tones of voice, Hale, Chamberlin, and one of Harper's students bore witness to what research entailed:

William G. Hale, on the life of the student and the professor: To begin with, the student must be gifted by nature with a certain amount of the celestial fire. Like the poet, the successful graduate student must be both born and made. In the case of either vocation, a stern self-training may possibly replace the training that should have been given by others of more intimate experience; but the being-to-the-manner-born is indispensable.

The second prerequisite is of almost the same supreme importance, though it is often sadly left out of the reckoning. . . . In every direction, investigation has been pushed so far that subjects once thought to constitute a specialty are now regarded as groups of specialties. Anatomy and physiology would, not long ago, have been supposed to come easily within the field of the biologist, or, at any rate, they would have been thought of as lying too close together for any separation from each other. Yet The University of Chicago, at the urgency of the department of biology, has separated these two fields from it and from each other on the ground that each forms so distinct and so great a specialty that no man can be a leader in both. Precisely the same thing is actually the case, though without resulting separation, with many subjects thought of by the public as one and indivisible. . . . To say, then, that a man is a specialist in Latin or a specialist in history, is to say almost nothing about his equipment. He must have a certain knowledge of most of the general province in which he works; but in addition he must have an extended and minute knowledge of what has been done and what is doing in some one field in that province. This, then, is the second condition of successful graduate work. It is not sufficient that the professed leader of it should be an estimable gentleman, he must have the knowledge of a specialist, in the severest sense of the word.

The third condition is still harder to meet. The leader of graduate students must not merely be a leader as toward them, while as toward the masters in his craft he is but a follower. He must himself be a master, or have the blood of mastery stirring in him. In this country, as in Germany, the professor that professes graduate work should be a man whose forum is, or at any rate is evidently soon to be, the world of scholars, the world over, in his province. This means that he must have the power of scientific divination. His scholarship must not be of the recipient type, but of the creative.[54]

Thomas C. Chamberlin, on the scientific spirit: It [the scientific spirit] has for its supreme attribute a controlling love of determinate truth; not truth in a vague mystical sense, but rigid solid knowledge. It is a thirst for facts and the immediate and necessary inductions from facts. It is a pervading desire for actualities, stripped of imperfections, and quasi-truths; stripped of mists and fogs and veils of obscurity and set forth in their pure naked simplicity. It is a zeal for uncolored realities. But it is not merely an affection or an enthusiasm, easily satisfied with what may come in the name of truth. It is a scrutinizing spirit, whose hatred of falsity is as great as its love of truth. One of its first steps is to demand the credentials of whatever offers itself for acceptance. If it be an observation, it is to be rigorously verified. If it be a generalization, its grounds are to be severely questioned. If it be a synthesis, the strength of every part is to be searchingly proved. If possible, the crucial tests of experimentation are to be brought to bear upon it. In the architecture of science, every beam is to be tested, every joint is to be put to trial. Conjectures, assertions, opinions, current impressions, preconceived notions, accepted doctrines, all alike are pushed aside to give free scope to untrammelled [*sic*] induction from carefully sifted evidence. The supreme endeavor is to present a disposition of fairness and openness to all evidence and all inductions. Whatever evidence demands, that it accepts. Whichever way the balance of evidence inclines, to that it leans. There is no resistance to the leadings of evidence, there is no pressing of evidence to give it greater or less than its intrinsic weight. All lines of inquiry are pursued with equal zest. All phenomena are welcomed with equal cordiality. The mind opens itself on all sides to every avenue of truth with equal impartiality.[55]

Clarence R. Williams, a divinity student, on his progress—under Harper's guidance—toward the higher learning:

October 4, 1900. Today President Harper lectured on Old Testament history, the early period, the descent into Egypt. He has a class of about forty-five. As I was leaving the room, being the last man, he asked me my name and where I was from, I said I had letters to him and he said he would be glad to receive them. The professors here seem pleasant and cordial.

October 10, 1900. Am taking a more advanced course with President Harper . . . Old Testament Tradition. He thought the one I was in too elementary for me. The new course meets at 7:30 which will get me up earlier, but I guess I can stand it if Prexy can.

November 20, 1900. Every man is busy. I do not think that I was ever at an institution where the men worked harder. We have to dig out our material from the original sources. As a result the departmental libraries are well used. Neither textbooks nor lectures are the basis of the work, they are but helps or outlines. . . .

January 8, 1901. Yesterday at eleven President Harper met his seminar on Micah. . . . He has arbitrarily divided the book into eleven sections, and under each eight topics are to be discussed: restoration of the text, literary form and authenticity, general exposition, etymological forms, syntax, lexicography, theme, condensed statement and teachings, and Scripture parallels. . . .

Dr. Harper gave us a bibliography of works appearing since 1870, twenty-two titles, many in Dutch, some in German, some English, perhaps some in French. These are placed in the seminar room for which each will have a key, but we are not expected to cover them all. In fact Prexy was agreeably surprised when he found among us one man who could read Dutch. So in this course we will have enough to keep us busy. . . . I must try to read Hebrew this term. Prexy wants us to be able to give him from the English Bible the Hebrew of Micah 1:2–7 on next Monday. A man who is thoroughly up in his work as a Biblical student ought to have a reading knowledge of Hebrew, Greek, Latin, French, German, and besides this if he knows a little Assyrian, Syriac, Arabic, Ethiopic and Dutch, they will come in handy.

But of course all this is not in itself so much Bible study as preparation for such study. We must first find what the Bible says, then what it means, then what it teaches. And I hope that I shall not forget that the last is the most important of all.

I am more and more convinced that I have come to the right place for my study. On the whole I believe that these methods are the best for me at this stage of my intellectual training. They tend and intend to make a man an independent student and investigator, and show us how to work and obtain results for ourselves, instead of giving us the results of others to memorize.

February 9, 1901. I must tell you about our meeting at President Harper's on Thursday evening. . . . President Harper wore a dress suit, as he had a social engagement later. We assembled in his dining room around the board, in the center a large plate of rosy-cheeked apples and we were told to help ourselves whenever we desired. The waitress brought in cups of tea and we went to work. . . .

Prexy says it [a chapter of Micah] is a dirge in 3 2 3 2 measure and called upon us to note the long *e* and *a* sounds giving it a mournful or wailing cadence. The Hebrew must have been a very beautiful language when read. Something after nine Prexy had to attend a reception on Prairie Avenue for no other reason than that he is President of the University of Chicago, so he announced, but begged us to excuse him and left the apples and ordered another cup of tea for us so we were not left unconsolable and after enjoying his hospitality we broke up. . . . He has the remarkable faculty of making you conscious of your great ignorance but at the same time inspiring you with a determination that you will know something about the subject.

March 5, 1901. I got through after a fashion and Prexy was very much pleased and took the trouble to speak to me about it personally after the session. The point which he especially commended was my restoration of the strophic structure. This was a piece of original work for which there is no book or paper published,—at least known to Prexy,—which goes into the matter as thoroughly as we did. Prexy's own arrangement was naturally somewhat different from mine, but it involved a change of text for which I was not prepared.

May 6, 1901. President Harper was not able to come out today and sent word for us to meet him at his house. As he began, he coughed considerably, nevertheless he dictated resolutely and seemed to grow better as he warmed up to his subject, and ceased to cough. For about an hour he lectured and for another hour did a good part of the talking. . . . I have learned HOW THEY MAKE COMMENTARIES . . . he is not only giving us material but showing us how he works. While it is improbable that I shall write a commentary on a book of the Old Testament, I can understand how to use them from knowing how they are written. This is the most advanced work in Biblical study I have ever done. What I have gained is a method of work, which has compelled me to get my material *first hand* and given me more knowledge of the methods of the great German scholars who are our chief authorities in the work here.

June 3, 1901. Prof. Shailer Mathews and Prof. Edgar Goodspeed examined me in New Testament at 3. At four President Harper, Prof. Robert F. Harper, his brother, and Dr. [John M. P.] Smith came in for the examination on the Old Testament. President Harper asked all the questions. Prof. Mathews excused himself. But at the

end President Harper said that my Old Testament work was satisfactory and he supposed the New Testament, congratulated me and shook hands, and said he hoped
that I would continue until I received the doctor's degree, which I told him I hoped to
do [and did do, ultimately, at Yale].

If I did not like him I would certainly dislike him, for he examined me upon Micah,
chapter two, which he himself once said was about the hardest chapter in the Old
Testament, and not only asked for a translation, but wished me to RECONSTRUCT the
text, at which I had scant success. . . .

As I say again, if I did not like him, I would certainly dislike him. But I cannot do
that.[56]

CHAPTER X

Outside
the Classroom

Inevitably, it became a joke: the University of Chicago was Harper's Bazaar. In one aspect, the Quadrangles did resemble a market place, a perpetual fair, an emporium, where members of the Faculty negotiated endlessly over the packaging of facts and ideas into programs, calculating exchange rates for courses in the complicated currency of academic credit. When in 1904 Thorstein Veblen, assistant professor of political economy, wrote a book entitled *The Theory of Business Enterprise,* he suppressed a chapter on the higher learning—not because it was irrelevant to his argument, but rather because he thought it would make a book in itself.[1] Eventually, in *The Higher Learning in America,* published in 1918, Harper would appear as a captain of erudition beside the captains of industry. Yet it was never Harper's intention that the University should become a place to which students would resort as buyers of education. The image of Alma Mater, the bounteous mother, had no conspicuous place among the icons of the University; but the ideal of a university as surrogate parent, serving a community of foster children, retained its force. Harper and his coadjutors sought to create an academic society: in the words of George E. Vincent, dean of the Junior Colleges, the students coming to the University should find a hearth, not a radiator.[2]

In 1891, Stanford University opened the doors of a plant that was nearly complete; when the University of Chicago first received students in 1892, it lacked the material apparatus of social unity. At the end of the first year, the view from the Ferris Wheel on the Midway of the Columbian Exposition revealed how much remained to be fulfilled of the architect's vision. The quadrangular plan promised something resembling the setting of medieval collegiate life; but the authorities of the University had not waited for the completion of a single quadrangle. Foster Hall, at the southeast corner of the campus, nearly opposite the Wheel, was separated from Cobb Hall, at a distance of almost two city blocks in the middle portion of the western side, by ground upon which no building had been erected. To house Faculty members and students, the University rented the Beatrice, a new apartment house. Another apartment house served the scientists until permanent laboratories were built within the Quadrangles. The Beatrice stood four blocks to the east, the laboratory building two blocks to the north; the actual, workaday campus of the University, if campus it could be called, was simply a scattering of buildings fronting upon public streets or, within the undeveloped property of the University, upon ground that became a morass in wet weather.

Expectation had to take the place of the amenities in the creation of a common spirit. Writing of her arrival at the University, Marion Talbot, a dean of women, wrote her parents: "Mrs. Palmer, Prof. Hale and I were met by Mr. Laughlin, who waved at us the first number of the *University of Chicago Weekly*. Isn't it like this great rushing city, to have a student publication out a week before the institution opens its doors?"[3] Yet the student arriving alone and unmet—as well as how many Faculty members?—might well have felt stranded. On that same day, about a week before the University opened, Bessie Messick, a young southern girl who had never before been away from home, was "in despair where to go till she succeeded in finding the president." She was brought to Marion Talbot, who had a cot installed for the girl in her hotel sitting room.[4] The gesture may have been impulsive, but it was not isolated. The young dean's response to Bessie Messick's loneliness was the beginning of an effort to provide a gracious approximation of home life. (Marion Talbot would become identified professionally with study of the household and with its reorganization around the educated woman.) Moving to the Beatrice, Marion Talbot, under the guidance of Alice Freeman Palmer and with the assistance of several high-spirited women holding fellowships, sought to convert a collection of lodgers and boarders into a familial society. The residents of the Beatrice indeed became "the family."[5]

The reception was perhaps the favorite social instrument of Marion Talbot, who presently remarked to Harper that the custom of giving receptions was a large contribution to the development of "an orderly and educative social life."[6] Yet she could unbend: "I threw my dignity to the winds," she wrote of Thanksgiving Day, 1892, "led off in all the games, danced and played the D.K.E. waltz ... to the rapture of all the girls."[7] Later in the winter, Alice Freeman Palmer said in regard to the men of the University: "Just let them wait until another year, and we will show them what good times are properly made of."[8]

Practical arrangements in the Beatrice were necessarily makeshift, and the women may have been somewhat self-consciously sociable; but a tradition of solidarity among them was established—perhaps the more firmly precisely because they were originally obliged to make-do. Listening to discussion of such questions as how and by whom should absence from class be excused, Marion Talbot believed that the sole principle involved was "the co-ordination of individual liberty and organic union."[9] It may be supposed that she listened to the questions put by the students with the sustaining thought that the "daily catechism" had to be endured in good spirit if the principle were to be observed: Where is the nearest letter box? Is there a night watchman? What are the best courses in the biological department? Will you change a quarter? Would baked beans make a good Sunday morning breakfast?

The Beatrice was the prototype of the "houses" into which students were organized as quickly as dormitories were built. Residence within the University was not thought of as simply a device for protecting women or the very young living away from home in a great city. The house system was designed to contribute positively to education. The student who lived in a private family, Harper said in 1896, did not enjoy the full advantages of University life:

I do not hesitate to say that *ideal* college and university life will be attained only in those cases in which the life of the individual is brought into closest contact with the lives of many other individuals, and this is impossible when students isolate themselves and maintain association in large measure with those who have no connection with the University.[10]

Later, when Harper reviewed the first ten years, he characterized the house system as the distinguishing factor in the social life of the University. "The theory of the system may be summed up," he said, "in the statement that the University is one family, socially considered, of which the President is the head. . . ." Six or more students living together might be constituted as an official house, for which the President appointed a head responsible to him.[11]

In fully developed design, a house possessed not only a head but a Faculty coun-cilor; a secretary and a treasurer; a house committee; and patrons or patronesses, who were not members of the University. Residence and membership in a house were not necessarily identical; a student might live temporarily in a house as a guest or become a member by election under the by-laws. All officers but the head were elected by the members, who also adopted rules of govern-ment by a two-thirds vote.[12] The principles which Alice Freeman Palmer and Marion Talbot had sought to establish were liberty, equality, and unity: so Marion Talbot said when the system was well under way.[13] Plainly that triad came to much the same thing as the co-ordination of individual liberty and organic union which she had had in mind when the University first opened.

The houses for women became residential clubs, if not family homes, thanks in part to several heads of houses who possessed a social flair. (Two of these heads, Myra Reynolds and Elizabeth Wallace, had belonged to the group of Fellows who had roughed it in the Beatrice.) Years after the first generation had retired, an alumnus who had been a student in their time recalled, as if the experience epitomized the reality of the houses, that the caller was met at the door of each by a gracious woman.[14] The houses for men had a different history, partly because the headship did not apparently become established so strikingly as an institution among the men as among the women and partly because some men found centers for their social life elsewhere, specifically in fraternities.*

The institution of fraternities and sororities had no place in Harper's original thought, which pointed in another direction. "I for one," Harper said to the students in November, 1892, "am a firm believer in the old fashioned literary society."[15] The comment was genuinely conservative; for Harper sought to per-petuate the informal education of the literary societies, which had obliged gen-

* The case might conceivably have been otherwise had that Scottish genius, Patrick Geddes, come to Chicago, as he thought of doing when Harper was assembling the first Faculty. Geddes wrote Harper: "You wish me, I understand, to run a Hall. Good: suppose we elaborate the idea of it somewhat thus? You want your new University not only to be alive, but (what is much more difficult to provide for) *to keep so*. How better than by putting it & keeping it permanently in touch with each of the great University systems of the old world, & through them also with the different nationalities to which they belong; & which have all their part in the ancestry of American culture as well as of race? Let my Hall then be a distinctively *'Scots College,' 'St. Andrews Hall,'* or the like; let one of your German professors do the same for Germany. Some Englishman for Oxford & Cambridge, a Frenchman (or for that matter if you have no one better, I am about Frenchman enough) for France. Of course I don't mean to emphasize the national idea in any narrow sense, but in the cosmopolitan one. . . ." The possibility of reviving the medieval or-ganization of university students into "nations," somewhat modified, had no visible impact upon Harper's planning; but later Geddes founded his Scots College at Montpellier, France, rather than Chicago, Illinois (Patrick Geddes to Harper, Nov. 16, 1891).

erations of students to practice rhetoric before their peers. At the same time, he read without demurrer a statement in which the Faculty expressed its disapproval of the newer institution, the fraternity. Debate over its merits and uses began early, did not reach an end for several years, and in the meantime raised the question of the power wielded by the University. At the first meeting of the Faculty of Arts, Literature, and Science, George C. Howland, a member of Psi Upsilon, proposed—it was the first motion to be put before the house—that secret societies be permitted in the University under restrictions "named by the President." Laughlin, alert defender of Faculty prerogative, immediately and successfully moved that the matter be considered by a committee to which Judson, Hale, Small, Tufts, and Stagg were appointed.[16] The committee shortly reported that, "on the whole," it would be better if fraternities did not establish chapters at Chicago. It was the opinion of the committee that it would be unwise for the Trustees to forbid students to form fraternities. If the Trustees should decline to authorize—while not prohibiting—fraternities, their institution might be discouraged "by moral means." When an informal poll revealed that Faculty opinion was divided between prohibition, non-interference, and permission coupled with a policy of discouragement, the question was referred back to the committee, which was enlarged to include the President and T. C. Chamberlin. A second report did not differ from the first. The general case was that "the end sought by these societies so far as they are laudable, may be secured by other means which shall be free from the objections of secrecy, of rigid exclusiveness, and of antagonism to the democratic spirit which is inherent in the highest scholarship and manhood, and the most exalted citizenship." The Faculty would be "deeply gratified if the high purposes and lofty feelings of the body of the students should lead them to co-operate with it by voluntarily excluding everything that makes against a broadly fraternal spirit, and a primary concern with the intellectual aims for which the University of Chicago was founded." Yet the Faculty did not deem "the necessary evils" connected with secret societies sufficiently grave to require absolute prohibition, provided they submitted to certain, specified conditions. The practical question was whether students should be permitted to begin organizing fraternities immediately.[17]

The report had the form of an address by the Faculty to the Trustees. Laughlin wrote emphatically to Harper of the damage that would be done to the prestige and influence of the Faculty and to the balance of governing powers within the University if the Board exercised its unquestioned right to overrule the Faculty.[18] The decision which the Board reached could have been construed either as tacit dissent from the general argument or as concurrence in its all but explicit expectation that fraternities would appear if they were not absolutely prohibited. The organization of chapters was permissible provided that each chapter submitted its house rules for approval, appointed a representative with whom the Faculty might confer, and restricted membership to students of the second year of the Academic (Junior) Colleges and of the University (Senior) Colleges. The University reserved the right to withdraw its permission for a chapter to exist. This policy was virtually the organic act of the secret societies.

The issue of fraternities remained alive. In his (unpublished) report for the first year, Harper noted the existence of clear evidence that a large number of fraternities desired to establish chapters, remarking that no doubt establishment of such societies was attended with many advantages. "It is equally certain," Harper continued, "that there are certain possible dangers which deserve careful consideration." He had in mind the conduct and life of the men inside the fraternity halls, the relations established with outside institutions through the fraternities, their effect upon the "literary life," and the danger of developing loyalty to the fraternities at the expense of loyalty to the institution.[19]

In May, 1894, the Faculty returned to the matter by voting the appointment of a committee to consider the social life of the men and the place occupied in it by the secret societies. The committee recommended, in February, 1895, that all secret societies be disbanded under the right reserved by the University to withdraw permission for a chapter to exist. (Presumably the Trustees had intended that the right would justify disciplinary action in particular cases.) The recommendation was tabled; but the question of the place of the fraternities had not been settled.[20] In October, Judson called attention to the incongruity in the position of the University. Some of the best fraternities, which would be of advantage to the University, had declined to organize chapters on the campus; and the attitude of the Faculty, "disapproving and permitting in the same breath," was not dignified. Judson thought that the Faculty should either forbid fraternities to exist in the University or withdraw the stigma of disapproval.[21] In response to that statement, Harper again raised the issue at a Faculty meeting during which Judson offered a substitute for the policy of 1892. The most striking feature of the proposal (which did not stigmatize the fraternities) was the statement that such organizations as might occupy distinct buildings or rooms as residences should be organized as University houses under the general rules already in existence. Before assimilation of the fraternities to the University system of residence was put to the vote, an informal poll indicated that no one favored either prohibition or simple hands-off; an overwhelming majority of the Faculty (34 of 38 votes) favored the general regulation of all student organizations—the policy underlying Judson's proposal. Judson's recommendation carried and was the rule through the remainder of the Harper administration.[22] (The following year, a Faculty Board of Student Organizations, Publications, and Exhibitions was created to oversee extracurricular activities and the terms upon which they were conducted, including eligibility for intercollegiate debating and sport.)

After incorporation into the house system, the fraternities won the approval of University officers but were still regarded with some wariness. The director of the house system remarked in 1899 that fraternity members, by their spirit of ready co-operation in the plans and work of the houses, had shown that they regarded themselves as integral parts of the system, not as members of private clubs.[23] George E. Vincent, dean of the Junior Colleges, believed in fraternities, "rightly used," but expressed concern over the possible growth of "contemptible, petty rivalries, political combinations, athletic wire-pulling, social segregation, and the like."[24] Harper wrote privately in 1902: "They [the chapters] accept certain rules of the University. I do not believe that they form cliques that would not be formed if they did not exist. . . . In the main, I think membership in them is a good thing for one. So far as our observation goes, the influence of the societies here has been beneficial rather than harmful."[25] Publicly Harper stated, with a suggestion that he was balancing pros and cons, ". . . their [the fraternities] presence in the University has been a source of great advantage rather than of disadvantage. In almost every case the fraternities have contributed each its share, not only to the social life of the University, but to its general welfare."[26] Yet when a student commission on a general club for men was tentatively organized by nomination of one man from each of nine fraternities, plus three other men, Harper responded: "This is *bad*. This must not be put exclusively in the hands of fraternity men."[27]

National sororities were never given opportunity to demonstrate whether their virtues outweighed the defects attributed to secret societies. Marion Talbot led in their exclusion from the life of the women. "Are sororities a desirable form of organization for our women?" she asked on one occasion, and answered with a battery of observations: we must realize that we are in a formative period; all must act together for the good of all now and hereafter; the ideal of organizations thus far has been utmost liberty; any decisions which we may reach should be independent of our opinion about other institutions; the fact that men have fraternities has no bearing on the case; the demand for sororities is to come from within, not from without.[28]

The words reflect a sense of present policy as the clay that would harden into the shape of the future and a conviction that the women of the University should find their own way without regard to pressures exerted either from outside the University or by the ways of the men within it. Marion Talbot was acutely aware of "our women" as a distinct entity or open sorority that should neither be permitted to fall into conflicting parts nor be denied autonomy as a whole. She believed in women's right to self-determination; and she was determined that the right should be exercised. She faced—but perhaps did not fully recognize—the dilemma involved in the transformation of a population into a democracy. If she merely obeyed the dictates of a still inchoate public opinion, her constituency might disintegrate altogether; but if she enforced her own convictions in regard to what democracy meant, her regime would verge upon dictatorship, benign but real. Plainly it was the better part of strategy to confront the "hydra-headed question" by insisting that the issues of fraternities and sororities should be dealt with separately. Her tactics were to encourage the development of indigenous organizations and to delay the importation of particular sororities. She had Harper's support. When in 1894 she said that she trusted he would be pleased with a proposed undergraduate society and would approve of the "dignified and self-respecting" way in which its formation had been made known, Harper answered: *"Very much indeed.* Please secure me the chance to express my feelings." The organization would be a help, Marion Talbot predicted, in meeting the efforts of secret societies "ambitious and eager" to found chapters in the University.[29] The flow of discussion in 1896 reveals the substance and temper of Marion Talbot's labors:

February 16, Marion Talbot to her mother: My special problem this week has been in connection with the girls' sororities. Under the present rules of the University, men's fraternities are allowed under regulations and there is really no reason why the sororities should not come, except the feeling that they are undesirable. You see I have no weapon to use except moral suasion and I don't know how long I can keep up the conflict.

March 5, Marion Talbot to Harper: There is some discussion going on concerning the formation of women's secret societies, but I think charters will not be granted to local chapters if we are frank in the statement of our belief that this form of social organization is not the best for the women under the special conditions which prevail at the University of Chicago.

Harper to Marion Talbot: I am with you.

March 19, Marion Talbot to the women officers of the University: You are invited to attend a conference . . . to discuss the question of the introduction of sororities into the University of Chicago. . . .

April 29, Harry P. Judson to Harper—after the women officers had found the introduction of sororities inadvisable: I doubt the wisdom of putting the women under different regulations as to fraternities from those that [are] given the men. I doubt whether the fraternities [sororities] will make any material difference with the halls. Many of the women are not in the halls. The Sororities can make no greater difference than the clubs already organized. It seems to me the best policy not to fight the Sororities but to work with them. I doubt the spontaneity of the action of the women students in condemning of the Sororities.

May 14, Marion Talbot to Harper: . . . I have on every possible occasion sought to learn the real preference of the students. The fact that for nearly four years no organization was formed, although there had been no prohibition and no general knowledge or discussion of our position, has led me to think that there was no demand for fraternities on the part of women. As a petition for recognition of a society has been lately received will it not be possible for you to call together the women of the senior colleges and ask for an expression of their opinion as to whether fraternities should be established now or postponed until some later time when there should be a general demand for them from within rather than without?

May 18, Harper to Marion Talbot: I have thought over the matter of your suggestion . . . , and have concluded that inasmuch as everything is quiet in reference to this subject, we would better let it go on without saying anything for the present until action is demanded. What do you think of this?

December 17, Marion Talbot to Elizabeth Kennicott Culver, a niece of Helen Culver, concerning the silence of the University in regard to the admission of a sorority in which Elizabeth and Helen Culver were interested: I should have acknowledged long ago your very courteous letter. . . . It seemed to me, however, that you and I did not have the same understanding of the action which had been taken by the University, and I have been making inquiries and consulting the record in order to ascertain the exact status of the matter. I find that the request from the fraternity was not refused, as you state, but action was deferred. . . .

My consideration of the subject has to be abstract, or in other words, I have to take into account both the few women concerned in this special group, and all types of women who might be concerned directly or indirectly, as well as the workings of the system, not merely in the present, but in the long years to come.[30]

A special committee of the Board of Student Organizations recommended that sororities not be admitted until some of the problems then engrossing the attention of the women were more nearly solved and a general demand had been indorsed by the women officers. The report was adopted by a vote of four to three; but one member of the majority, who favored granting the request, voted "in deference to the attitude of the representative of the women upon the Board." The petitioners seeking judgment of the Faculty were thus virtually presented with Marion Talbot's original decision. The Board voted (and the Council approved) a ruling to the effect that sororities should not be sanctioned "under the present circumstances."[31]

When Harper announced this action, he stated that further consideration of the question in all its details had been authorized "with the understanding that the present decision is temporary."[32] At the request of the Council, the question was referred once again to the women officers including the Fellows. Earlier, they had been asked whether it was not advisable to withdraw approval from local clubs that were secret. The officers decided that intercollegiate sororities were not, "at present," adapted to the life of the women of the University but that local societies should not be disallowed although they were to be thought of as strictly experimental. The officers also voted unanimously that all possible encouragement should be given by the Board to such organizations among women students as tended to promote a spirit of unity and democracy.[33]

Some five years later, when Edward Capps, professor of Greek, again raised the question as a courtesy to "an influential alumna" and with the confession that he had given the matter little thought, Marion Talbot, who was on vacation, wrote immediately to Harper that she differed from Capps in having given the matter a good deal of thought, and added, "I hope . . . that no official discussion of the matter will be allowed in my absence."[34] It had been her presence that had turned opinion, or at least the official decision of the University, against national sororities. In 1892, when the Faculty expressed disapproval of fraternities, a school superintendent who opposed secret societies had written someone in the University: "I had suspected that a great man was rising in Israel—I now know it. . . . You are not 'built' like a man who will yield."[35] It is likely that the recipient was Harper, but it was Marion Talbot who did not yield. It is impossible to know how many members of the University shared Capp's feelings when he wrote of the sororities: ". . . personally I should like to see a larger freedom granted them. . . ."[36]

Whether maintained by the University or by fraternities, the houses failed to provide space in which the student body could establish itself as a family. Every page of the student rosters in the *Register* is heavy with residential addresses far from the Quadrangles. Conversely, the paucity of University addresses within the Quadrangles indicates how impracticable it was to think of them as the center of all student life. The Alma Mater was young, but she had too many children for her handsomely made but narrow shoe. In 1897, Harper noticed crowding in the libraries and loitering in the halls, which occurred (it appears) because day students lacked better accommodations.[37]

In 1898, on Lincoln's birthday, a men's house bearing Lincoln's name gave its opening reception in a clubroom provided with games and magazines: "It forms a pleasant centre for daily gatherings of the members and their guests for lunch and recreation. . . . The House appreciates the kindness of the University in providing them with this college home, and believes that social hours spent there will cement friendships and strengthen the feeling of loyalty to the University."[38] In the same year and on the appropriate birthday, Washington House came into being, also for the use of men; and Spelman House was presently opened for women.[39] While Lincoln House was still in an experimental state, its head, George E. Vincent, found the outlook encouraging: at an initiation, "a good deal of corporate enthusiasm was manifested."[40]

Yet the establishment of *esprit de corps* produced a paradox within the terms of a plan that patently had been designed to provide houses for the unhoused. The twenty-six members of Lincoln House were inclined to resent a ruling of the Board of Student Organizations that their number should be raised to thirty-six. They felt it was extremely difficult, Vincent said, "to maintain any real unity in so large a group"; and they were also inclined to feel that occupancy of their quarters—a fourth-floor room in the Botany Building—was not so great a privilege that the University could afford to make any very stringent requirements. Experience had already shown, Vincent continued, that most of the best men in such houses would be drawn off into fraternities:

> If the houses are really going to meet the need of the men who join them, they are bound to take a fraternity bias; that is, the element of exclusiveness must be present in some measure in order to make the plan really satisfactory. . . . Important as it may be, to gather in the homeless and the friendless, the very success of that philanthropic work would tend to discredit the plan and make it unpopular. For example, the members of Lincoln House resent most emphatically the thought that they are to take in people because they have no place to go.[41]

Perhaps no institution striving at once after unity and catholicity can escape the problem of the Ins and the Outs that faced the University. Not impossibly, by giving one more group of students a room of its own, the University accentuated the solitude—perhaps sometimes enjoyed but how often lonely?—of those students who shared nothing outside the classroom but the unsociable experience of having no place to go.

In 1900, a writer in the *Weekly* spoke of the result produced by the situation of the University in a great city, by the exceedingly broad scope of the institution, by the fact that the Faculty was made up largely of specialists, and by the impact of the quarter system upon class spirit and class attachments. The writer argued: "The new student coming here feels, as he could not feel in a smaller institution, in a smaller city, that he is isolated from his fellow men and from his surroundings. He is impressed at once with the greatness of all but himself; he feels that for some reason he has got out of his element, and that this new world would not miss him, even for a moment, were he to suddenly disappear." In spite of all hindrances, conditions would be immensely improved ".... if there were some means by which members of the faculties and the students could become better acquainted with one another and with the work which the University is doing."[42] It may be that even in a college where Faculty members and students do live, as it were, *en famille* or at least dine regularly in the same hall, the students sometimes may feel left out. The inevitable differences between generations produce some sense of separateness, if not alienation, in both segments of the academic population. In a large university, without a commons that is literally the common table of Faculty and students, they cannot merge socially; but they may become (as the writer intimated) better acquainted, or not, in accord with the Faculty's intention—and that of the students (which the writer did not mention). It was one thing for the Faculty member to stand as an outsider, *in loco parentis,* and another for the college officer to be, in Harper's language, an older brother and fellow student.[43] Harper believed that such should be the relationship between college officer and student; and he acted accordingly, perhaps most memorably by gathering Seniors together for informal talk. "Weary at the week's end, he met us," an alumnus recalled after Harper's death, "and told of his experiences in building up the University. The little secrets of the business that sapped his vitality, the trials that he had met with men, his reverses and his victories—he told us all...."[44]

At the end of the University's first decade, Harper expressed the opinion that ".... in no other institution of its size had intimacy been more zealously cultivated." He immediately added that co-operation between the Faculties as such and the "student social interest" had been lacking: "There seems to have existed a strong disposition to leave the students to themselves in their various plans for social improvement, the Faculties restricting their energies largely to their own membership."[45]

Unprompted, many professors might hold themselves apart from the life of the students; but the Harper regime sought to secure a closer acquaintanceship between Faculty members and students, and also to give the students a voice. What were called divisions were instituted on the middle ground between regimentation and laissez faire. The students of the Junior Colleges and Senior Colleges were divided into groups, six for each set of Colleges, according to the majors of credit that the students had acquired. Thus the sixth division of the Junior Colleges contained those students who had less than three majors and so were the greenest of freshmen; and the first division of the Senior Colleges contained students nearly ready to graduate, with thirty-three or more majors of credit. A Faculty member was assigned to each division as adviser; and the students themselves elected a representative in a Junior or Senior College Council. Weekly lectures were offered to the divisions, at least partly to enable the students to view the various subjects offered in curriculum of study.[46] A motion was once made in the Faculty of Arts, Sciences, and Literature that "synoptical" courses, which might be taken for credit, should be offered by the departments; and Albion W. Small went further to propose that each student should be required to take at least six courses before graduating. The suggestions were voted down: the program of the divisions did not become a substitute for or a rival to the existing curriculum.[47] Harper did, however, hope that the lecture system would somewhat counteract the serious dangers which he saw grow out of too narrow specialization. The plan would also contribute something toward "the unification of student spirit and toward the broadening of student sympathies."[48]

In spite of Harper's bias against the idea of standing *in loco parentis,* his government leaned toward paternalism. Salutary neglect of the students would have been difficult to achieve psychologically and was, in strict logic, given the premises of the regime, a contradiction in terms. As Harper's views committed the University both to aggressive experimentation and to the pursuit of social unity, it could not but take the initiative in the organization of student life. In 1896, the *Weekly* observed guardedly that under some circumstances paternalism was an effective agency.[49] The question was implicit in the debate over secret societies. They represented a mode of life which, plainly, some students desired and which also, just as plainly, the President indorsed only after the fact. The issue was put explicitly in its most critical aspect by Dean George E. Vincent: "Is not there danger of too much Faculty interference . . . ? I believe that it destroys the spontaneity of the students."[50] The play of that spontaneity against the chord of paternalism made the conduct of student life a study in institutional counterpoint.

In 1897, the *Weekly* said: "Chicago is in many respects entirely unlike every other college, and it does not stand to reason that customs and institutions that flourish elsewhere will find the same congenial surroundings for growth here."[51] The comment was hortatory rather than descriptive. The actual direction of the students' movement was implied by a question which immediately preceded that comment: "In our mad rush to be and do like other colleges are we not in danger of overdoing things?"[52] The policy of the administration, however paternalistic, favored innovation. At the same time, the students were heavily influenced, their actions suggest, by a desire not to miss anything that going to college had come to mean in the land. They were spontaneously emulative and did not hesitate to borrow from the experience of other colleges to found a weekly magazine immediately; a yearbook (*Cap and Gown*) in 1895; a newspaper (the *Maroon*), published regularly from 1902; debating clubs; fraternities, local sororities, and secret societies—for example, Owl and Serpent, for senior men. The descriptive adjective for such names itself became a name when a group of women founded Esoteric. Contrary to Harper's hopes, the "old fashioned literary society" failed to take deep root in the esteem of the students.

Fending for themselves, although under the control of a Faculty board and with such counsel as Marion Talbot and others offered, the students created a varied club life. Its visible relics are the group photographs of stiffly posed, carefully dressed students in *Cap and Gown*. The Gold Club of 1896 was understandably short-lived; but other organizations, including *Cap and Gown* itself, survived as generations of students flowed through the colleges.

The graduate student was thought to stand in need of special attention from the University. Writing as dean of the graduate school of arts and literature, Harry P. Judson observed that the nature of graduate work was such as to make it essentially personal: "There is little or no cohesion among the students . . . for the mere reason that there seems to be few common interests."[53] The departmental club for his discipline was presumably the graduate student's first resort. Yet it could hardly be doubted, Judson had said, that students pursuing individual specialties would be benefited by frequent contact with those in other disciplines as well as by familiarity with the persons and the problems of the graduate school as a whole. Early in the history of the University, the departmental clubs were federated to create the University Union, which was intended to unify and elevate "the intellectual spirit" of the University in the face of departmentalism. It was not designed to furnish entertainment. Although in 1894 the *Weekly,* which looked for a social life in the Union, commented unfavorably on an attendance at one meeting of less than three hundred University people, it seems remarkable in retrospect that the interest in the Union should have been measured by hundreds of attendants before the total student population in Arts, Science, and Literature had risen above one thousand.[54] The Union did not gain momentum. As programs were devoted to the reading of papers from the clubs, success in the pursuit of unity depended upon the possibility that departmentalized studies would please a mixed audience. The papers were not supposed to be technical in form, but, according to the *Weekly,* so they were.[55] The Union died before mid-March in 1895. At the same time, it was proposed to organize a club to bring the members of various departments together for their mutual pleasure and advantage, and the last council of the Union called an organization meeting.[56] Its result was the Graduate Student Club of the University of Chicago, designed to afford its members both an opportunity to consider questions relating to graduate work and to meet socially. The club survived more than five years, during which time it combined with similar clubs, notably that at Harvard, to publish a handbook of graduate study in the United States.[57] For a time, a body called the Graduate Student Faculty served to anticipate the life that many such students would lead. Constituted as the faculty of a make-believe college but sitting in the real Faculty room, the students discussed such matters as the proper duties of the President and deans. The faculty was chaired by Harper, who, when a statute defining the duties of the college officers was presented, said the great question was: "Have the committee granted the President too much power?"[58] Harper's talk with the students was not perfunctory.

The most striking display of both paternalism and student enthusiasm occurred in athletics. Toward the end of the Harper era, the *Maroon* observed that the only place where members of other colleges and the general public could form any estimate of Chicago spirit was on the athletic field: the spirit of the college was gauged ". . . by the strength and staccato quality of its cheers and by the visual stimuli of colored ribbons."[59] The *Maroon* asked if that was fair, and answered no. The *Maroon* did admit that on the football field the University did not exhibit the spirit of Michigan, Wisconsin, Illinois, or Northwestern. The men of Chicago were more mature than other college men; therefore more conservative, the *Maroon* intimated—more undemonstrative. "The spirit of Chicago is a spirit that goes deeper than mere show."[60] The grapes may have been sour, but the influences which the *Maroon* found responsible for the greater maturity of the Chicago men—the city, the broad-mindedness of the

University rule, the scattering (rather than the concentration) of students, the commixture of law and medical students, the large number of graduate and "research students," the very size of the student body—may well have dampened college spirit of the usual sort and prevented enthusiasm for intercollegiate sport. Yet the football field was a rallying-point: *Go Chi-ca, Go Chi-ca, Go Chi-ca-go* did its part to make what would be the Big Ten famous in football. When the Congregation discussed athletics policy in 1900, "the present increasing interest" in athletics was taken for granted.[61] In that debate, George Herbert Mead, assistant professor of philosophy, stated his conviction that the University (or the Congregation) was helpless in attempting to regulate the social life of the students.[62] The opinion was heterodox but perhaps reflected some understanding of the force as well as the direction of student inclinations. Yet it was not at the demand of the students that competitive sport was brought into the life of the University. Unlike Johns Hopkins and Clark, the other universities emphasizing graduate work from their opening, at its beginning the University of Chicago adopted intercollegiate sports, which had become a tradition in the years between the founding of Johns Hopkins and the University of Chicago. In January, 1891, Harper indicated that physical education, which Amos Alonzo Stagg would direct, could be construed to include games. Stagg wrote his family:

I had been in doubt ever since accepting the position [at the University] what Dr. Harper's attitude toward athletics would be, fearing lest he, in his race for intellectual achievements, should discard intercollegiate athletics and be content with just enough exercise to keep the body in fair condition for mental work. But in answer to my question what his attitude would be toward intercollegiate athletics, he said: "I am most heartily in favor of them. I want you to develop teams which we can send around the country and knock out all the colleges. We will give them a palace car and a vacation too." These words made me very happy, for it means such a vast deal more pleasure to me. I am so very, very fond of outdoor sports. More than this, it will be sure to create a strong college spirit which means so much to a college boy's life. And last and best of all, it will give me such a fine chance to do Christian work among the boys who are sure to have the most influence. Win the athletes of any college for Christ, and you will have the strongest working element attainable in college life.[63]

Almost ten years later Albion W. Small, sometime college president and head of the sociology department, expressed the same idea: ". . . athletic sports in our colleges are among the most important moralizing influences at our disposal."[64]

Unlike the fraternities, opposed by Stagg, football was not received on sufferance; but like the fraternities, football came under attack within the University as well as in the country at large. The Congregation heard the now-familiar arguments. Increasing interest in athletics led the athletes themselves to neglect their college work, and the publicity of college games subjected them to "unhealthful influences." The interest injured the University as a whole because it caused scandal and tended to set up false ideals of academic success. Athletics was attended by the evils of professionalism, including the participation of players who were not bona fide students, and by the commercial spirit. It exaggerated hero-worship of athletes.[65] The Congregation was sufficiently disturbed to wonder whether the regulations contained all safeguards against abuses, but it found that "on the whole, . . . the advantages of college athletics as at present conducted outweigh their disadvantages."[66] The guarding phrase, *as at present conducted,* pointed directly to Stagg and the Board of Physical Education which had jurisdiction over intercollegiate athletics but also beyond the man and the Board to the heart of University policy. It was of its essence that worthy causes should not be left at loose ends and that the common guaranty of their worth should be their government by officers of the University. Stagg was not—as custom elsewhere indicated—a coach hired by an autonomous athletic association to produce winning teams but a professor appointed by the University to carry to success a segment of its own program. Coaching was part of Stagg's work, and victory was sweet; but it was not a condition of his tenure. Athletics became a part of the academic establishment. Harper did not flinch at the implications of the fact. To the charge that the sale of tickets was corrupting intercollegiate sport, he replied, let it be endowed.[67] This Utopian proposal jibed perfectly with Harper's opinion that ". . . the athletic field, like the gymnasium, is one of the University's laboratories and by no means the least important one."[68] Presumably the difference between a football game and a meeting of the University Union, where work in the other laboratories might be reported, was that only the one provided what Judson described as a never-ending fund of interest for students in general. He found it, on the whole, salutary but attacked the eagerness for competition among institutions that led to an overweening desire for victory.[69]

The enthusiasm of the students did not prevent them from wanting a voice in the management of athletics, an approach to that kind of government which Stagg's appointment as a Faculty member had forestalled. He edited the constitution of a proposed athletic association: where the draft read that the association should regulate the general athletic interest of the University, he substituted the verb "further" for "regulate"; and where it spoke of managers, he inserted "Assistant." He was not, he said, strenuous in regard to the additional word but remarked ". . . it presents my idea of duties much better and possibly may prevent any chance for assumption of the managers duties in other institutions."[70] The University accepted intercollegiate sport; but with Stagg unmistakably in charge, it kept to its own path. At the dedication of Bartlett Gymnasium, Stagg explained where the path led; he saw an unending procession of men passing forth: ". . . vigorous mentally, powerful physically, they take up life's burden and responsibilities. . . ."[71] As a young man only recently appointed to the Faculty, Stagg spoke of the pleasure he found in sport and of its service to religion; and as an elderly man he named his memoirs *Touchdown* and looked back upon his career as if upon a life in the ministry.[72] In the interval, as the Old Man—a nickname Stagg acquired before he turned forty—he exemplified, in his attitude and action, a paternalism that combined both gusto and righteousness. The University possessed that blend of qualities—it may be argued—in common with the heroes of its particular age. The students might resist the regime and yet find what it stood for irresistibly appealing.

The building of the University was presented to the students as a dramatic event. Harper possessed a sense of theater, which was revealed most directly in his taste for academic costume and pageantry. The cap and gown were frequently worn at the University—but not to everyone's satisfaction; and because the University granted degrees at quarterly Convocations rather than at a single Commencement each year, the ceremonies were many. It was Harper's practice to make a formal statement on the state and future of the University at each Convocation. The sessions did not altogether escape criticism, but they gave Harper an opportunity to offer a running account of the University, in quicktime, that may well have accentuated that the University was moving fast. At the end of the Harper era, an outside observer recalled, "I never heard any one who could read a table of figures with such eloquence as President Harper."[73] The Faculty members perhaps did not talk enough to students of work done in the University; but Harper's statements and their publication in the official gazette, the *University Record,* constituted a means of informing the students as well as the Faculty and the public about the affairs of the University. Not infrequently, the address of the day at Convocation dealt with higher education: at the first Convocation, Hermann von Holst, head professor of history, spoke on "The Need of Universities in the United States."[74] Attending meetings, reading the *University Record,* and—as a Senior—listening to the President's casual talks about the University, the student could believe that he was being offered an informal course in the development of a university; and the subject matter was constantly changing. Ceremony was especially prominent in 1896 and again, more spectacularly, in 1901, when the University celebrated its fifth and tenth anniversaries.* At the beginning of the tenth anniversary, Clarence R. Williams, a college graduate who had come to the University for a divinity degree, wrote to his family: "Great is the University of Chicago—the biggest ten-year-old the college world has ever seen. Beforehand I felt that as the B.D. meant little to me now but the ability to write a couple of letters more after my name, that I would not greatly enjoy the exercise. But in fact I am beginning to feel proud of this young, pushing, aggressive institution."[75] The University of Chicago did inspire enthusiasm.

The University invited its students to join in the advancement of a cause. Its immediate beneficiary was the University; but it was presented as a part of the academic world. Frequently, at Convocation and elsewhere, members of the University and visitors spoke about other institutions, universities at large, the nature of research—the list of topics is long. Harper described the bearings of the cause in terms of the "college man's" position.[76] In Harper's view, he was neither—in the language of a later era—a nonentity lost in the faceless crowd nor an alienated intellectual.

Because of his education, the college man already had lived one life when he entered what Harper called the world fellowship: ". . . he is beginning life a second time, and has before his eyes its probabilities, or at all events its possibilities. Such a man sustains a peculiar relation to the world and must occupy a peculiar place in its fellowship." It was the place of the parent in the family or of an elder brother: ". . . not elder, perhaps in years, but in experience; for experience comes not merely with days of life, but with days of thought and action."[77] A man received a special gift—either of education or of wealth—in order that he might help his brother, that humanity might be lifted higher. The obligation, more burdensome than that carried by the mass of men, was one of service:

* The age of the University of Chicago is calculated officially from 1891, the year William Rainey Harper formally assumed office as President. The University, in one sense, had been founded two years earlier when John D. Rockefeller made his first (conditional) pledge for a college in Chicago. In another sense, the University was founded in 1890, when the terms of the Rockefeller pledge were met and the University was incorporated. Its life as a teaching institution began in 1892 when it opened its doors to students.

... an obligation which rests upon you, my friends, in part because you may not deny your relationship to every member of the human family with whom you come in contact; in part because of the very constitution of your mind and body which brings you into close relationship with others of the human family; but especially because you have been accorded privileges not ordinarily enjoyed by the members of the human family.[78]

The doctrine had much in common with the ancient justification of an elite; it left ample room for the inference that the educated should feel themselves united by a special bond. Harper dealt explicitly with the service owed by the college man to those equally blessed with advantages: "These will need your help for themselves; for where you are strong they may be weak. . . . For your own sake you will serve them also; since where they are strong you may be weak, and the joint service thus secured will uplift you both."[79] Yet *elite* did not figure in his argument; in Harper's view, the college men had no exclusive claim to the special attention of God, from whom all gifts came. Did the few receive them because they deserved them? No! The inferiority of others to the college men was, Harper thought, a matter of the incorrect reckoning of the world: "There is no real sense in which they are below you. The world, as it is constituted, has not been able to furnish them the opportunity which it has given you—that is all."[80] Had the students—along with the preparation for service—the spirit of service? The question suggests a distinction (between capability and will) that is implicit in Harper's view of the University itself. It was not meant solely to prepare students for specialized activity; it was to convey the familial spirit in which all men should act.

It was not enough that the University should represent secular altruism. The institution was not narrowly denominational—Harper distinguished between a university and a college, which might be controlled by the "ecclesiastical" spirit. But the University had been founded upon religion, and religion was not, Harper believed, identical with what he called the higher life. Religion was ". . . something in itself and for itself, fulfilling a separate role, and not in any way to be confounded with art, or philosophy, or even with morality"—or with science.[81] Religion might have been the origin of those other phases of the higher life; but that did not mean that religion remained their mother—again the familial metaphor: ". . . the child, in time, may grow to be independ-ent. . . ."[82] Yet religion was essential in the higher life to the "full fruitage" of its other phases. In each, a particular faculty or set of faculties was predominant (for example, imagination and emotion in art); but in religion the various faculties had to be held in even balance.[83] Religion alone exercised a man's whole being. This view implied belief that it was in service to the cause of religion that the University would find its ultimate fulfilment and most nearly perfect unity.

Before his appointment as chaplain, Charles R. Henderson described the practical problem of assuring religion a place in the University. "The average college professor, however pious, is apt," Henderson wrote Harper, "to give chief attention, as he ought, to the more intellectual aspects of culture"; and the overworked pastors of Chicago could do very little for the students.[84] There was no reason to expect that spiritual culture, "the crown of glory" in the work of the University, would secure the prominence it deserved unless special and adequate provision were made for it. Speaking retrospectively, a decade later, Harper cut more deeply along the outline of the first proposition: "The life of the professional student has a tendency to become distinctly selfish."[85] Henderson's own appointment evinces Harper's agreement that the University itself had to organize the means toward its ends. The response was characteristic, as was the commissioning of an officer to take charge of the matter.

Harper did not think his duty was done when he arranged Henderson's appointment. Of his talks to students on religion and the higher life, Harper would say: "I have in this way discharged in a measure a responsibility which has weighed upon me more heavily than any other connected with the office which I have been called to administer."[86] The words could have been spoken by the most conservative clergyman-president in the land: Harper, too, had been called.

But what specific attitude should the University adopt? When the first Rockefeller gift and the matching pledges were transferred from the American Baptist Education Society to the University Trustees, Gates asserted that the prospective college would be evangelistic. The statement placed the University with the colleges, of which Amherst and Oberlin had been notable examples, where the success of a college year might be measured by number of souls converted to Christ. The thought Gates had expressed in 1890 may not have wholly left his mind when, in the course of December, 1892, he inquired into the state of religion at the University. He asked several professors for written statements, with the intention of committing them to the religious interests of the University. Gates's own views are suggested by his classification of Laughlin as an extreme liberal after receiving a letter from Laughlin and having a conversation with him.[87] Laughlin wrote that in his experience, "young men are apt to be repelled

... by open or evident attempts 'to save their souls'; they shrink from the expos-
ing of their inner religious life; and are influenced to practical respect for Christianity by seeing it in an attractive & manly form, in the indefinable atmosphere
of the place."[88] Gates did not take further action—and never again went so far
as to make a survey.*

The saving of souls became a concrete issue when John W. Mott visited the
University to organize a branch of the then evangelical Young Men's Christian
Association.[89] Mott talked to Harper in July, 1892, and argued his case again in
October just as the University was being set in motion. Harper did not immediately receive the YMCA but rather—it seems—objected to what he thought
was the narrowness of its program.[90] The question was not whether the YMCA
could find sponsorship within the University—Stagg had come from a post in a
YMCA training school—but rather whether an outside body with the orientation of the YMCA should take the initiative in religious work at the University.
Its response was to institute a body, the Christian Union, through affiliation with
which evangelistic and other religious groups might be identified with the University without the University becoming identified exclusively with a particular
mode of religious activity. Sponsorship of such activity was to be broad; but
the Christian Union was advisedly named. When its nature was being discussed,
there was a danger—in Goodspeed's words—that the organization would be
so broad that it would not be Christian, and so at once it was put "on a distinctly Christian basis."[91] Thus the University followed a middle way. It neither
evangelized nor shunned association with evangelistic groups which were
prepared to unite with the University on its own terms; it acted in the name
of Christ but did not deny the spiritual worth of other religions. It adhered
to the principle ". . . that no form of worship has any value that is not absolutely and sincerely free."[92] While reviewing his first ten years in office as
chaplain, Henderson wrote:

Those who lead in the conduct of worship are Christians, and their expression of
religion is in the language of the Christian world, sacred to most of us from the dawn
of consciousness. But this does not exclude other dialects of the common faith of the
world, and the freedom to voice the deeper feelings of the soul in any form hallowed
by reverence and family associations is permitted and encouraged.[93]

The Christian Union was both a confederation of organizations and an
association where Faculty members and students might unite on the basis of

---

* In his survey, in 1892, of the religious affiliations of 107 Faculty members, Gates found that
44 were Baptists, 24 Congregationalists, and 20 Presbyterians, with the remaining members scattered
among seven denominations or religions.

a common faith, "without inconsistency with the maintenance of individual religious conceptions. . . ."[94] As the Union was originally constituted, its membership nominally embraced all members of the University. Goodspeed wrote Gates in 1892: "Here the theory is that the professors and students are one body, all students together. They are therefore associated in its work of religious organization."[95] In 1901, the Union was placed "upon a more distinct University basis," under the control of a board similar to those created to oversee other activities sponsored by the University.[96] Toward the end of the Harper administration, all members of the University were no longer regarded "as *ipso facto* members of the Christian Union."[97] But a signature on the roll brought the student or professor into the Union. It remained a meeting place for any members of the University interested in religious work without requirement of conformity to creed.[98]

The latitudinarian character of the Christian Union may be viewed either as a cause or a reflection of diversity in the work conducted by the Union and its affiliates. Yet the more traditional kinds of religious work such as home missions were somewhat overshadowed by activities related to the Social Gospel. Henderson was himself a professor of ecclesiastical sociology as well as chaplain. Presumably without intending to echo Laughlin's words, he observed:

Students rarely permit anyone to uncover their inner life or to question them about their beliefs, which are in a state of change and ferment; but they frequently express their best purpose in plans of useful activity and friendly service. More and more the divine life takes human form, and goes out into conduct. It is on this side of the natural instincts of young people that we can hope to achieve most in educating them in the best experiences of the spiritual life.[99]

The University of Chicago Settlement grew out of the philanthropic work of the Christian Union, and it remained officially under the auspices of the Union after it was separately incorporated.[100] (The University of Chicago Settlement League was both a women's auxiliary and a women's club in Hyde Park.)[101] Before the Settlement was founded, Harper had thought of establishing a church mission and later considered the possibility of a settlement house in association with the Divinity School.[102] For a time, Clifford W. Barnes, later organizer of the Chicago Sunday Evening Club, a young clergyman with experience in church missions, served both as an instructor in sociology and director of the Settlement.[103] The Settlement owed less, however, to the church mission than to Hull-House in Chicago and indirectly to the prototype of the university settlement house, Toynbee Hall in the East End of London. "A

Settlement," the *Register* announced, "is a body of educated people living in a neighborhood for the purpose of co-operation in social work and for learning the concrete facts of life at first hand." Vast accumulations of knowledge lay dead for want of "mediators" to communicate it to the multitudes of people whose existence was intellectually and aesthetically barren: "On the other hand, the lives of cultivated people are frequently narrow, undignified, useless, and false from exclusiveness. The student of politics, economics and social philosophy can avoid provincial, individualistic and class prejudices only by mingling with people of varied experience." The residents of the Settlement aimed to promote every effort at local amelioration; they would not introduce "a foreign institution, but fertilize and cultivate the spring elements of good already found in the neighborhood."[104]

In the hands of Mary E. McDowell, the head resident, that broad charter was used to warrant what Charles R. Henderson called "useful activity" in the area surrounding the Chicago Stockyards, where the settlement house was located.[105] The work of the Settlement did not, however, become a regular part of the program of the University. Harper did not secure endowment funds for the College of Religious and Social Science, which might have become, in combination with the Settlement, a School of Social Service. The Settlement remained a direct outlet of philanthropic sentiment and an expression of distaste for exclusiveness.

When the Union was reorganized in 1902, the idea was broached that the Christian Union might be given some attributes of a church, and the creation of such a body out of University membership was discussed by Harper, Burton, and Barnes; but no congregation was founded.[106] The University went no further than to institute Sunday services with preaching by distinguished clergymen or "university preachers" such as Harvard appointed.[107] Weekday chapel services were instituted, but students were not originally required to attend. To Harper's distress, many did not; later, attendance at a weekly chapel meeting was made compulsory for each division of students. The endemic problem of collegiate chapel was aggravated at the University by the lack of a chapel building, either to symbolize religion or to provide seating space for the whole University gathered together as a community. Only in architectural drawings of the completed Quadrangles did the spire of a chapel rise above the roofs of the academic buildings. Yet the University did not so much need a building as an expression of the religious spirit to which the students would voluntarily give their attention in the midst of their day-to-day activity, which would be the more engrossing, the more nearly the University succeeded, department by department, in offering stimulating instruction. In 1900, the *Weekly* specified what every student would welcome in chapel, ". . . an opportunity to put aside everything for an hour that he may listen, in a simple-hearted way, to the teachings of earnest men."[108]

Harper himself spoke to the point of the gravest issue before an institution attentive to the claims of both intellect and piety. Harper saw no easy way toward their reconciliation; but it was possible and necessary. "It has sometimes seemed to me," he wrote,

that to think and to doubt were synonymous. Certain it is that in proportion as a man thinks, in that same proportion questions arise the answers to which are often hard for him to discover. And since it is the chief business of the student to think, he need not be surprised if doubts crowd in upon him thick and fast. If one's reading does not lead him to think and to ask the wherefore of things, the why this is true, if it be true, and the why this is false, though always believed to be true—it would be better for him not to read. If one's reading has taught him to think about the classics, and about art, about science, and about history, and has not also led him to think (and I mean by the word "think" the asking of questions, the testing over again of truth supposed already to have been tested, the interposing of a doubt as to this or that thing not yet based on sufficient evidence)—if, I say, one's reading has not led him to think about the great questions which are connected with our religion and our faith, that reading or study has been in part a failure. You must not misunderstand me when I say that unless your intellectual work has taught you to doubt, at least to an extent which will compel you in self-defense to make inquiries the result of which will be the furnishing you a basis on which to rest an intelligent faith, that intellectual work has not yet gone far enough. Although you will meet difficulties, if you think, do not, I beg of you, stop thinking because you are afraid of difficulties. They are certain to exist.

.   .   .   .

But suppose that you are not a Christian; are you waiting until all difficulties have disappeared? If so, you will wait until the end of life. If some good friend labors with you until he has persuaded you that these difficulties have been removed, and begs you now to accept the Christ, he is deceiving you; it is not so. Do not allow yourself to be thus deluded. Many of these perplexities will continue; but if your faith is real and simple, they will gradually become less and less significant, until by falling into their proper places they will leave you undisturbed. Be sure, thus, of this: If you wait until you are argued out of these doubts, you will wait long and hopelessly.

.   .   .   .

Just here someone may raise an important consideration. "How," he asks—and I understand him to ask it honestly—"How can I profess to accept that about which

I have doubt? A Christian life is inseparably connected with a full acceptance of Christian doctrines. If I cannot accept the doctrines, how can I lead, or profess to lead, the life?"

I answer: I know that life and conduct are affected by opinion; but I know also that the doctrines necessary to be accepted by him who would lead a true life, are not many, nor abstruse. I remember that the men and women of our Lord's times who accepted him, and in him found rest and peace, were not loaded down with theological systems; and, still further, that their theological beliefs, so far as they held such beliefs, were made up largely of the ephemeral notions and ideas of their day. The sum and substance of the Christian faith is found in two words, "Follow me." The belief in this or that thing may be important; it is not essential. The simpler one's faith, and the more childlike, the more helpful and satisfying it will prove to be.[109]

These were the words of an earnest man, who practiced inquiry, loved God, and sought to prepare the young, both in mind and soul, for life in the family embracing mankind.

PART FOUR

THE GREATER
CONSTITUENCY

Wherever Mankind Is

In Harper's view, the spirit of unity should extend far beyond the Quadrangles to bind the University to the people, both to the American people and, ultimately, to humanity itself. When he described the ideal university in print, he entitled his statement "The University and Democracy." Asking what relation one sustained to the other, Harper found his answer in the Old Testament analogy. As the prophet, priest, and sage of democracy, the university had been given a mission of righteousness in the world. Democracy was the outcome of movements that had been in operation for fifty centuries or more, but it had not yet been unified: "And without unity the doctrine of equality may not exert its full force. Spokesmen who understand this unity and appreciate its necessity in the economy of democratic progress must proclaim it far and near, until no ear shall have failed to hear the proclamation, no heart shall have failed to heed its clear injunction."[1] In the prophetic office, the university might speak to a downcast, downtrodden people—a democracy despondent: ". . . all oppression shall be removed, and all war shall cease, and a new government shall be established—a government of justice and righteousness which shall endure forever." When democracy became corrupt, it had to be cleansed and purified without pity until the evil had been expunged. "The clear voice of prophetic rebuke must be heard. . . ." And it was the university that fought the battles of democracy, its war-cry being: Come, let us reason together. The university was the interpreter of democracy—"the prophet of her past, in all its vicissitudes; the prophet of her present, in all its complexity; the prophet of her future, in all its possibilities."[2] As priest, the university was a mediator between man and man, between man and man's self, and between mankind and "that ideal inner self of mankind which merits . . . man's adoration." The university had devoted itself—again Harper personified an ideal as a woman—". . . to the cause of lifting up the folk of her environment— an act of consecration than which none is more holy." The university was the keeper, ". . . for the church of the democracy, of holy mysteries, of sacred and significant traditions" that would be marred if touched by profane hands. Yet the whole world might be included in the list of the initiated: ". . . the true university, the university of the future, is one the motto of which will be: Service for mankind wherever mankind is, whether within scholastic walls or without those walls and in the world at large."[3] As sage, the university answered demands for "severe thinking. . . . I mean the honest and unbiased consideration of all the facts which relate to democracy." Its problems involved the "philosophical" treatment of socialism—"the extreme and exaggerated form of democracy"; of the rapid increase of the population in large cities; of the accumulation of great wealth by a few men—what shall their place be in a democracy and by what determined?; of the great business corporations— how should democracy adjust itself to them and them to itself?; of the deterioration of popular government—is government really a democracy or is it rather an oligarchy of the party machine?; of the hostility of workingmen to the churches—they are not democratic institutions; and of education—it is the basis of all democratic progress. The expectation of mediocrity in the development of art, literature, and science, Harper said, is itself fatal to the highest claims of a democracy. Its future was the problem of problems, including all the others.[4]

Harper's amalgam of the ancient Hebrew example and of late nineteenth-century hopes and anxieties lacked incisiveness, but it was not mere bombast. The words were those of a strong-willed man. For the particular University over which he presided, his rhetoric weighed less than his program. If the larger mission of the University was to be fulfilled, Harper's colleagues had to adopt his plans as their own: did they think his sweeping conception of the professor's duty a mere pastiche? They committed themselves without second thoughts to inquiry, the work of the sage, and also to the priestly service of instruction on campus; but even before the opening day, Hale and Laughlin insisted upon scrutinizing one of Harper's plans to extend the University to the people beyond the Quadrangles. If made concrete, the office of prophecy might be opposed as a dangerous irrelevancy; and in the day-to-day life of the University, the unities Harper talked of might make incompatible demands. The specifications of Harper's university, the great design existing in his mind, called both for corporate harmony and for dedication to the democratic cause; but Harper and members of the Faculty could disagree upon the distance that the University should seek to throw its voice.

Once when the relation of the University to other institutions was being discussed, Harper wrote a Trustee: ". . . I agree with you that we must not undertake anything that is not strictly University. The only question is what the word 'university' in its fullest sense signifies."[5] Harper was leading his witness; but the question could not be thrust aside. The friends and members of the University were challenged to examine its reason for being and the nature of their own obligations.

CHAPTER XI

The Mission
of the University

The most conspicuous vehicle to carry the University to the people was University Extension, as it was designated. For its enthusiasts, University Extension was the secular counterpart of evangelism. The higher learning was to be carried across the land by the University as the Bible had been taken to the frontier by an earlier generation of itinerant preachers. (Perhaps the most famous University Extension lecturer, Richard G. Moulton, was the son of the superintendent minister of a Methodist circuit in Great Britain.) The evangelical purpose of Extension was unmistakable: "The whole movement . . . is primarily a missionary work. Its aim is to make people desire the things it can offer, to make people long for improvement."[1] "If culture is not contagious, it should be . . . more or less infectious, and every person who is reaping some of the rewards of the earnest labors of scholarly men should see that something is done to bring others into touch with the same spirit."[2] "University Extension . . . is for all classes, rich and poor, men and women alike, and in so far resembles the church in its comprehensiveness. Its work resembles, moreover, that of the church in another point, namely, that it is essentially missionary in character."[3] In short, it was to bring culture to the uncultured. To reach their audience, the lecturers did not have to ride horseback through forests or along prairie trails; rather, they lived like traveling salesmen, eating at lunch counters, sleeping on trains, and coming home, perhaps in a cold dawn, only to pack bags again. The great object of Extension was the cultural redemption of America.

William Rainey Harper could not take much part in Extension work, but he had known the lecturer's migrant life and was entirely convinced of its worth. For him, the diffusion of scientific knowledge and the creation of a desire for "a higher and better intellectual and aesthetic life" were no less important than the advance of scientific knowledge itself by original investigation and discovery: "Indeed, . . . the latter will not find the fullest support and the most satisfactory field of progress, except in a community in which interest in a higher education is widely spread."[4] The University was engaged, he said, not simply in supplying an existing demand but ". . . in the even more difficult and important work of creating in the community at large that demand for the best of everything in the intellectual, aesthetic and moral world which is at once the evidence of, and the surest means toward, the higher civic life."[5] Had Harper been carried into progressive politics, that phrase, the Higher Life, would surely have been his slogan. The elevation of the public was of the essence. The work of diffusing knowledge had to be popular, but "in a good sense," being systematic in form and scientific in spirit. The work had to be done under the direction of a university by men with scientific training.[6] University Extension would make self-education as easy as possible; but every member of modern society had the duty of pursuing that education systematically, persistently, and continuously.[7] The University would guide Everyman, provided he was prepared for a strenuous climb upward.

When Harper stated that University Extension would bring the University "into direct contact with human life and activity," he was not broaching a new idea.[8] Early in the nineteenth century, enough of the monastic atmosphere had survived in the colleges to justify Daniel Webster's approving reference to "the quiet retreats of academic life"; but reform had long been freshening higher education.[9] The original Morrill Act was three decades old, and dissatisfaction with traditional studies even older. Yet Harper's declaration had point; for the universities were not well equipped to carry instruction to persons who lived beyond the campus and who did not fall into the established categories of students. But how far should a university extend its arms; what *was* the community at large of which Harper spoke? The constituency of a state university had definite limits, set by law and public policy. In theory, a private university had no easily ascertainable frontier; at any given time, the sphere of influence would be the area over which it enabled its instructors to range and the segment of the population to which the university was determined to speak. If Extension was to benefit all classes and all ages and if its action was not to be limited "to this or that form of work"—as one director of Extension asserted—the character of the audience was indeterminate.[10]

The actual program was complex and malleable. Its evolution from Harper's original plan may have begun in December, 1890, when, as Moulton recalled, Harper met him and enthusiastically indorsed the conception of Extension ". . . as we understood it in England."[11] An announcement issued in the next month contained a reference to particular courses "in accordance with the best developed plans of University-Extension" (which were British) but did not specify the characteristic features of British extension.[12] If Harper did not then have their details by heart, he learned them quickly. For the University of Chicago soon appropriated the British machinery intact, even as it dropped Bible study, Harper's own specialty, as a major category of extramural courses.

By the summer of 1892, the plan for Extension had become so elaborate that nearly twenty-five pages were required to explain it, even without a statement of specific courses. Extension was to be organized in six departments, each with its own secretary responsible to a director of Extension. Lecture-study was the Chicago version of the original British text. Its courses included six or twelve lectures, discussions with the instructor at the time of each lecture, and weekly written exercises based upon a formal syllabus. Students were to be brought together into centers by local organizers, and the centers linked into circuits. (In modern terms, the result would resemble a network of subscription television stations offering a common series of educational programs, save that the instructor appeared in person at each center.) Classwork, shortly to be known as class-study, consisted of regular University courses, taught off-campus. Correspondence-teaching (or correspondence-study) was a generalized form of the instruction by mail in which Harper had excelled. The examination department was designed to accredit work done in Extension, and the department of library and publications to provide necessary books. Still another department was to train Extension teachers.[13] (When teaching actually began, the plan for a training department miscarried, and the work of the examination and library departments was absorbed by other agencies of the University.)

Because Extension work might compel professors in the University Proper to neglect their regular duties and occupy time which ought to be given to research, Extension was to be carried out by a separate Faculty, which would include not only such persons in the University Proper as might wish to do

Extension-teaching but also a group of teachers, distinct from the Faculty in the Quadrangles, who would give the greatest part of their time to extramural teaching.[14] With the growth of the Extension movement, one announcement read, "what is practically a new profession has been created."[15] Although the statement was premature, it was consistent with the intention of the University in regard to its Extension staff.

Extension was planned as an aggressive and autonomous enterprise and not as a catalogue heading to cover whatever appearances members of the Faculty might feel prompted to make in response to scattered requests for their services. The University would not wait to be discovered by the public, and it would not simply supply beyond the Quadrangles what was offered by the several academic departments. What the advocates of Extension were contemplating was as much a new medium of education as a wider application of traditional devices of instruction. It remained for the University to settle upon an arrangement whereby the University Proper and University Extension might live under one corporate roof without friction. Often, the more nearly work in Extension approaches that on campus, the more readily Extension invites the jealousy of its older sibling; and the farther Extension departs from established practice, the more vulnerable it is to charges of academic impropriety. In fact, the character of Extension never became the subject of a full-dress quarrel during Harper's administration—perhaps because of his conspicuous approval of the program—but it did give rise to an undercurrent of discontent. Then as now, the value of Extension work, most notably in the currency of formal academic credit, was a subject of abiding argument.

In the earliest plan for Extension, two kinds of courses specified there were described by the phrase "in college and university subjects"; but the question of credit was not answered.[16] Harper planned that credit should be given for work done *in absentia* and expected that a student would be permitted to fulfil up to half of his degree requirements in this way.[17] The vehement opposition of Hale and Laughlin to Harper's intentions foreshadowed the more restrictive policy which actually went into effect: not more than one-third of the work toward a degree could be done *in absentia*. In the specific case of the requirements for a Master's degree, no study away from the campus was permitted. (Though the University was taking a long step away from orthodox practice, it did not come abreast of the University of London, an alma mater known to some of its alumni as an examining body halfway round the world.) When in May, 1893, the University announced in bold type and capital letters that regular credit would be granted in Extension only after examination held at the University—a requirement already for such credit in correspondence-study, the University may only have wanted to forewarn students too unfamiliar with academic practice to take examinations for granted; or the University may have sought merely to discourage opportunists who might try to abuse Extension.[18] Members of the Faculty may have believed, however, that the University should publicly disclaim any intention to deal in shaved coin. In the same month, the director of Extension, Nathaniel Butler, acknowledged the existence of fears among Faculty members that Extension had been harmful and might prove more injurious in the future. Butler dealt specifically with the expressed opinion that Extension had been presented dishonestly. Extension pretended, Butler insisted, to offer no short cut, no newly discovered royal road to learning.[19]

When Butler asserted—at the same time—that Extension did not duplicate work done on campus, he must have been thinking of lecture-study. Class-study differed from work in the Quadrangles because of unavoidable failings rather than of intended virtues in the class-study program. Since each course was financed out of fees paid specifically for it, an offered course might be withdrawn if only a few students enrolled, which meant that students might be frustrated in regard both to particular courses and to any systematic plan in which those courses figured. The most striking changes in class-study occurred precisely because it was designed to duplicate studies on campus. The program attracted many Chicago teachers who lacked a college education and were encouraged to continue their studies while they were working, just as college-bred teachers of a later day were to be offered incentives to get a Master's degree.

In 1898, the demand in the city, coupled with the contribution of $5,000 a year for five years by Mrs. Emmons Blaine, called into being the College for Teachers. Like the "colleges" on campus but unlike class-study in its original form, the College received its students as matriculants of the University. It differed from the other colleges of the University, for example Commerce and Administration, because it drew its offerings from the full range of scholarly fields and not simply from those appropriate for study toward a single degree or class of careers. Potentially, its interests were far more diverse than those of any particular curriculum pursued in the Quadrangles. "We hope, as this experiment succeeds," said Edmund J. James, the first dean, at the opening exercises of the College, to add many more [courses], until all the courses offered to other resident students which may be of service to teachers, may be duplicated here. . . . In fact, my friends, we shall not rest content until we have organized here a great down-town college in which, so far as possible, all the work of the other colleges in the University shall be duplicated which can be of service to busy people in any line of active life—and this means something for everybody.[20]

The expansiveness of the institution was recognized formally in 1900 when the College for Teachers was renamed University College and carried into effect by the organization of classes for railway employees, an institute (proposed by Graham Taylor) for training students in social and philanthropic work, and a course of lectures for Sunday School teachers and other religious workers.[21] Thus, University College was both a device to draw Extension closer to residential study and a vehicle to bear the influence of the University outward along new roads. The mixture of centripetal and centrifugal tendencies which the College exhibited was a product of experience. Unlike the class-study department, which had been born of excogitation (and then devoured by University College at its birth in 1900), the College evolved through a process of adaptation to the environment. Harper hoped that Extension colleges would appear in smaller cities.[22] (In Great Britain, the extension efforts of the ancient universities encouraged the rise of institutions called university colleges, from which independent universities were to grow.) The process that produced the College in downtown Chicago failed, however, to work elsewhere under the particular auspices of the University.

Correspondence-study, also offering regular courses but in an unconventional format, was meant particularly to benefit those who had been cut off from their studies by the "hand of necessity"—such as the students who had to drop out of college to take jobs.[23] The first offerings were confined to the fields of history, Semitic languages, and mathematics; but the area covered by correspondence-study increased in size as the program gained acceptance. Ultimately, even courses in science, usually taught in a laboratory, were carried by the postman. Such studies made headway against the skeptics, it would seem, precisely because they did closely resemble or duplicate as nearly as possible the work done by students on campus and did not reveal signs of kinship to the swarming progeny of mail-order courses. (Some question was raised whether reproach might not come to the University, if only by association.[24] In 1901, Harper protested when the manager of a correspondence school used a quotation, attributed to Harper, to the effect that students coming to the University after a year of correspondence work were better prepared than those who had taken classroom work. Harper explained that the statement referred to correspondence work directly under his control, but he did not disavow authorship of the quotation.[25] Its point was once driven home at a rally for correspondence-study, when "one of those uncomfortably logically minded people"—in the words of a philosopher —asked why the University did not dismiss its classes if correspondence was superior. After a "short, but oppressively aphasic, interval" Harper answered, but with only a patent quibble: his enthusiasm for academically respectable correspondence-study had carried him into a rhetorical cul-de-sac.)[26]

For many of the persons who entered correspondence-study, the arithmetic of credits was extraneous to their intentions. In 1899, Edmund J. James remarked that the great majority of students in correspondence-study took the work because they desired to get help that came from supervision by the University ". . . and not at all because they care for University credit of any kind." Thus the University would perhaps do a far more extensive and useful work if it would adapt correspondence courses "more immediately and directly to the needs of the people who desire such work." The requirements set by the University in regard to the length of courses and the character of the work were "somewhat rigid," according to James. In addition, instruction was given by Faculty members whose time was mortgaged to other claims.[27] In 1903, Harper also urged a further development of correspondence-study. Its constituency could be enlarged and the influence of the University as a democratizing agency proportionately extended and increased if it could reach young men and women who had to take jobs. To do so, the University would have to accommodate correspondence work to their needs by providing curriculums designed to afford the necessary preparation for professional courses in education, law, medicine, technology, and so on. Harper asserted that the University would cheerfully organize such curriculums but did not specify precisely what they might be.[28] It is difficult to see how they could have been mounted without appearing as a challenge to the limitation on study *in absentia*. Either as an equivalent to degree programs or as an easier, alternative way into the professions, the new pattern was potentially a rival of the old.

Conservatives may have been reassured, as perhaps Harper intended, by reading his review of the first decade of correspondence-study. Very frequently propositions had been made, Harper said, to popularize its work and greatly increase the number of students who availed themselves of its service, but those propositions had been uniformly rejected: "Academic traditions have been respected. . . ." Harper added that the work had been conducted largely by men who were at the same time teaching on campus. He felt, however, that correspondence work was too much to ask of the regular instructors and put forward the idea of a separate staff—as had been contemplated for Extension as a whole when it was first planned.[29] The incompatibility of that proposal with implicit commendation of correspondence-study because its courses had been taught by departmental instructors was left hanging in the air. Indicating that correspondence-study was respected and appreciated throughout the University, Harper noted that the Faculty had been "rightly suspicious" at first. Did he fear that any but the most tentative reference to autonomy for correspondence would jeopardize its position? In 1904 Harper acknowledged the survival among the Faculty of cautiousness in regard to correspondence. Hervey F. Mallory, then secretary of correspondence-study, had suggested that every student in the Junior College be required to do a certain number of majors by correspondence —which would mean that the Faculty could be reduced and funds set free for correspondence. "What I can most earnestly recommend and urge," Mallory had written Harper, "is that as soon as possible this work, which has proved its worth, be put on the same basis as residence work and not be expected to pay for itself." Harper's response was to refuse to take the proposition seriously, saying that it was absolutely impracticable from the point of view of the Senate— and also that the Junior College produced more money than it cost and that correspondence-study ought to be, and could be, self-supporting. "I am afraid," he wrote, "that long thinking on the subject of the correspondence work has somewhat disturbed your equipoise."[30] He might have added that managing the diplomacy of Extension successfully was a feat that required a very fine sense of balance indeed.

Lecture-study, unlike class-study and correspondence-study, was not based upon assumed identity of particular courses as offered on campus and off. Although an early bulletin indicated that six courses of twelve lectures each would be considered equivalent to two majors of regular college work, the issue of credit did not play the same part in the development of lecture-study that it did in the other departments of Extension.[31] "It is understood," the University announced in 1893, "that the lecture studies are intended, not to extend to the general audience the same instruction as that given in the university class rooms, but rather to stimulate and direct reading and study along the various lines of literature, history, and science."[32] This statement was made simultaneously with the announcement that credit would be given (presumably in class-study and correspondence-study) only after examination; the University felt a need in its first year of teaching to define exactly the relation of the several parts of Extension work to studies on the Quadrangles. (The *modus vivendi* of adult education and the traditional activities of universities are still frequently based upon an explicit designation of the nature and intended purpose of particular offerings: some must be labeled "for external use only.") Lecture-study was not to be confused with a program of academic *courses,* but it was to deal with academic subjects. In the first decade of instruction, those most often studied were English literature and language, sociology and anthropology, history, and biblical literature, in that order. Art came in fifth place, far behind the others. The gospel of culture and enlightened citizenship touched the lives of persons in 368 centers in twenty-one states. The number of courses was 1,326 and of traveling libraries 715. A total of 272,967 seats were taken for lecture courses; and the number of admissions to the individual lectures was 1,637,802. The cost to the University for that effort was $75,000 or slightly more money than the total salary of one head professor over the same ten years.[33] The approximate financial equivalence of lecture-study and the direction of one department indicates the degree to which lecture-study was organically related to the University.

Qualitatively, lecture-study fell short of its original specifications; in 1902 Harper commented on the small number of persons who could be relied upon to do much systematic work.[34] Lecture-study was often—it would appear—no more than listening to lectures—which may be an entirely serious practice without being particularly studious. Near the end of the Harper administration, the governors of Extension even proposed the offering of single lectures, which could hardly have served to stimulate any sustained effort by the audience. Indeed, as the Board on Extension made this recommendation, it recognized the danger of undermining "... what is being recognized as the most solid result of the University Extension movement, namely the difficult step of raising the public mind from the idea of single lectures to that of continuous courses."[35] In the metaphor of evangelism, the Board might have said that it was one thing to attract an audience for one sermon by a famous preacher and quite another to inspire its members to attend church regularly and to study systematically the designated texts. Since the visible reward for faithful attention to lecture-study was a special certificate rather than credit toward a general degree, the student had only a weak incentive, in point of practical self-interest, to take a difficult step upward. A program which could not hold its students captive had to be remarkably captivating itself.

The quality of the lecturing was the crux of the matter. Many members of the Faculty, including a number of head professors, took part in lecture-study, but they were not universally successful (at least in the opinion of the advocates of Extension). Lecturing, no less than murder, Moulton once remarked, was a fine art that required practice.[36] A few men bore a large part of the teaching load: of some one hundred persons who lectured over a decade, three lecturers, Richard G. Moulton, Charles Zueblin, and Edwin E. Sparks, offered more than one-third of all the courses, while at least twenty-five lecturers gave only one course apiece.[37] The load might have been more evenly distributed—and perhaps increased *in toto*—if the training program originally proposed had been instituted. As it was, the University had no such certain source of professional lecturers as the regular departments had of trained scholars, thanks to the establishment of graduate studies. The hardship of the road made careers devoted to lecture-study physically trying, while academically the attractions of the Quadrangles exerted something like the pull of gravity. Thus, Edward W. Bemis, who was not conspicuously successful on the road, and Moulton, who was, both looked with longing to the campus. It was easier to talk of a distinct Extension Faculty than to maintain one where distinctions entailed important differences in the lives men led and where the distinctions themselves seemed invidious. One lecturer wrote Harper:

I could give you numerous instances of the distrust (perhaps the word is too strong) in which the [local] Extension Committees, especially in the small places, hold the "University Extension" lecturer. They think him a kind of adjunct to the teaching force of the University and they wish to have "University" instruction if they pay for it. ... The people have been deceived so many times by wandering literary tramps in the guise of lecturers that they are suspicious.[38]

Within the University, feeling about the lecturers often worked in the same direction, although in more sophisticated terms. When Moulton began to make headway in the organization of a campus department of his own, the reactions of nominal colleagues revealed their sense of the distance between proper university work and Moulton's interest, literature in English. "I regard this as a thoroughly legitimate part of educational work," wrote John M. Manly, head of the Department of English, "but there are people who look upon it with suspicion, as being not scholarly." So Manly suggested the addition of some "serious" work in comparative literature "in the strictest and narrowest sense of the word."[39] Paul Shorey, head of the Department of Greek Language and Literature, recognized Moulton's ability and effectiveness as a "popular lecturer for untrained minds" but declared that "his conception of a course on Greek literature in English would not be mine." There would be no guaranties "... of the accomplishment of a definite amount of scholarly work as in Latin, Greek, Political Economy, etc., etc."⁴⁰ (Shorey's linking of political economy and classical scholarship suggests compatibility of the men in those departments: the Winged Victory of Samothrace appears in the portrait of the head of the Department of Political Economy, J. Laurence Laughlin.) The existence of imperfect sympathies between extramural lecturers and professors on the Quadrangles left in doubt the position of lecture-study, for what is one to say of the missionary who is not entirely welcome in the home parish?

In 1893, one prospective lecturer expressed his joy in the willingness of the University to realize that constant contact with the sources of knowledge was as vital to Extension as to other work and that Extension would allow an unusual share of time for research. This provision as well as the co-ordinate rank of Extension would go far, he felt, to offset the unpleasant features of Extension—"night lecturing, night traveling, irregular meals, danger from travel, loss of time from long trips, and absence from home."⁴¹ In that expectation lay the major problem presented by Extension: how could it be maintained as a truly co-ordinate part of the University in the presence of forces that worked against the stability of the program? Judson had argued for the assignment of individual Extension professors to the appropriate Faculties in order to integrate the two branches of the professoriate. In saying "... university Extension *is* auxiliary to the work of the Faculties," Judson virtually subverted the doctrine of co-ordination in the interest of closer harmony and sympathy between Extension and the resident Faculties.⁴² But Harper was not persuaded. In his decennial report, he recommended two concrete measures based on the distinctiveness and independence of Extension: the payment of a premium for Extension teaching, either in increased salary or shortened annual service, and the creation of an endowment of $500,000 to $1,000,000 for lecture-study. Harper contemplated the existence of a staff of "Extension men" and also the occasional detachment of classroom instructors for a quarter of service with Extension, where they might come in contact "with life and work outside the University walls."⁴³ Did the University Proper, as Harper saw it, in fact too much resemble an ivory tower?

While extending its sphere of influence, the University did not ignore the printed word, which was at the very least a necessary adjunct of instruction by mail, instituted by Harper before he came to the University, and the Extension services established by Harper and his coadjutors. Indeed, Extension and the Press were paired in Harper's mind: "Like the University Extension, the University Press constitutes an organic division of the University."[44] When publication work was announced as one of the three great elements of University work in the *Official Bulletin, No. 1,* it might have been expected (and possibly it may have been planned) that a subsequent bulletin would be devoted to the Press.[45] The University Proper and University Extension were so publicized. In actuality, the Press came into being without the benefit (or embarrassment) of elaborate introductions, perhaps because Harper found it difficult (according to one director of the Press) to formulate plans for publication. In this case, Harper did think it dangerous to put too much on paper: "It is rather wiser to feel our way slowly and do even more than we promised rather than less."[46] Such restraint in the declaration of intentions was uncharacteristic of the administration of the University and set apart the early history of the Press.

That history was also distinctive because the Press was not originally a part of the University in law, however organic the relation of Press to University may have been in purpose. Before the University opened, it was proposed either by Harper or by the publisher of his journal that the Student Publishing Company should move its headquarters to Chicago and that Harper should place all publications, "so far as it is in his power," in the hands of that company.[47] Although this proposal came to nothing, the University did enter into an arrangement with another commercial publisher, D. C. Heath, of the Boston firm of that name.* According to the agreement with Heath, a stock company called the University of Chicago Press was organized and placed under his direction. Although the Press was legally independent of the University and of D. C. Heath and Company, its affairs actually touched the interests of both, to the eventual dissatisfaction of Harper and Heath, the one because the Press had come to a standstill in the summer of 1893, and the other because the firm bearing his name paid some of the debts of the Press and became implicated in the maintenance of its credit. Consequently the Press was given a fresh start in 1894 by a second agreement whereby the University acquired full ownership of the name of the Press and of its physical assets, the equipment consisting largely of

---

* The owner of the Student Publishing Company, C. A. Piddock, was decidedly offended by the failure of the University to use his services. To Harper he wrote: "You asked me to put my case in your hands and you would see that I came out all right." That language rings true to the key of Harper's relations with other men, as do Piddock's further words: "My love for you personally is in no wise affected . . . but I feel down deep very keenly that I have not been treated right in this matter" (C. A. Piddock to Harper, Sept. 27, 1892).

body type. Although the Press was thus incorporated into the University, it retained the marks of its early history as a business enterprise rather than as a strictly academic institution. Press assets were considered an investment of the University, and its transactions (even with other parts of the University) were accounted for in terms of profit and loss.

Serving under a succession of three directors to 1900, the Press was a harassed (and harassing) factotum. It was a purchasing agent for the University, a retail bookseller as well as a typesetting and job-printing shop, and a publisher of departmental journals, syllabi, and the very copious official matter of the University. It did not, however, publish books regularly. Arguing in 1895 for the publication by Macmillan of a series prepared by the Department of Political Economy, Laughlin, the head of the department, asserted that it was inconceivable that the publishing department at Chicago would soon become efficient. With perhaps unintended irony, Laughlin also pointed out that the materials he had in mind were such that both for the education of the country and for the good of the University they should reach as wide a constituency as possible—hence the need to bypass the Press. (As if to forestall any suggestion that Political Economy might aid in the development of the Press by giving it the series, Laughlin remarked, "I am quite ready to have some other department sacrifice for this purpose.")[48]

After the appointment in 1900 of a director, Newman Miller, who was deeply interested in book publication, and under the stimulus of subsidies for decennial volumes, the Press became more ambitious. Miller was a practical idealist. He believed that making the results of research available to students in general raised a question as serious as that of securing endowment for instruction; certainly raising money for buildings was vastly easier. In America, the output of learned institutions was published by commercial houses under uncertain and changing arrangements, and much that was commercially unprofitable remained unpublished. Miller faced the implications of that fact: "The responsibility for issuing publications [that cannot sustain themselves] . . . must always rest with the University itself, and the problem of the University Press will be that of distributing in the most economical way."[49] As director of the Press, Miller demonstrated that the economy he envisaged was far more than mere penny-pinching. In his view, the whole of publication work could be run in a businesslike way—an actual profit would have been embarrassing to a philanthropic corporation—if the total volume of publishing, including some subsidized items, was markedly increased. The premise of Miller's argument was the existence of a threshold over which the Press must pass to prosperity; and the corollary was enlargement of working capital. Harper's prescription was the endowment of university presses.[50]

Whether carried forward as missionary work or as a business enterprise, the effort to address the world outside of the Quadrangles, by the time of the decennial celebration, had given the University much practical experience. The larger constituency that was ever in Harper's mind was not wholly the stuff of aspiration. The University had appeared in Tonawanda, New York; in Constantine, Michigan; in Pueblo, Colorado; in Alhambra, California; and in more than two hundred and fifty other towns and cities; the mails did carry the words of University instructors; and the imprint of the Press was not a rarity. In its first decade, the Press published two hundred separate titles, including pamphlets but not official matter, and eleven journals, of which only two were discontinued.[51] The outward thrust of the University was both deliberate and continuous. Yet neither in the budget nor in the esteem of the Faculty did the work of Extension and the Press stand level with academic pursuits on campus. It is inconceivable that a proposal to strengthen the PH.D. offerings would have been questioned but very likely that some of Harper's colleagues were displeased to read in his decennial report that the possibilities of work toward the establishment of "Extension colleges" were without limit.[52] Plainly, indeterminate extension of the University had not become a common cause. Unlike Extension so-called, the Press did not constitute an alternative to—or as some Faculty members viewed Extension, the upstart rival of—academic work on campus; publication was the complement of research, literally its indispensable extension. Yet Harper did think to close his decennial report on the Press by admonishing the members of the University at large to cultivate a closer sympathy with its work.[53] Commitment of the Faculty to the sweeping program of Harper's ideal, and many-sided, university remained imperfect.

CHAPTER XII

The Presence
of the University

In 1903, the old *Life* published a cartoon in which Ye Rich Rockefeller University was depicted as a woman holding up a lamp resembling a soup tureen. It is labeled Standard Oil and gives forth a tiny flame of Knowledge.[1] Had the lamp-bearer borne the name Standard University upon her robes, which were covered with dollar-signs, the identification could easily have been taken as a play upon an old joke. In part because it was believed to be either Rockefeller's hobby or his incubus, the University received an immense amount of publicity in which derisive iconography became conventional. For Rockefeller's enemies, the laugh—often bitter—was on the University, or on Rockefeller for footing the bills. What the joking did not take into account was the intention of the institution to be not *the* university of Standard Oil but a *standard* university, dedicated to the elevation of higher education. The University indeed carried a standard in that cause. The act was not unique, for other institutions, from which the University took ideas and inspiration, had entered the field; but the University moved with striking ingenuity, adaptability, and aggressiveness. It might simply have offered superlatively good instruction to establish itself as a prime mover both among institutions and in the eyes of the public. By exercising its authority to grant (or to withhold) degrees, any university can demonstrate what it thinks scholarship to be without more ado: build a better mousetrap and the world will come to your door—but that was not the way of the University of Chicago. "It seems hardly necessary to call attention to the fact," Harper said in 1896, "that the work of the three great divisions of affiliation and co-operation, the extension and the press are virtually three phases of a single work. It is through these three channels that The University comes in contact with the outside world."[2] Harper could have said, more exactly, that through these channels the University put itself into contact with the world. From its opening the University was not only present in American education as a place of education and investigation; it was also a presence, a new but somehow ageless being actively at work in the land, to be watched sometimes with admiration and sometimes warily as if it might prove to be other than it seemed. One day, in 1893, a New Englander turned away from the Columbian Exposition to pay a call upon William Rainey Harper: "I have wanted for a long time to find out certain *facts* about the University which has started out in such a remarkable manner. Found Mr. Harper very courteous and ready to answer questions."[3]

AFFILIATION AND CO-OPERATION

Although University Extension went a perceptible and, in the opinion of some professors, a dangerously long distance beyond the limits of conventional academic work, Extension remained a vehicle of instruction. Affiliation was not designed to convey directly to human beings truth or intellectual power but rather to shape institutions and their policy. As a system of formal alliances between the University and other corporations, affiliation would convert an accumulation of separate institutions into a rationally organized and elevated structure. The program would disturb a regime of chartered but obsolete separatism and produce a new orderliness in education. In 1891, one of Harper's correspondents remarked: "Your plow-share cuts deep into the soil, and tears up many roots, and some old stumps . . .";[4] and eight months before the University opened, Harper himself wrote to Charles L. Hutchinson that a plan had been worked out ". . . which will, I think, be revolutionary in its work."[5]

The co-ordination of institutions was not new in the academic world. Frequently, complementary institutions, such as a college and a medical school, allied themselves, perhaps as parts of an at least nominal university. Rush Medical College, for example, was affiliated with the old University of Chicago before its dissolution. The new University was the product of an effort by a non-academic body, the Education Society, to provide for a group of schools and colleges. The plan for reorganizing collegiate education in the West, which Gates had outlined in 1889 while still leading the Society and described to Rockefeller as revolutionary, possessed a purpose similar to that of the plan for affiliation. In some states, a public board of regents had exercised a degree of control over the schools and colleges, which were thus tied to a common superior. Henry P. Tappan, an innovating president of the University of Michigan, had conceived at mid-century of a university as the elevated source of educational ideals and the arbiter of standards. Harper cited history when he said that ". . . so far as concerns educational work, important reforms proceed from the higher to the lower sphere of activity."[6] The distinctiveness of the program for affiliation did not lie in the novelty of the several parts but rather in the logic of their configuration. The proposition was that a private university should undertake to create by exercise of its power to make formal agreements something like an educational system answerable neither to a church nor the state but responsive to intrinsically academic imperatives, expressed in the standards of a university.

The machinery of the program consisted of a regulatory board like those instituted to control the house system, physical culture and athletics, and so forth; the office of director; and a set of agreements with other institutions.[7] According to the pattern announced in June, 1891, a secondary school might enter into either of two relationships with the University. An affiliated academy in the strictest sense of the term would resemble a department of the University, which would manage the academy jointly with a local board. A connected school, so designated, would be conducted by its local board "as an independent institution," except that the University would pass on appointments, conduct examinations, issue certificates and letters of dismissal, and publish the announcements of the academy together with similar announcements of the University.[8] The blank form designed to provide for affiliation of colleges read:

THE UNIVERSITY AGREES:—

1st. To offer its examinations at cost, in all subjects taught in the College.

2d. To confer upon the students of The College passing these examinations, the certificates and the degrees to which each student would be entitled if in the University [Senior] Colleges at Chicago.

3d. To grant diplomas and degrees conjointly with The College to such students as, pursuing a partial course in The College, complete the same in the Colleges of the University at Chicago. In virtue of this affiliation, the names of such students may be retained on the Catalogue of The College.

4th. To grant fellowships affording free tuition for one year in the graduate schools in the University, to three students annually who shall have earned the Bachelor's Degree....

5th. To grant free tuition for residence work in its graduate schools to all instructors in The College under regular salary from the same.

6th. To furnish The College for temporary service, at cost, teachers from among the University Fellows and special instructors and lecturers from its faculty.

7th. To furnish The College scientific apparatus and supplies at cost.

8th. To furnish books for the Library, students or Officers of The College at cost.

9th. To loan to the instructors of The College books and apparatus, where practicable, at net cost of transit and handling.

10th. To unite with The College in joint committee in nominating all instructors to fill vacancies in the faculty of said College.

11th. To unite with The College in joint committee in suggesting termination of service of such instructors in said College as may prove unsatisfactory.

12th. To elect the President of The College to membership in the University Council.

13th. To give preference, when engaging instructors for special service in the University, to approved instructors in The College, and to announce such instructors in the University Catalogue for the year or years in which such service is rendered. Such instructors shall thereafter be honorary members of the University faculty.

THE COLLEGE AGREES:—

1st. To employ only the University Examinations in all subjects taught in The College.

2d. To adopt so far as may be practicable the courses of study, and the general regulations of the Colleges of the University of Chicago.

3d. To elect only such instructors during the period of this affiliation as shall have been nominated by The College in joint committee with the University.

4th. To terminate the service of such instructors as shall have been suggested by the University and College in joint committee as unsatisfactory.[9]

In part, the program of affiliation was designed, in the immediate, practical self-interest of the University, to assure it a flow of able students:

In seeking to co-operate with colleges, high schools, and academies [Harper said in 1891], The University confesses frankly its desire so to affect the work of these institutions as to secure more thoroughly prepared students for college and university work. This ... may be called selfish, but The University realizes that the entire success of its future turns upon its ability to attain this end, for whatever may be the advantages for research and investigation offered in The University, the results of such research and investigation will be nothing or next to nothing, if the students who undertake it, have not been trained in a most careful and conscientious manner.[10]

Albion W. Small, who directed the program, also understood that "the selfish motive" was present in the interest that the University had in affiliation.[11] The unselfish motive of the University, Small wrote, was ". . . the desire to be an important factor in lifting the standard of collegiate instruction, and as a necessary preliminary to that [the standard] of academic instruction." The University, Small thought, could have pursued the even tenor of its ways and never troubled itself about the failures of other parts of the educational machinery; but that was not the spirit of the founders: "Its mission is to help make every educational institution within the circuit of its possible influence stronger, and more efficient than it could be without the co-operation of a great central educational clearing house."[12]

Supporters of affiliation might disagree as to whether the improvement of education was the *sine qua non* of success for the University itself. Whether affiliation was a necessity or not, the program, like the institution of the summer quarter, was an attack upon waste in education. Revulsion against disorder in education and the cognate emotion of admiration for devices calculated to make education more efficient were characteristic of Harper's reaction to his world. It is arguable that his commitment to affiliation owed less of its strength to conviction based upon reasoned inquiry into the state of education than to abhorrence of what seemed an obvious vacuum. "With our thousands of educational institutions," Harper said in 1893, "there is at present no trace of system and order."[13] Later he would say, ". . . there is no element in all our western civilization more conspicuous than the slovenliness which characterizes the earlier educational work. . . ."[14] Harper had already said that the time had come for the universities, as such, to take a hand in the whole question of secondary education: "The responsibility was no longer to be avoided."[15] Education was in disarray, therefore the University must attempt to organize it; such appears to have been the essential movement of Harper's thinking—or intuition.

In the West especially, academies and colleges had multiplied, subject to little restraint. In England the power to grant degrees was jealously watched by the ancient universities and sparingly dispensed by Parliament. Oxford and Cambridge possessed a monopoly of the power until the nineteenth century and then retained their hegemony. Only a few universities (including those later called Redbrick) were chartered, after presenting credentials for close examination. In America, by bestowing charters generously, the legislatures of the sovereign states had created an academic freedom of a peculiarly American kind, the prescriptive right of almost any respectable group to attempt the founding of a degree-granting institution. The University itself had been chartered, with the broadest of powers, under the terms of a general incorporation law. In 1890, the United States Commissioner of Education reported the existence of 597 institutions of college or university grade.[16] The spread of higher education, geographically and to some extent between social classes, was made easy, but the authority to maintain standards was dissipated. Viewing that scene and the lower schools as well in July, 1892, while Harper was organizing the University of Chicago, Charles W. Eliot argued that a "desirable uniformity" would be introduced into education if some national body—he did not say a single university—sanctioned an effort by experts in each subject of instruction to co-ordinate school and college programs.[17] In the pursuit of order, Eliot's chosen vehicle was the Committee of Ten which the National Education Association immediately created, with Eliot as chairman, to undertake precisely the work he described; Harper opted to commit the University in his charge to an independent campaign, sanctioned by the University in its own name.

Wherever the University spirit might work the ordering and elevation of education, there Harper would propose affiliation. The University would avail itself of the latitude of the law to offset the thrust toward laissez faire that the same quality of the law had authorized. At any given moment, the composition of the University in its largest aspect would be determined by the number and variety of the institutions over which the University Proper, at that moment, was exerting influence through affiliation: the extended University would be an indefinitely expansible flux of academic enterprises. In describing the University in 1895, Robert Herrick spoke of "this complex organism" as if it were a living creature of unfamiliar morphology. Of all parts of the University, affiliation was, Herrick said, perhaps the most tentative and yet imaginatively the most fascinating.[18] When the University had been open less than a year, Harper stated that no feature of the organization of the University contained greater possibilities than affiliation; but he declined to pass judgment upon its initial results: "More time is needed. . . ."[19] In retrospect, it appears that Harper had glimpsed the outlines of a new dispensation in higher education but hesitated to discuss affiliation, at least publicly, as anything more than an experiment. In Small's opinion, the affiliation policy of the University was the beginning of a larger movement:

. . . of a co-ordinating process which will in time take in every University and college in the country, in a perfectly adjusted federation; each member independent within its own sphere, but each getting the benefits of a carefully calculated reciprocity with the others. In order to bring this about there must be on the part of some University a demonstration of its economy and consequent desirability. We have undertaken to make this demonstration.[20]

Perhaps inevitably, affiliation inspired a number of variations on the theme of academic imperialism. One writer, who was friendly to the University, spoke facetiously of Harper taking a trip around the world to organize the alumni of the University: "... as a side issue he was to affiliate the universities of Europe, Asia, and Africa, and reorganize them in accordance with our general plan for secondary schools."[21] The *Chicago Tribune* referred—in 1899—to the "expansionist powers of President Harper."[22] Harper himself was aware that "... the word 'affiliation,' borrowed from English educational terminology, has not come to be popular. In the minds of many the act of affiliating an institution is equivalent to absorbing the institution and taking away its independent existence."[23] Small spoke of a fear that in affiliation there was "... something covered up, some trap in which the college is to be caught."[24] The observation was realistic: in 1891, the president of Des Moines College, which was considering affiliation, reported that the trustees feared that affiliation would give the impression that the College "... is no longer an institution under the auspices of the Baptists of Iowa, but it is a Chicago school, run for the benefit of the University there." Some of the trustees of the college opposed affiliation, saying its terms implied—and announced to the world—that Harper (or the University) did not have confidence in their ability and did not trust them. The president added: "They resent that."[25]

Affiliation was supposed to hold promise for the schools and colleges—specifically as a channel of wealth. "If the school," a letter to Harper runs, "were to be put into exact harmony with the University as to method and purpose, and to use its influence to send its students to the University under conditions agreed upon, would it be worthwhile to the University to guarantee a certain financial backing?"[26] And the president of Des Moines College to Harper: "Of course I understand that you have no money you can pledge personally to our college, but you and Mr. Gates can get it when it is necessary. Your hearty co-operation is what I want promised."[27]

Robert Herrick remarked that affiliation contemplated "a college trust."[28] In light of the conspicuous connection between Standard Oil and the University at one remove, the phrase is striking and may have been provocative at the time it was written; but it was more impressionistic than precisely descriptive. Rockefeller offered the University no money to enable it to help other institutions financially or, in any sense, to buy into them. He was indeed consistently wary of the affiliation program, which he viewed, insofar as money was involved, as a potential drain upon resources needed in the Quadrangles. When in 1894 Harper (apparently) interceded on behalf of three institutions regarding funds "for purposes of affiliation," Gates wrote Harper: "I have had an interview with Mr. Rockefeller on the subject and he instructs me to say that he cannot make the contributions for this purpose, which you desire. Of course, Mr. Rockefeller regrets that he must disappoint you in this matter."[29] Although conceivably Harper may still have dreamed of the educational trust of which he had spoken before the Education Society had decided to campaign simply for a college in Chicago, he lacked a financial fulcrum for his lever. What the University could actually offer prospective affiliates were academic privileges and advantages of only marginal cash value. Small explained where the larger gain to the colleges was to be found:

During the last twenty years . . . there has been a relative decline in the reputation of the institutions that confine themselves to strictly collegiate work, especially if these are country colleges. Even among educators themselves there has developed a tendency to depreciate the colleges, and to glorify the universities, as though the universities could exist without the colleges as a foundation. Irrational as the sentiment is, it is a fact that there is today no country college which has relatively the repute of Williams, or Union, or Bowdoin in their best days. Many of these colleges [are] doing better work than they ever did before, and this work may be superior in important respects to that done for and by the average student in the great city institutions, yet the prestige of the latter is so imposing that the majority of patrons, and of persons before whom college graduates have to pass muster when competing for employment, take it for granted that the education received in the country college is inferior. Affiliation is a plan to secure revision of this judgment, and to retain to the country colleges the reputation which their work warrants. . . .[30]

To the institutions which Harper designated as "so-called colleges," without sufficient endowment to support the last two years of college work, the University offered the suggestion that they should limit themselves to a two-year curriculum—become junior colleges. Harper added that these colleges were defrauding their students.[31] Edward Capps, speaking as dean of the Junior Colleges of the University, argued that it was manifestly to the advantage of the weaker colleges and the stronger universities

. . . to emphasize more distinctly the essential difference in cost and in quality between the two portions of the usual college curriculum; for the latter to aid and encourage the former in that part of the collegiate work which they are prepared to do well, and for the former to recognize the superiority of the latter in the more strictly university work.[32]

The case was logical; but what (precisely) the colleges feared, as Harper said on occasion, was that the step into affiliation would be followed by a second, the removal of the last years of work and withdrawal of the privilege to confer degrees.[33] The University could not, however, push a reluctant college even into the first step. Herrick might have written that of all the parts of the University, affiliation was the most fascinating and yet necessarily the most tentative.

Ten years after the University opened, it was connected by affiliation with nine academies. Originally, Harper had planned for collegiate work on the supposition that in some large part the student body would be recruited from schools under control of the University through affiliation or direct ownership. The *Official Bulletin, No. 3,* of June, 1891, stated that as an important feature of its work, the University would conduct academies—in the plural. The public high school had not been dealt with; but in fact it provided large battalions of students. When the doors were first opened to students, the *University Record* later reported, the University and the schools of its region, "its natural constituency," were practically strangers to one another.[34] In the nature of things, the director of affiliation remarked, the public high school could not be subject to the close educational supervision possible with private schools.[35] The University would have rejoiced exceedingly (in the language of one letter) if it had been able to establish allied preparatory schools—"and that may be a plan for the future."[36] In the present, the University turned toward the public high school. The dean of the Junior Colleges pointed the moral: "The absence in the West of large preparatory schools . . . makes it absolutely essential that western institutions of higher education should adapt themselves to the public secondary schools."[37]

Very shortly after opening in November, 1892, the University initiated what was to become a series of annual or semi-annual conferences on matters of common interest to the University and the secondary schools. The University acknowledged that ". . . it could not decide all questions which arose in connection with secondary education purely for its own point of view, but must confer freely and on equal footing with the leaders and teachers in the schools from which its junior students must come."[38] (The word *must* was realistic and perhaps somewhat wistful as well.) In free conference, affiliation in its original form was quickly brought into question. In December, 1892, a speaker, Clarke B. Williams, professor of mathematics at Kalamazoo College, argued that the first and most important way in which the University might make its influence felt in the schools and upon their students was "by doing good work itself and by turning out genuine students and furnishing men who can be successful teachers." The University should not direct the work of the schools: "The University has its work, the preparatory school its work. Neither should encroach on the ground of the other. Neither institution has the right to dictate the work of the other."[39] Williams did not argue that the University should never be represented in the schools; on the contrary, he believed that the University could do much to meet a danger of degeneration in secondary-school teaching by sending professors to visit the schools and to talk to the pupils. In fact, as it gained experience, the University directed much of its effort in behalf of secondary education toward the training of teachers and the visitation of schools. A relationship called co-operation, which entailed visiting, was the practical expression of a common interest. Under the terms of co-operation, the principal of the high school and the teachers whose instruction was approved were entitled to certify a student's work toward fulfilment of the University requirements for admission; examination over such certified work was waived.[40] Thus, without giving up control of its curriculum and teaching, the school gained recognition of its merit; the University could be assured that its incoming students were well prepared; and the student, who suffered most immediately from disorder in education, was spared the pain of stumbling on the step between school and college. In 1902, the number of co-operating schools, including no more than a dozen private schools, was 129.

In that year, six institutions of higher education were affiliated with the University. Four were liberal arts colleges, Des Moines College, Kalamazoo College, John B. Stetson University, and Butler College; one, Bradley, was a polytechnic institute offering two years of college work; and one was Rush Medical College. The fact that three of the colleges, Des Moines, Kalamazoo, and Stetson, had Baptist ties raises the question whether the program would have gained any perceptible momentum among the colleges if the Baptist associations of the University had not prepared the way. Yet in his decennial report Harper stated that "enough . . . has been done to prove beyond question that something of the kind proposed is possible and most desirable." He did not specify what he meant by "something of the kind" and added that no considerable effort had been made to increase the number of affiliated institutions, partly because machinery had not been perfected and partly because ". . . it was thought wise to move very slowly in a matter of so much consequence."[41] A favorite idea had again been indorsed; but was the program indeed practicable? Speaking as dean of the Graduate School of Arts and Literature, Small would presently pass judgment that in the case of the colleges where the plan had been enforced, its operation had been sufficiently successful to justify the relationship. "It is hoped," Small said, "that provision may be made for extending it to other colleges." He also intimated, however, that affiliation as it was had not solved "the problem of conditions of graduate work";[42] too many students in the colleges had not been taught to see that there was a horizon entirely beyond their experience. That affiliation might be as beneficial in practice, to both the colleges and the University, as it was in theory a greater amount of time had to be devoted to the exchange between institutions than the University had been able to give.[43] Years earlier Harper had told Gates: "I find that personal contact with these institutions [the collegiate affiliates] accomplishes a great deal. If I could only stay in the field all the time, I believe that results would be magnificent."[44] In brief, the task was too big. Had the University entered more deeply into the affairs of the affiliates, it might have become seriously embarrassed. In two of them, rebellion against the president occurred. Explaining why he did not intervene in one instance, Harper said, ". . . I did not wish to have the University of Chicago mixed up in a quarrel."[45] Small bluntly described the situation of the University: "We can't publish to the world what we know about our experience with College affiliation so far. The Colleges whose association with us would help us, don't want affiliation, and we can't afford to carry the burden of any more Colleges that are dead weight."[46]

Small was a friendly if rueful critic. "I have no desire," he once wrote Harper, "to encourage pretentiousness on the part of schools that have neither past, present nor future, but we are on the wrong track until we properly recognize the real and potential merits of smaller schools. . . . The need of making our own faculty see these things constantly looms up more than ever."[47] The other side of the question was put by William G. Hale, head of the Latin department, when he said privately to a Trustee—apropos of the affiliation of an institution Hale thought to be quite without standing: "I am not quotable, but I wish there were a majority among the Trustees who . . . preferred to see this University concentrate its strength upon itself."[48] Harper observed that more opposition had arisen from the Faculty and students of the University than from the colleges.[49] The *Weekly* in 1898 objected to the creation of "pseudo-alumni" by the awarding of University degrees, as the program allowed, to graduates of the Colleges after a quarter of study in the Quadrangles: the plan was unjust to the regular University student, would lessen the value of the degree "from our Alma Mater" in the eyes of everyone, and was designed to increase the graduate school at the expense of the undergraduate department.[50] The affiliation program did not prevent the undergraduate department from growing—if that is what the writer meant to imply—but it did offer at least a potential threat to that *esprit de corps* which the University sought to cultivate. Looking back over the first decade of the Senior College, the dean, James H. Tufts, observed:

If a sentiment of solidarity and a fairly consistent standard of method and efficiency are to be maintained, it is certainly desirable that our Bachelor's degree should not signify, for the most part, that only a portion, and perhaps a very small portion, of the work has been performed in the University. It would practically transform the University, so far as its undergraduate work is concerned, from an institution which gives a course of training and cultivation, to an institution which estimates the work of various smaller institutions and confers degrees.[51]

The University of Chicago could not be made to resemble both a family and the University of London. Had the University shifted the instruction of Junior College students to the colleges and had they been content to offer a two-year curriculum—in short, if the original plan of the University had been carried into effect—affiliation would have been the complement of a strictly university program in the Quadrangles. But success in affiliation was incompatible with fulfilment of the purposes which emerged as the program of the University actually developed.

The affiliation of Rush Medical College stands apart. That controversial action was patently the result of circumstances and intentions, on both sides, that the general program had not been designed to cover. The origin of the Rush affiliation was awareness of a situation offering a specific opportunity. Dr. Ingals talked, and Harper's imagination was fired: stimulus and response. In the early nineties, Harper had been moved by general observation of higher education to devise the program of affiliation; in later years, other experiences inspired him to organize more particular enterprises. By 1902, collegiate affiliation as a formal program had receded so far into the background of University life that the affiliated colleges were not listed in the decenial report; but the impulse to bring institutions together remained. In his portion of the decennial report, Harper suggested a conference between the University and the colleges of the West and South, to discuss the problems of the college in its relationship to the university "from the point of view of both college and university."[52] The proposal may have had its specific stimulus. In 1901, Small had toured the far West and the South, and Shailer Mathews, professor of New Testament history, also toured the South, as representatives of the University. Their reports had an unmistakable point. "I am simply overpowered," Small wrote from San Antonio, "at the sight of the undeveloped possibilities of every sort here."[53] And Mathews wrote Harper:

It is almost pathetic to see how the men in the faculties of these [southern] colleges want private talks with me. . . . The men are full of unrest, are open to conviction, but have no one who can put them in the track. I never was so convinced of the importance of the position we hold, for man after man has thanked me for helping him to surer ground. And it is simply that I have done the thing we are doing in the classroom. Of course with the students it is not possible to talk except very guardedly, but they will sit with you, ask private consultations, and for all the world act as if you were a deliverer. . . . At Athens [Georgia] last night a group of the faculty waited for half an hour in a similar way. You understand it is not I they are interested in, but in a Christianity that asks no odds and claims to be honest in its investigations. But I never felt the need of our work as much. . . .[54]

No more potent appeal could have been made to Harper. What he thought of was such a conference as had succeeded among the schools, not such affiliation as only a few colleges had tried. Somewhat earlier, Harper had predicted what the future would be, as the colleges and universities conferred:

It is only within a few years that there has been any co-operation worth mentioning among colleges and universities, and the co-operation which has so far been inaugurated is of an exceedingly superficial character. Enough of it has been worked out, however, to make those who have tasted it desire still more, and the few steps already taken are but precursors of many that are to follow.

It is not enough that there should be associations in which, once a year, the representatives of certain institutions may come together for the reading of papers and the passing of resolutions. With better classification of educational work, with the greater similarity of standards for admission and for graduation, and with the variety of type secured, so that individual institutions will have individual responsibilities, there will be found a basis for co-operation such as has not hitherto existed. This association will be similar to that which men in all divisions of the business world have found necessary and helpful. Such relationship will serve as a protection for all who thus stand together, against misunderstanding and ignorance. It will secure results which no institution of its own strength could secure.[55]

Harper thought that rivalry between institutions would continue, but without petty jealousies. There was humility, learned from experience, in his suggestion that no university was strong enough to perfect the higher teaching by itself.

PUBLIC OPINION

"Already the institution has become very extensively known." Gates made this comment in May, 1892, while attempting to dissuade Harper from arranging a formal public opening of the University.[56] Gates's advice prevailed over Harper's original intention, and the opening ceremony on October 1, 1892, resembled a family service. After classes had met in the morning as if but another year were beginning, the members of the University and some friends met in Cobb Hall. The Doxology was sung, Harper led the assembly in the Lord's Prayer, and after other expressions of religious feeling, the service ended. A notice or two was given, but no one made an address. The simplicity of the occasion suited Harper's prepossession with work (and that of the University), but privacy was untypical of University life. To the chagrin of University officers, even the classrooms were invaded by the press, for it was the practice of newspapers to buy stories of students who doubled as reporters. In public, Harper said:

The eagerness of the daily press not only in Chicago but in all the larger cities of the country, to publish items, both true and false, concerning The University, indicates, it must be inferred, an attitude of interest on the part of the public at large. It is greatly to be regretted that the information thus promulgated is, in so many instances, without foundation; for even when denial is made of this or that statement, its publication is by no means as broad as was the publication of the statement itself.[57]

Privately, Harper fumed over some of the publicity that the newspapers gave to the affairs of the University: "N.B. I wish very much that there could be enacted a law in the state of Illinois, inflicting the death penalty upon irresponsible reporters for the miserable way in which they misrepresent the truth. I some times get weary of life in seeing how they twist the simplest matters."[58] And to Marion Talbot: "We are helpless in the hands of the press, and I do not know what can be done."[59] (Toward the end of the Harper administration, the University appointed a press officer; apparently it had not previously thought to provide the papers with any regular source of news.)[60] Sensationalism had its effect. It was presumably after reading his newspaper that an anonymous correspondent wrote Harper in 1901: "If rewards were offered for the most stupendous fools on the face of the Earth, they would be sought & found among the Professors of the 'University of Chicago,' commencing with that dutch fool, Von Holtz [*sic*], including Triggs & Starr."[61] Frederic Starr, an anthropologist with a lively mind and a striking personality, had said something that

223

came out in the headlines as: AMERICANS ALL TO BE RED MEN.[62] Von Holst had perhaps offended by being articulately anti-imperialist; Oscar Triggs, an instructor in the English department, was frequently a source of remarks that were bizarre or became so in the retelling. (When, somewhat later, the iconoclastic judgment that Longfellow's poetry was drivel and stuff was attributed to Triggs, he explained to Harper that he had spoken of Longfellow as a minor poet—"which he is from my point of view.")[63] The University was sufficiently stung by sensational stories to deny that the Faculty contained men who said or did things for the sake of a sensational result; the men against whom the charges had been made were removed the farthest possible distance, Harper said, from any such desire for notoriety.[64] Nor (obviously) was it desired by the University, although it could not dispense with some such service as the general magazines and newspapers provided. Had the University been content to remain a Baptist college, coverage of its affairs by the Baptist *Standard* would presumably have served to keep a circumscribed community of supporters in touch with its modest needs. As a University in the making, the institution required a constituency which had only begun to take shape on opening day and could be augmented only if the public paid attention to life in the Quadrangles. The alumni of the old University of Chicago were, at most, a constituency at one remove, and of course a body of its own alumni belonged to the future. (In 1900, a general alumni association was formed to combine four associations previously organized for collegiate, divinity, law alumni, and PH.D's.)[65] Although as a private institution the University was not dependent upon the People, it could not grow, because it was private, unless a number of persons turned to the University either as students or donors. Notoriety smarted; obscurity would have meant malnutrition.*

---

* The gratification which the press could afford Harper personally appears in the correspondence between Harper and James Keeley, managing editor of the *Chicago Tribune*:

"I do not know whether I ought to trouble you with a letter like the following or not. I certainly should not have done so if it had not been for your uniform kindness toward me as manifested in so many ways. The point I have in mind and at heart is the following:

"When I left my work in New Haven to come to Chicago I was laying greatest emphasis on the scholarly side. Up to that time I had given myself very largely to scholarly work. On coming to Chicago I had to turn aside for the next ten or twelve years to secure money for the University and in doing this I was compelled to throw myself into that side of the work. The consequence is that Chicago and the North West think of me as a 'money-getter' and that is the reputation I have everywhere—a reputation which is hardly fair in view of my antipathy for this kind of work and my love for the other.

"I have had a measure of success also in the scholarly work. I am taking the liberty of sending you a copy of the Commentary on Amos and Hosea. I do not think you will be personally inter-

Like Chicago among cities and the United States among nations, among academic institutions the University seemed a blatant *arriviste,* particularly—in the eyes of Harper's critics—as it was personified in its President. Because it could live down a reputation for bad taste and impropriety if its work was sound, the critical question was not whether it was charged with sensationalism from time to time but whether it could, through the years, retain public confidence in its capacities and so have opportunity to do such work.

In his letter arguing against a formal public opening, Gates observed that public expectation had been carried by the press to a very high point: "May there not be danger that your speakers [at a public opening] will vie with each other in the exuberance of oratory to magnify the greatness of the institution, and thus involve you in the risk of disappointing public expectation."[66] The University ran that risk for years after the publication of the *Official Bulletins.* Observers of the University were inclined to see no limit to its possibilities. In July, 1891, before Ernest D. Burton came to the University, he wrote Harper, ". . . nothing respecting the Chicago University can now surprise me except that there should be no new surprise."[67] In 1897, a sometime member of the Faculty was quoted in the *Chicago Tribune* as saying: "All sorts of ideas are experimented with at the University. They have gone into everything."[68] And well past the mid-point of the Harper administration, Hugo Münsterberg, professor of psychology at Harvard, wrote in *The Americans:* "The University of Chicago has everything and offers everything . . . and, whatever it lacks today,

---

ested in this, but I should like to have you look at it carefully. This book represents more hours of work than I have spent altogether in the administrative work of University of Chicago in fourteen years. In other words, I have given more time to the writing of this book than to the raising of money for the University and its organization. The volume has been received very favorably in England, Scotland and the Continent. The reviews in this country have been throughout favorable but it is a volume which the daily papers do not care to review and it is so technical in its character that the friends of the University do not even know of its existence" (Harper to Keeley, Oct. 23, 1905).

Keeley replied: "Your letter did not bore me. It interested me intensely. Whatever I can do to dispel the erroneous estimate which so many people must have of what constitutes your life work, I shall be more than pleased to do, and I think I can do it in a manner that will be effective.

"In a few days I expect to print on the editorial page a review of your commentary on Hosea and Amos and I intend to use that as the vehicle for 'lifting the veil.' Rest assured that the whole thing will be done *con amore*" (Keeley to Harper, Oct. 25, 1905).

To which Harper responded: "I had no idea that you would take up the matter of my last letter in so tangible a way. I cannot tell you how grateful I am to you for the appreciation you show of my work and the sympathy with which you have met me on so many occasions. . . .

"I can assure you that your willingness to help me throw off the danger of being known only as a 'beggar' is more fully appreciated than I can here tell you" (Harper to Keeley, Oct. 27, 1905).

225

it is bound to have tomorrow."[69] (Münsterberg added that possibly the University was still not equal to the older eastern universities as the home of quiet maturity and reflection, but for hard, scholarly work it had few rivals in the world.) As it was communicated to the public, such enthusiasm presumably secured the University the attention that it needed; but it may be asked—as Gates was asking in 1892—whether there was not a point where it would become dangerous for the University to arouse further hopes or to provide occasion for greater excitement. It was one thing for the University to be known for looking forward, another for it to be expected to accomplish everything at once. Gates set only the barest terms of the issue in his letter of 1892: "The intentions of the institution are well known. Its achievements . . . are still in the future."[70] He patently feared an inflation of publicity.

The issue had a corollary. In logic, the University could have decided to let its achievements speak for themselves. The public could discover on its own whether the work of the University came up to expectations: let the University simply get on with it. The idea was not wholly unthinkable at the time: apropos of a proposal to give official notice to each paper written by Faculty members, Von Holst once said, "It seems to me much more important, that all the departments be as quickly as possible put into a position to do the work undertaken by the University in a thoroughly satisfactory manner, than to have everything it does and that concerns it published—down to the minutest detail."[71] Von Holst conceded that nine out of ten institutions, styling themselves universities, might make quite a respectable show with the departmental equipment available at the University; but he argued ". . . it is so out of proportion to the standard which the University of Chicago has proclaimed to be that adopted by it, that a candid statement would, in the eyes of every person at all able to judge, amount to the humiliating confession: We are thus far unable to make good the promises we have made to the public. . . ."[72] (The proclamation of high standards would appear itself to have been an appeal to the public, the response of which helped the University to acquire such equipment as it had.)

In fact, the University did labor actively in the field that is now called public relations. True, Harper reported accurately on his own premises when he declared in his decennial statement that the University had not sought the prominence that it had: from the beginning, the University had not had, as Harper thought many people believed, a Bureau of Publicity "conducted at great expense for the purpose of advertising the institution."[73] But the University did regularly address the public in its own name and not simply through the lectures and writings of its Faculty members. In his quarterly statement for the spring of 1896, when the *University Record* had just begun publication, Harper indicated that the *Record* was intended to supply the Trustees, the Faculty members, the students, "and particularly the friends of The University at a distance," with a correct statement concerning everything of importance which transpired at the University. He added that many more subscriptions would be needed to insure continued publication.[74] That word-of-mouth advertisement was presumably directed toward persons who were already friends of the University. Other passages in Harper's quarterly statements—his descriptions of material needs—were obviously meant for everyone within earshot or within reach of the press. The Convocation exercises were themselves conspicuous: since the exercises were often held downtown, the University itself and not only its several members moved toward the public. Harper explained:

Experience has shown that it [the convocation] is also a most desirable educational agency, inasmuch as in a community as large as that of Chicago, it is necessary for the University to contribute something to the general life of the city, in order that the city may continue to be conscious of the existence of the University. It is not sufficient to have the University's existence kept in evidence merely by athletic contests and student wranglings, the two subjects which the modern newspaper seems particularly interested in presenting to its readers.[75]

There was pageantry each season and for Harper the opportunity to discuss the University before the community at large as he did, less formally, before the Seniors. "I have spoken to you freely and frankly," Harper said at one Convocation. "It has been the policy of the University from the beginning to conceal nothing from its friends—the public."[76] If to conceal nothing means to reveal everything, the words do not convey the exact truth; for the University kept some matters back from public view—for example, the fact that the tension created by disagreement over academic and financial affairs was sometimes extremely acute. Perhaps only a naïve auditor would have supposed that Harper meant his words to be taken literally. That the University was not invariably candid is suggested by evidence that Harper took pains, perhaps not quite to pad the enrolment figures—as was suspected—but to inquire, on one occasion, whether graduate students from small colleges, having attended the University for a year, might like to take a Bachelor's degree, or, on another occasion, whether a Fellow away from campus might be counted against a net loss in enrolment.[77] But the sum of information possibly offered disingenuously is small indeed when compared with the total mass of information issued by the University.

The climax of Harper's efforts as a spokesman was his decennial report, in which he said again that the University had from the beginning adopted the policy of making its affairs known to the public. The University had not done so with the desire to advertise itself: a charge to that effect, Harper remarked, had been made by those who were perhaps disturbed by the rapidity of the growth of the University:

Our feeling has been that the institution is a public institution and that everything relating to its inside history, including its financial condition, should be made known. Its deficits have been published as well as its surpluses, and we attribute largely to this policy of public statement, not only the interest of the public, but the confidence which has been shown on so many occasions. It is generally understood that everything relating to the internal history will be made known within a proper time; in other words, the books of the University, both financial and educational, the minutes of its Faculties, and even the record-book of the President are open to all. *Nothing is concealed*. Even that which at the first sight would seem to be disadvantageous is made known. The amount and character of its investments are published annually. Perhaps no other institution has shown a greater readiness to allow its internal affairs to be known and criticized.[78]

Yet was not the report itself a kind of advertising? The University did seek to draw attention to, and thus to advertise, itself; but it need not be supposed that Harper was speaking as a purist. In an editorial on the "portly volume," the *Nation* stated that Harper was supplying matter for much debate, ". . . for he has conducted fearlessly a vast experimental laboratory of education."[79] Perhaps Harper had intended to offer a laboratory report—to the world of education and also to patrons whose continued support of the laboratory was necessary to further investigation. The *Nation's* chief (and accurate) criticism of the report was its paucity of general ideas: Harper could have answered (with equal accuracy) that the subject of the report was specific work in progress. For Harper part of the work was to make its results known; and to him—it may be supposed—such work was not advertising.

Harper's report is almost 150 pages long. It was published with 574 supplementary pages of text, statistical tables, and financial summaries—reports by the deans and other officers, and a historical sketch. A separate volume was devoted to a bibliography of books and papers written by members of the Faculty. Harper's report was in part a critique of how a university comes into being, in part a prescription for the future, and in part an appeal to the public. Harper was fully aware that the period under review was short: "In these modern times ten years count for as much as one hundred years did formerly." The remark was a truism, but it possessed important implications, as did many of Harper's sententious remarks.

It is worth the while of those engaged in any important undertaking, educational or otherwise, to sum up the results of the work accomplished in ten years, to consider the policies which have prevailed, and to decide whether, in view of all the facts, these policies have been correct and have secured the results desired. Moreover, it is to be remembered that many policies, at least those of minor importance, may wisely be changed from time to time even under the same administration. . . . It has been customary in educational administration to wait for the change of administration before introducing or adopting new policies. This is a mistake.[80]

Directing his attention in turn to the roles of the Trustees, the Faculty, the public, the students, the alumni, and the Founder; to the parts and programs of the University; to its social and religious life; and to its most important experiments, Harper covered the items of what today would be called a development program. After reviewing each group or activity within the University, Harper made "suggestions," calling for changes in practice and often for money: larger endowment for salaries; more halls for the residence of students; endowment of from $500,000 to $1,000,000 for Extension lecturing; the erection of the buildings and the endowment of the work in five hospitals at a cost of $1,000,000 each; the expenditure of $6,000 or $7,000 a year for University College; establishment of a well-equipped museum of commerce and of chairs of Russian and Chinese studies in the College of Commerce and Administration (there was no more important field lying open before the college student "than work in these great empires"); a larger number of scholarships for undergraduates; increases in the sum given for fellowships; a central library building; an endowment of $500,000, or even $1,000,000, for the purchase of books; laboratories for geology, physical chemistry, anatomy and pharmacology, and hygiene; expansion of instruction in Morgan Park Academy; a building for commuting students; clubhouses for men and women; a student hospital; and a chapel—to be the most beautiful ecclesiastical structure in the Mississippi Valley. At the close of the report, Harper did not claim that the University was or would be *the* great university: "The institution promises to become a university, and not simply a large college."[81]

The issuance of decennial reports fitted into a scheme of decennial publication, which ultimately yielded twenty-six volumes of papers and monographs; and it was but one aspect of the decennial celebration.* It was a Convocation writ large: the public was offered a view both of the work of the University and of academic ceremony. A feature of the celebration was the laying of a number of cornerstones: when in doubt, George E. Vincent said, lay a cornerstone.[82] On June 15, 1901, an academic procession, led by a band, marched to the site of the Press building, and then to the site of Charles Hitchcock Hall; resuming three days later, the procession moved on to the sites of Hutchinson Commons, Mitchell Tower, the Reynolds Club, and Leon Mandel Hall. At each stopping point, words of affirmation: not money, but truth; the unfolding promise of the best manhood of this great city; a new covenant between the men of business and the men of scholarship in Chicago; co-operation between progress and reverence; now and forever, to tolerance and truth; the higher uses of the soul; the growing unity of the University; the unity of our University life; the unity of this many-sided republic.[83] Such were the sentiments of a golden moment which Harper called the end of a beginning.[84]

THE UNIVERSITY OBSERVED

A visit to the University in 1895, from a newspaper story by an irreverent reporter:

An hour's ride southward from the center of the city in the old, blue-bottomed Wabash Avenue cable cars, a few blocks eastward on Twenty-Second Street, with a passing glimpse of Michigan avenue, then a sharp turn and thirty-six blocks of Cottage Grove Avenue, with its panorama of gayly-colored theater posters, meat markets decorated with yellow hams, cigar shops with fly-specked windows and dark blue curtains, followed by the fresh green vistas of Washington Park, and at last the University of Chicago is in sight.

If the journey has been made on a Jackson Park car there is a turning at Fifty-Fifth Street, and soon the conductor, who begins to look about for university passengers as he nears Ellis Avenue, gives a warning look, and the traveler knows it is time to get off. The first landmark encountered is the red brick Home for Incurables, the university ball grounds, inclosed by a high board fence, occupying the next block, and then the university proper is reached.

There are advantages in making the trip on an Oakwoods car, which continues straight down Cottage Grove Avenue, with a "jumping off place" for students at Fifty-Eighth Street into a region which very much resembles a cemetery, so well

---

* There was an egregious mistake of omission in one of the decennial volumes, *The General Register of Officers and Alumni, 1892–1902,* as originally published. The name of Frederick T. Gates was omitted from the list of Trustees. "I hope," he wrote Harper, "this is not my punishment for so diligently restraining people from contributing to the institution." Goodspeed's accurate comment was: "This is pretty bad" (Gates to Harper, Oct. 14, 1903).

covered is it with white board signs erected by hopeful real estate agents before The Fair. By approaching the University from this direction exactly 300 steps are saved, at least this is the result of careful calculations made by students who have tried both routes, and it is probably correct. . . .

. . . .

In order to acquaint oneself with university life from the inside, the chapel is as good a place as any to begin with. It is in the northern end of Cobb Hall, on the first floor, a plain, bare room, except for the magnificent life-size portrait of Mr. Rockefeller hanging on the wall. At 12:30 o'clock students begin to assemble, while the organist sits dreamily, playing an "Invitation to Prayers," or something of that description, as a prelude to the entrance of the president, in black gown and cap, followed by half a dozen of the faculty attired in similar fashion. Although among other multifarious duties the president numbers that of officiating as high priest at chapel services he is usually assisted by different members of the faculty in turn. If the instructor upon whom this duty devolves does not happen to be eminent for his piety he is merely expected to accompany the president to chapel services without taking an active part.

. . . .

But if the elect member of the faculty comes from the divinity school or has any reputation at all for orthodoxy he is not permitted to sit quietly, but is expected to give out hymns and read the scriptures himself as a means of grace and preparation for a ministerial career, and sometimes deliver a short "sermonette." Whatever may be the effect of these spiritual ministrations upon himself his trepidation sometimes furnishes amusement to his hearers, and the sigh of relief with which he closes the Bible is joined in by every one who sympathizes with his embarrassment. Yet in spite of occasional episodes of this character, the chapel services, though simple, are marked by the dignity and impressiveness which characterize every ceremony at which the president officiates. The flowing black gowns, the responses, short pause for meditation at the close, during which the students remain seated while the president and his retinue leave the room to the accompaniment of slow marching music, are all calculated to give solemnity to the occasion.

The next door [beyond the University Press] on the same side of the corridor leads to the room where the dean of the graduate school, Professor Judson, gives advice as to the expediency of studying for the degree of doctor of philosophy or master of arts, the former degree being the only one that is much in favor at the university, although a few A.M.'s are given every year to satisfy the popular demand for that title.

. . . .

In another department of this office sits Miss Marion Talbot, in student's cap and gown, at her desk, in earnest consultation with the girls of the undergraduate school, and here also Mrs. Alice Freeman Palmer is often seen. The university extension headquarters, which comes next in order, have a somewhat domestic air, owing to the neat little curtain which the typewriter girls have put up to screen themselves from curious glances. Beyond this is the lecture hall, where the Wednesday afternoon lectures by different members of the faculty are given, the seats here being arranged on the regular dissecting-room plan, rising steeply above one another, a well-known device for making the late comer, who has to take a front seat, feel as if he were descending into a bottomless pit.

Across the corridor is the examiner's office, which is also used as an ante-room to the president's headquarters. Here visitors are received by an usher who introduces them to the president when their turn comes with all the solemnity of a Mercury conducting shades of the lower world, but here the resemblance ceases, for many of these callers are substantial looking matrons, who have come to intrust their offering to the president's care and direction. The room in which he is interviewed, however, is the capacious faculty room, dreary enough for Acheron itself, with its long table and rows upon rows of empty chairs, the president sitting in state and alone at one end.

It has always been one of the necessary formalities of becoming connected with the university to have an interview with President Harper, who briefly possesses himself of the important facts in each student's history. Faces he does not often remember, but his memory for individual biographies is something marvelous, and is probably effected by his own "inductive method" somewhat after this fashion: When a young man presents himself for admission to the graduate school with the statement that he comes from "a little denominational college, of which you've probably never heard," the conclusion is reached that the youth who is so ready to betray the insignificance of his alma mater will not do great credit to the university, while the boy who answers proudly: "Boggs College, sir," with an air which makes his questioner hesitate to ask where in the world Boggs College may be, is set down as likely to succeed in impressing the world with his achievements later on.

Besides the offices already mentioned the first floor of Cobb Hall contains nothing but the registrar's office, which is also a banking establishment for the cashing of students' checks, besides being a general information bureau, and the faculty post-office in charge of different students, who receive their tuition as compensation for the service.

The second floor is devoted to ancient and modern languages, the former being at the south end and the latter at the north. These are again subdivided into the romance library on the east and the Germanic on the west, while the classical library is also subdivided into Latin and Greek departments. The walls of the corridors and of all the rooms in this building are of red brick, and the woodwork of oak, giving a substantial air to the interior, which would be rather gloomy and dark if it were not that the upper half of all the doors are of glass, a convenience which is greatly appreciated by the student who wishes to convey the information to his brother in football on the inside that he is to be on the field at the earliest possible minute. It also gives the late comer an opportunity to survey the situation beforehand and calculate the chance of entering without attracting the teacher's attention.

The Latin and Greek library is one of the first rooms to which visitors are generally escorted, but they are seldom shown into a small room at the east end, which is devoted to Sanskrit and comparative philology, and, strange to say, it seems to be an object of dread to the undergraduates, who very seldom venture to open the door into this little room. . . .

Every morning he sees a young and beardless professor, with light brown hair, blue eyes, and glasses, rushing frantically through the library, his legs making a vain attempt to keep up with his body, which is bent forward at an angle of forty degrees, and he has seen this same man bolt out of the room at the end of an hour with the same air of frantic haste, and this it is which makes him afraid to enter a room from which the learned Dr. Buck retreats so precipitately. Another man who makes an equally rapid transit through the library to his inner sanctum is Professor Paul Shorey, the head of the Greek department, a little man, black-haired, black-eyed, and pugnacious to the last degree when one of his favorite theories is attacked.

On the west side of the library is the room usually occupied by the Latin seminar on Tuesday afternoons. The hour for meeting is 3 o'clock, but it is often later than this when Professor Hale enters the room with the calmness of a man who knows how to keep people waiting. Extremely tall, with dark gray hair and beard, he has an elegance of bearing which suggests the cultured gentleman of the days of Cicero and Catullus, a resemblance which is heightened by the white-duck suit which he sometimes wears as a modern substitute for the more graceful toga of the ancients. But when he has taken his seat at the head of the long table there is not a moment's delay before the celebrated champion of the subjunctive mode and author of the expression "forward-moving 'cum' clause" begins a questioning which keeps his class on the alert quite as much as a game of progressive whist, which it seems to resemble so far as the chances of "trumping" any of his subjunctives by their scientific names are concerned, and at the end of two hours he departs with the air of a man who has triumphantly slain and trampled underfoot a number of popular errors in regard to certain much-discussed questions of syntax.

Thus all these men have their peculiar "exits and their entrances" which do not escape the observation of the occupants of the library, but nothing causes quite so much commotion as a number of giggling schoolgirls ushered in as visitors by one solitary young man, who after gazing helplessly around at a place where they are not permitted to talk, are led off by their escort to their more congenial ball ground or tennis court.

After inspecting the Latin library, visitors are generally taken to the German library, where, at the farther end of the corridor, may often be seen the three men who constitute the Germanic faculty, a loving trio apparently, for they are all young men and capable of ardent friendships, which consist in exchanging confidences in German that are supposed to be unintelligible to the rest of the world. Professor Cutting is tall, slender, and handsome, with light brown hair and sparkling brown eyes, the embodiment of energy and vivacity. Von Klenze is also a slender youth, with an intellectual looking face, while Herr Doctor Professor Schmidt-Wartemberg has the thickset figure, florid complexion, fair hair, and blue eyes of the typical German.

The third floor is devoted to history, political science, etc., where there may be seen occasionally the Titanic-looking Von Holst, with his immense forehead and eyes that seem always to be gazing at the departed spirits of the founders of the constitution, as well as Thatcher, the author of a church history, who, as might be expected, is as solemn looking as the first deacon in the first Christian church, although his usual companion is Schwill [Schevill], the mediaevalist, a herr doctor with a wicked-looking, pointed beard, who apparently holds heterodox views on the subject of apostolic succession, to judge from the violent discussions, which apparently only strengthen their friendship for each other.

The fourth floor is given over to the divinity students, and has a rather forlorn and dingy air. At the south end is the Semitic library, where, at a certain hour in the afternoon, may be seen the familiar figure of Rabbi Hirsch, through whose own generosity and that of his church many of the books in the library have been purchased, and a fellowship in that department provided for, his own services as instructor in rabbinical study being also given to the university.[85]

The place and the people, viewed from within the Quadrangles by a Faculty member and future novelist, Robert Herrick, also in 1895:

The Midway is no more; in its place stretch two broad driveways separated by sunken gardens (some time they may contain a canal and varsity eights), which connect two great parks, an English-like bit of country with Gainsborough trees and level sod to the west, and the site of the Fair beside the blue lake to the east. One wishes, in mortal fashion, that the omnivorous city were kept at bay by a special park encircling the university to the north. Then the peaceful calm, in the world but not of it, the fitting atmosphere for an academic place, would be ever possible. The present suburban section immediately about the university will probably grow more and more into a college town, protecting the campus, rimmed round by unbroken walls of buildings from the roar and smoke of the city. For the existing halls, already an enviable equipment, merely indicate the plan. When the tropical growth of Chicago has done its good work, the twenty-four acres of campus will contain homes for several thousand students in many small halls, as well as many times the present number of buildings for general purposes. In this swift country the future is upon us before we have well realized the present, and for this future the founders of the university have provided none too extravagantly.

· · · · · · · · · · · · · · · · · · · ·

One seeks curiously in the system of the University of Chicago for the predominating type or ideal; is it the American college with its group of professional schools, or the English Oxford with its care for the individual soul or the German university? ... It is a truism that the most distinctive move in American college life of the last decade has been in the sudden interest in post-graduate study. But hitherto no Western institution, whether college or so-called university, has had the means to provide liberally for advanced studies. This open field, therefore, it has been the ambition of the University of Chicago, situated in the centre of a vast inland constituency of small colleges, to develop. A serious limitation in the way of accomplishing this ideal at Chicago as at the older universities has been the low standard of admission to graduate work. An American "graduate" is often (pretension aside) merely a graduate of an academy. Some day this laxity will be remedied by concerted action among all the American universities which aim to do advanced work. In the meantime it may be questioned whether the graduate school can maintain its integrity without a strong under-graduate body, and further whether the emphasis is not placed too heavily upon the creation of specialists, rather than the developing of men—the older ideal of the New England college. The presence of a large number of graduates at Chicago creates a serious, scholarly atmosphere, prevents boyishness, and sets standards of accomplishment; it stimulates the student and instructor alike. As a result of the interest in graduate work the university has done much to elevate the position of the doctor's degree in the West. Whether or not it may seem desirable to follow German ideals of mere scholarship to their logical conclusion, it is clear that for a long time Western colleges and high schools can absorb with advantage doctors of philosophy.

In the midst of all this novel machinery in which the university has expressed itself, the thoughtful observer remembers Newman's wise warning: "The personal influence of the teacher is able in some sort to dispense with an academical system, but the system cannot in any sort dispense with personal influence. Such is the history of society; it begins in the poet and ends in the policeman. Universities are instances of the same course; they begin in influence, they end in system." We have begun the other way at Chicago: the system was created of a piece, and then the life was breathed into it. But if the faculties, drawn from many intellectual centres, cannot amalgamate and supply this influence of culture and scholarship and character, then the university becomes a machine-shop indeed, in which there is much doing, but little worth remembering.

. . . .

Among the women there are many students from Eastern and Southern homes; the undergraduate men are almost without exception from the central West. What is this student like? How does he act in college? What are his amusements? He is decidedly in earnest—too much so, I am inclined to think. Frequently his conditions of life force him to struggle for existence at the university. Students who are earning the means to study are the rule, not the exception. Every possible occupation that a large city affords, from lighting lamps on the street to tutoring or writing for the newspapers, furnishes the few needed dollars. This condition of strenuous poverty necessarily produces a very different atmosphere in the college world from the opulent spirit of our older institutions. The poor man is the dominant person; to be rich and idle would be almost unfashionable. To be sure, the atmosphere is not the dreamy half-lights of an Oxford garden; rather the harsh, invigorating breeze of a Colorado desert. Unrelieved, that, perhaps, is the word; unrelieved by prejudice, past and present. The student is unprejudiced in scholarship, accepting no traditions of what is really excellent to know; unprejudiced in social life, despising the tame amenities of a reticent society; unprejudiced in athletics, and therefore, thank Heaven! still willing to regard his amusements as avocations. He is untrained; even the ambitious candidate for a higher degree in the graduate schools is often lamentably unprejudiced about his foundation of knowledge, but he is eager, sensitive, industrious. College means for him work, and I am sure that the faculty rejoice in the fact that an industrious poverty will for a long time prevent any other conception from becoming universal.

I have emphasized the industrious aspect of the student at Chicago. We may think of him only as an academic artisan, but he has his festivities. It is almost amusing to consider the eagnerness with which he has entered upon all the activities supposed to be peculiar to "college boys."

. . . .

All these clubs and athletic teams exist not merely for amusement, but also because the students feel that one cannot have a full-fledged university life without them. They make up the American idea of a university, just as the graduate school, the laboratory, and the elective system go to make a modern university. And this is noteworthy that the students feel a responsibility to construct a great university as much in their way as the faculty and the trustees in theirs. They feel the exhilaration and loyalty to the scope of the institution as men working shoulder to shoulder in a new country, planning for a brilliant future. This sense of personal interest and co-operation which goes far to make men of the students, not college boys, manifests itself most strikingly in the relationship or camaraderie with the faculty, and especially in loyalty to the president. I believe that nowhere in the United States is a college president so thoroughly known and heartily liked and admired by all students as President Harper. Not only does every student feel that the president knows him personally, but he knows that the president has an individual interest in him and his affairs. He feels that he may go to him about his private concerns, and as far as his position will permit it, the president may be depended upon to see the college life from the student's point of view. He does not impress them as merely an august and powerful personage at the head of a great corporation. This is more than mere popularity—it is loyalty and devotion. The students, one may say without exception, would be unwilling to commit any act that might place President Harper and the new university in an ungracious light before the public. They would care little for the possible punishment as compared to the pain and difficulties they might give the president. The result is that student government is one of the least perplexing problems at the university. This fact may be due in part to the large proportion of mature graduate students, who sober the usual college spirit; but I think that the deeper cause is the truer one—a sense of loyalty to the young university and its responsible executive.

. . . .

A young man may walk, some fine May morning, down the flag-stones of the yard at Harvard; the sun comes flooding in through the time-honored trees, the vines in tender green are creeping about the stiff deformity of this building or softening the angular lines of that, and the very breeze flutters the dignified air of the place; those

236

isolated buildings, each in itself so awkward and plain, with the wide openings between, through which the breezes and the sunshine play—subtly they present themselves to him like a slowly making picture of a past, a puritan past, with its rigidity, its scorn of beauty, its clean correctness and integrity of life. The wide spaces, the uncompromising architecture of the halls, are an incarnation of New England, softened now by time and its associations. And this sense of a fine New England past grows richer as he wanders up Brattle Street or Kirkland Street, that have seen so much which has had distinction in our America. Emerson, and Lowell, and Longfellow— the inadequate but just expression of our early life—all those and many others have left a benediction to Cambridge. Surely nowhere else on our continent is life so precious in its past possessions and subtle influences, as just here in this cluster of puritan buildings, in this fresh air that comes in from the sea.

And if it be his good fortune to take up his home there, to live that life for four or perhaps seven years, he will find that the place is not merely of the past: it has to-day a very definite life of its own. If he is carefully conscious of it all, he will note that this definite ideal of life, made of tradition and sure innovation, is moulding him inevitably, has moulded him irrevocably. If he has given himself up to it freely, he will leave it all with a sad homesickness, a regret of going away and leaving himself. His critics will say that his training has been snobbish, that he belongs to a class, that he is too "indifferent" (let us hope that he is to cheap affairs!), and that he is not American —whatever that may be. And if he is frank with himself, he will own a part of this impeachment, but not as an impeachment. What has been valuable in his past training is not so much any one piece of work, any one great scholar's influence, as the spirit of the place, its standards of work, its ideals of excellence—in short, its aristocratic bearing. In so far as he has already absorbed that intolerant love for the most excellent and but one excellence, he has come out a Harvard man.

We meet a new order of things at Chicago. It is not my purpose to contrast the worth of the two ideals of life, or to judge them; indeed, I have said that Chicago resembles Harvard, paradoxical as it is, in many vital respects. The complete intellectual, unsectarian independence in spirit is the same at Chicago as at Cambridge; the desire for high standards in scholarship is the same; the manliness and maturity of the students, born of great freedom, resembles the Harvard way of life. The multitudinous subjects and teachers are characteristic of all large universities. The one fact that at Chicago professionalism in athletics is absolutely unknown, although the Western colleges have not outgrown the habit of buying success if possible, places the new university with its older sister.

But at the University of Chicago the student graduates as a person, not as a member of a class. His work and student life are individual from the very first. He enters the university when he pleases; he graduates when he pleases. His course has been individual and democratic. The conventions of an old society, the ambitions of a select set, do not trouble him. He has had great freedom, great opportunities, and the stimulus of an eager, emulous life. He goes away certainly not without some insight into what learning and scholarship mean, but without class loyalties, without the intimate personal life so dear to us who have had it.

We look to a new order of things in learning, as in national and social life. In the new life, one fancies, the dominating forces will be traditionless. The uninterrupted appreciation of intellectual goods will no longer be true. The subjects taught will increase without number, and the most catholic means of estimation or valuation will be employed. Our new student will be contemptuous of mere culture, of anything that derives its respect from the past alone; he will despise forms and ceremonies, but he will be powerful in life.[86]

John D. Rockefeller and William Rainey Harper

The Founder did not see the University until 1896, when he attended the celebration of its fifth birthday. This photograph was taken in 1901 during the decennial celebration when Rockefeller made his second visit to the University. Martin A. Ryerson, President of the Board of Trustees, follows Rockefeller and Harper.

David A. Robertson, a student in the Senior College, lays the cornerstone of the Reynolds Club, the student clubhouse, during the decennial celebration in 1901.

At this ceremony, President Harper remarked: "College life, in a word, is the close association of a body of men who have in general common sympathies. . . . It includes friendships and animosities, struggle and achievement, disappointment and victory. The college world is the most democratic world that exists."

George E. Vincent, associate professor of sociology and a dean, at the same ceremony: "The University takes pride in her laboratories, but she also covets for her students something of the charm of life in the cloisters and quadrangles of Oxford and Cambridge; she would preserve in some sort the democracy of the old-time New England campus; she would unite in a larger brotherhood all student groups, and foster among them a spirit of wider fraternity."

The Tower group, completed in 1903: the Reynolds Club at the corner, Mandel Hall to the left, Mitchell Tower and Hutchinson Hall to the right.

THE BOTANY BUILDING AND HULL COURT, dedicated 1897

The contrast between the Botany Building, designed by Henry I. Cobb, and the Tower group, designed by Charles A. Coolidge of Shepley, Rutan, and Coolidge of Boston, indicates how the appearance of the University changed when Cobb's free interpretation of the collegiate Gothic style gave way to a greater fidelity to the prototype. Mitchell Tower, Thomas W. Goodspeed wrote, was modeled after the famous Magdalen Tower of Oxford.

Foster Hall, built in 1893, was extended to its present size in time for a dedication ceremony during the decennial celebration. President Harper stands on the speakers' platform with George E. Adams, representing the donor, Mrs. Nancy Foster, while John D. Rockefeller sits at the right, just above Professor Thomas C. Chamberlin. Alice Freeman Palmer, sometime dean of women, sits at the left, under the window from which students watch. This and other photographs of the decennial celebration belong to a series of handsome photographs taken on that occasion by Allen Ayrault Green, then a Senior College student.

SNELL HALL, ONE OF THE UNIVERSITY HOUSES, AND THE HEAT, LIGHT, AND POWER PLANT

Set back from the street, west of the Quadrangles, and built of brick without Gothic ornamen
the plant was not designed to embellish the campus. This source of energy for the Universit
was not only paid for by John D. Rockefeller but constructed under the eyes of his engineer. Th
construction received special notice at the time because many Negroes were employed, some fo
skilled and supervisory jobs.

The southern portion of the campus in its state of completion at the close of the Harper administration, viewed from the smokestack of the power plant. The line of sight here is the reverse of that in the photograph taken during the winter of 1892–93. A corner of Walker Museum is visible to the left; the women's houses, Beecher, Green, and Kelly, stand slightly behind the Museum to the right, with the view of Foster Hall cut off by the Law School building. Haskell Oriental Museum is in the center, and Cobb Hall and the Divinity Halls stand to the right. The roof of the University Press building is in the foreground.

HENRY A. RUST
First Comptroller and Business Manager

WALLACE HECKMAN
*University Counsel and Rust's Successor
as Business Manager*

A football game in 1904. During the World's Columbian Exposition, the public viewed the University from the south. Later, when football attracted crowds, the northern front of the Quadrangles became better known. Spectators in the stands of the football field, then popularly known as Marshall Field, looked at the one side of the Quadrangles to be completed during the Harper administration: the Tower group to the left; the Zoölogy building, the gateway given by architect Henry I. Cobb, the Anatomy building, and Hitchcock Hall to the right.

EMMONS BLAINE HALL, OF THE SCHOOL OF EDUCATION, designed by James Gamble Rogers, 1902–3

Pupils in the Elementary School on the terrace in front of Blaine Hall. When this photograph first appeared in 1905, it bore the caption: "Third-grade children melting metals in furnaces made by themselves." The children belonged to a history class then studying the Greeks and Norsemen. The photograph illustrated an article which explained that the work offered the children an opportunity, while making arrows and other objects, to realize the difficulty experienced by primitive man in dealing with a new material, metal.

And Adults

The University Press, Headquarters of Publication Work, completed in 1902

University Extension

Richard G. Moulton
Senior Member of the Lecture-Study Staff

Edmund J. James
Dean of University College

For a period of weeks during the summer of 1894, Rollin D. Salisbury, professor of geographic geology, directed a party of students who surveyed the evidences of glaciation and erosion in Wisconsin, principally in the Devils Lake region. The work was described in *Cap and Gown* the next year as the first student geological expedition. Although the accumulation of vacation credit made it possible for individual professors to travel widely, Harper's original plan had not included the mounting of expeditions of any sort. Work in the field, however, was an appropriate supplement to summer instruction on campus and a necessary extension of investigations conducted within the laboratories.

YERKES OBSERVATORY

A week after the University opened, Thomas W. Goodspeed announced that Charles T. Yerkes, traction magnate, had arranged to build one of the most complete astronomical observatories in the world as a gift to the University. A telescope for the Observatory was exhibited at the Columbian Exposition, but it was only after a long delay that Yerkes Observatory was dedicated in 1897 at Williams Bay, Wisconsin, near Lake Geneva. The Observatory was devoted principally to research. Courses were offered only to advanced students and not as a major part of the program.

President Harper was unsuccessful in obtaining funds for a marine laboratory belonging to the University, but Professor Charles O. Whitman served for years as director of the Marine Biological Laboratory at Woods Hole, Massachusetts, where other members of the Faculty conducted summer work and students were invited to enrol. In marine investigation, as in the organization of secondary and collegiate education, the University had greater success in co-operating with other institutions than in pursuit of its early plans to become entirely self-sufficient.

In 1903 the University was able to send an expedition abroad, with the support of the Oriental Exploration Fund established by John D. Rockefeller. Work at the site of the Babylonian city of Adab (Bismayah) was interrupted by the Turkish government after two seasons. The residue of the Fund was then used to finance the first Egyptian expedition of James H. Breasted, professor of Egyptology and Oriental History. In the winter of 1905–6, his party copied inscriptions at Abu Simbel.

James H. Breasted and His Family

January, 1906: the dahabiyeh of the Breasted party, the Nubian Epigraphic Expedition, moored astern a second vessel on the bank of the Nile at Abu Simbel. With other Egyptian monuments, the temple inspired Charles L. Hutchinson in 1892 to write Harper, then President-elect, that they must build well if they were to leave behind them such enduring evidence of their work. If we reckon by the clock of Abu Simbel, the buildings that Hutchinson helped to plan and pay for have endured less than a minute. Yet that has been time enough and more for the damming of the Nile to threaten the temple. But, thanks in part to the efforts of the intellectual heirs of Breasted, the temple is being lifted to the top of the cliff and will continue to testify to the works of man.

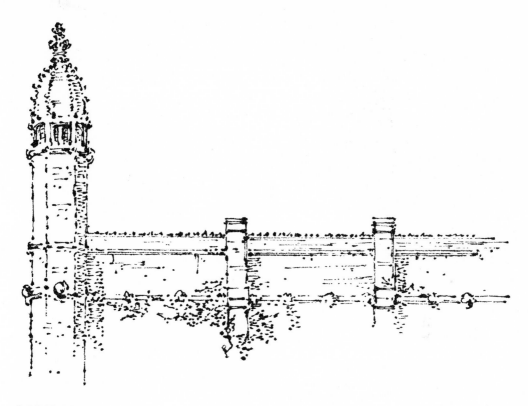

PART FIVE

DEMAND AND SUPPLY

Too Far
or Not Far Enough

Talking to students about behavior—or "policy of life"—in the complicated maze of the world, Harper once put a question directly applicable to his own conduct of the University's affairs:

How are we moving? . . . Has it occurred to you that the dividing line between good and bad is very difficult to draw; that the character of the policy is often determined, not by *what* it is, but by the extent to which it is carried; that mistakes are made—not simply in going, but in going too far or not going far enough?[1]

Exaggeration either way, Harper said, brought ruin and disaster. The health of the University depended upon the preservation of balance between enterprise and prudence, between boldness of strategy and restraint in tactics. Contrary to myth, Harper could play the role of nay-sayer, especially to departments that sought to expand at some cost to the University as a whole. "My work . . . ," he once told the Trustees, "consists very largely in denying requests for additional money and in opposing plans which require for their execution the expenditure of money."[2] Harper found that duty more onerous than any other: his refusal to approve further movement in particular directions was typically the consequence of shortages produced by his general commitment to a policy (or impulse) that knew no bounds. During his regime, the University always ran the risk of going too far—of asking too much of men and of all too exactly copying the history of the old University of Chicago. Yet the resources of the new University, being spread too thin, did not go far enough in any given department to satisfy its needs.

Outside observers could wonder if activism did not subvert the idea of a university as a house of thought, while men working within the University bore witness to the pressure put upon them. Edgar J. Goodspeed: "The only trouble is that WRH doesn't give us any time"; Albion Small: "At all events I have felt myself hounded by the next duty every moment. . . . I have not been able to concentrate on any one thing . . ."; J. Laurence Laughlin: "We have today stopped marching & dropped into the ditch of one of Harper's so-called vacations"; and William D. McClintock: "I came back home . . . with the determination not to make complaints to you [Harper] about overwork; but I am almost bitterly discouraged."[3] That "almost" was critically important to the welfare of the University; when Faculty members ceased to temper their complaints, aspiration could give way to fatal despair. Testifying to the loyalty of the professors, Harper remarked, it would seem with well-warranted carefulness of phrase, that there were no reasonable sacrifices to which they would not consent if it were necessary. They knew, Harper said, that their own highest interests were connected with the prosperity of the University.[4] If that prosperity were seriously jeopardized, however, would the individual members of the Faculty—indeed could dedicated academics—stay at the University? A mood of depression did penetrate to the innermost circle, the corps of head professors. William G. Hale reminded Harper:

I was the first man formally called to the place of Head Professor. I was, so far as I know, the first who came here, looked over the ground thoroughly, and pronounced a belief that a great University could be created here. When I cast in my lot with you, it was in the expectation that my department, which seemed well provided for, was to be as strong as any Latin department in the country. I certainly should not have left my quiet & my opportunities for study & writing to take charge of a second-rate department. Yet that is what the department has turned out to be. In one of the great provinces, it is not even up to the level of strong undergraduate work of the modern kind.[5]

Albion W. Small and Harry P. Judson agreed that a lack of historical material undoubtedly cut off a large part of the supply of graduate students in history and put the work of cognate departments under a handicap.[6] (Small was of course head of the sociology department and Judson of political science.) On the scientific side of the University, C. O. Whitman, head of zoölogy, reported on one occasion: "So far as men are concerned we have had the best dept. in the country; so far as equipment is concerned we have the *weakest* in nearly every respect. That has crippled us and led to dissatisfaction and steady decline."[7] At another time, Whitman said that he really felt humiliated at the state of the departments, "as compared with what we had planned, and were promised."[8] The neurologist Henry H. Donaldson thought it only just to graduate students in many instances to suggest that they work elsewhere: ". . . they cannot be asked to await the development of facilities by us."[9] And the man to whom the professors addressed their complaints was himself obliged, in 1901, to write Martin A. Ryerson, President of the Board and donor of the physical laboratory: "I am sorry to have to report to you that in view of the lack of funds for the department of physics the investigation work has practically come to an end."[10]

CHAPTER XIII

Trial Balance

The causes of frustration and disenchantment were not imaginary. In the first year and long thereafter, the aspirations and resources of the University were far out of balance. As one editor accurately observed, the University of Chicago occupied ". . . the anomalous position of being at once one of the richest and one of the most needy of American institutions of learning."[1] The Rockefeller gifts of 1892, totaling $2,000,000, were designed solely to support instruction. The large sums necessary to purchase laboratory and museum equipment, to pay for buildings, and to provide books for the libraries were lacking. Want of funds for such purposes continued to plague the University throughout Harper's Presidency. "Unless somebody comes forward with a large sum," Harper wrote George C. Walker during the first academic year, "we are hopelessly lost."[2] Harper was not simply crying wolf; within four months of the opening, the costliness of floating even the initial program had become apparent. In January, 1893, the President of the Board, Martin A. Ryerson, directly confronted the overlapping problems of delivering the University from the burden of debts which it had already incurred and of creating a large fund with which to meet the exceptional expenses of organizing the University. Ryerson was aware of pressing demands for general improvements and for equipment in keeping with the endowment. He may also have hoped that the fund would assist the

University to meet its expenses for the fiscal year 1893–94.[3] In another age, he might have said that an extraordinary thrust was required to lift the University into the air. The necessary force had either to be paid for by borrowing or out of special donations; and Ryerson no less than the Founder abhorred deficit financing. Ryerson himself undertook to give the University $100,000, if $400,000 could be raised from other sources by May 1, 1893. A half million had to be raised immediately, not to increase endowment or to expand the University program but to stabilize what was already under way.

When Harper and Goodspeed set about raising the $400,000, they were received cordially in the city, but gifts were small. A flurry in the money market and the ensuing depression of 1893 ruined any hope of meeting Ryerson's conditions on time. Although he extended the term of his pledge, the momentum of fund-raising had been lost; Harper's dark words to Walker were written in March, 1893.[4]

The financial future of the University was very obscure in April when Harper and the Board attempted, in many anxious exchanges, to make plans for the 1893–94 academic year.[5] Harper hoped that Rockefeller would promise $1,000,000, income from which might begin on October 1, 1893, the opening day of the second year of operations. Gates could hardly have been encouraged to read that Rockefeller's money was needed partly to meet building deficiencies. Harper assumed that the $500,000 would be raised and also that it might provide for the academic year 1893–94. But to what extent? The fund had not been designed primarily to support an annual budget.[6]

Rockefeller was deaf to Harper's proposal; but he did promise to contribute as much as $150,000 to cover a deficit for the year 1894–95 if the terms of the Ryerson gift were fulfilled. Presumably the Founder understood that part of the half million would indeed cover any deficit for the year 1893–94. The Rockefeller pledge would be paid, not at the beginning of the year but at its end if the Treasurer's books showed that the total cost of running the University for the year had not exceeded $500,000. Also, all proper economies were to be employed and every endeavor made to secure other funds to reduce the deficit as far as possible. Gates stated explicitly that all moneys available for the expenses of the year in question were actually to be so employed. If the University received funds for special purposes, not in the budget for 1894–95, which would increase expenditures above $500,000 or if for any reason it became necessary to increase the outlay, Harper must consult with Rockefeller before raising the limit; but it was hoped that he and the Board would find the limit satisfactory and work-able. "A capital point," wrote Gates, "will be, the limit having been once fixed, to hold the expense within it."[7] Shortly after the offer of $150,000, Gates sug-gested an alternate condition, which revealed the Founder's intent: by July 1, 1894, all debts were to be paid.[8] Thus did Rockefeller encourage the University to bend every effort in the direction of financial stability. In pledging money for running expenses, however, he departed from his practice of giving only to capital: the Founder of the University was becoming its sustainer.

Harper's response to the original announcement of the gift was to say that the condition paralyzed him. All arrangements for the coming year would have to be postponed until July 1, 1893, the new deadline for the Ryerson gift—and the Rockefeller proposition. But Harper added: "We are sure at any rate of success."[9] That remark Gates answered by telegraph: "If Board is sure of suc-cess why hesitate on Budget."[10] Harper wired back: "In passing budget two risks one of raising half million other of Mr. Rockefeller's gift [stop] board will take first but not second [stop] am greatly embarrassed."[11] Harper was certain, he repeated by letter, that the $500,000 would be raised; but he be-lieved, with Goodspeed and Ryerson, that it would not be safe to appropriate money for 1893–94 with the risk that, if the University failed to raise the $500,000, it would also lose the $150,000 Rockefeller promised for the following year. Were the University sure of having the Rockefeller money for 1894–95, Harper said, the University could take the absolutely necessary steps toward preparation of announcements for 1893–94. Harper then came to the nub of the matter: a crisis was brewing in the fundamental affairs of the University. Ryer-son was so concerned over the situation that he was proposing (1) to cut out all appropriations for books or apparatus (which, said Harper, would be simply ruinous), (2) to eliminate absolutely every additional expense in every depart-ment, (3) to trim down several departments, and (4) to give up the summer quarter—in short, drastic retrenchment. "Should any considerable portion of this policy be adopted [said Harper] my resignation will be in the hands of the Trustees next Tuesday. I will not face the country on this issue. It would be humiliating and degradation I could not endure. The last three days here have been little short of hell."[12] The particular sticking point for Harper was the dropping of the summer quarter.

Gates saw but one danger, that of not raising the half million:

The whole difficulty resolves itself after all into this, that the board are [*sic*] not pre-pared to act in view of the risk of failure to secure the $500,000. Suppose Mr. Rockefeller was to waive this condition, the arrangement remaining in other particulars the same, wherein would the board be relieved. The board would then be assured of what? Simply of $150,000 payable June 30, 1895, or such portion thereof as shall be required for the actual deficit of the year closing. None of it would be available for either of the two years [*sic*] deficit [*i.e.*, that for 1892–94] sought to be covered by the raising of this $500,000. If the $500,000 be not raised, you would have to carry any unraised portion as a debt for current expenses—precisely the thing we are all seeking to avoid. It has seemed to me, and I think Mr. Rockefeller shares the view, that if the $500,000 be not raised, we would have to reconsider the whole question of expense and have a new deal all round. It might in that contingency be necessary to consider more seriously than hitherto the question of retrenchment.[13]

Harper apparently gave no answer to that statement but did accept the alternative condition to the Rockefeller pledge, which meant much the same thing, that the University should not be in debt at the end of its second year. He also reminded Gates that he (Harper) had made a great and fatal mistake when he had allowed Gates to persuade him to come to Chicago.

On May 9, 1893, a special meeting of the Board considered the proposal of several men who wished to make personal loans to the University, each promising $25,000 (or more), with the patent intention of temporarily carrying the University's indebtedness. (In 1893, Martin A. Ryerson stood ready to make loans up to a total of $100,000.) The President and Secretary of the Board were authorized to execute notes in the name of the University, payable one year after date and bearing 6 per cent interest, for an amount not exceeding $250,000. A committee was appointed to devise a schedule to be presented regularly to show the financial operations and condition of the University. Since in the midst of depression it was becoming plain that the $500,000 would not be raised by July 1, the deadline to which Ryerson's pledge had been extended, the Board thus sought to buy time in which to raise sufficient funds by subscription to pay off debts.[14] Credit in Chicago had to be maintained unimpaired, which would be impossible if the University borrowed two or three hundred thousand dollars from the banks of the city. Harper believed that Ryerson had not given up thoughts of retrenchment, which would put the University, Harper also believed, in such a position that it could not regain in ten years the place it occupied. To avert this possibility, Harper asked Rockefeller either to contribute $150,000 toward the $500,000 giving the University leverage great enough to save itself before the public, or to bring closer the offer of $150,000 for use toward general expenses. If the University could have $150,000 for the second year as well as the third, it ought to be able to carry on its work as organized and to collect in Chicago the money necessary to pay off its debts by July 1, 1894.[15]

Less than a week after this appeal, Rockefeller pledged $150,000 to the Ryerson fund, to support the University for the first two years.[16] The reasons for Rockefeller's acquiescence in Harper's view remain obscure. Perhaps Rockefeller and Gates had come to see some inconsistency between meeting deficits more than two years away and allowing the University to hang on the brink of retrenchment during the year immediately ahead. Once he had agreed to contribute toward deficits, Rockefeller may have found it hard to draw a line between 1893–94 and 1894–95. As long as the terms of Ryerson's pledge remained unmet, the finances of the third year would be decidedly hypothetical. For whatever reasons, the Founder gave evidence by his gift that he did not intend to make the raising of $400,000 in Chicago a test of the ability of the University to survive without retrenchment; but he did not accept sole responsibility for the financial health of the institution. Even his support of the deficit for one year was made contingent upon the raising of $250,000 elsewhere.

The gift brought joy to Harper. His life had been saved: ". . . I could never have gone through another six weeks under the strain."[17] But Harper still had a suggestion to make: payments should begin on July 1, 1893, instead of October 1, as the terms of the gift specified.[18] Gates answered that he would bring up the matter if Harper and Ryerson so desired but he wished that Harper would squeeze along without a readjustment if he could manage.[19]

Apparently the element of contingency in his offer of $150,000 for 1893–94 did not prove entirely satisfactory to Rockefeller. In June he proposed a substitute for his subscription to the Ryerson fund, a gift toward current expenses in 1893–94 on the understanding that Ryerson would extend his offer through the year, that every effort would be made to raise the $500,000, and that Harper believed that it could be raised. Rockefeller assumed that in view of his new pledge the Trustees would finance the existing debt of the University to relieve the institution of danger and embarrassment on that account.[20] In effect, Rockefeller was underwriting the budget for 1893–94 with the expectation that another crisis would not occur. Significantly, the new gift, like the old, was to be payable on October 1, not July 1 as Harper had suggested. Harper would have to squeeze along: perhaps Rockefeller thought that the experience would be a wholesome astringent for Harper's hopes.

At the beginning of July, 1893, the indebtedness of the University, including $225,000 owed banks, was more than one-tenth the size of its assets, or $393,400 against $3,171,506.37. Before the second academic year had started, a large number of bills had accumulated at the Press, which served as purchasing agent for the University: ". . . a good many of the people from whom we have bought goods want their pay, and it is only right and proper that they should have it."[21] By August 4, 1893, the University had fallen behind in its payments for the library it had acquired in Berlin.[22] On the same day, Gates wrote Harper of the financial difficulties confronting the Rockefeller office: "Some faint idea may be had when I tell you that I have declined to loan money to responsible corporations at 5% per month. . . ."[23] (Gates's letter probably crossed one in which Harper alluded to ". . . something which will shock you, as it shocks us to refer to it."[24] What had happened Harper in fact never explained except to say that it had only to do with himself. Had Harper been, at least momentarily, overwhelmed by the pressure of financial crisis?) On August 10, Harper wrote Gates: "How are we to keep up our credit and allow the bills and salaries to stand unpaid . . . is more than I can imagine. We are likely, for lack of $25,000 or $30,000 to do ourselves more injury than we can recover from in many years."[25] By August 20, the University could not write checks for at least ten salaries.[26] It had reached the point where it could not pay its own officers—October 1 and the receipt of the first payment on the Rockefeller gift of $150,000 was a long way away.

On August 21, the *New York Daily Tribune* carried a story with the pregnant headline "Chicago University Pressed for Cash." After noting that the University was severely affected by the depression, the *Tribune* reported:

The institution is practically out of funds and the prospect for replenishing the exchequer is not encouraging. While there are no debts pressing heavily on the university [to the knowledge of the journalist], the trustees find it impossible to carry out at present plans for the development of the great school as projected, and an unpleasant postponement of certain proposed improvements is unavoidable.[27]

While there was no question but that the University would open for its second scholastic year at the appointed time and with substantially increased enrolment, it was certain that the grounds, building, and equipment would be less complete than the Faculty and Trustees had desired and expected. The tone of the paragraph was friendly; but the public might ask, did the *Tribune* protest too much? Harper had fallen again into a black mood. The thing which he had dreaded for days had happened:

The injury [he said of the *Tribune* piece] which such a statement will do is incalculable. The smallest possible sum of money was all that was needed to prevent it. I maintain that under the circumstances, notwithstanding the heavy pressure, it has been a piece of strange and peculiar management that has allowed matters to get into this shape . . . $15,000 on the first of August would have paid all the bills that were necessary to be paid; $30,000 on the first of September would have more than covered everything. This amount and more too is due us on the first of October from various sources; but with newspaper paragraphs going the rounds like that in the *Tribune,* we shall be crippled immeasurably. It seems to me that now something radical must be done.

Harper added, in regard to his own feelings, "The fact is a man could not be much more nearly crazy than I have been during these days."[28] To that outburst, Gates replied that he had no more reason to believe than he had had formerly that Rockefeller would be able to respond with cash; and he cautioned Harper against making any appeal to Rockefeller without first consulting Ryerson and Hutchinson.[29]

The University continued to rely on hand-to-mouth financing. When it was found impossible to discount notes from at least two men close to the University, the University secured $10,000 from John J. Mitchell, a Chicago financier; and Ryerson offered to furnish $25,000 on condition that on October 1 the University should pay a bank that much of $50,000 owed it. With money in hand, the University paid all salaries for August and made arrangements for those of September. "This carries us through the hard times," wrote Harper, "and my anxiety has come to an end."[30]

Neither Rockefeller nor Ryerson had seized upon a financial crisis as an occasion for cutting back the activities of the University. Both acted to rescue the University from acute embarrassment, Rockefeller by a gift that was inconsistent with his original policy of giving and Ryerson by loans which in effect anticipated his gift of $100,000. What exactly went on in the minds of these men and between them and Harper is unknown. Perhaps Harper's reference to resignation hardened into an ultimatum: maintain the University as it is or find another President. Conceivably, both Rockefeller and Ryerson felt their own reputations to be tied to the success of the Harper regime; but it is equally possible that Harper's actions at the moment of emergency had less to do with the nature of its outcome than the insight of Rockefeller and Ryerson into what Harper might do as an educator and leader of educators if he were not immediately checked as an executive.

Neither the academic promise of the University of Chicago nor its financial history could be separated from the nature of Harper's genius. His qualities held promise of greatness for the University but also made its ruin entirely possible. In 1893, Rockefeller and Ryerson enabled the University still to aim at greatness although the rules of strictly businesslike management indicated retrenchment. Had Harper been a cautious administrator, the University might not have had a brilliant beginning in which to fire the imaginations of its supporters; and had its principal supporters been Philistines, the University might not have survived the crisis without losing its distinctiveness. The founding would now be thought merely a curious aberration in the history of a good, sound college that once tried, unwisely, to become a university.

After the emergency of the late summer of 1893 had passed, Rockefeller offered to contribute $500,000 in four quarterly payments, beginning July 1, 1894, if the terms of the Ryerson fund had been fulfilled by that date. Of that half million, a sum not to exceed $175,000 (distinguished from the remainder as an unconditional gift) was to be employed against current expenses for the fiscal year beginning July 1, 1894; the remainder (or a sum up to $325,000) was to be devoted to the general purposes of the University.[31] In October, 1893, Harper estimated that a somewhat smaller sum, $250,000 or $300,000, would put the University "on its feet for the first time. . . ." The University was, he said, in the position of a contractor who had 150 carpenters at work on a building and tools for only one-third of that number. Presumably Rockefeller had such a thought in mind.[32]

In November, Harper was moved by an opportunity to acquire specimens left over from the Columbian Exposition to declare to Gates: "It is a fact that we are in a dreadful state because we cannot purchase the absolute necessities. . . . The ability to spend $50,000 now should make the work this year easily three times as effective as it will otherwise be. The spirit of all concerned will be different and the results accomplished vastly greater."[33] Harper had the enthusiasm of the Faculty as well as the credit of the University to think about. Rockefeller did not move for more than a month; but on the day after Christmas, 1893, he announced that, if the Ryerson fund were not made up, he would (even so) provide $50,000 for books and apparatus.[34] The pledge brought a profound sense of relief to the Trustees, who were under increasing pressure to make appropriations, and had felt powerless to provide for the urgent needs of the departments.[35] The beginning of the new year also brought relief to the head professors: "It is understood," Goodspeed wrote as Secretary of the Board, "that you are at liberty to send in new orders for books and apparatus. . . ."[36] Goodspeed took care, however, to insist that buying be kept within the limits of appropriations. An officer of the Press was asked to keep track of the amount of orders as a guard against an overdraft.[37] To the acting Librarian, Goodspeed wrote: "I am held to a strict account for expenditures and have been charged to permit no orders for books not authorized by an appropriation";[38] and to Isaac A. Hourwich, a junior member of the Faculty, he pointed out a University regulation that expenses could not be incurred by the professors without previous authorization. "This was a rule not known to you . . . [when Hourwich had spent some $26 more than he was entitled to], but you will readily see that in this matter of making expenditures we must be governed by fixed regulations."[39] That courteous but firm remark illuminated past practice and future intentions.

Goodspeed's correspondence was but a part of a drive to rule out the inadvertence which had helped to create debt and deficit. In April, 1894, the Board established a system for policing expenditures. Appropriations should be spent under the direction of the Executive Committee, to which the President of the University and the Secretary of the Board should submit a written report of changes, such as promotions, made within the appropriations. The Secretary was instructed to enter these changes in the minutes and to notify the departments and persons concerned.[40] Somewhat later, he was required to provide the Executive Committee, at each of its meetings, with the books containing budget items in detail and a full account of all new appropriations not in the budget, so that at all times the Committee would know the total amount of appropriations.[41] (Had the Committee not always had an exact notion of where the University stood financially?) The Board also decided to appoint a comptroller, the first being Henry A. Rust, a Board member and retired businessman.[42] Goodspeed summed up the series of reforms:

In the expenditures of the University we are working this year under a most rigid system of appropriations. So rigid is it that no one is authorized to expend any money until it has been appropriated, save only the Comptroller, Mr. Rust. And if under the pressure of an emergency he authorizes even a small expenditure he is required to report it at the first meeting of the Executive Committee. The Executive Committee itself does not authorize expenditures outside the appropriations made in the Budget, but restricts itself to recommending them to the Board of Trustees. The President of the University even has no authority to spend money.[43]

But borrowing continued to be a necessity. After June, 1893, the Board was morally obligated to Rockefeller to "finance" the debt, by which he presumably meant the raising of funds to pay off the debt. From time to time, for months, even after the time when indebtedness was supposed to have been resolved, the Board secured new loans from banks and elsewhere. In January, 1894, Ryerson suggested to Gates that Rockefeller might loan the University $25,000 or $50,000 to carry everything safely through to July.[44] Just previously, while traveling with Ryerson in the Mediterranean, Hutchinson had written Harper: "How goes the deficit? . . . Don't be led into temptation now that we are away."[45]

When July 1, 1894, arrived, the Ryerson fund of $500,000—and with it Rockefeller's matching $500,000—had been secured, but only after both donors had agreed to accept subscriptions which did not comply wholly with the original terms set for the pledges.[46] Notably, a gift of $20,000 from Mrs. Caroline E. Haskell was earmarked for endowment of a lectureship on comparative religion, which added to the intellectual resources of the University but did not help to pay for established programs or to pull the University out of debt. Just after the opening of the summer quarter, Harper could rejoice over the attractiveness of the University academically: "Over three hundred new students matriculated. This is something phenomenal. They are nearly all professors of colleges."[47] Financially the condition of the University remained critical; and in December, 1894, Rockefeller pledged up to $175,000 toward the current expenses for 1895–96, the pledge to be paid, beginning July 1, 1895, in four quarterly installments.[48] The Board understood that the money was to be used to maintain the University as it was and not to encourage expansion: in the event that expenditures exceeded income, Rockefeller would be free to withhold payment.[49]

The University had undertaken more than it could pay for, quite apart from the drains caused by the extraordinary needs of the University when it opened and by such financial insouciance as Goodspeed, Rust, and the Trustees sought to check. The program itself had been scaled to a larger endowment than the University possessed, if indeed Harper had made his plans and conducted his negotiations with exact matching of means and ends in mind. By the end of 1894, he had become convinced that the University required additional income of $175,000—or a sum equal to what Rockefeller was willing to contribute toward the budget and (presumably) to the difference between ordinary income and regular expenses. Yet Harper was uneasy about asking Rockefeller for a large gift to endowment. Indeed, Gates cautioned Harper against coming to Rockefeller for more endowment money, and Harper listened for the moment. But he soon came to feel that deference to Gates's opinion had been a mistake.

On December 18, 1894, Harper drafted a request for another gift—if possible $1,000,000. The plea was prepared, Harper stated, without the knowledge of any member of the Board. Such independence upon Harper's part ran counter to another bit of counsel from Gates, that Harper should not approach Rockefeller with a request for money before consulting Ryerson and Hutchinson. ("You will agree," Harper said to Gates, "that my instinct has shown itself to be right where the judgment of much better men than myself has been proven to be wrong.")[50] Harper's request of Rockefeller patently needed a prefatory explanation:

I know in my heart that the action which I now take may seem to you unreasonable and unwarranted, and that you may lose the regard for me which I have fondly hoped you entertained. I know on the other hand that you wish those who work in connection with you to be free to express their opinions and their beliefs, and because I know you feel this I write. . . .[51]

Possibly Harper was seeking to manipulate Rockefeller's emotions; but he did not behave like a man who had confidence in his power to succeed in his cause—or who really felt free to speak. Harper sent his letter—not directly to Rockefeller—but to Gates with the suggestion that he transmit it, at his discretion, to Rockefeller. Seemingly, Harper had more confidence in Gates's magnanimity than in the strength of his own position vis-à-vis the Founder.

In his letter to Rockefeller, Harper explained that the need for an additional $175,000 a year would not grow less in the future, but that the amount required for work already undertaken would not increase. Until the divisions of law, medicine, and technology were organized, the University would not need to ask for more. The development of the departments could be cared for by additional fees, once $175,000 had been capitalized. It was public knowledge, east and west, especially among the businessmen of Chicago, that the University needed three million for endowment (or, at an interest rate of 5–6 per cent, an income of about $175,000) to be put on a sound basis: a movement in that direction would be very significant. As it stood, a gift would be a step toward a permanent arrangement and by so much would reduce the danger of a backward step. Harper reminded Rockefeller that it had been two years since he had made a gift to endowment—with an effect that had been "simply tremendous." Another gift of one million (the first of three to endowment) would enable the University to secure a second million in Chicago, within twelve months, for buildings and equipment. To go forward with a "profound want" of money to meet expenses for the next year would be disappointing and disheartening—a temporary and temporizing policy, Harper said, which already had had its effect on Ryerson. It merely put off the day when the University should possibly, or probably, cut down.[52]

Either Gates chose to pocket Harper's letter for a time or Rockefeller read it without immediately finding Harper's anxiety compelling. The University continued to live from hand to mouth for more than ten months after Harper made his appeal. Then, on October 30, 1895, Rockefeller announced the largest pledge that he had yet made to the University. He would, without condition, contribute $1,000,000 for endowment, payable January 1, 1896, and, as of January 1, 1900, would also give the University up to $2,000,000 more for endowment (or other purposes designated later) to match, dollar for dollar, new gifts contributed by others.[53] It could hardly have been coincidence that the Rockefeller portion of the funds thus anticipated was $3,000,000, or the amount which Harper had said would provide the University the endowment it needed to wipe out deficits. In effect, Rockefeller was promising to provide permanent ballast for the budget of the existing program on condition that the University could find elsewhere the $2,000,000 to meet the kind of extraordinary expenses that had been brought to his attention from time to time. If they had had any anxieties over the future of the University, the Trustees wrote Rockefeller, he had entirely removed them.[54]

Robert Herrick, assistant professor of rhetoric and a frequent critic of the regime, remarked acidly that he supposed the gift would make Harper more cocky and Philistine than ever: "If he could only secure another ten millions and then die!"[55] Less than two months after the Rockefeller gift was made, Harper himself was moved to say: "Providence again smiles upon us."[56] Helen Culver, cousin, business associate, and in 1889 devisee of Charles T. Hull, whose home was to become famous as Hull-House, had approached Harper in regard to a gift to the University. The Hull-Culver benefaction, having a value of more than a million dollars, was devoted to building and endowment for the biological sciences. Chicago was honoring the Founder's intention not to bear the principal weight of the University indefinitely. At its launching, the University had lacked necessary gear and had also listed badly, even as it had been put under way; but by the end of 1895, a more nearly complete vessel might have seemed to be gaining equilibrium.

In 1889 it had been hoped that a college with assets of $1,000,000 might gradually become a university. Rockefeller's second gift, arranged to meet the only terms upon which Harper would accept office, had enabled the institution to provide for some of the graduate studies characteristic of a university. Immediately, Harper's activity as President had propelled the University into deficit financing beyond the limits of even its enlarged resources. Crisis followed crisis; and the Founder moved into close contact with the ordinary affairs of the University. He acted repeatedly to save the University from the immediate consequences of overspending, but *ad hoc* donations toward current expenses and equipment did not reach to the cause of deficits. In 1895, several deep intentions could have been read into Rockefeller's gift of $1,000,000 and his conditional pledge of an additional two million. Perhaps he was seeking to extricate himself from the affairs of the University at the price of a last great donation; perhaps he recognized the merit of what had already been accomplished and at once wished to preserve it and to test the confidence of other donors before moving on himself. Perhaps he was acknowledging that the expenses of organizing the University had been justified but wanted evidence that they were indeed extraordinary—that Harper could run a going university on a balanced budget. Plainly, Rockefeller did believe that, until 1900, every effort should be bent toward removing the University, as it was, from a state of crisis. The work of the years just ahead would be to consolidate gains already made beyond the limits of a college pure and simple. The consequences of the immediate past, both good and bad, required attention before the claims of the future were considered.

The first million of the Rockefeller gift of 1895 was payable on January 1, 1896. On January 2, Harper addressed the audience at Convocation:

Do the friends of higher education in this western country appreciate what higher education costs? Do they realize that the University of Chicago, with all its millions, is not half equipped, even in the departments which it has undertaken to establish? Is it necessary to explain that if the University is to be a university, there must be a school of law, a school of medicine, a school of technology? Does anyone imagine that at the University today work can be properly conducted so long as there is not a single room in the Quadrangles in which more than one-third of the University body may assemble at one time? Do the friends of religion appreciate the fact that the University has no such thing as a chapel or headquarters of any kind for its religious work? It may be difficult to understand how a university with eleven or twelve millions of dollars is in need, but when one remembers that this money has come in nearly every instance designated for a particular purpose, and that not half of the work of The University has been provided for, the case will perhaps become more clear. Why should The University of the city of Chicago be satisfied to do a work with an income of six hundred thousand dollars a year when the university located in the city of New York, Columbia, and the university near the city of Boston, Harvard, have each more than a million dollars of income?[57]

This general theme was appropriate to the situation in which the University had found itself: fulfilment of the terms of Rockefeller's latest gift meant the mounting of a vigorous campaign for funds. But to what purpose? Legal, medical, and technological schools might be necessary to the creation of an ideal university; they did not constitute the need that concerned Rockefeller, Gates, and Ryerson when they examined the finances of the University as it existed. Conceivably, Harper sought to create a situation where the benefactors of the University would again have no option but to increase their support or to watch the enterprise languish. Without intending to twist any donor's arm, Harper may have spoken so emphatically of expansion on the argument that a university will not be prepared tomorrow if it refuses to take some risks today. It need not be supposed, however, that Harper's activity was altogether the product of cool reasoning, at the levels either of coercive tactics or far-sighted strategy. Perhaps much of what may seem policy was in fact an impulsive response to necessity as Harper comprehended it. Perhaps he drove affairs—as others thought—too far because he was himself driven by awareness of how far the University still had to go.

CHAPTER XIV

New York
and Chicago

"The work of the University inside was never so satisfactory and the great machine moves along almost without friction." Harper conveyed this information to Gates in early December, 1896; but, Harper continued, ". . . we cannot go forward with the budget with much satisfaction until we know what the future is to be." Gates might like him to come east and talk over everything again.[1] But Gates did not invite Harper to New York. The University men continued to work on the budget, "more carefully than ever before because we have had data . . ." and yet what did they know of subsidies?[2] On the day before Christmas, 1896, Harper again proposed a visit to New York. He and Goodspeed would bring the budget to Gates. By his own admission, Harper had been almost unstrung. "I am quite sure you cannot understand how anxious I have been . . . ," Harper wrote as he testified to the nearly frictionless movement of the University.[3] In February, 1897, he would be in "absolute torture . . . torture which grows worse and worse every day"; he thought, he told Gates, of introducing a lecture on life after death among the Hebrews by saying that he had spent two weeks in Hell and so could speak realistically.[4] Although Harper himself stayed in Chicago, Goodspeed and Henry A. Rust, the Comptroller, went to New York to discuss finances.

Harper's anxiety was well-founded. The Founder's partly conditional pledge of $3,000,000 in 1895 had not been designed to solve immediately the problem of current expenses. Less than two weeks after the pledge had been given, Harper informed Rockefeller that the income from endowment was expected to increase in the fiscal year 1896–97, thanks partly to the return on the segment of the gift that was not conditional. Yet the University would need somewhat more than $100,000 beyond income on endowment to maintain itself as it was. Harper expressed his confidence that the University would have secured that much before the year began; but Gates had said, Harper wrote, that Rockefeller would consider making a payment of $100,000 on the $2,000,000 that he had promised conditionally—that Rockefeller would designate so much of his pledge for the current expenses of 1896–97. The $100,000 would be payable quarterly.[5] Rockefeller promptly adopted the plan.[6] In acknowledging this action for the Trustees, Goodspeed remarked that it would please Rockefeller to learn that ". . . we have very flattering prospects of some large gifts."[7] As such gifts were received, Rockefeller's payments would automatically cease to be advances and become simply matching gifts. Yet of Harper's negotiations with prospective donors, Goodspeed added: "What the outcome will be we cannot yet say."[8]

The financial condition of the University did not improve. On July 15, 1896, near the beginning of the new fiscal year, Goodspeed observed that almost every gift that the University received was designated for some particular purpose while for many purposes the University stood in the utmost need.[9] During the second quarter of 1896–97, the deficit again came under discussion, as did a floating debt in the form of short-term notes. The estimate of the subsidy needed for the year had been far too low; and the time intervals between payments from Rockefeller were far too long, given the actual flow of expenditures. They had once again resisted control, it seems. Arrangements were made for an accountant, who had served many corporations in which Rockefeller had an interest, to make an audit, which—Gates said—should be thorough.[10] The accountant was assisted by Trevor Arnett, who came to the University as a student, was presently appointed its auditor, and eventually became a national authority on academic finance. "The time has come," Goodspeed wrote, "when it will be necessary for us to act upon the repeated direction of the Board and decline to pay bills if the appropriations are overexpended."[11] In early November, the floating debt amounted to $227,000, roughly equivalent to one of Rockefeller's quarterly payments against the deficit plus $200,000 not covered by budget estimates.[12] Harper hoped that Rockefeller would decide to provide that much: "These bank flurries in Chicago have made it more difficult for us to arrange things than ever before."[13] And the budget for 1897–98 had to be worked out. Rockefeller expressed surprise and pain over the floating debt—and Harper had reason to be in torment as the second quarter of the year gave way to the third.[14]

Contrary to Rockefeller's larger intention to found a university that would move on its own momentum, the University had worked itself into a position where its velocity was determined by what Rockefeller intended to do about running expenses. Specifically, by deciding whether or not to grant the University subsidies, annually or even more frequently, in effect he decided from time to time whether the University should or should not retrench. The University proposed, and the Founder disposed—hence the conference in New York during the winter of 1896–97.

Since the conditions which made that visit desirable, or even necessary, obtained while the terms of the $3,000,000 pledge remained unfulfilled, it became the practice of the University to send a delegation to New York each year to present the problem of the budget. The Founder himself did not appear at the conferences, either to listen or to speak his mind. Indeed, he left all direct negotiations over University affairs to Gates or to Gates and John D. Rockefeller, Jr. (after he graduated from Brown University). Ordinarily, University business did not reach Rockefeller's desk until one or both of his lieutenants had been consulted. Socially, the men of Chicago might meet Rockefeller on easy terms; but officially they seldom enjoyed the intimacy which had marked his early visits with Harper in Poughkeepsie. Soon Harper was restrained from approaching him to discuss the business of the University. In 1898, at Rockefeller's express wish, it was agreed that all official correspondence or communication between his office and the University should be carried on by the Trustees through their President or Vice-President. Careful observance of that agreement, said John D. Rockefeller, Jr., would insure perfect understanding and avoid the possibility of misapprehension on either side—". . . which is of vital importance in order to facilitate the carrying on of this great enterprise."[15] Harper replied that he had no desire to question the preferences of the Rockefellers but did wonder whether an action of the President of the University, "the chief executive officer of the institution," ought not to be regarded as formal and official. In 1899, Harper began to write Gates a series of long, quasi-formal letters about the University; and Gates encouraged the practice: "There are so many things constantly pressing themselves upon our attention here, or being thrust upon us, that unless we have some reminders from outside of the University the interest would be likely, insensibly and unconsciously, to wane."[16] Rockefeller was not pushing aside University business, but the New York office continued to address its business to the officers of the Board. Once, after a visit to Chicago, Gates went so far in observing the proprieties of communication as to write back to remind Harper that University matters should be "somewhat formally presented" by the representatives of the Trustees to John D. Rockefeller, Jr., and himself: ". . . we have not thought of taking action on the new questions brought up in the conversations incidental to my visit."[17] (If ever Harper prayed for money in Rockefeller's presence after being forbidden to speak directly—as myth suggests—the act violated all rules of procedure as Rockefeller laid them down.)

The essential point at issue during each conference on the budget was the justifiability of the deficit which Rockefeller was asked to underwrite. In getting at that point, the conferees ranged widely over University policy and management. The New York men aired their doubts about policies and activities, and the Chicago men answered. Gates, or John D. Rockefeller, Jr., would give the University officers an opportunity to see which way the Founder's mind was running on specific matters and—most important of all—his attitude toward the University in general. The Founder's representatives frequently aired misgivings over expenditures for specific programs, but they did not insist upon the curtailment or elimination of those programs as the condition for a renewal of subsidies. The query, not the ultimatum, was the characteristic sentence addressed to representatives of the University. They could learn what was likely to strain relations between the University and its principal supporter; in his absence, the all-important matter of his intentions could be discussed openly without personal embarrassment on either side. Discussion did not invariably lead to complete agreement, but it enabled University friends to know each other's minds. Misunderstanding was not allowed to fester in darkness. Gates was truly discriminating in speaking of a "somewhat formal" relationship. The Chicago men came to New York as official representatives of the University, but in Gates they met a man who was a tested champion of the University as well as a personal friend of its leaders. The Founder's son was disinclined both to silence his colleagues and to suppress his own opinion. No false politeness, arising from a sense of strangeness in each other's company, kept such conferees from speaking plainly. The exchange of ideas took place in the language neither of the bazaar nor of a foreign ministers' meeting but rather in that of attorneys at a most serious but amicable hearing.

Because the recurrence of deficits was the *raison d'être* of these meetings, economy was their dominant theme: was the Morgan Park Academy unduly expensive; should University Extension pay for itself; was too much money being allocated for astronomical work, which was very costly and attracted few students; did the character of learned journals justify their subsidies? Behind these queries lay the question of the absolute or relative worth of the activities which the University had begun. The opinions of the professors were never touched upon; an inspection of the financial condition of the University did not become an inquisition into teaching; and the need for economy was not made an excuse for censorship. Professors were identified in the record only as recipients of loans.

Gates was at his trenchant best when the budget for 1897–98 came up for discussion in the conference of 1897 between Gates, Goodspeed, and Rust. A stenographer was also present and took down a verbatim report as if the conference were indeed a hearing. When the prospective budget had been prepared, the Trustees had not desired to increase the expenditures of any department but rather had aimed at as large a reduction in each as was possible without materially diminishing its work. It was believed that the University ought to be able, after four or five years of experience, to systematize and arrange its work more economically than before.[18] Yet even such a careful manager as Judson found practically nothing to cut from his department and said that he should greatly regret not having more funds available for books.[19] The pressures working toward expansion had not relaxed. Gates began by reviewing the past; he looked back to the ruin of the old University by debt; to the promise made by Goodspeed and himself that the management of the new University would be prudent and that the character of the new Board, with its first-class businessmen, would be a pledge of conservatism; to Goodspeed's alarm and his own over the "too extensive" plan which Harper had prepared; to an awakening, in 1893, to the fact that the University had a debt and fixed expenses running more than $175,000 beyond income; to Rockefeller's acceptance of the situation and his willingness to underwrite the deficit; and to

Rockefeller's conditional pledge, made in the hope that ". . . this deficit would be entirely wiped out, with perhaps a handsome margin for other purposes."[20] Rockefeller had understood that the University, as its first duty, would persist rigorously in the policy of balancing expenditures and income from permanent funds. Such was the situation, said Gates, when Rockefeller made his pledge of $3,000,000.

Gates went on to examine the state of University finances in 1897. Notwithstanding all of Rockefeller's gifts for current expenses and his attempts to prevent deficits, a debt had grown up of about $150,000 for current expenses alone, in addition to an old debt of $100,000. The University, therefore, was behind some $250,000, a sum which would increase to $300,000 by the close of the year. Further, notwithstanding the million dollars from Rockefeller for endowment and the Culver gift, the income of which Rockefeller matched, the deficit for the coming year was estimated at $200,000. The questions arose:

(1) Can we, without permanent injury to the institution, cut down this budget for the year beginning July 1, 1897, and if so, where can we make the cuts? (2) How much of the expected deficit can be raised otherwheres, and how much must we ask from Mr. Rockefeller? (3) On what terms shall we ask Mr. Rockefeller to make a contribution, if any? (4) What suggestions can we make, if any, which shall serve to encourage Mr. Rockefeller in the belief that the institution has come to its limit of deficit?[21]

Gates argued that the income, at 5 per cent of the unassigned residue of the conditionally pledged $2,000,000, plus $2,000,000 to redeem that pledge, or some $3,000,000 to $3,500,000—"a vast sum"—would not fill the gap in the budget: "It is a natural and, indeed, inevitable question with Mr. Rockefeller where this matter will end."[22] That question colored the whole of Gates's reflections.

In response to these comments, Goodspeed also looked backward in time. He confirmed the accuracy of Gates's recollection that economy had been a felt necessity; he recalled that Gates had charged him personally with the responsibility of making certain that the University did not exceed its income; and he spoke of differing a thousand times with Harper.[23] "If my views had prevailed," Goodspeed said, "we should have had in Chicago an institution located on a single block of ground with three or four small buildings, and the character of the institution would have been simply that of a small but respectable college." But Harper's ideal of a university had prevailed, with the result, Goodspeed freely conceded, "that we have an institution which in five years has taken a position beside the great universities of the country which have existed from 150 to 250 years."[24] Owing largely to Rockefeller's liberality, the University had accumulated large funds—not to be compared with those of Harvard and Columbia but much greater than those of almost any other institution in the country. These gifts and Harper's enlightened views had produced the wonderful success that had given the University a position of eminence. Chicago alone had added quite $3,000,000 to the funds of the University in a period of five years, when the times had grown increasingly hard and most educational institutions had languished. The University had been unwise in estimating income from the extraordinary growth of the first two or three years; but it had acted in accordance with the best light available. With this preface, Goodspeed justified the deficits:

... we have been laying the foundations of a very great enterprise. It was greater than we, ourselves, apprehended. The largeness of the plan upon which it was conceived involved the expenditure, year by year, of more money than any one of us, from Dr. Harper down, believed possible. This difficulty was inherent in the beginnings of the undertaking. The present year will close five years of our history. The University is now complete, so far as it is essential to the President's plan. He, himself, has no thought of increasing the work of the institution beyond its present compass, except through the addition of two or three great departments, by special contributions, such as Medicine, Law, and Technology. We know now for the first time just what the work on its present basis involves, what it requires, and what it will annually cost. ... The growth of the institution, on its present basis, will no doubt require additional expenditures, but such additional expenditures will be easily provided by the additional income from the growth of the institution. I ought to say, in concluding, that Dr. Harper has expressed himself to me, personally, in the strongest terms as to his own personal purpose to see that the University is conducted with economy....[25]

Goodspeed was inviting Gates, and through him Rockefeller, to consider the deficit as the product of an abnormal phase of University development and to look upon the University of the future as a virtually self-propelling institution. Ryerson had long since spoken of the extraordinary expenses of organizing the University. But was it so near to completion? Goodspeed, in his desire to persuade Gates to let bygones be bygones, gave less than full weight to the difficulty of creating great departments.

Gates did not reject the implication that the task for tomorrow was to stabilize the University as it was—a view upon which the $3,000,000 pledge had already been made; but he did refuse to move immediately from an examination of the past to consideration of the future. "You have made . . . ," Gates answered, "a forcible plea in justification of the general policy of expansion which the University has pursued."[26] Rockefeller was familiar of course with that argument, Gates indicated—in what dry tone? Gates did not suppose Rockefeller questioned the policy of expansion. But Rockefeller's eyes were wide open to the fact ". . . that this policy involved, of necessity, in order to save the large funds already contributed by him, and to save the institution from ruin, three or four millions from himself. . . ."[27] Not only had he not been consulted in advance on the policy which rendered those immense gifts compulsory, but every injunction he had given in advance had been distinctly against that policy. Thus Gates came close to suggesting that the University had neglected to respect Rockefeller's wishes. Gates did not press the charge directly; rather, he reasoned with Goodspeed and Rust, as if with colleagues:

You, gentlemen, would understand his point of view more clearly, than you can now possibly do, if you lived in the atmosphere of this office. Mr. Rockefeller is known to be a man of very large wealth. That wealth is sought very diligently by the business community, and with scarcely less diligence by the philanthropic community. The method of securing Mr. Rockefeller's funds in the business community is to generally secure such a combination of capital and circumstances as will make a contribution from Mr. Rockefeller compulsory. This is a situation which we are constantly meeting in business. The State, the Legislature, the Municipalities, and other public interests look upon Mr. Rockefeller's funds with the same earnest desire, and they are constantly introducing bills in the shape of rail rates, taxes, etc., making contributions to the State and to the Municipality compulsory on his part, and of such size as to be practical confiscation. It is the very frequent experience of this office that private persons seek to create situations in which Mr. Rockefeller will feel obliged to contribute funds to themselves. It is frequently true, also, of philanthropic institutions, with which Mr. Rockefeller comes into association, that if they do not actually create situations which will make the giving of large sums very nigh compulsory, they do, unfortunately, make it appear as if they did. One of the misfortunes of the present situation is that in every instance, within recent years, in which the University of Chicago has appealed to Mr. Rockefeller for funds, the appeal has not been for new enterprises about to be undertaken, in which he might exercise his judgment as to whether they should or should not be undertaken, but the appeal has been, in every instance, to make up deficits already created to meet exigencies in which the University is committed, and from which, if it be not extricated, it will suffer irreparable damage. You do not think of it because of your remoteness from the atmosphere of the office, but this set of circumstances is the very first thing which we here look for, from long experience and long habit, so that Mr. Rockefeller comes instinctively to feel that the methods of securing his assistance are too often methods of compulsion. The appeals come to him in the shape almost of forced contributions.

If you were to ask wherein lies the element of compulsion, I reply, his name and his fame have become indissolubly associated with the University of Chicago; its disgrace is his disgrace; its shame is his shame, and more than this, how dare he imperil the vast sums already bestowed by the failure to rescue the institution? This fact ought, of course, as we all recognize, to lead the management of the institution to avoid situations which might seem to involve compulsion.[28]

Goodspeed acknowledged the force of Gates's words, saying:

I trust it will not be considered by anyone for a moment that President Harper, in laying out the plan of the University and in increasing its expenditures, has deliberately sought to involve Mr. Rockefeller more and more deeply. The fact is that Dr. Harper has had before his mind a great ideal, and somewhat oblivious to the practical side of the question he has been seeking to realize this high ideal.[29]

The beauty and glory of it had been generally recognized; but in making plans, Harper had not himself understood the expense involved. But, interrupted Gates, Goodspeed was speaking as if in defense of Harper, the implication being of course that he was the responsible party. It was the Trustees who were charged with final responsibility for the conduct of the University. Gates had already expressed his belief that they had approved expansion and so allowed the University to run deficits against Rockefeller's wish. So the question hung in the air: had the Board erred? Yes, but not wilfully, Goodspeed answered. The original plans had involved all that the University had to bear for current expenditures in 1897. When, for example, Harper had added the biological department to the original plan, neither he nor the Board had any conception of what it would cost. The Trustees were in charge of a wholly new enterprise without parallel. After assurances had been given Rockefeller in 1895, there had been absolutely no additions increasing expenditures except the appointment of a professor of botany, based upon the Culver contribution. The deficit was as great a surprise to the Trustees—"and to President Harper" —as it must have been to Gates and Rockefeller. "Indeed," Goodspeed added, it would seem in distress and with near-incoherence, "it was simply to our surprise and grief and dismay to be involved in what was already in progress, and it could not be avoided." If ever any body of men were guiltless of desiring to involve another in expenditures beyond what he himself freely desired to give, the Trustees had been: to that Goodspeed bore witness, from six years spent in meeting the Trustees publicly and privately.[30] In brief, the Trustees had made the mistakes of novices: "They now have had experience. If they err in the future, in the same direction, they will, indeed, be without excuse."[31]

Gates explicitly denied that he was charging the University or any member of it with intent to compel Rockefeller to give, but he did ask if it were not true that Rockefeller was left practically without a choice in the use of his funds.[32] Gates also questioned Goodspeed's interpretation of the past. Gates had been under the impression that from year to year there had been very considerable expansion, involving increasing expenditures, numerous advances in salaries and increases in the number of journals, in the expense of the astronomy department—without a corresponding increase in students, in the expenses of the Morgan Park Academy, and, very heavily, in the care of buildings. That the buildings were involved in the very plan of the University was an effective answer, Gates continued, only on the supposition that there was "an inherent, necessary and inviolable law" compelling the management to carry out continuously and immediately the ideals on which the institution was originally projected, regardless of deficits, debts, or expense. The fact remained that increases had been made not before but after it was known that the institution had a deficit of from $175,000 to $225,000 a year. Moreover, Harper's own ideals had enlarged with the growth of the institution and presumably would continue to do so.[33] Rockefeller's pledges for current expenses had been made with the understanding that any other funds which the University might receive should be used to reduce the deficit and to release a corresponding portion of the Rockefeller pledge. Yet, although large contributions had been made to the University during all of the years in which the pledges had been given, no single dollar had ever been applied to the deficit. On the contrary, hundreds of dollars had been expended to erect buildings—costly to equip and maintain— which increased the deficit.

Goodspeed answered that in all but one case the projects in question had been part of the original plan and that in the exceptional case Gates was mistaken about the facts. Although the historical issue remained unsettled as the conferees began to examine the budget itself, Gates took care to point out where expansion had taken place. Gates had yet to be convinced that the financial difficulties of the University stemmed solely from indiscretions in its more remote past, but he did not demand explicit agreement with his own position.

Once, in the course of the conference, Gates entered the sphere of academic policy for the University Proper. In discussing the astronomy department, he reported Rockefeller's fear that the funds essential ". . . for instruction on earth would be diverted to investigations in the heavens."[34] Goodspeed asked —perhaps testily—whether the University was intended to do any work in original investigation or to be devoted solely to instruction; but Gates did not answer. Again, he declined to demand agreement—and may conceivably have been loath to take up the essentially academic issue which Goodspeed had extracted from Rockefeller's reported comment.

During the conference, Gates explained Rockefeller's principles in regard to the growth of the University. Gates said:

He feels that an institution of learning should be far more conservatively managed than, for instance, a bank, or even a savings bank or a trust company. These companies need only assure the depositor or investor that his funds will be duly cared for during the limited time in which they may be deposited. But a university invites the funds of those who are seeking to make an investment of money for the good of humanity, which shall last, if possible, so long as the world stands. Such contributors delight to contemplate their contributions as going forward in their beneficent purpose, generation after generation. Such contributors look upon the great universities of England and of the Continent, whose history runs back for ages, and observe their solidity and are inspired by the sight of the permanency of these institutions to make those contributions. They love to consider these gifts as perhaps the only lasting impression that they will make on mankind. Indeed, Mr. Rockefeller himself no doubt contemplates his gifts to the University of Chicago in some such light, and to him the question of a mere present success, such as vast numbers of students, great and numerous buildings, magnificently manned and equipped departments, or what not, of present glory, is of little moment compared with the question of what this institution is to be in the generations and ages to come. Far beyond any present successes, therefore, he is looking to the character and policy of the Board of Trustees as it may affect the future history of the institution.[35]

Reviewing the record of the conference somewhat later, Gates amplified that statement by interpreting Rockefeller's disapproval of debt and deficit:

. . . it does not follow from this that Mr. Rockefeller's conceptions of a university are, or ever have been, less broad than those, for instance, of Dr. Harper, or that his ideals of what the University of Chicago may become are now, or ever have been, less expansive or magnificent. Before he had even been approached in behalf of an institution at Chicago, he had visited great universities in our own and in foreign lands, and he had intimately contemplated for years the plan of an institution involving far greater expense than any now involved at Chicago. His conservatism is not now, nor has it ever been, due to any narrowness of conception.

Nor have his prudence and caution arisen from any reluctance to contribute. . . .

Why, then, these frequent and earnest admonitions to avoid debt and deficit at any cost?

I reply, for one thing, in order that public confidence might be secured and maintained. The University has never put forth a Treasurer's report, because, as the Treasurer truly says, it has never dared to disclose to the public the facts. The public confidence is maintained only because the public is not informed as to the true situation. Instead of inviting funds, debt and deficit, if known, are the most certain means of destroying confidence and repelling funds. The debts and deficits of the University of Chicago have not made the institution. On the contrary, the institution has been saved from their ruinous effects only by Mr. Rockefeller's assuming them.

Then again, Mr. Rockefeller, cherishing views perhaps no less broad than those of Dr. Harper, and ideals no less high, has perceived the importance and value of time in an undertaking so vast. He has not been urgent that the University should spring up in a night. He has realized his own inexperience in this great work and the inexperience (to quote the substance of Dr. Goodspeed's remark) of the management of the University, from the President down. He has felt that nervous haste would naturally follow inexperience and has sought to restrain it.

Then again, Mr. Rockefeller has distinguished between mere external expansion and real growth. The actual magnitude of the University is measured only by what it has the money to pay for. All beyond this is deceptive and fictitious. He would avoid unreality. He would avoid the appearance of power not justified by the substance thereof.

Again, Mr. Rockefeller has his eye not on the transitory present, but on the long future. He is unspeakably [*sic*] more interested in the tendencies, policies and character of the management than in any present successes, however brilliant.

Lastly, he has known from the first what he has only lately disclosed to others; this namely, how largely he might, under favorable conditions, become interested in the University at Chicago, and he has known that he would himself give not only far more cheerfully, but also far more largely under a conservative and prudent management that avoids debts and deficits.

Finally, let me add that Mr. Rockefeller, rejoicing in all that has been achieved, recognizes and extols the great qualities of leadership, enthusiasm, and organizing ability in Dr. Harper, without which the present development of the University would have been impossible. He looks to the Trustees, whose invaluable services he also heartily recognizes, not to chill this ardor or to discourage it, but to guide it into channels of solid and permanent prosperity.[36]

Thus, according to the Founder's strategy for the University, the Trustees' mission was to exploit Harper's genius without allowing him to commit the University to financially risky ventures. Rockefeller was content to wait without "nervous haste" upon the future if only it was not jeopardized by a striving for factitious grandeur in the present. What the Trustees' incentive to accept that view would be was implied in Gates's suggestion that Rockefeller might support the University far more largely. Gates did not allude to the fact, of which the conference was in itself evidence, that Rockefeller had been compelled to intervene in University managment against his wishes; but Gates left no room for doubt that the Founder would give more voluntarily than under compulsion. The conference and Gates's commentary plainly touched a vital nerve. Years later, Gates recalled that Rockefeller read the whole (stenographic) report including the addendum, requested that every member of the Board should read it, and ordered it laid away with his securities in his safe in order that it might be available in future years.[37]

The specific sum asked of Rockefeller was $200,000, not for the floating debt plus the new budget but rather for the budget alone.[38] The Trustees presumably believed they could cope with the debt by enforcing economy. Gates responded that Rockefeller was inclined to maintain the status quo—to give $100,000 for 1897–98, as he had for 1896–97. As if to suggest that the renewal of a $100,000 gift was a concession, Gates remarked that Rockefeller might logically have dropped the figure to $85,000 because he had been committed annually, after 1895, for a sum equal to the income from the Culver property. Gates added that Rockefeller might be induced to loan the University funds at a low rate of interest—4 per cent—if exigencies so required.[39] Rockefeller was concerned not only over the existence of a debt itself but also over the need to siphon off income to meet high interest charges.

Shortly after the conference adjourned, Rockefeller promised the University a gift of $100,000—charged to his conditional pledge—and a loan of so much as $100,000 at the rate of interest Gates had mentioned.[40] Thus he made the requested sum of $200,000 available to the University, but on his own terms —to the dismay, Harper remarked, of some Trustees. Harper understood that it was Rockefeller's hope to encourage the elimination of indebtedness and the reduction of expenditure: "He thinks that we will use a smaller amount of the [second] $100,000 if we borrow it than if he had given it to us."[41] It was Ryerson's opinion ". . . that we . . . should at an early date trim our sails" unless the University had very good assurance that Rockefeller intended to place it in a position to continue on its existing scale.[42] Rockefeller had not stipulated retrenchment, if that was what Ryerson had in mind; but Rockefeller's promise had a sharp edge. Appropriations for 1897–98 were to be reduced to leave a margin of $35,000—in effect a contingency fund—between total appropriations and estimated income including a subsidy.[43]

A desire had been expressed in the New York conference ". . . that all obligations should be cleared up and got out of the way preparatory to a new start and a new policy."[44] Rockefeller probably thought of the arrangement for 1897–98 as a reversal of the tide; but, short of retrenchment, a policy of economy, as distinct from its practice, would not be an innovation. The rub had always been to carry proposed conservatism into effect. Just before Goodspeed and Rust went to New York, the Trustees had acted to tighten the financial management of the University by ruling that no expenditures of any kind should be made without the Comptroller's written consent and that he should authorize no expenditure and approve no vouchers for which an appropriation had not been made.[45] After the conference, the Board decided that annual budget appropriations should be merely provisional except for those items such as salaries for which appropriations had to be fixed. The head professors would have no absolute right to spend what the budget allowed. Also, the complete schedule of appropriations was to be known only to the members and officers of the Board; and the President of the University, the Comptroller, and the Secretary of the Board (its President serving ex-officio) were to constitute a standing committee on expenditures. It was duty-bound to consider carefully all proposed expenditures and to make actual appropriations by authorizing such expenditures as were absolutely and unqualifiedly within the limits of the provisional appropriations. The committee was prohibited from authorizing any expenditure whatever which was not clearly provided for in the budget. These measures were buttressed by a commitment which Gates phrased for Goodspeed's acceptance:

. . . as Secretary of the University I will make it my business to keep Mr. Gates informed, as a member of the Board, in advance, of any action contemplated which would either directly or indirectly involve any expenditure beyond the Budget. Also any policy proposed which directly or indirectly would affect the funds of the University along lines not now pursued or as viewed from the standpoint of present expenditures. My aim will be to keep Mr. Rockefeller so constantly informed, in advance, of contemplated action, that it will be possible to get his views in advance and prevent action which he may not approve relating to the financial affairs of the institution. . . .[46]

This procedure would forestall action without the Founder's consent—a practice which Gates singled out as the source of deficits. Official communication between Goodspeed and Gates would keep Rockefeller in constant touch with the condition of the University. Harper grasped the point. Rockefeller desired,

Harper wrote Ryerson, ". . . that we should consult him beforehand on all matters relating to the financial side of things."[47]

Shortly after the New York conference, Gates systematically reviewed all parts of the University and their costs, penetrating even to the level of mailing charges. In the course of this examination, he looked jealously at the outlay for Morgan Park Academy and for University Extension and he took a dim view of the museums, about which he differed radically from Harper.[48] He also noticed the fact that the journals operated at a loss.[49] But in spite of all this, he did not recommend far-reaching retrenchment. The truth was, he remarked, that in institutions of higher learning the salaries of professors usually formed the great bulk of expenditures whereas at Chicago, Extension, Affiliation, the Press, and other unique features nearly doubled total expenditures. Gates was not persuaded that the University should be made to conform to a pattern set by other universities, most of which had grown gradually from a central nucleus. The history of the University had been altogether different: "It is more like the erection of a building." The University had gone up from foundations to roof on the general scale of the architect's ideal: "What we have now may be fairly estimated to be the cost of a fairly complete university, excluding the applied sciences, law, medicine, and technology." Retrenchment would mean tearing down the building to save heat, light, and service.

You may take the budget and scrutinize it from beginning to end and the moment you attempt to retrench you will find that you cannot do it at all, or at least do it to any appreciable extent, without simply dismembering the institution. Here we have an annual deficit of about $200,000.00. Let us suppose now that we go to work to save that amount of money. Where shall we begin and what shall we do? If we cut down the faculty say 10% or 20% in salary, we have only saved from $30,000.00 to $60,000.00. We will cut off an entire department, or two or three departments, and we have only saved the salaries of these particular men, say $50,000.00 or $60,000.00 and we would have still the vast expense of administration, of grounds and buildings untouched. In other words it is utterly impossible to make any saving without amputation, and if you amputate you have amputated at enormous waste.[50]

It was utterly impossible to save the deficit without practically destroying the institution. However unpalatable the fact might be, it was the cold truth. The institution simply could not retrench without closing: ". . . the University is one whole. Every part is dependent on the other parts. It is like a living organism and any attempt at change of its present basis, involves all of the frightful wastes of amputation and disease."[51] The University that resembled a building in its creation had become a living thing: the rising Chicago architects of that day could not have asked for a more expressive shift of metaphor.

Retrenchment did not threaten the University immediately, but it continued to face the old problem of paying for what it had already undertaken in such fashion as to maintain the Founder's confidence. In September, 1897, Gates gave warning on precisely that point. Harper had alluded to a margin of some $28,000 for the fiscal year of 1897–98, to which Gates responded:

. . . the margin ought to be $35,000 . . . I fear this margin has already been cut into to the extent of $7,000. I don't want you to feel a bit comfortable about this margin. Your receipts are likely to fall more than $28,000 below your estimates and you ought not to allow yourself one dollar of extra expenditure above the amount actually fixed in the budget. I will not answer for the calamity which may come to the University if the year ending June 30, 1898, proves again to be a financial disappointment, and I don't want you to feel one minute's comfort. If you know of any point at which the University is spending more money than the estimates, the expenditure should be rigorously cut down. I fear that a comfortable sense of margin may somehow take away the sinew of your resistance to the clamors of the departments. They cannot know, as you and I do, that absolute and irrevocable loss of confidence on the part of Mr. Rockefeller in the financial administration of the University is to be feared and confronted should we be met with another disappointment at the close of the current year.[52]

Perhaps it was awareness of that danger that, in October, made Goodspeed uneasy about an overexpenditure of $2,500 for the theological journal. Goodspeed was anxious beyond measure not to call upon the Founder to make up its deficit: "He has done and is doing so much [and] we must necessarily call upon him to do so much more that we feel that we must not call on him for this item."[53]

However embarrassing it was, the cost of the journal—and that of the Morgan Park Academy and University Extension—came under discussion at a preliminary conversation about the budget for 1898–99. Harper declared his expectation that the journal would be self-supporting in the course of two or three years. The Academy received attention, as it had previously, because of costs for physical plant. In regard to Extension, Harper argued for increased expenditure: a larger staff at work in the field would increase receipts in a greater ratio than expenses, the fixed charges of Extension being constant. Gates remarked that, to reduce the general deficit, University Extension should be made self-supporting, "as was the original expectation"; but he did not relish

Harper's stratagem.[54] Harper maintained that economy could be exercised at other points with less detriment to the University.

Harper: There is no $5,000 which is better spent and which reaches a greater number of people than this $5,000. The lectures reach at least 50,000 people.

Gates: Granting that this statement of Dr. Harper's is true, yet, still, if the department can be made self-supporting, it is a point to be most urgently sought.[55]

In the same conversation it was pointed out that the University was borrowing from Rockefeller faster than warranted by the budget arrangements for 1897–98. Further requests for loans should be accompanied by a full statement, showing the necessity for the current excess and for any additional loans.[56]

The formal budget conference for 1898–99 proceeded from a review of the year then in progress. Again Goodspeed rather than Harper represented the University.

Goodspeed: We estimated the total expenditures of the year at $703,000. The statements made January 1st [1898] indicate to us very clearly that the total expenditure of the year will not exceed this estimate.

Gates (interrupting): Is it quite accurate Dr. Goodspeed to say that $703,000 is the total estimated expenditure? My understanding is that the budget provided for an appropriation of $666,000, but it was believed that there ought to be a leeway or a margin for possible error in the estimated receipts or expenditures and that some provision should be made for a possible expenditure of $703,000.

Goodspeed: I was going to say, I have no doubt that the total expenditure of the year will fall considerably below this sum of $703,000, but they are just as certain to exceed the definite appropriations. . . .[57]

Following this exchange, discussion returned to the journals, the Academy, and University Extension. Comment on the journals was sharp but not, between the conferees, argumentative. The Founder was, Gates said, quite sensitive about the *American Journal of Theology,* ". . . which was a late addition to the family of journals—never welcomed by those who had the financial conditions of the University under serious scrutiny."[58] It had always proved a disappointment financially: ". . . it seems to me that right here is a very good time to test the question whether there is to be a limit within which these matters must be brought."[59] Either the journal should be cut down or other friends of the University should pay for it. It should not be made a charge upon the University; at least, Rockefeller should not be involved either directly or indirectly. Goodspeed had already tried to forestall such comment. He had, he remarked at the conference, made himself exceedingly offensive in fighting the expense of the journal, laboring with Harper and others until he had made himself—so he feared—a general nuisance on the subject.[60] Gates and Goodspeed were in agreement.

They differed, however, in regard to the affiliation program, which was also examined. In earlier conversation on the new budget, the cost of the affiliation program had been questioned: should that cost be charged to the affiliated institutions? Goodspeed explained that the Trustees' course in regard to affiliations, specifically those with Shimer Academy and the Chicago Manual Training School, had been misunderstood. These affiliates had not been united with the University and had no financial relationship with it; but some of the Trustees of the University (seven in the case of Shimer and nine in that of the Manual Training School) were also trustees of the other institutions. Gates conceded that technically and legally the institutions which had recently become affiliated with the University, in what Gates called a departure from the original design as the New York office had known it, were separate from the University; the University was not responsible for their debts or their financial prosperity; and trustees served in their individual capacities. But they were trustees of affiliated schools because they were also Trustees of the University. They had to take the time needed to care for those schools and to "shin around and collect the money to run them from their friends,"[61] who were also friends and supporters of the University. If those institutions got into financial difficulties, although nobody could sue the University and recover, their difficulties also became those of the University. The schools would have to look to the constituency of the University for financial recovery.[62] Obviously it was the University and its own recovery—and nothing else—that concerned Gates.

Rockefeller again agreed to support the budget; but, Goodspeed reported, Harper was greatly distressed. From the report of the conference, he drew the inference that Gates did not fully trust him. "He is so deeply moved," Goodspeed wrote of Harper's attitude, "that I am quite certain this thing is going to work a radical change in him."[63] His absence from the two budget conferences, whether accidental or not, had provided occasion for detached comment upon his work: quite possibly, feeling some isolation, he was unduly touchy. His personal integrity had not been attacked, but the wisdom of the administration he headed had been put partly into doubt.

Harper attended the conference on the budget for 1899–1900. Again, much of the discussion revolved around old issues. Gates scrutinized the cost of publications, and Harper gave somewhat incompatible assurances that under no circumstances would the debt of the *American Journal of Theology* be increased but, if it should be, Rockefeller's subsidy would not be drawn upon.[64] Gates also asked why University Extension, which was mainly self-supporting, could not be wholly so. Ryerson, who was present, answered that it would not be unless fees for administration were increased, which would probably not be wise. He argued that the possibilities of University Extension work in departments not then occupied would justify a large annual expenditure beyond probable income; but Ryerson agreed with the other conferees that, because of the deficit, Extension should become self-supporting as rapidly as possible without serious loss in efficiency.[65] Gates again invoked the principle of self-support in connection with affiliation. The program had been started on that principle and should return to it.[66] The gist of Gates's thought is clear: the greater constituency of the University, which Harper cherished, should not be served out of endowment income, at least until the future of the University Proper was financially secure.

The effort to conserve resources continued. During the conference, a review of endowments revealed that the University had made loans to some professors and had invested in buildings used for its own purposes. The size of its income had become partly dependent upon the amount of money its members could afford to pay out: a potentially vicious circle had been created. It was also noticed that at least one fund—established by Rockefeller—had been drawn upon to anticipate cash payments from other sources. (The Trustees subsequently disallowed the first practice and permitted the others only with safeguards.) When Rust reported that about $29,000 of Rockefeller's gift toward the budget of 1897–98 had been used to pay arrears on previous budgets, running as far back as 1893, the conferees also agreed that, in future, funds applicable to a particular budget should never be used for any other purpose without the donor's consent.*

But was new money being raised to match Rockefeller's conditional pledge, which had been designed to wipe out the deficit? In May, 1898, Goodspeed had written optimistically to Gates about the campaign:

* Years later, Trevor Arnett was to incorporate such reforms in the canon of sound academic management in the volume *College and University Finance* (New York: General Education Board, 1922), pp. 24–53.

In Chicago the time has not been propitious for securing subscriptions but the tide has now turned. Everything looks hopeful. We can approach men with confidence and courage and they will hear us with patience and favor. We have not neglected this work. We have waited for our opportunity and we believe it has now come.[67]

At the conference, in December, Gates asked for detailed information on actual cash receipts. It had been understood, Gates said, that insofar as possible the University would direct the minds of future donors to endowment and the bridging of the $200,000 deficit rather than to buildings and so forth.

Gates: Can the gentlemen report progress in that direction? What has been the use of the funds thus far received?

Harper: We have not received much.

.   .   .   .

Ryerson: So far as there is any opportunity of directing the application of the gifts to the University, the policy of the Board now is to provide for work already being done by the University rather than for any expansion of the work.

Rockefeller, Jr.: What is the chance of getting enough money to make good the pledge of my father?

Ryerson: I do not think the chances are favorable.

Rockefeller, Jr.: Has every effort been made up to date in that direction? Have all the energies possible been bent toward that end? That, of course, is the great considera-tion. We have often felt here that it was not so considered in the West.

Ryerson: I think the Board has in mind the importance of that fact and any delay in making efforts has been caused by the hopelessness of doing anything rather than through forgetfulness of the Board. It is now planned to renew the efforts at an early date.

Harper: For instance, a gentlemen said to me (I speak of Mr. Hutchinson) do not touch it until after the first of January: you will do more harm than good until after that date. His opinion was that we would lose time and money by starting in too soon.

Rockefeller, Jr.: You think every effort has been made to raise money on this pledge?

Ryerson: Yes. Every opportunity that has presented itself has been taken advantage of.

Rockefeller, Jr.: I mean you think it would not have been wise to push the matter more?

Ryerson: Yes, that's it; that is, it would not have been profitable.[68]

Rockefeller again subscribed to the budget; and Harper threw himself into the campaign. The deadline, January 1, 1900, lay halfway through the year that the budget covered. "Every hour during which I am not able to withdraw my mind from the financial situation is," Harper declared to Gates in October,

1899, "an hour of agony."[69] It seemed clear that the money could not be raised in small subscriptions. Also, the men who were ready to give wished to put their money into buildings: in every case, Harper tried, he said, to secure a sufficient amount to provide for maintenance.[70] He also reported that he had to do most of the soliciting alone. Although Goodspeed was entirely willing to accompany Harper, the work was "largely of a personal nature," which was presumably Harper's way of saying that donors appealed unto Caesar.[71] In mid-November, Harper was becoming "somewhat desperate."[72] Less than a fortnight before the deadline, Gates was asked how strictly the Founder would interpret the terms of his pledge: would gifts promised before January 1, 1900, but payable later, be acceptable, and also gifts on which life annuities were to be paid?[73] Mrs. Charles Hitchcock, for example, offered a property interest valued at $250,000 on conditions including annuity payments.[74] On Christmas morning, 1899, Harper reported to New York that the University would probably fall short of its goal by at least $300,000, perhaps more. The direct loss of funds, including an unmatched portion of Rockefeller's pledge, would thus be at least $600,000, Harper reasoned. According to the logic of the campaign, he might have measured its results another way: since Rockefeller might match as much as $1,700,000 given by others, the University would gain nearly three and a half million, or far more than it had previously received as the result of one drive. What Harper actually saw was "our first failure"—a failure to carry through a great undertaking, which would mean a distinct loss of public confidence and would have a moral effect upon the mind of Rockefeller himself.[75] Yet on December 28, when the campaign had less than a week to run, Rockefeller pushed the deadline back three months at the request of the University.[76] Then, on January 2, 1900, Gates and John D. Rockefeller, Jr., wired that they could not commit the Founder to the severe terms of the Hitchcock gift, but that, if announcement of the gift could not be avoided, they would help the Trustees to find some way to meet the conditions.[77]

During January, the University men were preoccupied with making arrangements for the coming year; and in the six weeks after February 1, they made little progress in securing large gifts. Harper dreamed in March of the great comfort it would be if there were some way of reducing the amount to be raised: ". . . but I suppose there is nothing to be said along that line."[78] As he had in other moments of crisis, Harper declared his concern over his own ability to persist. To George C. Walker, Harper wrote that the six months just past had aged him ten years: "The agony of it and the anxiety cannot be described . . . after this last effort I must be relieved of such responsibility. Or, to put the matter in another form, the University is now at a point where we can not afford to do work in this way."[79] To Gates: "It is now more than two years since I have had much of a let-up, and I suppose the results are beginning to appear. . . . The stress of the situation is . . . beginning to tell on me."[80] To Ryerson: "I find that I am not personally in as good trim as in December, and in spite of extra care taken these last two months, it is quite evident that I am not equal to the strain through which I passed in the month of December. Three times within the last ten days the evidence of this fact has presented itself in no uncertain way."[81] What had happened Harper did not say.

In the last month of the campaign, Harper argued, from either intuition or undisclosed indications, that more than the conditional pledge was at stake: "Everything depends upon this effort. If we succeed we shall enter at once into the promised land, for I am confident that Mr. R. is ready to capitalize the deficit by giving five million dollars, and in this way we shall be put in splendid condition."[82] Then, writing Gates as the last week of the extended campaign drew near, Harper reverted to his thoughts of late December: ". . . if we fail, it will have a very pronounced effect upon the public mind. It will mean that we have reached the end of our rope here in Chicago, which of course is not true— for there are a great many people who wish to give but are not quite ready to do it, and who will not be forced by the representations of the present situation." Many people had already snubbed the University, wanting to know why it was in such serious condition when the Founder had shared in a large—and widely publicized—dividend from the Standard Oil Company. "I repeat," Harper wrote, "that it will be tremendously to the advantage of the University in the future if we have the moral effect of success in this effort. . . ."[83] If we succeed; if we fail: these contingencies were the poles of Harper's thinking.

Three days before the end of the campaign, Harper reported several substantial gifts, including a conditional gift from Hutchinson.[84] Earlier in the month, Gates had intimated to Hutchinson that Rockefeller might join a syndicate to finance building if Hutchinson should organize one. That, Gates took pains to point out, was a marked departure from Rockefeller's usual procedure. On the last day but one before the deadline, Gates asked to be told by wire, at the last minute, ". . . how much you lack of fulfilling conditions."[85] Harper replied the next day that of $405,000 lacking on January 1, $205,000 had been subscribed and that two subscriptions were pending: ". . . any adjustment should be flexible enough to allow these subscriptions to be counted if made today or tomorrow. . . ."[86] On the same day Gates telegraphed that friends of the University had pledged enough to cover whatever actual shortage there might be: ". . . you can therefore announce the success of the movement."[87]

Gates did not formally identify its saviors but indicated that Rockefeller himself had suggested that friends could be secured in New York.[88] Rockefeller allowed the University neither to depart from strict accounting nor to fail in a campaign that demonstrated the willingness of others to support the University.

Unquestionably, Rockefeller had hoped, in 1895, that the campaign would provide the University a sound foundation. But most of the gifts were earmarked for purposes other than endowment, and parts of Rockefeller's $2,000,000 were used to meet deficits and to pay for building, or were otherwise diverted from investment. It was, Goodspeed recalled afterward, a great disappointment to Rockefeller that so little could be saved for that use.[89] The problem of operating deficits remained. Rockefeller continued to support the budget, and for three years he also added $1,000,000 to permanent funds each December. The timing of the gifts implied the warm sentiments of Christmas; but their assignment to the endowment of the University expressed the cold logic of its financial history.

PART SIX

THE UNIVERSITY
ESTABLISHED

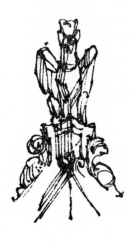

After the Beginning

" 'To begin is poetry; to continue is prose.' I think we all realize that the romance of the beginning days of the University is a thing of the past, and that we are now down at work in the prosaic period."[1] Harper made that observation to John D. Rockefeller, Jr., after the decennial celebration, in December, 1902. The effects of the successful campaign that had ended in 1900 were becoming visible in new buildings; the learned papers and monographs available for publication in the decennial series provided evidence that the Faculty was not merely giving lip-service to the idea of research; the decennial report of the President and his coadjutors would shortly indicate, with massive documentation, that the University had gained a vast amount of experience in spite of its youth; the celebration itself marked the fact that the precocious institution had passed beyond childhood; and the Founder was regularly demonstrating his confidence. (In 1901, his son had indeed asked how much it would cost to round out the work of the University.)[2] Harper's remark, in his decennial report, that "the essential characteristics of the institution have been determined," was that of a President looking backward, not forward, to the most critical work of his administration.[3] What had been accomplished, however, implied that more remained to be done in the institution that promised to be a university and not simply a large college.[4] Harper combined historical observation and prognostication in making that statement. In his logic, the past of the University was indeed prologue. Thus during the period of the celebration and afterward, Harper labored over plans to enlarge and to improve the program of the University. As always, he had to be concerned over money. In 1901, the new capital required to round out the University was, by Harper's estimate, $26,-635,000, a sum almost twice as large as the value of all resources (fourteen million plus) at the end of the fiscal year 1901–02.[5] Plainly, Harper's hopes were large in comparison with the results of past financial efforts. Yet measured against other universities, Chicago did need much more wealth than it had. Following a procession from cornerstone to cornerstone, a visitor to the University of Chicago might have missed the fact—but it was the fact—that Chicago was not the richest university in the United States. The total of University resources, including buildings, grounds, and so forth, was not much greater than the *productive* funds of Columbia or Harvard.[6] Under that rubric, the University also stood below Cornell but above Yale.

The financial and academic needs of the University were great; but, seemingly, time was on Harper's side. He was in his mid-forties and could sensibly have supposed that his administration might last another two decades. (Charles W. Eliot had presided over Harvard for more than thirty years and did not retire until 1909. Without holding office as long as Eliot did at Harvard or as Nicholas Murray Butler would at Columbia, Harper could have served until 1929, the year in which Robert M. Hutchins was to come, as Harper had, from Yale to the University of Chicago.) Yet in the forecast with which Harper closed his decennial report and in which he read the future from the record of the past, he spoke only of the second ten years. What he hoped they would bring amounted to a great expansion of the University program.[7]

CHAPTER XV

Toward the Higher Teaching

The first of Harper's specific predictions for the second decade was that professional work would be placed on a level with graduate studies and would ". . . indeed itself be graduate work of the highest order."[1] A law school was already "in substantial shape," Harper said, and a medical school was "practically arranged for"; schools of technology, music, and art remained to be organized.[2] According to Harper's estimate of 1901, which did not cover schools of music and art, the cost of adding the new schools was $7,050,000—or $500,000 for law, $4,550,000 for medicine, and $2,000,000 for technology.[3]

During Harper's administration, the foundation of schools of music and art was nothing but a dream, justified by only the flimsiest prospect of material support.[4] The academic program did not fulfil the culminating prediction of Harper's forecast, that in its second decade the life of the University would be enriched aesthetically.[5] In the field of technology, Harper's expectations were no less wide of the mark. Almost immediately after the death of Philip D. Armour in 1901, Martin Ryerson expressed his hope that a union of the Armour Institute and the University might prevent the necessity of duplication: the obligation to have an unsurpassed school, if the University entered the field, must be impressed upon Mrs. Armour and her son, J. Ogden Armour.[6] Harper approached him; but before Armour had reached a decision, the Trustees of the

University also approached John D. Rockefeller. He refused to support technological education, "for the present at least"; but, taking up those words, Harper sent John D. Rockefeller, Jr., an emphatic appeal that lacked only specification of a time for action.[7] Harper had in mind a gift of $1,000,000 outright and $2,000,000 pledged conditionally. "I sometimes get the feeling," Harper wrote, "that all that we are now doing is of little value in view of the demand for technology."[8] Harper visited New York and on his return told Ryerson that the friends of the University were willing to go forward in regard to the Armour Institute. Harper added: "The Armours are just on the point of settling the matter."[9] In what he called a very interesting situation, Harper argued for a merger of two great benefactions in a common cause, i.e., that the resources of the Institute should be used to match a conditional Rockefeller pledge. Did he suggest to the Armours that the University would compete with the Institute (as Ryerson had intimated) if union were not arranged? After an interview with Armour in November, 1902, Harper again visited New York and came home to report to Armour that Gates was enthusiastic.[10] Armour immediately wrote Harper, in a friendly vein but without explanation, "I do not believe there is much use in our figuring to put the two schools together."[11] Still refusing to give up, Harper forwarded Armour a letter in which Abram S. Hewitt, the son-in-law of the philanthropist Peter Cooper, indorsed a proposal to put Cooper Union in the hands of the trustees of Columbia University. Such disposition of a philanthropy by the heirs of its donors was advantageous: a university was organized expressly for the supervision and administration of educational work.[12] Armour thanked Harper for sending the letter but remained unpersuaded: ". . . I don't believe that we would care to part with the Institute now."[13] Rockefeller was no more responsive; and Harper's plan aborted. The University had been opened without technology in expectation that sooner or later, in the environment of Chicago, the practical side of education would be included.[14] Technology did receive support, but not in fulfilment of Harper's grand design for the University.

In medicine—and according to Harper's decennial testimony a school had been all but arranged—the University had chosen to accept affiliation with Rush Medical College. In 1902, Doctor Ingals again recommended union; and, contrary to their earlier policy, the Trustees accepted the proposal, with the understanding that no better arrangement for the future development of medicine could be proposed and on the condition that Rush raise $1,000,000 within a year.[15] Presumably the Board had been converted by the results and possibilities offered by affiliation once it began to take effect. During the years from 1898 to 1904, accumulating changes in medical instruction transformed the original Rush program. Admission requirements were raised, and the entrance examinations were placed in the hands of the University, which meant a more rigorous weeding out of unprepared candidates. Large classes were divided into smaller sections after the pattern of instruction in the University; and an elective system was introduced into the latter part of the medical curriculum. A library for students was organized at the suggestion of the University; and the laboratories of the University were used by many of the younger instructors, sometimes for original work. Perhaps the most significant of the changes following upon affiliation was the transfer of pre-clinical instruction to departments of the University so that half of the medical course became University study.[16] Repeatedly, the *University Record* preached the moral that the program taught by example: medicine was an experimental science.[17]

The thought of medical research as a specific career had occurred to Ingals and Harper even before affiliation took place. In 1902, what came to be called "full-time" medical education was advocated publicly by Lewellys Barker, professor of anatomy, as he addressed the alumni of Johns Hopkins University, where he had lately taught. Before coming to the University, Barker had written to Harper: "It appears to me that in the near future, medicine, surgery and obstetrics could best be advanced if these subjects were, like the subjects of Anatomy, Physiology and Pathology, placed on a University footing and dealt with in the spirit of, and by means of the methods which prevail in modern education of the highest type."[18] It would be a pity, Barker thought only a short time later, if the credit for first establishing academic clinical work should be lost to the University. Its friends had at that moment ". . . a grand opportunity to *mark an epoch* in medical education."[19]

The process that Barker had in mind was evolutionary. Semi-university schools, in which the subjects of the first two years of the medical curriculum were taught by professors rather than practitioners, should become "real university" schools when men, bred to university careers, were placed in charge of hospitals especially constructed and endowed for university purposes and were permitted to devote their whole time and strength to teaching and investigating. A distinction should be drawn between men who gave their whole time to the College and those who did not. Practitioners should not be altogether excluded from instruction; but as rapidly as money was available, the University should fill the various chairs of medicine with men of the other class.[20] In this direction lay the absorption of Rush by the University. (One wonders if Barker knew that Ryerson had hoped that "extension of the work of Rush" might lead to this result.)[21]

Rockefeller's representatives approved the proposal of union, on the premise that the aims and ideals of the Rush faculty were substantially those that Barker had expressed in his address and that Frank Billings, a Chicago physician who became president of the American Medical Association in 1902, had outlined in conversation. Gates and the young Rockefeller set other conditions: Harper and the Trustees must feel that, if the University were to establish a medical school *de novo,* they could do no better than to make the Rush faculty the basis of the school; no funds should be requested of the Founder on account of the union, or as a result of it, for at least five years; the name of Rush should presently be dropped; and the University should not be inconvenienced in its administration.[22] Within the year allowed, Rush raised $1,000,000 to meet the Trustees' condition, thanks largely to Billings' effort; but about two-thirds of the total consisted of funds earmarked for purposes not taken into consideration in 1902.[23] Even so, the Trustees continued to consider arrangements for union; but the Founder demurred. Rockefeller had to be convinced that research had been provided support. He would not be hurried in his decision. In July, 1903, he proposed to Harper by telephone that the whole matter should be postponed a year:

This [Harper reported] I succeeded in showing him would be unfortunate. He still maintained his position that he could not give favorable decision if pressed. I then proposed to . . . take the thing up leisurely; have Hutchinson come on, but to this he replied no, that by a leisurely consideration he did not mean one week, or two weeks, but longer. He, with Mr. Gates, insisted that the best plan was to take a year. I insisted that this meant a decision on their part unfavourable to the proposition which was made. This he admitted.[24]

Harper finally secured Rockefeller's consent to postpone a decision of any kind until the first of October. John D. Rockefeller, Jr., pointed out that if Rush brought for immediate improvements $700,000 less than was originally contemplated and if that sum was not raised within five years, the Founder would then be asked to provide these needs.[25]

When negotiations were resumed, the Trustees and the Founder's representatives agreed that the Rush campaign had failed and that the question of union between the University and the College should be renewed—in the words of John D. Rockefeller, Jr., and Gates—"untrammelled by engagements of any kind on either side."[26] The Trustees proposed that union should be effected upon a fund of $225,000 or more, in cash and without restrictions, to be used for endowment or building. The Trustees would endeavor to conduct the work for four years without calling upon the Founder. (Harper's original draft had read that the Trustees would undertake to conduct the College on these terms "except perhaps in the case of an unexpected emergency.")[27] Presumably the Trustees hoped that immediate union would enable the University to salvage the pledges made to the campaign. The proposal left the Founder's representatives unmoved. By close economy and special arrangements with some professors to work for little remuneration, the University might conduct the school and still avoid debt; but such an arrangement would be increasingly irksome to the professors and at best could not fail to be exceedingly embarrassing to the University. Without a large outlay, at the very least several millions, the high ideals shared by the University and the College could not be carried out; and if they were not, the medical college would not be placed on a parity with other departments of the University. John D. Rockefeller, Jr., and Gates reminded the University that they had originally regretted the Rush affiliation, mainly because they feared ". . . that on the part of some or all of the trustees and professors of the two institutions, and on the part of the public as well, the affiliation was understood to contemplate union and was a preliminary step thereto. . . ." The contrary view in New York had been ". . . that any medical department of the university should be devoted mainly, if not exclusively, to research, and should be independent of any medical school or any school of medicine." In view of these and other considerations, including a University deficit of more than $150,000, union seemed unwise.[28]

The Trustees held the issue open for study until the summer of 1904. Then, speaking directly to the argument of the Founder's representatives, the Trustees asserted that affiliation had not carried an implied commitment to union, that affiliation had been fruitful, and that they sympathized profoundly with Rockefeller and Gates in their emphasis upon research. But, the Trustees continued in a statement of fundamentals,

. . . we believe it would be unwise for the University to depart from its general policy in this particular division of its work. In every other department of the University provision is made for instruction. This is necessary, in part, because only in this way can we secure men well prepared for the higher work of research; and further because in the work of instruction investigators most frequently find their greatest inspiration. It is the experience of most investigators that a certain amount of teaching, especially with advanced students, is a distinct advantage. Moreover with schools of Law and Divinity and other professional work organized for the education of students of whom high standards of preparation have been required, it would be manifestly a peculiar policy to restrict work in the Department of Medicine absolutely to a few research professors. . . . We sincerely hope that it will not be thought wise to differentiate medicine from other subjects in the method to be adopted by the University. . . . As trustees we do not contemplate the establishment of research in any other department of the University, without at the same time providing instruction in connection with such work, and we see no good reason for making exception in this general policy in the case of medicine.

. . . .

The instruction of students—the preparation of medical practitioners of the best type, is quite as much the function of a University as is the promotion of research. Such instruction can only be given in an Institution where research of the highest order is being conducted. . . .[29]

In brief, investigation *and* teaching were required of a university. The Trustees asked that the Founder give an endowment of $500,000 to the University for medicine, provided Rush and the University secured another $500,000 elsewhere. That request was read by John D. Rockefeller, Jr., and Gates and submitted to the Founder, who declined to consider a gift, as his son reported, "to Rush Medical College." In New York, the institution being organized did not appear to be the Medical School of the University of Chicago. When the income and the expenses of the University had been brought together (instead of tending each year to separate further), John D. Rockefeller, Jr., remarked, he and Gates would as Trustees have ". . . better grounds upon which to present to my father and other friends of the University its needs for growth and enlargement."[30] The Trustees believed in union and argued their case stoutly; the Founder did not believe in union and did not move his hand, either in deference to the Trustees' decision or in anger at the fact that they defended it. There rested the effort to create a medical school until after the Harper era ended.

Why did a stalemate occur? The Founder had shown himself prepared to endow medicine; the Rockefeller Institute for Medical Research was created in 1901. The University also sought to advance medicine as a science. No one doubted that the advancement of medicine depended upon inquiry. The Trus-

tees did insist that *in the University* research and teaching should be combined.*
Was union finally rejected in New York, then, because the University was, and
refused not to be, a school? Having been shocked to learn how little was known
of the pathology and therapy of diseases, Gates had become convinced that discovery should take precedence over other medical work; but neither Gates nor
the Rockefellers flatly rejected Harper's plans on the grounds that they embraced medical education as well as research. What the New York men opposed
—or accepted only under protest—was the Rush affiliation. In their view, it
threatened to implicate the University, already deficit-ridden, in the affairs of
another financially precarious institution. Their imaginations were never fired
by the possibility that affiliation—or union—might offer the compensating advantage of a new departure in medicine. Did they think that the University was
inclined to make do with half-measures? Perhaps it asked for support of too
little rather than too much; but as long as the University was running on a
deficit, it was not well situated to make a large request for new schools. Possibly
$4,550,000 would not have been out of the question after 1901 had the University
in earlier years spent only what it had in hand. Stalemate was perhaps a product
of history. Bold expansion in the beginning had its price: its financial results had
taught the Founder to be wary of Harper's optimism. Ironically, the Rush
affiliation, as seen in Chicago, facilitated a movement that was both aggressive and evolutionary, the kind of growth for which Gates, Goodspeed, and
Ryerson as well as others had argued but with which Harper had not originally
been content. The University, it was hoped, would advance medicine by improving the best of the old education until the better new education had been
achieved. The principle of gradualism had been set aside often and was invoked
too late.

"You have got the doctors, now Doctor Harper, get the lawyers, or you will
be like a bird with only one wing. . . ." So wrote a Trustee, Hermann H. Kohlsaat, in 1900.[31] Harper's effort to add law to the curriculum began after the
affiliation in medicine had been arranged, but it succeeded without compromis-
ing the future. In law, no attempt was made to graft another institution on to
the University. Although in 1893, President James C. Welling of Columbian

---

* In his decennial report, Harper advocated the establishment of research professorships, the occupants of which might lecture or not according to the best interests of their work (Harper, PR,
1892–1902, p. xxv). Harper remarked that such was the character of the professorships in the Yerkes
Observatory, but he did not propose that any other department should be organized, in its entirety,
as a research institute.

University in Washington, D.C., had suggested that the law school there might be placed under the direction of the University of Chicago, neither consolidation nor affiliation figured in the establishment of legal education. Harper was not dogged by the frustrations he met in technology and medicine. A law school was thought to be far less expensive than the other proposed schools and so was less menacing to the hope of a balanced budget. Rockefeller authorized the purchase of books from the unexpended portion of his 1895 gift and also guaranteed a building on condition that his pledge would remain known to the Trustees only and that they would try to solicit contributions elsewhere.[32]

As did professional education in business, legal studies might have evolved from the interests of a professor in the Faculty of art, literature, and science. When Ernst Freund joined the Department of Political Science in 1894, the *Weekly* asked editorially if the appointment meant only a desire to put the department on a broader basis or if it signified that the University had taken the first step toward establishment of a great law school without waiting for an endowment.[33] The University had acquired the services of a lawyer who held a doctorate in law from Heidelberg and would earn a Ph.D. in political science from Columbia University. In the winter of 1901–02, when the Trustees decided to establish a law school, Freund was prepared to advise Harper about the experts in legal education and to draft a curriculum which would embrace social science as well as strictly legal topics. In March, 1902, the Senate ruled tentatively that law students would be given an opportunity, within limits, to carry studies which were not strictly professional and not required for admission to the bar: "As many lawyers enter public life, and by reason of their technical knowledge have in many respects a controlling influence upon the framing of laws, they should be enabled to study principles of legislation as well as principles of law"[34] The law school would be affiliated with the work of Political Economy, Political Science, Sociology, and Commerce and Administration. Harper remarked that a scientific study of the law involved history, economics, philosophy—"the whole field of man as a social being."[35]

The impact of Freund's thought was immediately and materially reduced by the men to whom, as it happened, he referred Harper. "I . . . think it extremely desirable that you should at some time have a talk with Professor James Barr Ames of the Harvard Law School . . . ," Freund had said; and he also mentioned Joseph H. Beale of the same faculty.[36] The successor to Christopher C. Langdell as dean of the School, Ames represented pre-eminently the reform of legal education as Harvard had conceived of it. The mastery of jurisprudence meant the extraction of principles from the record of cases actually tried in court; the process should be directed by professional teachers of law, not by practicing attorneys teaching part-time, and the students should be liberally educated men. Kohlsaat had testified backhandedly to the success of the Harvard Law School by measuring the prospects before the University by the yardstick of rivalry with Harvard. Harper was advised by one colleague that the Harvard Law School was "theoretical, doctrinaire" and should not be imitated in the more practical environment of the University; but Harper did listen intently to Harvard men.[37] The University quickly decided that Beale should be borrowed from the Harvard Law faculty to preside over the founding of the University of Chicago Law School, which meant that Ames was in a position not only to offer advice but also to give or withhold consent to the appointment of the prospective dean. Harper's situation was unlike that which he occupied while seeking to arrange affiliations or mergers involving the amalgamation of staffs and resources as well as programs. The issue raised by the proposed infusion of Harvard talent was academic in the most strict sense: how was the law to be studied in a university; or, more specifically, given the Harvard Law School as a model, wherein did its excellence lie?

Harper did not question (and indeed had long accepted) much that the Harvard Law School represented. In 1893, he had said that the law school in the University would be a school of jurisprudence and of jurists. Its field would be the higher study of law; its professors would devote their entire time to their work in the University; and its students would be college graduates.[38] In March, 1902, before the arrangements for Beale's temporary release from Harvard had been completed, Harper announced the Trustees' belief that the larger part of legal instruction should be given by men who made a profession of teaching law.[39] But was a particular mode of study essential to academic education in the law? Differing meanings could be read into Harvard's experience. "It was not," Freund was shortly to recall,

chiefly or primarily the method of instruction [at Harvard Law School] . . . that challenged admiration—on that point the attitude of the University was that of the open mind; but the spirit of earnestness and devotion to their chosen work on the part of the students, for which that school was distinguished, it was deemed essential to transplant and reproduce. . . .[40]

Beale also paid tribute to the spirit of the Harvard students; but neither he nor Ames put the method of Harvard in second place.[41] The higher study of the law pointed to the casebook. The law must be taught, like every other science, by putting the sources of knowledge into the hands of the student and leading him, by investigation, by comparison, and by the gradual formation of a scientific judgment on which he may depend. . . . The original sources of our law are the decisions of our courts, the official depositories of legal learning; and only by a study of these decisions can we know the law as a science.[42]

The implications of that difference in emphasis may not have been fully explored when in the spring of 1902 Harper arranged—as he believed, satisfactorily—for Beale to come west on loan from Harvard. When Freund subsequently visited Cambridge, however, Ames and Beale discovered a gulf between their thought and his. Both of the Harvard men wrote Harper to reopen discussion of the terms on which Beale would come to Chicago. "We were perhaps not quite justified," Beale said, "in supposing that . . . you had in mind a school in all respects like ours."[43] Hardly *not quite;* Freund had not only left the impression that he was predisposed against the casebook method, he had also suggested that political science and sociology should be taught in the law school and that professors of prelegal subjects should be admitted to its Faculty. "We have no such subjects in our Curriculum," Ames declared, "and are unanimously opposed to the teaching of anything but pure law in our department. . . . We think that no one but a lawyer, teaching law, should be a member of a Law Faculty."[44] Beale asked for assurances that none but strictly legal subjects would be taught in the school, that policy would be formulated in the first instance by a Faculty consisting entirely of lawyers, that no person would teach who did not frankly concur in adopting the spirit and methods of the Harvard Law School, and that Harper would himself heartily support Beale in an effort to establish ideals and methods similar to those in the school. He could not be of any use, Beale asserted, in such a school as Freund had in mind: "These differences of view are so fundamental that it is obviously necessary to choose one conception of the school or the other."[45]

That bleak option exhibited the point of law, as it were, upon which the Harvard men stood. Beale did not demand, however, that the University should choose between himself and Freund. Had he done so, Harper would have been obliged to allow the negotiations to collapse or to drop the original architect of legal education at the University. By distinguishing between principles and persons, Beale made use of the Harvard model practicable and immediate organization of the school possible. He was willing to act as a mediator between Harvard and the University. In that role, he wrote privately to Freund:

Perhaps Mr. Ames was more disturbed than I by what he (and I) consider your heretical ideas about law. The hard fight which he and Mr. Langdell had . . . made him anxious that I should not meet a similar difficulty and he very probably feared when there was no need. . . . I thought while our ideas differed (only on that one point) we could get on charmingly; but it was regarded here as essential that I should have certain assurances before going and I wrote accordingly to Dr. Harper. . . . Allow me to say that your own ability and position will naturally give your opinion great weight; but you are a lawyer and have taught law, and it is therefore a matter of course that you shall have your share in the formation of the school's policy.[46]

Beale assured Harper that he did not need to fear an exclusively Harvard faculty while Dr. Freund was able to exercise "a healthy restraining influence."[47] Beale was willing to organize a school with colleagues who were not devotees of the Harvard system, provided they were first-class lawyers. The Law School was opened in 1902. At the end of the academic year, the regular Faculty contained five Harvard LL.B.'s, including James Parker Hall, who soon succeeded Beale as dean; two men with degrees in law from other universities; and one who had been admitted to the bar, after the older fashion, and had taught law without taking a degree.[48]

To secure Beale's services from Harvard, the University had virtually consented to honor the Harvard precedent at some expense to its own original views. The terms of Beale's coming precluded, in the basic curriculum, a strikingly new departure onto new ground where the law might have met the studies that were to become behavioral sciences. The "first and foremost vocation" of the school was to train lawyers, by offering a three-year curriculum composed entirely of professional work. The method of instruction was announced to be the study of cases, "designed to give an effective knowledge of legal principles and to develop the power of independent legal reasoning."[49] Bringing eastern standards west was the initial service of the school to legal education.[50] That was, one supposes, the reason for Harvard's co-operation, and that rather than sheer innovation was the measure of accomplishment. But the training of lawyers was not to be the sole concern of the school:

. . . it understands that its duty to the University requires it to cultivate legal science in its less practical aspects. Opportunity, therefore, will be given for the pursuit of graduate studies in Systematic and Comparative Jurisprudence, Legal History, and the Principles of Legislation. This branch of the work . . . will be closely affiliated with the work of the Departments of History, Political Economy, Political Science, and Sociology.[51]

The words echoed Harper's original intentions, and also anticipated the future. The "graduate studies" contemplated would have been described more accurately as postdoctoral; the second and third years of the regular curriculum were identified as graduate work, and the degree was Doctor of Law—J.D. rather than LL.B.—the form of the degree having been chosen, the University explained publicly, "as appropriate for *graduate* professional work."* The emphasis suggests an intention that legal study should not only follow liberal education in the life of the student, but also that the work itself should have the intellectual characteristics implied by "graduate work" and advanced degrees in the arts and sciences—in short, an orientation of study toward the unknown. It was near the time when the Law School was founded that Harper made his decennial forecast: professional education would indeed itself be graduate work of the highest order. In 1902, the University began—in law—to move toward that ideal.

In pedagogy, the University had begun to plan for graduate studies in 1893–94. The Department of Philosophy, to which John Dewey came the same year as head professor, announced its hope that psychology, then taught in the department, would be "a welcome ally . . . to those fitting themselves for the work of teachers and physicians," and that a fellowship would soon be available in pedagogy.[52] In 1894–95, a Department of Pedagogy (later Education) appeared as the twin of Philosophy; John Dewey was head professor of both departments, which were listed under the same Roman numeral in the *Register*. The aim of the new department was "to train competent specialists for the broad and scientific treatment of educational problems."[53] That formulation of purpose remained intact throughout Harper's administration. As a departmental study, pedagogy was concerned with inquiry. Dewey observed a division of labor between those schools designed to train the rank and file of teachers and those educating the leaders of systems, persons who had as a rule already been to college—teachers in normal and training schools, professors of pedagogy, superintendents, principals of schools in large cities. The latter schools should devote themselves more directly to discovery and experimentation: "It is obvious, without argument, that this higher type of training must be undertaken for the most part, if it is to be done in America at all, by universities and

* In effect, the idea of legal studies beyond the regular curriculum revived the substance of an old proposal, that the LL.D. be granted as an earned degree for studies beyond the doctorate.

to a considerable extent as graduate work."[54] As a departmental study, pedagogy was hardly more "professional" in its intellectual bearings than philosophy, or the other disciplines taught by the Faculty of arts, literature, and science; inquiry lay at the heart of them all. Educational theory had to be tested; otherwise, theoretical work would partake "of the nature of a farce and imposture—it is like professing to give thorough training in a science and then neglecting to provide a laboratory for faculty and students to work in."[55] For the school bore the same relation to the work of pedagogy that the laboratory did to biology, physics, or chemistry.[56] In the pedagogical "laboratory" principles might be tested and demonstrated.[57] (The school Dewey had in mind might have been as aptly called a clinic as a laboratory. Harper was to compare the school to a hospital serving a medical department.)[58] In Dewey's view, then, philosophy and psychology led into pedagogical research and into the practice of teaching —although not, in a university, to practice-teaching. That orientation of studies resembled the extension of political economy into business and the early alignment of political science and law. Each using his own fulcrum, Dewey, Laughlin, and Freund sought to push the University program toward the meeting place of the disciplines and the vocations; and in 1902 Dewey did become the director of a professional school. The way was roundabout and sometimes rough.

In 1896, an elementary school was opened as an adjunct to Dewey's departmental work.* The world knows how strikingly influential the school was as a testing ground and a demonstration of what has become known as progressive education; but, as a laboratory, the school was organized too late to become part of the regular establishment. The sciences had absorbed the funds granted for laboratory work, and borrowing had become necessary to sustain the existing program of the University. For the most part, the school was on its own financially. Dewey, indeed, asked that the school be allowed to prove that it could fend for itself:

... it would be the work almost of chance to find in advance persons of means who realized the importance of this new line sufficiently to endow it. The school itself furnishes the required demonstration. Moreover it tends of itself to arouse the interest needed for its own development. As a matter of policy, it would be hard to suggest any way in which the University could so easily get such a strong hold upon the interests

* Officially called the University Elementary School, the institution was also known as the Dewey School. The school descended from it is not unnaturally called the Laboratory School.

of a number of persons as by affording their children with as nearly as possible an ideal education.[59]

That prediction and implied commitment were in Harper's own style; the school was floated on its expectations. The actual response of parents was not universally friendly. The comment of one father upon his son's experience may be the prototype of the now-standard complaint against progressive education: "One year at the University Preparatory Laboratory, otherwise known as the D—— School (supply the proper word, not on Sunday, please!) nearly ruined him. We have to teach him how to study. He learned to 'observe' last year."[60] But many parents were devoted to the school: the Parents' Association pledged $500–$800 a year to the school. Other donations ranged up to $3,500. The school received publicity officially through a serial account of its work in the *University Record* and less formally but more stirringly through Dewey's book *The School and Society,* made up largely of three lectures delivered to parents. (The early history of its publication suggests how quickly interest in Dewey's laboratory spread: first edition, November, 1899, 1,000 copies; second impression, February, 1900, 1,500 copies; third impression, July, 1900, 5,000 copies—and other impressions followed.[61] It remains in print today.) Professor B. A. Hinsdale of the University of Michigan, a pioneer in the academic study of pedagogy, observed that more eyes were fixed upon the school than upon any other elementary school in the country, ". . . or probably the world";[62] and Harper reported that judgment to the Trustees. Dewey's ideas were indeed demonstrated, and favorably received; but funds for endowment were not offered. The school was thus in the now familiar position of a project floated on grants for current expenses—today money would come from foundations or the public purse. The project acquires a devoted staff, produces exciting and widely publicized results, and yet has no assured future financially.

As early as May, 1896, Dewey requested an appropriation of $2,500 for the year 1896–97. At first the Trustees took no action, and then the Executive Committee of the Board decided that the appropriation should be made, on the condition that $2,500 was secured before the beginning of the fiscal year. The money could be spent if it could first be found. In June, Mrs. W. R. Linn agreed to give or secure the money, and the appropriation became effective. By such financing, the school was maintained. On the same day that the Trustees received Dewey's request for $2,500, Harper presented a proposal that the University celebrate its fifth anniversary at an estimated cost of exactly the same sum. The Trustees at first voted that the expense was not justified and then reconsidered. It was finally decided to appropriate $1,200 (or possibly $1,800) to the celebration, which cost $2,565.31 after all.[63] Dewey might have felt some jealousy of an expenditure, partly beyond appropriation, so close to the sum that the school had to find; but he could not have struck at financial optimism without hitting himself. Whether the University might better have spent its money to support the school than to celebrate its anniversary is a moot point. It is impossible to say what part of the support given Dewey's work—or that of any other professor—represented a return upon investment in general public enthusiasm.[64] The work of the school may have been the sole inspiration of direct gifts; but that work was exciting partly because of counsel from such men as George Herbert Mead in philosophy, John M. Coulter in botany, Albert A. Michelson in physics, Frederick Starr in anthropology, and of course Dewey himself, and their presence was provided for out of the general (unbalanced) budget.

By 1899, Dewey had become dissatisfied with the scale of the school as an institution for the preparation of specialists: "The demand is likely to exceed the supply here; but lack of funds is the only thing which stands in the way of a very large expansion."[65] The theory upon which the school was run was not the chief obstacle, Dewey said. The school needed both a building designed, constructed, and equipped expressly for its own use and a permanent endowment: ". . . the school must be on a precarious basis and make undue demands upon the thought and anxiety of all concerned, until it has an assured annual income upon which it can count."[66] In effect, he was arguing that the school should be treated like the other laboratories, but Harper found no endowment comparable to the Ogden and Culver funds. To the suggestion that the University was making money from the school and that gifts to it ought to be matched by funds from John D. Rockefeller, Harper responded that probably the Trustees would be in favor of disbanding the school if they became aware of that feeling. But to do so, Dewey retorted, would evince a very small degree of sympathy with the school.[67] Hand-to-mouth financing was making both Harper and Dewey edgy; but Harper was enthusiastic about the prospects of the school. "I am confident," Harper wrote, "that nothing is being done today from which greater good may be expected for the public school system . . . than the work of the Elementary School, which is, after all, a pedagogical laboratory."[68]

But what kind of a laboratory had it become? Originally, Dewey had spoken of testing and demonstrating principles; by 1899, he intimated that the chief purpose of the school was ". . . to demonstrate certain principles as fundamental in education" rather than to turn out methods and materials for slavish copying elsewhere. The simple existence of the school as a systematic innovator helped insensibly but positively to modify the educational atmosphere and to prepare public opinion for similar changes elsewhere.[69] But had the fundamental principles of education been discovered already? In Dewey's opinion, the school faced unsolved problems; but, he said, the period of experimentation with the elementary program was practically at an end.[70] Insisting in the same year that the work of the school was, in the truest and highest sense, University work, Harper also spoke of problems in elementary education which might be worked out in the school; but he did not suggest that the fundamentals had been established. He asserted that work in the elementary school was as important as that in any laboratory in the University and expressed the hope that its investigations would be endowed; but he did not specifically pledge University support to the existing program of the school or to the results of the investigation at that point in its progress.[71] Dewey had begun to cherish a particular school while Harper applauded the work of the school as the vindication of a method. The two attitudes were not identical. Harper could ask if the time had not come for the department to look upward from elementary education to the problems of the higher schools, which Dewey had pondered but had not brought into the laboratory.

Circumstances immediately forced Harper and Dewey to consider the future of the school. In 1899, Mrs. Emmons Blaine decided to free the work of Colonel Francis Parker, a veteran educational reformer and principal of the Cook County Normal School, from dependence upon public authorities. She would provide $1,000,000 for the endowment and building of a teacher-training institution and an attached elementary school under Parker's direction. His program and staff—and thus his model of reformed education—would be transferred to the control of an independent board of trustees.[72] Mrs. Blaine had apparently subsidized the original publication of *The School and Society,* which Dewey dedicated to her; but by the disposition of her large gift, she indicated that the endowment of the new education should benefit Parker's version of it.[73] In the interval between the founding of the school, called the Chicago Institute, and its opening, Harper sought to arrange a merger of the Institute and a new division of the University, the School of Education, which was created to make the scheme practicable. The pattern of Harper's labors resembled his work in behalf of medicine except that in education Harper was negotiating for a million-dollar gift that came, unlike the million pledged to medicine, from a single donor with a single purpose. The University would secure training and elementary schools with a million dollars or nothing at all; a financially marginal "union" such as that with Rush was out of the question. To make the merger possible, Harper and the University had to assure Parker, Mrs. Blaine, and the trustees of the Institute that the work begun in the Cook County Normal School and then projected as a separate enterprise should not be hampered by being placed again in a larger system of education. Harper also undertook to bring into the School of Education two secondary schools, the Chicago Manual Training School and the South Side Academy, a preparatory school. Control of these schools plus the school of the Institute, which extended through the eighth grade, would enable the University to achieve on its own campus the educational equivalent of vertical integration in industry: a child could enter the orbit of the University from the nursery and remain until leaving with a ph.d. degree. Logically but without immediate prospect of financing, the effect could have been achieved either by inserting one of the two secondary schools between the Dewey school and the colleges or by extending the course of the school through twelve grades. Harper was characteristically pertinacious, however, in attempting to incorporate the staff and work of the Institute into the University. What of the laboratory school? Harper suggested that Dewey should turn his attention to the problems of secondary education. Since in 1899 Dewey had designated the approach to the secondary school as one of the problems before his school, Harper in effect was proposing that investigation by the department should be raised the next step beyond intermediate education along a line extrapolated from Dewey's thinking. Had that shift been made, the Dewey school might again have become a testing ground, as well as a demonstration, of progressive education. Dewey made plans for secondary-school work but did not drop the lower school. The parents of children in the elementary program insisted that the school should be maintained, and they agreed to subscribe up to $5,000 against deficits. Thus when the University succeeded in satisfying the several parties to the merger, it found itself in control, not of a single tier of pre-collegiate institutions, but of two elementary schools, as well as two high schools, a teacher-training program, and an academic department preparing specialists in educational investigation.

Of practical necessity, the direction, staff, and budget were bifurcated. Parker was given charge of the School of Education, which embraced the Parker elementary school and the teacher-training program (called the College of Education); and Dewey remained in control of the laboratory school and of the departmental work in which the school had originated. He would also oversee secondary-school work. Nomenclature was simplified by the consolidation of the Departments of Education and Philosophy; but, to Dewey's distress, the existence of two University Elementary Schools caused confusion. It was decided that the original (Dewey) school should continue to bear the old name, the University Elementary School, while the Parker school should be known as the University Elementary School on the Blaine Foundation.[74] The Dewey school preserved its identity, but its unaugmented name bespoke its continuing lack of endowment.

When plans for new buildings were being made, Dewey angrily concluded that Wilbur S. Jackman, Parker's aide and dean of the School of Education, was slighting the interest of the Dewey program; Jackman's suggestions in regard to new buildings were "absurdly exaggerated . . . too absurd for serious attention."[75] In retrospect, it is plain that Dewey had arrived at an immensely frustrating position; he worked in sight but not in reach of such money as the endowment of his laboratory called for. Although the prospect before him had been somewhat improved financially by the parents' readiness to guarantee his elementary school against deficits, Dewey's situation had worsened psychologically. Had he withdrawn immediately and utterly from school management to devote himself to the philosophical investigation of education, in which other men did not so excel, he would have saved himself pain. What he actually did was to appoint to the principalship of the laboratory school a colleague whose clear and experienced intelligence was, Dewey said, wrought everywhere into the texture of the school.[76] The colleague was his wife, Alice Dewey. Harper had not been consulted in advance of the act, but he did not abruptly disallow it.

The several schools of the University opened under the new dispensation in the autumn of 1901; on March 2, 1902, Francis Parker died. He was succeeded as director of the School of Education by John Dewey. During his first year in office, he arranged—as the rule of simplicity plainly indicated—for the consolidation of the two elementary schools, which meant that the two staffs were united on the Blaine Foundation. The pedagogical laboratory had become part of the University establishment.

The offerings of the Colleges were affected by the developing interest in professional work, as in his decennial report Harper intimated they should be. In the College of Education students might enter either a "general program" containing many courses of direct interest to prospective teachers (e.g., the Teaching of Reading) and leading to the Bachelor of Education degree alone or a program that was designed to prepare "special teachers" in the secondary and normal schools.[77] It consisted of a set of optional studies in the arts, literature, and science as well as in education. On completion of the requirements, the student qualified for both the ED.B. and the A.B., PH.B., or S.B., as indicated by the student's field of concentration.* The concerns of the College were explicitly but not exclusively professional. The granting of a professional degree for undergraduate studies in law or medicine would have run counter to the fundamental intention to convert preparation for those professions into graduate study. Yet the University had given its blessing to candidates for the A.B., PH.B., and S.B. degrees who anticipated the requirements for the medical degree by electing the courses in pure science that constituted almost half of the medical program. Similarly, when the Law School was organized, the University allowed prospective lawyers to take the first year of the professional course as the last year of Senior College work and also created a prelegal program for the first year of that work. In each of these instances, half of the undergraduate's program was oriented toward a profession, although professional work in law did not begin as early as in medicine. In his last year as an undergraduate, however, the student in law turned to professional *subjects,* contracts and torts, for example, while his classmate in medicine was still at work on the preclinical sciences.[78]

By initiating these programs in medicine and law, the University virtually—but not formally—created two more Senior Colleges, which offered something resembling prescribed programs. Given the whole range of offerings available for Senior College work, the student had a right to pick those courses that pointed toward medicine or law just as he might pick other courses to gain some understanding of ancient civilization or modern politics. The choice was his to make; but if he decided to accept the invitation to move as quickly as

* The College of Education was distinct from the older College for Teachers, an offshoot of the University Extension program that became the downtown University College. In addition to degree programs, the College of Education offered a two-year general course and another two-year course in arts and technology, which could be taken, after 1904–05, as the Senior College division of any four-year course provided the student met all of the other requirements called for (see *Register,* 1904–1905, pp. 121, 128).

possible toward medicine or law, he ceased to have a wide range of options. In a university that was becoming more and more involved in professional education, the elective principle worked to limit freedom in practice.

In the oldest of the quasi-professional programs, that of the College of Commerce and Administration, specialization became increasingly pronounced. By 1904–05, all of the five groups available for election contained at least nine "recommended" majors; and two groups contained nineteen or one major in excess of the standard program of eighteen majors. (Did the elective principle work in reverse, to permit the student to omit one of the recommended majors?) Practically all of the majors dealt directly with a vocational interest or with its context.[79] The student in Transportation, for example, would devote six majors of his work to railway transportation; comparative railway legislation; railway rates; government ownership; tariffs, reciprocity, and shipping; and law of public service companies and carriers; and he would also study economic history, law of contracts, modern business methods, accounting, American agriculture, trusts, labor and capital, finance, and the economic geography of North America.[80] Studies within the groups were, one announcement reported, "more technical" than Junior College work: the comment was accurate.[81]

The last of the colleges to be created during the Harper era was announced in 1903–04. The College of Religious and Social Science, offering the ph.b. degree, was designed to serve prospective ministers who could not afford separate undergraduate and divinity programs and those students who intended to do religious and philanthropic work outside of the regular ministry—perhaps in the YMCA and charitable bureaus.[82] (The device of allowing undergraduates to take professional courses had been applied in the realm of theological education as early as 1896–97 when Senior College students had been given permission to elect Divinity School courses.)[83] The new College offered two programs, in each of which the student was asked to take a mixture of divinity and other courses including psychology and philosophy. Sociology also appeared in both programs, the prospective ministers being required to take an ecclesiastical variant of the subject.[84] The nature of the programs suggests that the University sensed the presence of a fresh opportunity to unite the old and the new learning in the service of religion. In retrospect, the College appears to have served two distinct purposes—the provision of modern yet inexpensive preparation for an old profession and the inauguration of training for social service, which had not then taken a clearly defined shape. The University was laboring, without perhaps being fully conscious of what the attempt involved, to create a new profession by gathering already existing courses together to form a protoprofessional curriculum.*

Perhaps the University was groping, but it was not moving absent-mindedly. In 1901, Albion W. Small asserted:

We are actually revolting, in practice, against the dominance of the culture conception of college education, and we are adopting in practice the calling conception of education. . . . We are about to declare in practice that we will no longer defer and defraud preparation for our vocations out of deference to an illusory standard of mental depth and breadth. We are about to demand that culture shall be obtained by most college graduates as an incident of preparation for their callings. In other words, college education is become rudimentary professional education.[85]

The judgment was extreme, but by the end of the first decade and at the beginning of the second, the Senior College programs unmistakably showed the combined effects of Harper's effort to round out the University and of a transformation within the elective system. James H. Tufts, a philosopher and dean of the Senior Colleges, noticed the change; writing his decennial report as dean, he observed that the range of courses had widened but that "the tendency is undoubtedly just at present toward the closer definition of curriculum."[86]

The original regulations for Senior College work were not dropped; obliged to take only a few specified courses and restrained only by general rules on concentration and distribution, the student, if he wished, still could devise a program of his own without regard to explicitly professional training. By far the greater number of students did elect to study under the old regulations after the new programs had been introduced. In 1901–02, only twenty-four students out of 311 graduated under the new dispensation—seven from the College of Commerce and Administration, and seventeen in s.b. and a.b. premedical programs. In the succeeding years of the Harper era, the figures were: 1902–03, 33 graduates in new programs out of 270 taking Bachelor's degrees; 1903–04, 58 out of 270; 1904–05, 47 out of 269; and 1905–06, 39 out of 303 graduates.[87] Plainly, the great mass of Senior College students preferred the well-worn paths; but they did seek more advanced courses than they were formally entitled to take.

* Before the summer of 1899, a *graduate* school had been proposed, to prepare (a) teachers of the Bible in colleges, academies, churches, and Sunday schools and (b) "competent Christian workers in missionary fields, both home and foreign." The course of instruction would include psychology, pedagogy, and sociology as well as biblical literature and other subjects conventionally associated with religious work. The school was to be co-ordinate with, but independent of, the graduate school of Divinity, and it was to be connected closely with "the religious and philanthropic forces in the city, such as the Social Settlements and other forms of Christian activity, which would be virtually laboratories for the work of its students . . ." (typed Circular of Information: Graduate Schools. The Graduate Schools of Christian Methods Biblical Training Christian Work of the University of Chicago, n.d.).

Indeed, the undergraduate body as a whole contained many students who migrated into courses above (and also below) the level of their colleges. With the consent of individual instructors, students frequently violated the frontiers between more or less elementary work of the Junior Colleges, the intermediate work of the Senior Colleges, and the advanced courses of the graduate schools. In four of the twelve quarters between 1895 and 1898, more than 10 per cent of the Junior College students took graduate courses, and in one quarter 39 per cent did.[88] (The Junior College dean was disturbed.) In 1898–99, as professional education was being introduced at the undergraduate level, crowds of Senior College students took graduate courses, the highest numbers of registrations being 76 in history, 75 in political science, and 62 in sociology. It may not have been an accident that the first of the new programs, that of the College of Commerce and Administration, encouraged specialization in the social sciences, where the students had already displayed a strong desire for advanced courses. The University policy was consistent with, although it may not actually have followed, the election returns. Yet the University did not simply regularize the students' habit of fusing elementary, intermediate, and specialized studies; the University formally accepted professional utility as a valid reason for undergraduate study of a subject, and it deliberately organized programs with that rationale. "The question may arise," Tufts reported, "as to whether this does not introduce undue preparation for professional work into the undergraduate course."[89] In Tufts's opinion, the answer lay in the students' motives for studying; it was a fact not usually taken into account that a large amount of the Senior College work elected by students who were actual or prospective teachers was really professional work. Might not the distinction between liberal and professional study need some restatement? "It seems arbitrary," Tufts remarked, "to say that a student who is studying Latin with the intention of teaching it is not getting from it the value of a liberal study, as we should certainly be obliged to say if we made the 'professional' equivalent to the 'non-liberal.' "[90] The University was indeed working to soften or even to abolish the distinction—by making the professions truly liberal and the content of liberal education in part frankly professional. The first *Official Bulletin,* of 1891, had ended with the words ". . . a truly University spirit."[91] For Harper, it meant the difference, not between pure and applied learning, but rather between inquiry and preparatory drill. In the programs for professional and other advanced instruction, the spirit found expression—but not complete fulfilment. For the University offered less than the whole constellation of curriculums which Harper had envisioned in 1891—and still hoped for in 1901.

CHAPTER XVI

The Academic Way Re-examined

The University of Chicago had been conspicuously self-conscious during the first decade of the Harper administration: the decennial *President's Report* is a monument of institutional introspection and of dedication to self-improvement. The University did not rest as the season for celebration passed; it continued to experiment—yet it did so as an institution where some habits had already become settled, some policies had been transmuted in custom, and some disagreements had hardened into political issues. The attitudes of Harper and his colleagues toward their work disclosed much of what academic life stood for at the University: what the degrees meant; where the professors found themselves united—or at odds with each other; where the student was expected to find education; and how, it was hoped, the higher teaching as a whole might be advanced.

DEGREE PROGRAMS

As a school for the PH.D., the University displayed marked conservatism. True, the University was not insensitive to the heat generated by friction as the system touched the lives of students. Details of the requirements were adjusted from time to time; but the essential form and rationale of the PH.D. program remained what they had been. No Faculty body reviewed the long-standing declaration that the PH.D. was given as the recognition and mark of high attainments and ability, shown first "by the production of a thesis evincing the power of independent investigation and forming an actual contribution to existing knowledge" and second by the passage of an examination.[1] Harper was concerned that the existing system should work efficiently and according to design. He once asked Dean Judson if it would be a good thing to prod graduate students who had been on hand some time; but he had no reason to prod the departments. Their complaint was that lack of equipment forced them to stand still.[2] The Faculty barely mentioned the possibility—now often supposed to be the reality—that theses might contribute little more than inert or insignificant facts, unknown because they were not worth knowing. Perhaps it was taken for granted that dry as dust scholarship made no actual contribution and so deserved no attention. Yet the degree did not pass uncriticized in the United States. In 1903, William James attacked the "PH.D. octopus" and the "doctor monopoly": the terms harmonize exactly with the rhetoric of progressivism. James argued that America was rapidly drifting toward a state of things where no man of science or letters would be accounted respectable without being stamped with some kind of badge or diploma: "It seems to me high time to rouse ourselves to consciousness, and to cast a critical eye upon this decidedly grotesque tendency."[3] Not all of the Faculty members at the University were PH.D.'s; and some, such as Robert Herrick and Robert M. Lovett, acquired tenure without being committed to the preparation of PH.D. candidates. Admiration of the degree was probably not monolithic: recently Laurence R. Veysey has demonstrated that the emerging American university contained a number of men of humanistic bent, as were Herrick and Lovett, who did not embrace the ideal of objective or "scientific" research with which the PH.D. was associated.[4] As an institution, however, the University spent no time debating over the danger James saw ahead. Apparently the University was not worried by, if indeed it was roused to consciousness of, a future where a *curriculum vitae* without a PH.D. might mean for the American scholar a course of life leading to a dead end.

The attitude of the University was not a product of sheer complacency. Although the degree was not new in America when the University was founded, the PH.D. symbolized a cause that inspired a still fresh enthusiasm, especially in new institutions without a collegiate tradition. The need to build universities was more impelling than anxiety over possible misuse of what was being built; and in Chicago, even after the turn of the century, the evidences of unfinished work were everywhere. The head professors had enough to criticize, where the ph.d. was concerned, in the partial failure of the University to provide adequate means; disappointed in that regard, the professors were less likely to feel disenchanted with the end in view than to become more fiercely devoted to its attainment. Many of them had come to Chicago primarily to conduct and supervise such work as the ph.d. represented, and they had not completed their mission in ten years.

In 1904–05, what concerned Albion Small, dean of the Graduate School of Arts and Literature, was not a threat of monopoly but the debasement of the degree at the hands of universities which, to retain students, offered the degree without being able to create the environment for graduate work, "the graduate atmosphere." The University, he said, had no more important and timely task than to emphasize the marks which ought to distinguish graduate from undergraduate work. In effect, Small responded to James's assertion that it was high time to criticize the uses to which the ph.d. was put. Small was preoccupied with widening the circle in which the true meaning of the degree was understood. The graduate atmosphere had had no effect upon the student who would say "I have had" physiology or chemistry or English; the outlook of students who made that remark contained, in Small's opinion, "no provision for unexplored territory beyond the range of their present point of view." Thus Small implied that the cardinal virtue of the ideal graduate student was the urge to explore; James in turn spoke of intellectual distinction. The two qualities of mind are obviously not mutually exclusive, but the connotations of the terms differ: Small's *exploration* pointed toward things, whether facts or laws, to be discovered—traditionally the collective object of ph.d. research. James's term implied the primacy of intellect, whether applied to the unknown or the familiar.

In his general prescription for graduate work, Small had the faults of other universities in mind, but he did not say that the students whose conversation distressed him were matriculated elsewhere, and he presented his specific recommendations as a summary of those emphasized "by the departments," that is, by men within the University. Graduate work required adequate library facilities; collections and apparatus not merely for illustrating known principles; instructors with time freed from undergraduate instruction, administrative duties, and other demands; facilities for publication; and scholarships and fellowships—needs only partially supplied by the University. Two of the items constituted a virtual gloss upon official policy toward ph.d. requirements.

Small reported that "actual experience in the enlargement of knowledge, and not mere theorizing about it, is a necessary factor in adequate training for independent investigation," and he recommended "the utmost absence of arbitrary requirements or conditions in the choice of work, and in using time as the demands of one's special subject may indicate." William James scornfully proposed, as one way of keeping the hold of the octopus in check, that the universities might lower their "fantastic standards" and give the doctorate as a matter of course "for a due amount of time spent in patient labor in a special department of learning." The two men were both attacking routinized scholarship, but in their differing ways. James wanted a new dispensation; speaking for himself and his colleagues, Small was asking for opportunity to make the old complete.[5]

Small did not discuss an issue implied by the entry that the University was making into professional education. Preparation for the law and for medicine was to be brought up the level of graduate study in the arts, literature, and science: conversely, was such study to be considered a form of professional education? The doctorate was being required increasingly of the college and university teacher for advancement in his profession, and presumably many (or most) students sought the ph.d. in some part as a passport to academic careers: should the program be designed explicitly to supply the classroom and lecture hall with professors? Although several departments announced an intention to train teachers as well as investigators, the University did not directly confront the question.[6] Yet, plainly, the University offered study for the ph.d. on terms unlike those governing the award of the doctorates in law and medicine. Candidates for the j.d. and m.d. knew exactly how long they were expected to study before beginning professional life; and they moved up a ladder consisting entirely of courses or subjects. The ph.d. candidate could expect to remain a student not only until he had acquired competence in a subject which might have vocational uses but also until he had demonstrated his possession of a power to which no profession had a particular claim but of which (the University believed) the practitioners of all learned professions should have an understanding. The ph.d. stood for investigation—generically considered—for the ideal of research into the unexplored, for inquiry per se; and the University accepted its ph.d. program as if it were but the inevitable embodiment of the true academic spirit.

In regard to the Master's degrees programs, which lacked a single, established meaning, the University did have fleeting second thoughts. In December, 1902, the Congregation asked the Faculty to reconsider the non-specialist Master's degree (that not requiring a Master's paper); and a Faculty committee defended the degree.[7] Work for it was "definite and advanced in character" and had to be approved in advance by the heads of departments. In fact, the committee continued, the degree was not easy to obtain; students were frequently unable to comply with the requirements because of inability to do graduate work in diverse departments.[8] On receiving the report of the committee, the Congregation immediately declared itself satisfied.*

The conduct of graduate study in the arts and sciences, as well as of professional education, involved what appears in retrospect to have been a twofold question. How specialized should education be in reference to the several stages of a student's progress; and to what extent should the University prescribe studies, both to enforce specialization where it was desirable and to check it where general culture was the desideratum of education? Inquiry and preparation for it constituted the primary work of the University, to which the institution owed its essential character and from which, in logic, its other activities were derived; but, in practice, the ideal of inquiry did not plainly indicate what broad learning the University should require as a foundation for investigation. As the attainment of that learning came first in the student's progress, the question of prescriptions in the Junior Colleges possessed particular urgency.

From the time when the University opened, professors had disagreed vehemently over the ingredients of the culture upon which true university study should rest. The argument had continued right up to the time of the decennial celebration and had not been settled then. In 1905, William G. Hale reminded Harper of the hope "which you expressed a couple of years ago, namely that we should hear no more of this question [the Junior College curriculum] for five years"; in actuality the Faculty gave itself little respite.[9] In April, 1902, a commission on the Junior Colleges was created with George

---

* Reporting for the academic years 1902–04, Harry P. Judson, dean of the Faculties of Arts, Literature, and Science and also the proposer of the cultural Master's degree, asserted that it supplied a need. The number of such degrees granted indicates that some actual demand for general studies existed—Judson spoke of the "Master's degree, general"; and the center of gravity in the whole Master's degree program shifted somewhat toward its more broadly cultural part. In 1902–03, the distribution of awards was 40 Master's in the several departments and 5 general Master's; in 1903–04, 41 and 5; in 1904–05, 36 and 6; in 1905–06, 40 and 12. The general degree was gaining strength both absolutely and relatively; but the specialized program obviously remained by far the more popular (Harry P. Judson, "The Faculties of Arts, Literature, and Science," Table IV A and IV B, P.R., 1902–1904, pp. 63–64; Tables III A and III B, P.R., 1904–1905, p. 21; Tables III A and III B, P.R., 1905–1906, p. 28).

E. Vincent as chairman. Contributing to the decennial report as dean of the Junior Colleges, he asserted that it was evident the limits of flexibility in the program were being approached rapidly: "If provisions for substitution are multiplied, the time will be reached when the exceptions will far exceed in number the original general principles."[10] (Although the opponents of required Latin had failed to secure its outright abolition in the ph.b. and s.b. programs, a regular procedure for replacing Latin in particular cases had been instituted; also, the Faculty sometimes granted petitions, for a miscellany of substitutions, as an act of grace.) Two kinds of proposals had begun to appear, Vincent reported; one kind aimed at minimizing requirements and the other at "enlarging" the clearing-house system—or the measurement of the student's attainment against the model curriculums for high school and Junior College. The system could be made more flexible, and enlarged, not by reducing the total amount of specified majors but by formulating more of the specifications in terms of interchangeable subjects, grouped together—for example, by demanding four majors of mathematics and science instead of two of mathematics and two of science.[11]

In 1897, the Congregation had tabled a proposal by Thomas C. Chamberlin that the requirement for the Junior College student should be three majors of work in each of five groups of studies relating, respectively, to the individual, his physical and natural environment, his sociological relations, the means of communication, and qualitative relations: now Vincent was recommending that a similar idea be given thought.[12] He was suggesting in light of experience that the permitted exceptions in the existing program might be made the rule. After making what Harper described as an exhaustive study of present conditions and educational tendencies in schools throughout the country, the Junior College Commission, in 1905, reported a plan that was based on a "proposition" very like Vincent's suggestion—that in entrance and college requirements "there be included fewer specified subjects and more electives from groups of subjects."[13]

Many of the recommendations of the commission were essentially conservative. The clearing-house system was amended but retained in substance. (The phrase itself was not used; it never did appear in official announcements.) The University would continue to offer three Bachelor's degree programs with a variant ph.b. for graduates of the College of Commerce and Administration— which meant that debate would revolve about its old axis. What studies, in what amounts, should be common to three distinct programs, in each of which particular departments or segments of the Faculty were more or less tacitly admitted to have a special interest? The commission proposed that a core of ten units—two in mathematics, three in English, and three in foreign languages plus two units to be chosen by the student—should be required for admission to all programs—a plan that was new only in form because nearly the same requirements appeared piecemeal in the several programs then in force. The commission proposed a new departure when it recommended that it should be possible for candidates for the ph.b., s.b., and professional degrees to take them without Latin or Greek. Classical studies would not be considered a necessary part of liberal education and would be demanded only of students who sought the traditional degree of a.b.[14]

The report was attacked. A dissenting minority within the commission prepared its own report; and Hale again appealed to Harper. Vincent worked for conciliation, saying ". . . the differences will gradually simmer down to Latin in the ph.b. in Lit."[15]—the advocates of Latin would no longer insist upon its presence in the s.b. program. (Possibly, Vincent suggested, the ph.b. could be split into one degree with Latin and one without Latin.) Harry P. Judson was profoundly disappointed with the general character of the report:

> I am ready to give up the theme of a specifically required curriculum, but want something of value in exchange. The report does not give it. The new plan should be simple, should be some sort of a system, and should be based on intelligent and intelligible principles. The report is complicated, is not a system, and rests on no principles which I can discover of any material value. It is a confused jumble of incoherent ideas. We need something very different—something on which we can rely as worth fighting for. This is mere patchwork. I am ashamed to have it go out as our new curriculum. Is it not possible that we can do better than this?[16]

The same criticism came to Harper from Marion Talbot, who said, some time after discussion of the report began, that while in the beginning there were some principles underlying the report, they had been practically eliminated.[17] Harper wrote Vincent: "It is unfortunate to go before the public with something that we cannot fight for, or at least those of us who are the chief administrative officers."[18] Harper's comment was not idle. The undergraduate curriculum had long since become a subject of wide debate, and Harper would have been foolish to suppose that warfare over the report could be kept private. He asked Vincent, ". . . when the Latin question is announced outside, cannot we revise the whole matter and put it into a shape that will be intelligent and intelligible?"[19] Vincent thought he could establish that the curriculum was based upon principles, that it was as simple as the situation permitted, and that it would reflect credit upon the University.[20]

What the situation was not thought to permit, the nature of the report suggests, was a philosophical reconciliation of the issues that had divided the Faculty. Seemingly, the commission considered itself a political broker, with the task of producing a compromise that would satisfy a sufficient number of professors to become a practicable schedule of requirements. Just before the final version of the report was drafted, Vincent wrote of caucusing.[21] The designations of the groups in Chamberlin's earlier plan had implied a systematic rationale of learning; the groups named by the commission were somewhat mechanical: ancient languages, literatures, and institutions; modern languages, literatures, and institutions; sciences; and professional and technical courses. The greater part of the report was written as if it were copy for the *Register*. Specification followed specification, with signposts to the reader seeking his way. The content of the plan was complex, providing, for example, a choice between varying amounts of one subject, listed as being interchangeable with other subjects within a group which was both divided in two and itself partly interchangeable with others; and the format of the plan was complicated. The applicant for admission to the University would read that he was advised to select his preparatory work as indicated in this table:

REQUIRED WORK		ADDITIONAL ELECTIVE WORK	
English	3 units	From Group I	2 units
Mathematics	2 units	From Group II	1 unit
From Group I	3 units	From Group IIIA	1 unit
From Division B of		Free elective,	
Groups I–V	2 units	Groups I–IV	1 unit

Looking back to an earlier passage, the applicant would find that Group I, for example, contained:

LANGUAGES

A. Latin	4, 3, or 2	B. Advanced Latin	2
Greek	3, 2, or 1	Advanced Greek	1
French	3, 2, or 1	Advanced French	1
German	3, 2, or 1	Advanced German	1
Spanish	3, 2, or 1	Advanced Spanish	1 [22]

The report was a compilation of details; and it was dealt with as such.

Receiving the report in early February, 1905, the Junior College Faculty resolved itself into a committee of the whole, which became virtually another commission. As discussion opened, the Faculty almost immediately decided to start—what would be five days of debating—from the old question of required majors in single departments, and not with a discussion of the fresher issue, that of grouping studies.[23] The Faculty proceeded from vote to vote on particular studies as if it were acting upon a simple motion to review whatever recommendations the members had in mind. Some may have been influenced by the report of the commission; but the Faculty as a whole neither adopted nor rejected it. Rather, the Faculty produced its own report. Splitting of the ph.b. was proposed and approved by an informal ballot taken in writing after the fourth session, but at the fifth session the specific requirement of Latin for the ph.b. was formally voted down by a vote of 31 to 22. An editing committee was appointed in part to prepare an intelligible public statement of the action taken by the Faculty.[24] The chairman was Judson.

The new report was forwarded to the United Faculties with a request that Vincent appear before the group ". . . to make some explanations."[25] In that body, a member who was not a classicist moved that in the opinion of the Faculties the University should not grant the ph.b. in Literature without Latin. The motion was voted down; and then Hale, who was of course not a mathematician, proposed a comparable motion that no degree should be granted without some college mathematics. Voting that motion down also, the Faculties proceeded to give an ambiguous indorsement to the report of the Junior College Faculty: the report was not amended but approved "subject to changes in detail submitted in writing as recommendations to the Senate."[26] In the Senate, Hale and any other department head who disapproved of the proposals had a right to vote to disallow the new curriculum, in detail or as a whole. After a day of debate, Hale remarked to Harper that the temper of the Senate had been conservative; had the propositions for the ph.b. come to a vote that day, Hale speculated, they would have been defeated and Latin would have been conserved: "The side which I believe in had a clear majority." Hale had no desire, he said, to win a victory through the absence of anyone; but he did wish that at the next meeting of the Senate, "we should have the vote of every man who has a right to vote," and he argued for the eligibility of two particular men.[27] Less than a week later, Hale moved that there be a fixed requirement of six majors of Latin in the ph.b. course in Literature; and after a long discussion, he was defeated by a margin of two votes, 15 to 17.[28] He did not attempt to restore Latin as a required subject to the s.b. program. The Senate appointed a special committee to prepare a statement for the Congregation; but the next

Register did not explain to the public what principles the University was applying. The machinery was described, however, in three relatively simple tables.

The new program was indeed more flexible than the old; but the Senate did not let down the bars as low as the Junior College commission had proposed to do. The commission recommended, for example, that four majors of mathematics be required of A.B. candidates; and the Senate voted six. While the Junior College Faculty were debating, a committee chaired by Robert A. Millikan, then an assistant professor of physics, had systematically polled the Faculty of the University to discover what each of its members thought the subjects desirable to all programs were. The committee concluded "... that the faculty as a whole deems it desirable that all of the courses have a little more [required] breadth than is provided for in the commisison's report."[29] Indeed, the general commitment of the University to specialized studies was matched by an abiding concern lest preparation for them might cease to be broad.

Except in the case of Latin, changing the prescriptions did not undermine the existing collegiate program; rather, its area was enlarged by the addition of modern studies. Including secondary school studies, the A.B. requirement in mathematics was six majors both in 1892–93 and in 1905–06, and two of science in the earlier year and two in the later, plus two in a new group of science and mathematics. At the other pole of the curriculum, the S.B. candidate needed ten majors of English and history (listed together) in 1892–93 and eleven (listed as three in history and eight in English) in 1904–05; also nine majors of French or German (plus Latin) in 1892–93 and ten majors of French, German, or Latin in 1905–06. In that year he was also required to have one major in philosophy or psychology and two in political economy, political science, history, or sociology.[30]

Throughout the Harper era, the University kept to a middle way in undergraduate education. Before the final vote on the Latin question was taken, Hale remarked to Harper:

We have held constantly thus far the moderately conservative position which you laid down at the outset. We have neither a free elective system nor a system of complete requirements. We have a system which allows a man to choose one of four groups [including the PH.B. program in Commerce and Administration] as he enters, then to exercise his own discretion for a part of his second year, and so to attain to practically complete freedom in his third and fourth years, after having obtained a sufficiently wide survey of human activity to enable him to judge with some wisdom.[31]

316

Hale himself must have thought that the University took a downhill road toward the radical left when the Senate rejected his motion; but the Faculty members, voting in their several legislative houses, gave no indication—at least for the record—that they had revolution in mind.

The elimination of Latin from the s.b. and ph.b. programs was not an unprecedented break with the past. The classical foundation of the s.b. had been sapped by the mitigation of requirements until the permitting of substitution for Latin left its requirement a contingency. It was demanded only of those students who did not opt to avoid it. In 1905, when the shell was cast aside, it was consistent with that act to drop Latin from another curriculum of modern studies or, conversely, to conceive of the a.b. program as being distinctly classical and of Latin as being necessary there (and there alone), not because every liberally educated man needed Latin but rather because as a specialty it bore the same relation to the classical program that chemistry (for example) bore to the scientific. The new curriculum departed from the past more by indirectly redefining the a.b. than by applying the precedent of the s.b. to the ph.b. degree. A paper which was probably prepared in the Junior College Faculty to explain its report to the United Faculties, put the case for a ph.b. without Latin: the modern, non-scientific field

. . . has such rich educational material and resources that it is thought these can be made the core of a college education in the same way that the sciences and the classical languages form such a core for the educational lines leading to the s.b. and the a.b. degrees respectively. One of the questions involved in the recognition of such a degree is whether students should have the privilege of such an education only when presenting four years of secondary school Latin, in spite of the fact that Latin while desirable is not at all essential per se for college work in that field or whether an adequate substitute for the educational value of the four years of secondary school Latin could be secured in the modern field itself. A large majority of the Commission and now a large majority of the Junior College Faculty are of the opinion [and a slender majority of the Senate was to agree] that there should be a college degree with education in the field of modern thought as its core; that the privileges of such a degree and education should not be limited to those who have had four years of Latin, and that an adequate substitute for the educational value of Latin could be found by requiring three or four years' work in some one department of the modern group, including over one year's work in Senior College courses in that department. The value of Latin in a purely educational sense, not in a technical one [as a tool of scholarship?], is thought to lie less in the subject than in the fact that it is pursued continuously for four years.[32]

The paper invoked the principle of "the essential equality of all departments of the University as a source of liberal college education." The nature of that education was not formally defined; but the paper did refer to the cultural advantage of the student being compelled "to master some one subject, to see the same subject from different, ever advancing points of view, to learn how to deal with intricate, fine distinctions, to acquire the power to use and apply his knowledge critically."[33] Thus in some part a Bachelor's degree stood, as did the ph.d., for a *power* equally attainable in the several departments regardless of differences in subject matter.

Although the argument against requiring Latin across the board was consistent with much history and policy, the fact was that it expressed the opinion of Latin held by only a minority of the Faculty members. Responding to the inquiry of the Millikan committee, two-thirds of them indicated that they would advise students in all of the programs to study Latin. Its exclusion from the s.b. and ph.b. programs, in spite of these findings, testifies to the nature of the situation that the Junior College Commission had confronted and indeed to the temper of the Faculty as a political body. Its members had not been brought together either to defend or reform the traditional curriculum; the primary interest of the most powerful professors did not lie in the instruction of undergraduates; and the President was not persuaded that prescribed studies belonged on a university campus. By 1905 the grinding processes of legislation had produced little to justify hope of philosophical reconciliation and much to make concession attractive to the majority.

The Millikan committee found that 100 per cent of the Faculty members believed that English was indispensable; 98 per cent felt the same about mathematics; 95 per cent voted for history; 94 and 87 per cent, respectively, for two groups of sciences; and 81 per cent for philosophy, political economy, political science, and sociology together. Thus the support of Latin was markedly weaker than that of some other subjects or several groups of subjects. Yet the consolidated vote on languages, including Latin, indicated that 94 per cent of the Faculty members favored requirement of studies from that group. This calculation was heeded by the committee as it constructed an ideal core: it was defined by assembling subjects or groups, the votes for which approached unanimity or, in the case of English, achieved it.[34] As disclosed by statistical analysis, the consensus may have been somewhat artificial; but the admissions requirements plus several of the prescribed majors of college work in the new curriculum, as formally voted by the Faculty, bore a close resemblance to the plan of the committee, suggesting that its calculations were essentially realistic—and also that the Faculty tended to require only those subjects that everyone, or nearly everyone, wanted or might be expected not to disapprove of as required studies. (The Faculty did require one major of philosophy, which only 64 per cent of the Faculty members polled by the committee thought indispensable; but prescribed philosophy had not been the *bête noire* of a minority, as prescribed Latin had become.)[35] The paper on educational principles might have carried a footnote on procedure—that the Faculty found its way by consulting concurrent majorities. The same process may have been employed in the Senate, where the rule of suffrage was one department, one vote. The decision against required Latin in the Senate—indeed the *Senate*: did Hale hear the shade of Cicero weeping?—carried no necessary implication that opinion among the senior professors had turned against the traditional liberal education judged upon its own merits. Sheer exasperation with the running debate over Latin may have influenced some senators: the head of zoölogy, Whitman, had withdrawn from the debate years before. Its cost had been high, in the hours of professors who had none to spare and in the occasions it presented for the airing of antagonism. Given the strength and pride of the departments, peace—or an end to parliamentary conflict—was more likely to be attained by constructing a core curriculum of the subjects that every department wanted than by forcing any department to acknowledge the indispensability of Latin. A division of opinion among the scientists had once given the classicists a tactical advantage; seemingly, in 1905, insistence upon Latin was understood to imply an invidious distinction between the claims of the departments, a distinction that placed the classical party in an impossible position strategically. A negotiated peace, based on the principle of departmental equality, gave the Latinists no option. They were obliged to withdraw to the A.B. program, with a classical culture which the majority of the Faculty members admired but thought they could not specify as an essential ingredient of liberal education.

While the debate was going on, Hale commented to Harper upon a university, Michigan, that had ceased to require Latin: "Here and there, however, there are signs of greater wisdom. . . . As I have said to you before, I believe saner views about classical study are going to come in; and I hope that we shall not lose our sanity after holding a wise position for so many years."[36] Speaking of another university, Wisconsin, and looking into the future, but after the new curriculum had been enacted, Chamberlin wrote Harper that the thought of an engineering-commercial course, which was being considered in Madison, was an exceedingly happy one: "The idea is susceptible of considerable extension in various modern lines."[37] Confronted by such divergence of views, the University tested cultural pluralism as a working premise. The fundamental issue that had produced conflict between Hale and Chamberlin was virtually tabled.

SOCIAL ORGANIZATION OF THE STUDENTS

Unlike the traditional college program, the University system of granting Bachelor's degrees carried no logical implication that the undergraduate would live within academic society for any particular period of time or as a member of a veritable college class. The curriculum was a race course: if the rules of the track only required the individual student to move from marker to marker, or from credit to credit, at his own pace until he had passed thirty-six, might he not speed along too fast or plod too slowly to acquire any sense of sport enjoyed in the company of teammates and competitors? Was going to college merely a lonesome run? In his report for 1898–99, Dean Tufts had noted with disapproval ". . . the tendency of some minds to set up as an ideal the acquisition of the greatest number of credits in the minimum of time."[38]

The students' rate of progress in relation to each other was in fact markedly uneven. At the turn of the century, less than half of the students (and at least once as few as 28 per cent) earned a degree without some study elsewhere, which Dean Tufts said made "an additional element of irregularity."[39] In the University of Chicago, he observed, only about one-third of the members of a class graduated in the normal time, about one-third in less than the normal time, and about one-third in more. Of 208 students who graduated from the University during the academic year 1900–01, only 58 had entered four years previously. Three had come to the University as early as 1892–93, 44 in all had come more than four years before graduation, and 101 had been at the University less than four years. Lastly, three students took degrees without residence. (Tufts pointed out that in a graduating class of about the same size in one of the "typical institutions of the East," only 24 students had joined the class after the conventional starting point.) Of the students who had entered the University of Chicago as Freshmen in the autumn of 1897, less than half graduated in the spring of 1901, or at the "normal date"—the number of those graduating was not much larger than that of students in the same entering group who had dropped out and the number who remained in the University.[40]

Although Tufts criticized the tendency of some students to hurry through their courses, he also noted that there was little disposition "to consider residence at college as simply an agreeable means of passing four years."[41] From the time Marion Talbot converted the rented Beatrice into something more than a dormitory and developed the house system, the University had sought to make residence in college a positive contribution to the education of its students. In its second decade, it attempted to advance along the line indicated by that earlier experience. The Junior College received particular attention. The University failed to achieve unity of spirit in planning the curriculum of the College; but it strove unremittingly to foster a spirit of unity in the life of the students.

The ideal of academic society was expressed by two officers, who were directly responsible for student life, Dean Talbot and James W. Thompson, who was director of University houses as well as a medievalist. Miss Talbot spoke of the hope that the Women's Union, an organization founded in 1901 and designed to include all women of the University, would unite them "in a large and generous fellowship."[42] Thompson pointed out that higher education in America had been curiously backward "in developing the social instinct in the student during the formative period of life, when character is most adaptable and the lessons of experience are most easily learned. . . ." He continued:

Broad, genuine, sympathetic *social* life is still an unknown element in far too many institutions. But the change is happening—has happened. It is only tardily that American college authorities have become aware of this deficiency in student life, and have grown to appreciate that liberal culture implied the development of the American college student in all right directions, intellectual, physical, aesthetic, social.

The building of a well-equipped clubhouse for men at the University of Chicago confirmed the Trustees' intention to provide a four-square education, in the liberal arts, in science, in gymnastics, and in "the manners that make men."[43] Thompson was referring to the Reynolds Club.* Perhaps the tradition of chivalry, shortly to be portrayed in stained-glass and murals at Bartlett Gymnasium, entered into Thompson's thought; but it was to the corporations of the learned clerks that he turned for illustration. The colleges of the Middle

* Designed to resemble a city club, the Reynolds Club was a gift from the estate of Joseph Reynolds, the proprietor of the Diamond Jo Line. He left an imperfectly prepared will indicating that he wanted to assist young men, and his money was used for the clubhouse, it must be supposed, at the suggestion of the University (Thomas W. Goodspeed, *The University of Chicago Biographical Sketches* [Chicago: University of Chicago Press, 1922], I, 225–41).

Ages had grown out of student eating clubs: "Table talk is doubtless one of the most ancient forms of literature, and now as always one of the most universal. Man relaxes when he eats, and becomes social." And again: "The most ideal institution of learning, so far as the word *home* is concerned, is Oxford, where the colleges are only houses developed."[44]

Neither Thompson's concern nor his choice of an English model was untimely. In 1904, President James M. Taylor of Vassar wrote Ernest D. Burton: "I have been thinking for years of the possibility of some adaptation of the Oxford system. . . ."[45] The German university was still admired, but it shed little light upon the problems of undergraduate life, which had been atomized partly because the German example had encouraged Americans to build universities. Remarking in 1904 upon a wave of reaction against the individualistic and intellectual standards originating in Eliot's Harvard, the editor of *Harper's Weekly* declared that

the new ideal, or rather, the renewed emphasis on an old ideal involves the finding of great humanists once more as leaders of youth, as men who can preside over the colleges within the universities, and shape youth as Jowett did at Balliol by daily intercourse in the common living-room or in the quiet of the master's study.[46]

In 1902, a year before the first Rhodes scholars were chosen, English collegiate life was described in a book entitled *An American at Oxford,* by John Corbin.*

* In his Preface, Corbin reported the "curious coincidence" that the last proof for his book was sent to the printer on the same day that Cecil Rhodes's will was published. In the body of his book, Corbin was concerned with the lessons that American institutions, most notably Harvard, might learn from the collegiate mode of education. Corbin's general conclusion dealt with several matters directly relevant to discussion at the University of Chicago:

"The American institutions of the present are usually divided into two classes, the university, or 'large college,' and the 'small college.' The merit of the large colleges is that those fortunately placed in them gain greater familiarity with the ways of the world and of men, while for those who wish it, they offer more advanced instruction—the instruction characteristic of German universities. But to the increasing number of undergraduates who are not fortunately placed, their very size is the source of unhappiness; and for those undergraduates who wish anything else than scientific instruction, their virtues become merely a detriment. It is for this reason that many wise parents still prefer to intrust the education of their sons to the small colleges. These small colleges possess many of the virtues of the English universities; they train the mind and cultivate it, and at the same time develop the social man. If now the American university were to divide its undergraduate department into organized residential halls, it would combine the advantages of the two types of American institution, which are the two types of instruction the world over. Already our college life at its best is as happy as the college life in England; and the educational advantages of the four or five of our leading universities are rapidly becoming equal to those of the four or five leading universities of Germany. A combination of the residential hall and the teaching university would reproduce the highest type of the university of the Middle Ages; and in proportion as life and knowledge have been bettered in six hundred years, it would better

It was brought to Harper's attention by Vincent, who was especially interested in the system of dons. He said that ". . . mere residence in the halls, commons, and the like will not produce the unity which is essential. Could we not introduce a new kind of fellowship which would be valid for five years and pay enough to a man of cultivation and first rate ability to devote that amount of time to developing this unity, as well as giving advice and direction?"[47] It is striking that Vincent should have singled out fellowships for particular commendation. They had been the feature of English academic organization which the early advocates of graduate instruction had frequently combined with devices of German origin. They had thought of fellowships as a way of hiring students to stay in the university, not as a way of bringing mature talent into undergraduate education.

Oxford had already been observed by University men interested in the physical aspect of academic life. In 1900, Charles L. Hutchinson visited Oxford with a member of an architectural firm. "I am coming home," Hutchinson wrote Harper, "with great ideas of what our future buildings ought to be and only wish that we might begin all over again."[48] At a time when ill health forced Burton to give up teaching temporarily, he was commissioned to plan systematically for building as well as for library arrangements. (President Faunce of Brown University wondered why a kindly fate had not given Burton a position in some country retreat ". . . far from the lash of that tyrant, Dr. Harper.")[49] In 1902, Burton stayed for a month at Oxford, which he examined from the inside as a privileged visitor. While there, he reported that he had discovered little that ". . . would be possible and desirable to reproduce in Chicago," but later he looked back upon that visit as the most interesting part of his trip and prepared a talk about Oxford.[50]

The University was also affected by other stimulants, of which one was the example of the small college. In 1900, Harper was not ready to think a small college might be superior socially to a university; but by 1904 he had apparently changed his mind.[51] With the rapid increase of numbers in the great universities, several of the valuable features of the old college life began to disappear: "It has been conceded not only here but elsewhere that the build-

that type. England has lost the educational virtues of the mediaeval university, while Germany, in losing the residential halls, has lost its peculiar social virtues. When the American university combines the old social life with the new instruction, it will be the most perfect educational instruction in the history of civilization" (John Corbin, *An American at Oxford* [Boston: Houghton, Mifflin and Co., 1902], pp. 308–9).

ing up of undergraduate work in which hundreds or even thousands are gathered together under large faculties, is attended with serious disadvantages to all concerned."[52] The small college offered the student the possibility of closer association with a limited number of other students in the same class, a democratic social life in which the social qualities of each man became known to his fellows, and a more intimate relationship with a few instructors, in class and out. To the instructor, the small college offered opportunity for co-operation in administration, social life with a smaller number of colleagues, and an opportunity to know a limited number of students personally and to aid that number effectively.[53] The task, Harper said, was to combine some of the benefits of the small college with the resources and "cosmopolitanism" of a great university.[54] When, in his decennial report, Harper had said that in no other institution of its size had intimacy been more zealously cultivated, he had chosen his words carefully.

In no institution of its *size:* in 1901–02, the enrolment in the Junior College was 772, the total attendance in the colleges and the graduate schools of arts, literature, and science being 3,471 for the year, and the greatest attendance for one quarter being slightly less than 1,900 students.[55] Measured against enrolments today, the University was not big; but the population of the Junior College had more nearly trebled than doubled in less than ten years. Even in 1892–93, before the Junior College contained two regular classes of students who had entered as Freshmen, the College had been large in comparison with the institution which Harper had known as a college boy and from which presumably he derived something of his idea of the small college. In 1870, when Harper graduated, Muskingum had less than 50 students.[56]

Sheer numbers of students produced crowding; space in the lecture rooms and laboratories was growing scarce. Yet the size of the Junior College did not pre-empt the attention of the Faculty. When the University was ten years old, the instruction of younger men and women in the same class came under direct attack. True, the University had sought to create distinctive modes of student life according to sex. Marion Talbot, a champion of women's rights, had seen no inconsistency between the provision of educational facilities equally to the sexes, which the terms of the foundation entailed, and her own regular reporting upon the women of the University as a separate entity. In 1900, she protested to Harper against the possibility of losing an opportunity "to strengthen the social and physical life of the men and women on different lines."[57] In the classroom, however, the University had been unambiguously co-educational. No other kind of instruction had been seriously thought of after the committee appointed by the Baptist Education Society had recommended the building of a college in Chicago; but the Faculty had probably never been united in support of a practice more common in the West than in the East, where the University found many of its professors. In 1890, while still president of Colby, Albion W. Small had proposed the institution of co-ordinate colleges for the men and women there. The separation of the sexes that he had in mind was not Draconian, but it differed markedly from the plan followed at the University in 1892.[58] In 1902, Small—and others—advocated separation.

The question of separation or "segregation" divided the Faculty as nothing else did during Harper's administration.* The larger part of the Faculty, including Harper, favored the new departure. Harper agreed that the arguments for separation, taken absolutely, were arguments against co-education in general; but he denied that the University was "... shut up to the alternatives of indiscriminate approval or disapproval of co-education."[59] The opposition was not intimidated by the persons or the numbers on the other side of the question. Frederick T. Gates was impressed by the fact that more than fifty Faculty members were prepared, as he said, to lock horns with the President. Protest came from most of the men whom he had been accustomed to regard as the ablest men of the Faculty: he observed "... how acute the spirit of irritation is in the institution."[60]

That the topic of co-education in the Junior College contained explosives is patent; why it exploded when it did may perhaps be explained by the fact that the number of Junior College women, who in 1892–93 had constituted a minority by a ratio of about two to three, increased not only absolutely as the University grew in size, but relatively; in 1901–02 the enrolment of women outstripped that of men. In the light of ancient inequity, co-education was a righteous cause; in the light of statistics, for some members of the University, it became a source of concern—and conceivably, in the eyes of at least a few, it began to seem a threat to distinctively masculine life at the University.

The University decided to create residential colleges, but only after much

---

* The action denoted by the word *segregation* was not intrinsically discriminatory. When Marion Talbot heard that a young man in a crowd at Cobb Hall had said: "This won't last much longer. The women will soon be put off the campus," she pointed out that the men of the Junior College would go at the same time as the women, if not before. The student's remark and the tone of Marion Talbot's response do suggest the invidious connotation that segregation acquired: the segregation *of women* was spoken of (Marion Talbot to Harper, Nov. 10, 1902).

deliberation. In 1904, *Harper's Weekly* spoke prematurely and inaccurately when, citing Jowett's Balliol College as an exemplar, it used the heading "Oxford Transplanted to Chicago."[61] Explorations of the options before the University continued into 1905. In June, Harper reported to the Trustees that nowhere (among the larger institutions) had any very definite steps been taken to secure the advantages of the smaller institutions. Harper proposed that Junior College students should be distributed, in numbers not exceeding 175, among several colleges, each of which would possess a dean, faculty, and distinctive character. For example, one college would stress the classical curriculum and another the curriculum for commercial and industrial life. While he was in the Junior College, the student would be required to take at least half of his course of study under the faculty of his own college. He might remain a member until he had taken his Bachelor's degree. The students of each college should ultimately form a residential community.[62*]

According to plans finally adopted and put into effect on October 1, 1905, the Junior College students were organized, for purposes of "administration, instruction, and personal association," into eight colleges, or one for men and another for women in Arts, Literature, Philosophy, and Science. Each college was administered by a dean and separate Faculty responsible to a united Faculty of all the colleges, the deans forming a board chaired by the dean of the Junior Colleges. Each Faculty was free to adopt its own methods within the limits of the general regulations set by the united Faculty. At least one-third of every student's work each quarter was to be taken with instructors assigned to the student's own college; and the student was entitled to receive of them "friendly counsel"—as Harper announced—"not of a vague and general nature, but specifically and practically related to his studies, his private reading, his future plans, and other personal problems."[63] The divisional lectures were superseded by college meetings; and certain rooms were put at the disposal of the colleges as social centers.

That last arrangement signified that the University lacked the money either for college buildings on the Oxford model or for additional houses in extension of its own more modest plan of residence. Harper, with justification, had been sensitive to cost while Burton was studying the problem of space.[64] A room was

---

* Another plan combined the English model and the existing system of residence at the University. A *college* would consist of not less than four *houses*. Each college would have a distinct budget, a device that would have constituted the inward substance of a collegiate autonomy expressed outwardly by buildings (memorandum, "A Plan for Development in the Junior Colleges," inclosed with a letter from Judson to Harper, Nov. 29, 1904).

assigned each college, the dean of the Junior Colleges said, ". . . with the hope that ultimately this would be replaced by some permanent building."[65] The adverb was the operative word. In spite of physical handicaps, the colleges did have vitality and unity in their first year; in the opinion of the dean, the new organization had made a significant beginning. Yet the record was imperfect. The attempt to keep instruction within the college boundaries broke down from the start, partly owing to the complexity of the curriculums. Similarly, segregation became an anomaly whenever a Junior College student was permitted to take an advanced course in a co-educational classroom or a department found it difficult or undesirable to offer Junior College courses in two, segregated sections. Moreover, the Faculty members, with individual exceptions, failed to find ". . . occasion and time to establish close personal relationships with the student body."[66] In that brief statement, the Junior College dean described a principal cause of the academic malaise for which the creation of small colleges within a university had originally been prescribed.

When *Harper's Weekly* applauded the transplanting of Oxford to Chicago, it had predicted that the President would find bricks and stone for dormitories with comparative ease but that it would not be so easy to find the men who could preside over the destinies of the colleges: "Still longer must he wait for that atmosphere to gather around them which so insensibly yet so powerfully alters the lives of men who enter the classic shades of Oxford."[67] The University had indeed to wait, even for completion of the easiest task.

BEYOND THE QUADRANGLES

During the decennial year and after the University was deeply involved in the remodeling of education within the Quadrangles, but Harper continued to look far beyond them and to concern himself with University Extension and the extramural work that had gone under the name of affiliation. Because Extension was more a product of Harper's enthusiasm and perseverance than of concerted purpose and effort within the Faculty, the final reorganization of Extension appropriately was triggered off by Harper's activity in behalf of an institution, the American Institute of Sacred Literature, which he had founded and carried forward. The Institute, which conducted instruction by mail, stood in line of descent from the evangelical-scholarly enterprises which Harper had floated when the promise of his career lay wholly in the advancement of Old Testament criticism and the encouragement of Bible studies. (In 1898, Harper had tried unsuccessfully to bring parts of Chautauqua within the orbit of the University. He proposed to move to Chicago the headquarters of the Chautauqua Reading and Scientific Circles and two publishing enterprises working under contract with Chautauqua and, according to one version of the plan, to associate them with University Extension and the University Press.)[68] Harper estimated that the Institute of Sacred Literature reached some 10,000 persons; but it was heavily in debt, in some part to Harper himself.[69] Presumably, he had been helping to keep the Institute alive by meeting bills out of his own pocket. In 1903, when he was about to travel abroad, Harper deputized Judson and Burton to make new arrangements for the Institute in conjunction with a reorganization of Extension.[70]

Negotiations over annexation fell into a familiar pattern. The financial condition of the Institute was an obstacle. Burton talked with a committee of Trustees and, without consulting Harper, presented the facts of the case to Gates.[71] The timing of debt payment was of the essence; Judson and Burton argued that money could be raised after annexation and on the basis of it, especially if Harper campaigned; but the Trustees were reluctant to anticipate the results of a drive for which the University would be responsible. Because money to meet the liabilities of the Institute was not immediately forthcoming, the proposal hung in the air for two years. Then, in 1905, Harper arranged that his vacation credit (or the dollar equivalent of unused vacation time) owed him by the University be used, at least temporarily, to offset a debt of $6,000 owed to the University Press by the Institute.[72] An additional indebtedness of $4,000 was also provided for, and the Institute was incorporated into Extension.[73] It was simultaneously reorganized into a series of five sections according to subject matter taught. One section conducted the work of the sometime Institute.[74] Thus, Bible study, which in the early years had been given a place in University extramural work only to be quickly dropped, reappeared as one of its constituent parts and perhaps as the model of their form. A circle had been completed and a chord in Harper's life resolved.

Although it may possibly have been to inject new life into the original plan for affiliation that, shortly after 1900, Albion W. Small made a junket of institutions in the West and South, the University did not become the center of such a constellation as Harper had once envisaged. The few schools and colleges with which the University signed affiliation agreements supplied neither a copious stream of students nor the leverage to raise general standards of education. Yet Harper continued to attempt the extension of the influence of the University in particular situations as opportunity arose, either through agreement with other corporations or by independent action. The union with Rush Medical College and creation of the School of Education represented affiliation carried to its highest power. Harper also became involved, to no avail, in plans to reorganize the government of the marine laboratory at Woods Hole. Its scientific director was C. O. Whitman, head of the Department of Zoölogy. The University had wanted a marine biological laboratory of its own, and Harper's plan would have given Chicago men, if not the University itself, great influence in the board.[75] In 1901, Elizabeth Wallace opened a school under University auspices in the Latin Quarter of Paris; but too few students appeared to justify the experiment.[76] In 1901–02, Harper negotiated an arrangement which fell somewhere between an academic appointment and affiliation of the University with a single free-lance investigator. W. Alleyne Ireland, a young man without any degree that the University knew of, asked for support of a massive inquiry into colonialism in Southeast Asia, or what today would be called an area-studies project. He wanted far more money than the University was willing to provide; but Harper allowed the correspondence to continue. He found $500 of University money and helped Ireland to secure more elsewhere; and he also arranged for Ireland to be appointed Special Commissioner of the University.[77] (Later Ireland wrote of being Colonial Commissioner.)[78] The University used its corporate power to vouch for virtually independent research to be carried out by an enterprising but previously uncertified investigator in an area geographically remote from the Quadrangles and intellectually unrelated to the research of the Faculty. The agreement proved in practice to be unique; but in principle it projected the University into the coming age of grants-in-aid and also into the general licensing of research. How wide should the umbrella of University sponsorship be opened?

Although the affiliation program was conspicuously fruitful in so few instances that they seem the exceptions proving that affiliation as such was ill-advised, the pursuit of order in education was speeded along other new paths which the University and the men who knew its experience helped to open. With the presidents of Harvard, Columbia, Johns Hopkins, and the University of California, Harper called the conference at which the Association of American Universities was organized; and the University of Chicago was the host of that conference. Two expected results were greater uniformity of the conditions under which students might become candidates for higher degrees in different

American universities and the raising of the standards of the weaker institutions.[79] Harper had been one of the men who called the organizing convention
of the North Central Association of Colleges and Secondary Schools, and he
chaired the committee which drafted its constitution. As the host of the first
annual meeting, he had occasion to point out to the members of the Association:

Each institution is an individual. It takes many individuals to make the whole, of
which each forms a part. . . . Individualism in institutions has grown in the last ten or
fifteen or twenty years, but after all we have at heart the same work, we have in mind
the same purpose, we are doing the same thing. . . . Perfection in method and work
is far beyond us. We may never hope to reach it, but we must strive for it, and in that
effort the experience of our brethren will count for more than all other things combined.[80]

That sharing of experience, Harper might have said, was the conference idea
writ large. The North Central Association did not long confine itself to consultation. Soon after its founding, the Association established a commission
on accreditation of schools, of which Harry P. Judson, a University of Chicago
dean, was chairman and George N. Carman, sometime head of Morgan Park
Academy, was secretary. It was Carman's question—shall we accredit the colleges?—that opened debate on a policy which put the Association in the fore-
front of the effort to maintain standards in undergraduate education. One of
Carman's reasons for advocating college accreditation was the impossibility of
drawing a line of separation between the secondary school and the college.
About half of the combined school and college requirements for the Bachelor's
degree, said Carman, might be and as a matter of fact were pursued either in
school or college. Carman added that failure to co-operate in fixing and maintaining standards had led too often to an unseemly scramble for students, which
sacrificed what was best for them to the seeming advantage of the college.

By defining courses of instruction [Carman suggested] and inspecting and accrediting
institutions much waste and confusion may be prevented and the interests of students
conserved. When all elementary courses in English, mathematics, science, history and
foreign languages are thus standardized, the student may pass from one institution
to another at that stage in his advancement which is most to his advantage.[81]

Neither the diagnosis nor the remedy was new.

As if Harper realized that the University could not itself provide a sufficient
remedy for the ills of the colleges, especially without funds for the purpose, he
proposed in his decennial report that a corporation be organized under the
auspices of the University but legally independent of it, to receive and invest

330

money for the support of college work and to investigate the financial affairs and general management of colleges—in short, that the University be the nursery of a foundation for the advancement of undergraduate education.[82] In 1904 or 1905, Harper presented the same proposal, amended and enlarged, to Andrew Carnegie. An institution should be founded to encourage the work of the colleges—not the universities. The institution would aim to increase the efficiency of existing colleges; to discover where new colleges might be built; to encourage the union of some colleges and the discontinuation of others; to assist in fixing a common standard of college work—together with greater uniformity in admission requirements—in securing and investing endowments, in informing the public about such investments, and in making lecturers and teachers available for joint service among the colleges; to provide financial aid to exceptional men and women—whenever and wherever found—who needed educational opportunities; and to publish the results of the investigation of college education in relation to what preceded and followed it: the proposal was sweeping.[83] Out of his imagination and (can it be doubted?) his frustrating experience with collegiate reform conducted by one university without financial leverage, Harper produced what in retrospect seems a forecast of foundation work in collegiate education, including a national merit scholarship program that would wait a half century for fulfilment. His part was prophecy; but in June, 1905, John D. Rockefeller pledged $10,000,000 to enlarge the General Education Board, "to promote a comprehensive system of higher education in the United States."[84] The purposes of affiliation were carried forward most powerfully by other means than the University and by men commanding far greater funds than its President was granted to bring his hopes into reality.

When in March of that year Harper wrote to Carnegie of the proposed college scheme, he remarked that he had been thinking many hours of its possibilities "as I have lain upon my bed in these last weeks. . . ." Cancer had set in. Harper's mind continued to range forward as it always had; but the man could not stand constantly on duty. He had written George E. Vincent in February: "I am bequeathing to you the responsibility for carrying through the plan for the development of the small college. I sincerely hope that you will take this upon your heart and make of it what I am sure it can be made. The possibility is simply magnificent."[85] Harper's influence had never been absolute, but never before had his presence been withdrawn. The University without Harper was being foreshadowed.

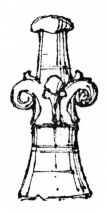

CHAPTER XVII

"Work Still To Do"

The future of the University depended upon the character of its Faculty, upon the material resources it could devote to education and research, and upon the quality of the self-consciousness and the other imponderables that established its identity. After the tenth birthday of the University had been celebrated, Harper believed an age of prose had begun. Yet the sequel to the first decade was again a history of crisis. The outcome of events occurring then affected the prospects of the University more profoundly than the experience to which Harper looked back with his kind of nostalgia in 1902. His death in 1906 cut short a regime and ended an era, but the last years possessed a significance not to be found in the bare fact that they were indeed the last before the first President of the University ceased to direct its work.

THE STATE OF THE FACULTY

Following a visit to the University, less than a year after the decennial celebration, Albert Shaw, the editor of *Review of Reviews,* wrote Harper:

. . . Not least was I impressed with the presence in your university of what I most like to find in an educational institution, namely, a spirit of mutual respect among the professors and instructors, and of real content and harmony. I found divers and sundry of the men I knew quite free to express their opinions on all university subjects, but I found none of them other than loyal and hopeful, and of good-will. It all seemed pretty "strenuous," but of course you could not have accomplished so much in ten years by the exclusive cultivation of the virtues of repose and serenity.[1]

In spite of their serious disagreements, particularly over the undergraduate curriculum and the segregation in Junior College classes, the members of the Faculty did not fall into civil war. The life of the Quadrangles was disrupted neither by unbridled rowing nor by threat of the massive secession that sometimes cripples an academic institution. The University of Chicago never suffered such damage as half wrecked Clark University when much of its faculty withdrew to Chicago; history did not repeat itself.

Yet the Faculty worked under strain, produced partly by the same shortage of funds that had distressed Clark University. The strain sometimes showed itself in sheer irritability. In 1902, James H. Tufts, writing as dean of the Senior Colleges, inquired whether any account was taken of the fact that their work had practically doubled in three years and whether the authorities of the University cared to have the work of his office conducted in a businesslike and efficient manner. Tufts had been denied a cabinet in which to keep the records of conversations with students: "It is, of course, not anything that I have any personal interest in," Tufts wrote Goodspeed, "as to whether such accounts are kept or not, and personally, of course, I do not care whether we have any registration cards or any other facilities for doing the work of this office. It is simply a question of what the University wants done. . . ."[2] Harper commented that Tufts's letter did not seem to have been written in the proper spirit; nor did it show, in Harper's opinion, a proper appreciation of the circumstances and situation: "The success of the administration of the office does not depend upon any particular piece of furniture. There are economical ways of taking care of correspondence which have been employed in the past and which can be employed in the future."[3] The exchange made no lasting mark; but the correspondence in a similar vein between Harper and another professor-administrator, John Dewey, no doubt contributed to what, in the light of history, may be considered a disaster for the University as an intellectual center. In April, 1904, Dewey resigned both as head of the Department of Philosophy and as Director of the School of Education. In the second capacity he had immediate control of an endowed laboratory school, but he was not content. His staff included a large contingent of men and women who followed Francis W. Parker rather than Dewey to Blaine Hall; his wife, Alice Dewey, was not allowed to remain principal of the elementary school; and Dewey himself as the chief administrator of the school was expected to give a close accounting of its finances. Dewey protested against financial reports that showed a deficit for the School of Education; but in May, 1904, a Trustee was writing John D. Rockefeller, Jr., of an overdraft of $120,000 that had been caused by accumulating deficiency balances. The school was responsible for one. Rockefeller's views forbade the incurring of indebtedness, and the bank objected to overdrafts.[4] Dewey had become a central figure in the most painful of difficulties, and he resigned, writing Harper of the way he had been hampered. He referred to "a history of years."[5] Although the evidence bearing upon Dewey's experience in the University fails to indicate that Harper was hostile toward him—rather, Harper sought to provide Dewey with the closest possible approximation to his ideal laboratory— Dewey's remark points, however obliquely, to a truth. Through a history of years the University had asked its professors to take account of present circumstances, to do the best they could with what they had, to serve as part-time administrators, to have confidence in the future, to be patient. The patience of John Dewey cracked.

Other incidents created (or revealed) similar fissures between men or between individual Faculty members and the University. For example, James H. Breasted, already an ardent but not yet famous Egyptologist, and Robert F. Harper, an Assyriologist and the brother of the President, clashed over Oriental studies. For years, Breasted found himself in a tantalizing situation, enabled to pursue his specialty, then not an established discipline in American universities, and at the same time frustrated in his effort to move from the library and the museum in order to make what he thought would be his particular contribution to Egyptology, the exact recording of inscriptions from which a history of Egypt might be written. All the same, he was not lost to the University. Toward the end of the Harper administration, he was enabled by the Oriental Exploration Fund, established by John D. Rockefeller, to take his first expedition to the Nile.[6]

In another instance, the inability of the University to satisfy the requirements of a Faculty member, the physiologist Jacques Loeb, meant his departure to California. In October, 1902, before Loeb left the University, Harper wrote Gates: "There is no man to-day working in biological science, or in fact, in any other science, who occupies a position in the world more creditable, or more widely known than Loeb. For him to leave the University of Chicago means the world-wide inquiry—Why did he go? The answer must be—lack of support."[7] The search for fuller opportunity which brought gifted investigators to the University could also take them away.*

In that same year, George C. Walker, donor and Trustee of the University, indicated his dissatisfaction with an improvisation that had become custom. He had intended that the building which he gave the University should be used as a general museum—a designation entirely consistent with Harper's early conception. The establishment of museums was an important part of the work to be done by the University. Walker had consented to the use of the Walker building for geology classes because there was no other place to put them: ". . . no one had any idea this would continue for any great length of time."[8] In 1903, the Trustees agreed that they should provide other quarters for the classes as soon as possible and that the Walker Museum should be conducted as a general museum, related to the departmental museums as the general library was to the departmental libraries.[9] Yet in 1904, Harper remarked that the University museums had been neglected and asked: "What is to be the future policy of the University regarding Museums?"[10] Presently a joint Museum Commission of Trustees and Faculty was created. To the commission, Thomas C. Chamberlin, head of the geology department, was obliged to report disputes over the location and arrangement of a general museum: "Indeed we seemed to be farther from uniting on a practicable and workable scheme than ever before. The essential difficulty lies partly in diversity of departmental interests and partly in a failure to appreciate what is requisite to give a museum its greatest productiveness."[11] The obstacles to agreement, it appears retrospectively, were the same as those the Faculty had encountered in its running debate over the undergraduate curriculum—some incompatibility between the constituent units of the University and the lack of common understanding as to the concrete means best fitted to the ends the University was meant to serve.

During the year 1902, in formal action involving the Faculty as a whole, the polity of the University was brought into question before the Congregation. In

---

* Perhaps the loss of Loeb taught Harper that the University could not expect to keep all of its Faculty members. Not long after the University failed to hold Loeb, William G. Hale wrote Harper that Carl D. Buck, whom Hale described as the first philologist of the world, might be called to Harvard. If he went, Hale said, the blow to the prestige of the University, with the double loss of Loeb and Buck, would be terrible. Harper answered: "I do not think myself that any institution is dependent on any one man or even two men, and I think we might contribute to other institutions even three or four and have remaining a very much larger number of investigators than the other institutions. We cannot, of course, hope to have all investigators, but we must try to keep our share." Buck did not in fact leave the University (Hale to Harper, Dec. 12, 1902, and Harper to Hale, Dec. 12, 1902).

1895–96, as the Faculty of Arts, Literature, and Science was being divided into the separate Faculties for government of the several colleges and schools, the partitioning of power had been criticized, by Ryerson, who thought it carried the University away from simplicity toward elaborate organization which would add to the President's burdens and by Robert Herrick, who remarked on "Harper's bête, ward-politician method of bottling up his faculty in three small bottles to be carried about in the pocket."[12] In March, 1901, the Congregation had resolved that the establishment of a general Faculty in arts, literature, and science with supreme authority within those areas was desirable, and a committee of five was appointed to make specific proposals. When the committee reported months later, in January, 1902, it was deeply split. The majority held that the jurisdiction and functions of each of the governing bodies as well as legislative procedure should be clearly defined; that the number of Faculties should be as small as possible; that a single Faculty should govern each branch of the University that formed a unit according to subject matter (rather than a program and students at a particular level of studies, for example, the Junior Colleges); and that the actions of each Faculty should be final within its jurisdiction unless the President exercised a written veto or an appeal was taken to the Senate. The majority, in effect, recommended the re-creation of the Faculty of Arts, Literature, and Science, but with a difference. The Senate should have original jurisdiction over matters pertaining to the whole institution (for example, Extension), but not within a single branch of the University; there, the report of the majority asserted explicitly, the Senate should not legislate. The several branches were to be arts, literature, and science; theology; medicine; education; and (prospectively) law; technology; and so forth. This division of authority meant the abolition of distinct Junior College, Senior College, and Graduate School Faculties, for which boards were to be substituted. The distribution of administration among these boards, committees, and a new administrative board of the Senate would eliminate the old Council. Finally, the majority of the committee turned toward its parent body, proposing that the Congregation should meet once a year, rather than each quarter and at special call, and that the Congregation would "record its opinion," rather than "make recommendations."[13]

A minority report, by Small and Judson, presented as "fundamental principles" that initial responsibility for work should rest with those engaged in it and the system of legislation should be bicameral, "whereby is secured an independent review of all measures from the point of view of the University as a whole."[14] Small and Judson recommended, in accord with the first principle, that the Junior College Faculty be retained, and in accord with the second, that all enactments on educational questions should continue to be reviewed by the Senate. The Council would remain a distinct body in charge of administration. The Senior College and two graduate Faculties would be merged to form a general body with standing committees on curriculum. Small and Judson agreed with the majority that professional Faculties should stand beside those of Arts, Literature, and Science.[15] Harper supported the minority report.

Throughout the majority report, Small found the implication that the organization of the University had been a bungle from the start.[16] The gist of the report as summarized by Laughlin, a supporter, was local self-government.[17] The report appears to have been aimed in part at the exploitation of vaguely defined powers by a central administration, and it enlarged the power of the academic commonalty, organized as a single Faculty insofar as arts, literature, and science were concerned, at the expense of a body with general jurisdiction, the Senate. To alter the work of the Congregation would screen Faculty members from the view of a body not made up entirely of Faculty men. The report, at the least, implies such jealous regard for academic prerogative as Laughlin and Hale, who belonged to the majority of the committee, had displayed to Harper in Ithaca in 1892. The Senate had answered their need, then, but became a target of their criticism in 1902; did they believe that the Senate had ceased to serve constitutionalism?

When the reports were put to a vote in the Congregation, it adopted the Small-Judson recommendation by a ballot of 62 to 38. With the approval of the Senate and the Trustees, a United Faculty of Arts, Literature, and Science was established, without alteration of the powers of the Senate or of administrative machinery. The status quo had been preserved without striking amendment, but against opposition by about one-third of the voters. A substantial part of the Faculty was restive; but the question of the majority report had not been put, and so cannot be interpreted, as a formal motion of no confidence in the administration—although Small must have thought this was what the report signified. The minority vote expressed distaste for the way in which the University was governed and administered (as distinct from the administration as such) and also—possibly—dissent from policies with which the administration was associated. Nearly five-sixths of the minority was composed of Faculty members who had no administrative responsibilities and who may conceivably have resented the autonomy of the administrators. Marion Talbot, who was an administrator, may be supposed to have voted with the minority in indirect protest against the adoption of segregation of the sexes as in the Junior College classrooms. The opponents of segregation formed a perceptibly larger part of the minority than did supporters of segregation. Similiarly, it may be that some of the humanists who voted in the minority, and many did, were disturbed over the failure of Harper or the Senate to give absolute protection to Latin in the curriculum. Yet Chamberlin, too, voted in the minority, perhaps because he thought a new Faculty would grant the freedom from Latin that the Junior College Faculty was then still denying s.b. candidates. Academic ranks, general areas of subject matter (e.g., arts), and departments were split in the vote. The members of the departments of arts, literature, and science were indeed divided almost equally. Without the votes of full-time administrators and other non-departmental voters, some of whom were enfranchised because of Harper's ideas of a larger University community, the balloting would have been very close. The regular Faculty did not lose; but it was Harper's conception of the University, rather than a patently dominant view within the Faculty, that won.

Shortly after the event, Laughlin complained that only a "presidential kitchen cabinet" attended meetings of the Senate, which in his opinion was merely a rubber stamp.[18] Attendance by senators who had voted for the more drastic plan of reorganization declined at meetings in February and March, 1902, but increased in May.* Discontent had been deep enough to produce rebelliousness but not rebellion, a distinction critical to the stability of the regime.

Harper was fully aware that some members of the University felt hemmed-in, or deprived, as he said, "of an opportunity of joining themselves more close-ly with the various fields of university work"; but he believed that no single person could possibly keep in touch with all the departments to the point where his judgment would have value on every specific point.[19] The officer who wished to ask questions about a particular action had a right to speak in the Congregation. If one root of Harper's attitude was a desire to divide and rule, another was probably concern lest the government of the University be irre-sponsible and ineffectual. A memorandum in the presidential files—possibly written by Harper—argues that responsibility for administration had to be fixed and could not be located if decision was reserved (as the majority report had

* On Harper's suggestion, acting heads of departments were given places in the Senate—as the majority report had recommended.

proposed) to a "large body" like the Senate; it was safe to say that if the Press, Extension, and affiliation had been in the hands of the Senate, ". . . most of these interests would have long since ceased to exist."[20] It had been Harper's proposal of credit for Extension work that had alerted Hale and Laughlin to the need for a Senate to give professorial opinion a strong voice. It may be that Harper was afraid that the body he had allegedly captured would not unwillingly neglect the administration of the University beyond the Quadrangles. The tensions within the University were complex.

In the month when the committee of the Congregation was submitting its reports, John Dewey published an article, "Academic Freedom," which constituted a gloss on the attitudes reflected only fragmentarily in the record of the business of the University. Dewey believed there was no longer reason to fear out-and-out suppression of freedom in the true universities of the United States; he set aside the case "as regards academic freedom in the popular sense, that is to say, of dictatorial interferences by moneyed benefactors with special individual utterances." A subtle and refined danger lay within the university itself.

Money is absolutely indispensable as a means. But it is only a means. The danger lies in the difficulty of making money adequate as a means, and yet keeping it in its place —not permitting it to usurp any of the functions of control which belong only to educational purposes. To these, if the university is to be a true university, money and all things connected therewith must be subordinate. But the pressure to get the means is tending to make it an end; and this is academic materialism—the worst foe of freedom of work in its widest sense.

The university did need to expand to be true to itself, and to expand it had to have money. A new type of administration had been called into being by the great material expansion of the university. Dewey argued:

A ponderous machinery has come into existence for carrying on the multiplicity of business and quasi-business matters without which the modern university would come to a standstill. This machinery tends to come between the individual and the region of moral aims in which he should assert himself. Personality counts for less than the apparatus thru which, it sometimes seems, the individual alone can accomplish anything. Moreover, the minutiae, the routine turning of the machinery, absorb time and energy. Many a modern college man is asking himself where he is to get the leisure and strength to devote himself to his ultimate ends, so much, willy-nilly, has to be spent on the intermediate means. The side-tracking of personal energy into the routine of academic machinery is a serious problem.

Yet the absorption of energy that ought to be spent in dealing with the larger issues of life would not have been very threatening had it not been associated with a tendency toward specialization. It led to withdrawal:

It means preoccupation with a comparatively remote field in relatively minute detail. I have no doubt that in the long run the method of specialization will justify itself, not only scientifically, but practically. But value in terms of ultimate results is no reason for disguising the immediate danger to courage, and the freedom that can come only from courage. Teaching, in any case, is something of a protected industry; it is sheltered. The teacher is set somewhat one side from the incidence of the most violent stresses and strains of life. His problems are largely intellectual, not moral; his associates are largely immature. There is always the danger of a teacher's losing something of the virility that comes from having to face and wrestle with economic and political problems on equal terms with competitors. Specialization unfortunately increases these dangers. It leads the individual, if he follows it unreservedly, into by-paths still further off from the highway where men, struggling together, develop strength. The insidious conviction that certain matters of fundamental import to humanity are none of my concern because outside of my *Fach*, is likely to work more harm to genuine freedom of academic work than any fancied dread of interference from a moneyed benefactor.

The expansion of the material side of the modern university also carried with it strong tendencies toward centralization. The old-fashioned college faculty had been a thorough-going democracy in its way, and the executive was but *primus inter pares:*

All that is now changed—necessarily so. It requires ability of a very specialized and intensified order to wield the administrative resources of a modern university. The conditions make inevitably for centralization. It is difficult to draw the line between that administrative centralization which is necessary for the economical and efficient use of resources and that moral centralization which restricts initiative and responsibility. Individual participation in legislative authority and position is a guarantee of strong, free, and independent personalities. The old faculty, a genuine republic of letters, is likely to become an oligarchy—more efficient from the standpoint of material results achieved, but of less account in breeding men.[21]

Dewey's experience would illustrate his generalization: argument over the deficits of a school drowned out discussion of education. The University might lose its vitality not under assault from without but by ossification of its own tissue. The bonds between specialists and between specialized departments could become brittle and weak; unity like that of a family, in Harper's metaphor, might be replaced by conformity under a bureaucratic government. The fault would not lie in sheer need of money and in its pursuit. With unimpeachable intentions, Dewey pleaded for financial support; but, when he received it, his frustration was only intensified. There was slight danger that the members of the University would be denied freedom to think but a somber possibility that, while the University moved forward as an institution, they might be hurt badly enough to be distracted from thinking. Clarence L. Herrick, the professor of biology who resigned his post before the University opened, probably never recovered from the impact of his encounter with the University; Edward W. Bemis became a sacrifice to unrealistic expectations; and other men, who did not leave the University, spent time writing letters of complaint as well as monographs. John Dewey lost confidence altogether in having opportunity to work unhampered in the University. Yet many Faculty members did benefit from Harper's willingness to pledge the future; much of his achievement was risk justified. Were the tragedies of his era but the price any institution must pay for attracting talented men and women whose brilliance carries unusual vulnerability to disappointment; or did the way of the University necessarily produce a peculiar threat to personal feeling—a sapping of humanity that endangered the University itself? Harper's presence was a standing promise that the life of the University would transcend ordinary, humdrum existence—he punched a hole through the ceiling of the currently possible—and Harper's University, as an ideal, implied greatness; but was Harper's University, the actuality, to be checked short of greatness by the accumulating effects of the pressure it put upon human nature? Did that University indeed go too far in the demands it made upon the human beings who supported and served it—upon John D. Rockefeller, who hated deficits but was asked year after year to underwrite them; upon the Trustees, who had the task of at once bringing Harper's genius to fulfilment and of keeping the University solvent; upon the Faculty members, who felt the centrifugal force of curiosity and the restraining leash of economy; and also upon Harper himself? The weight that he put upon others bore down upon him, too; for the burden of the University was his to carry. His life tested the capacity of personality to survive in a university.

THE STATE OF FINANCES

The laying of the cornerstones during the decennial celebration had symbolized the power of the University to attract support; but the new buildings themselves were a mixed blessing. Increased maintenance costs unmatched by corresponding additions to endowment accentuated the problem of deficits. Indeed, the University lacked sufficient working capital to pay its bills promptly

341

and was unable, when economy was especially desirable, to take advantage of discounts. By the end of March, 1903, there existed an overdraft of nearly $88,000, while vouchers amounting to almost $53,000 were still to be paid. When, at the request of the Trustees, Rockefeller loaned the University $200,000 to establish a working fund (to be kept intact), the pressure of monthly payments was somewhat eased; but there remained the weight of an overburdened budget threatening the stability of the University.[22]

In the winter of 1903–04, financial management became the subject of extraordinary investigation by lieutenants of the Founder. In November, at a time when the merger of the American Institute of Sacred Literature and University Extension was pending, Gates sent inquiries meant only for Ryerson's attention. ("What a pleasure it is," Gates wrote, "to have a friend to whom one can write a confidential letter, and feel perfectly sure that it will be held confidential in fact!") Noting that the Institute, Harper's "private philanthropy," was $5,000 in debt to the Press, Gates questioned the system that made such things possible. Rejecting Harper's description of the Institute as to all intents and purposes the Extension department of the Divinity School, Gates suggested to Ryerson ". . . putting our heads together to see if there is not some way by which this and anything else like it may be corrected."[23] Ryerson replied that the director of the Press did not feel it incumbent upon himself to use great caution while extending credit at Harper's behest: the debt of the Institute had been counted as something Harper would soon take care of—"and so it grew, until it reached its present excessive amount." Ryerson attributed unauthorized expense less to a defect of system or organization than to personal elements in the situation. "It is difficult . . . to keep Dr. Harper from interesting himself in all the details of affairs at the University and in cases where he thinks an emergency exists, from exceeding his authority. . . ." It might not be expedient, Ryerson added, to run the risk of discrediting Harper's proper authority by making it possible and even necessary for employees to question its extent.[24] On the other hand, how far should consideration of the "personal element" be carried? To the proposition that transfer of the Institute to the University would relieve Harper of a burden, John D. Rockefeller, Jr., responded, "I dislike on principle to take on new work for the University under pressure of this sort."[25]

The attitude of the Founder toward the use of pressure was critically important in the affairs of the University. The office at 26 Broadway was patently a
generator and a focal point of immensely powerful forces. Perhaps because of
that fact, Rockefeller sought to deal with philanthropic appeals upon their own
merits rather than under duress. A man of power, he resented being pushed.
In the winter of 1903–04, a lawyer, Starr J. Murphy, examined the University
on behalf of the Founder; at Gates's suggestion, Murphy had already conducted
a survey of medical schools—while the Rush affiliation was being considered.
Unlike Gates's November inquiry, the investigation undertaken by Murphy
was conducted under Harper's eyes and in accord with his desire (or so Gates
thought) to have Murphy look at the University as John D. Rockefeller, Jr., or
Gates would have done.[26] Murphy's commission was to search for financial
leaks in whatever he might observe—particularly in the Press, including the
journals (were they "of real living and vital interest" or was their content so
much lumber?); in University Extension; in affiliation; and in the course offerings, where he was to look for uneconomically small enrolments. Of the journals, Extension, and affiliation, he should ask why the work was not self-supporting—the same question that Gates had put during discussion of the
budget.[27]

Murphy was impressed by the astonishing vigor and vitality of the University; the productive power of the Faculty, "especially along lines of original and
creative work"; and the monumental beauty of the buildings. He missed an
atmosphere of scholastic repose and of refining and uplifting culture, like that
at Harvard; but he reported a virile energy and enthusiasm, ". . . more characteristic of the great young West." The whole atmosphere of the place reflected
the personality of the President. Yet the absence of a chapel moved Murphy to
wonder if the institution had a soul.[28] His searching (but somewhat incomplete) report on the specific activities of the University was similarly mixed.
The journals appeared to be interesting and valuable and the management of
the Press had been reconstituted along promising lines, but its actual practice
had not been radically changed. "I suspect," Murphy remarked in regard to the
Press, "that the President will do about as he pleases in the future as he has in
the past." In University Extension, correspondence-study was unique in that it
was self-supporting; but lecture-study did not impress Murphy. The lecturers
appeared to be men of high ability and the lectures excellent, but they were not
taken more seriously, as education, than commercial lecturing. Moreover, the
foundation of the work was unstable, for it rested on unassured local responsi-

bility and interest. As to affiliation: the idea of raising standards of secondary education throughout the Mississippi Valley was lofty and noble, but the task, if attempted seriously, would take the resources of all the universities of the country. Other universities exerted influence on the secondary schools without having a special machinery for the purpose. "In other words," Murphy wrote, "I think the affiliated work of the University of Chicago exists largely on paper.... The whole movement impressed me as illustrative of President Harper's tendency to absorb into the University everything that is loose."

Looking at the financial management of the University in general, Murphy was pleased by the work of the auditor, Trevor Arnett, and the business manager, Wallace Heckman, but pointed out two weaknesses in financial administration: an easygoing and unwarranted optimism in making up the budget (much more accurate estimates than those for 1903–04 must be possible) and a tendency to disregard the limits set by the budget after discovering that its estimates were not being fulfilled. Notwithstanding the growth in endowment and a larger income from student fees, the demands upon Rockefeller to make up annual budget deficits showed no decrease but, on the contrary, "a steady and alarming" increase in absolute amount. The tabulation of budget income indicated "a totally unsound financial policy." Should Rockefeller's support be withdrawn for any reason, the work of the institution would be very seriously crippled. Asking how such a situation was to be explained, Murphy confronted the naked question of the relation between Rockefeller and the University:

... There is, of course, an obvious suggestion which lies upon the surface, ... that there is a feeling that the founder cannot afford to allow the institution with which his name is so closely identified to get into financial disrepute, and that therefore it is safe to deliberately incur large obligations with the idea that he will be under a moral compulsion to provide for them. I should, however, be extremely loath to attribute such motives to the Trustees. It must be remembered that they are busy men of the highest standing, and that they are devoting a great deal of most valuable time gratuitously to this work. While it is of the utmost importance that administrative errors and harmful tendencies should be frankly recognized and promptly checked, it would be unfortunate to misunderstand the position of the Trustees and wholly calamitous to unjustly attribute to them unworthy motives. I think that we shall get a more accurate view of the situation, and thus be able to arrive at more hopeful remedies, by trying to look at the subject dispassionately, first from one side, that of the Trustees and Administrative Officers, and second from the other, that of the founder and those who are called upon to furnish the financial resources. During my visit to the University I made it my business to get as nearly in touch with the spirit of the institution and with the men who are doing the work as possible, and I stayed there long enough to see something of the inside workings. There is a splendid spirit of enthusiasm which characterises all departments of the University and almost all of the men on the Faculty. Each man is keenly alive to the needs and possibilities of his department and is constantly exerting a pressure upon the authorities for the furnishing and development of the things which seem to him to be important. When you consider that this is the attitude of almost every man on the Faculty, you can see that the accumulated pressure upon the authorities must be almost irresistible. This pressure is sincere and enthusiastic, and in almost every case the thing asked for is in itself desirable. When one is familiar with these needs and in a position where the pressure of them can be exerted directly upon him, it requires great determination to resist it. This situation is, in itself, a most helpful one and a condition of the most vigorous growth. The study of the principles of evolution shows us, that, throughout the entire organic world, the condition of progress is this intense and persistent pressure upon the means of subsistence, which is the primary means of assuring that the unfit shall perish and only the fit survive. The same principle applies in the case of the University, which is, after all, a great living organism and subject to the laws of organic life. One cannot stay at the University and get into intimate touch with it, without realizing and being profoundly impressed with the enormous vitality of the institution, and it is this very vitality which accounts for the tremendous pressure which is brought to bear upon the authorities. The President is a man of the widest optimism. This is a quality of first importance provided, only, [that] it can be restrained by a cool and deliberate judgment. It is almost impossible to find those two qualities united in the same individual, but it would be a great misfortune to eliminate this optimism from the President, provided some means can be found in other quarters to control it. It is this quality which has led to the really phenomenal growth of the institution, and to it is largely due the inspiration of the other men in all departments. The President is a man of great persuasiveness, and it is easy for him to present to his Trustees, in a very convincing way, the importance and necessity of the things which he desires to see accomplished. Being subjected as they are to this pressure, and realizing the value and the need of the various things recommended, it is not surprising that the Trustees should be disposed to acquiesce in his plans, so far as the resources of the institution will permit; and to be optimistic with regard to the possibility of increasing those resources. The situation is unusual. The founder is well known to be a man of great resources and of great liberality, and the Trustees are justified in believing that he has a profound interest in the institution. Year after year he has added princely sums to its endowment, and year after year as the annual budgets have been presented to him and his immediate representatives, the annual deficit has been provided for, and, so far as I am able to ascertain, this has been done without any very grave protest. It would not be fair, moreover, to charge the Trustees and Administrative Officers with leaving the whole financial burden to rest upon the founder. They have exerted themselves most diligently and most successfully in procuring funds from other sources. In the twelve years of the institution's life contributions from people other than the founder have exceeded the total aggregate resources of all but a very few of the larger institutions of learning in the country, and this result, apart entirely from the gifts of the founder, entitles the Trustees and the Administrative Officers to the highest praise. . . . But . . . the existing financial situation, and the course of financial administration for the past few years is intolerable and must be altered. While it is desirable and necessary that the Trustees should be men of broad intellectual sympathy and of keen appreciation of educational needs and possibilities, it is also necessary that they should be men of iron resolution, capable, notwithstanding their full appreciation of these things, of appreciating, with equal force, the limitations imposed by financial considerations. This is where they have proved themselves lacking, and it is in this direction that a change must be sought.

The growth in the past has been magnificent and rapid beyond all precedent, but inevitably it has lacked the solidity which would come from a slower development. The time has now come, in my judgment, when further expansion should be checked so far as possible, and all the institution's energies devoted to solidifying the work which has already been done, and establishing it upon foundations which can never be shaken. The present situation is perilous in the extreme.[29]

In New York, a remedy had been prescribed, first in application to the proposed merging of the American Institute of Sacred Literature with the University. After consultation with his father and Gates, John D. Rockefeller, Jr., wrote:

The University has now of necessity so many heavy financial burdens which properly belong to it and will have for some years to come, that we feel as though it should be the aim of the officers and trustees to keep it scrupulously free from any and all relationships which involve added financial responsibilities in so far as this is possible.[30]

This opinion soon became formal policy. At the budget conference of December, 1903, representatives of the University reported an estimated deficit of $206,266 for 1904–05. When eleven new items deemed essential were added, the total came to $245,761. This need was the outcome of forward steps taken several years in the past, with results that were making themselves felt in added cost of maintaining buildings, grounds, and the power plant.

Three years before, at another conference, it had been agreed, and so reported to Rockefeller, that $5,000,000 in endowment would prevent the annual deficit. Since that time, he had contributed $3,000,000 toward endowment. Yet more than $6,000,000 rather than $2,000,000 were required to wipe out the deficit. "It is therefore evident," the conferees stated, "that the tendency, instead of being toward a decreased deficit as we had all confidently hoped, had been decidedly and alarmingly toward an increased deficit"—in spite of policy looking the other way. More radical steps toward reduction of the deficit had to be taken:

It is the unanimous sense of this conference that until this deficit is wiped out by endowment or retrenchment the University must rigidly decline to consider the enlargement of any departments now existing, or addition of any new departments of work which do at the time or may in the future involve the University in additional expense, unless adequate funds are especially provided therefor. This policy the gentlemen here assembled commit themselves to carry out to the full extent of their ability.[31]

This was an explicit pledge to do what the Founder had hoped for in vain over the years. Several times in the past, the University had seemed about to free itself from deficits. The "new policy" of 1897 and the campaign concluded in 1900 had been designed to bring together income and outlay; but new construction, which the campaign had made possible, had upset the apple-cart. In December, 1903, first the conferees and then the Trustees, by approving the memorandum of the conference, declared that from this time there would be no further resort to deficit financing. To this declaration, John D. Rockefeller, Jr., added a paragraph of exegesis which was also accepted by the Trustees.[32]

We conceive this step to be a step in advance and the most important and the most exigent now before the University. If we shall demonstrate our ability to conduct the institution within its income and thus place it on an assured and permanent financial foundation we shall have placed the institution in a position to invite the confidence of men of means in Chicago and in the East, and will be in a position to assure them of not only the permanency of the institution but that it can and will conduct its affairs annually without financial embarrassments and without financial crises, which may either threaten its usefulness or embarrass its friends.[33]

This gloss summarized a long history, beginning with the collapse of confidence in the old University. John D. Rockefeller, Jr., proposed a virtual reaffirmation of the program that Goodspeed had broached in 1888: the University was to grow, but not on a diet of borrowed money.

Although the Founder perhaps felt himself embarrassed by involvement in the difficulties of the University, as his son may have meant to intimate in the choice of his final words, no recriminations appeared in the statement of 1903. Indeed, Gates acknowledged that the Trustees in New York were as much responsible for the predicament as were those in Chicago. Earlier, Rockefeller had given practical evidence of his conviction that the University would grow by buying more than $1,500,000 worth of property on the north side of the

Midway; and after the budget conference, he gave the land to the University.[34] Following the December conference, he also agreed to underwrite a deficit of $245,000 for 1904–05, but he did not add another million to endowment at Christmas time as he had each year after the campaign had been successfully completed in 1900. Almost simultaneously, Murphy wrote:

While it would be unwise, and even unjust to the institution, to suddenly cut off the annual contributions toward the budget deficit, I think it would be unwise for the founder . . . to make large contributions to endowment until the policy in this respect has been changed, and changed in such a way as to indicate a firm conviction of the necessity of maintaining the changed policy in the future.[35]

Harper had listened to the Founder's representatives and to the Trustees. Discussing the possible establishment of a social science center in University Extension, he wrote Graham Taylor, a pioneer in education for social service: "We must be careful not to incur expense until we know where the money is coming from to pay it. You know how businessmen feel in matters like this."[36] Yet neither Harper nor the Board refused absolutely to consider expanding University work already under way.

In May, 1904, Harper called the attention of the Trustees to the desirability of purchasing the James Hall paleontological and mineralogical collection and library. Statements by Stuart Weller, assistant professor of paleontologic geology, and others, represented the value of the material so forcefully that the Board voted to forward the papers to Rockefeller, on condition that the purchase could be arranged. At the same time, Harper also recommended an appropriation for astronomical work to be carried on by George E. Hale at Mount Wilson in California. The Board made its approval contingent upon the views of John D. Rockefeller, Jr., and Gates. They answered that the memorandum of 1903 precluded both the purchase of the Hall collection and the appropriation for astronomy. The first proposal could only be regarded as an enlargement of the Department of Museums, and the second was made necessary only by contemplated enlargement of the astronomy department: "Valuable as this research work is," wrote John D. Rockefeller, Jr., and Gates, "we cannot but feel that of greater value to the University will it be to adhere rigidly to not only the letter, but the spirit of the agreement. . . ."[37]

Patently, the policy of 1903 brought Harper up short, although he declared himself entirely in sympathy with the central proposition of the agreement.[38] At the first meeting of the Board after its approval of the New York memorandum, Harper requested, as he had years before, an annual leave of six months from his presidential office. Had Harper concluded that full-time administration of a university which was not to develop further until it had a surplus in hand was too unfruitful an activity to justify such a diversion of time from his research as he had countenanced, to his pain, during the first, expansive years? In 1897, it will be recalled, Rockefeller had looked to the Trustees to guide the University into channels of solid and permanent prosperity without chilling Harper's ardor.[39] In 1904, the pursuit of prosperity along the road marked Economy had Harper's consent but left him cold. When the Trustees refused to permit him to take time from his role as President of the University, he acquiesced but warned Rockefeller not to expect too much of him, ". . . even after these many years." And he added, surely in self-flagellation, "I shall certainly expect more of myself in the future than in the past."[40] Another cloud of frustration formed in Harper's mind as he contemplated his responsibility for the religious life of the students. He had noticed that with each year it required a greater effort to undertake that kind of service. "I have asked myself whether, as a matter of fact, it was growing more and more difficult to deal with subjects of this kind in a university atmosphere?"[41] Harper worked on but with his reasons for despairing: was an academic official a fit instrument of Salvation?

In April, 1904, Wallace Heckman, the business manager, reported that the working capital had been absorbed, and remarked that the obvious, appropriate course would be retrenchment to release the capital.[42] In May, Harper went to New York to arrange for the Trustees to send Murphy or someone else to Chicago for first-hand information. Although Harper spoke of several needs, including an item of $43,000 for lost capital which he had neglected to mention at the regular budget conference, he pointed out that it was retrenchment rather than a remedial gift that he had in mind. Substantially this conversation took place:

Gates to Harper: Do you want a check . . . ?

Harper: No. I am not authorized by the Board to make any such request. The trustees regard themselves as assigned to the duty of administering this splendid benevolence. They consider it their duty to place this situation before you. They do not, as I understand it, feel justified in abruptly retrenching, cutting out departments, or in the stopping of branches of the work without the full knowledge of the trustees in the East. In a new institution, difficulties are encountered which do not exist in older ones. These difficulties have to be met. The trustees challenge the closest investigation of their work and invite criticisms of it. They wish to know Mr. Rockefeller's desires as to the course being pursued and the views of the two trustees who are more intimately acquainted his.

Rockefeller, Jr.: My father does not desire or expect that the institution should be retarded or recede. One or two items with which we are all familiar have gotten away from those in charge of them. But these matters even are now well in hand and will be held so.[43]

John D. Rockefeller, Jr., also expressed full confidence in the business methods of the Trustees and said that further information could only confirm what he had already learned from his experience and observation.

At the end of the fiscal year, 1903–04, Heckman offered a report as heartening as Rockefeller's words: the bills of the University were being promptly met as they matured.[44] Gates, however, found disquieting information in the record for the same year. By his calculation, an unfavorable discrepancy of more than 15 per cent appeared between budget estimates and actualities. "Anybody ought to be able to make a budget that would come closer than that. I could make one myself"—these words stuck in Harper's ears. He argued that 7 per cent was the correct figure, but Gates would not agree.[45]

Gates continued to worry over the costs of constructing and maintaining buildings. When news came to him that the University was to receive $150,000, informally earmarked for building, he reminded Harper of past experience: costs were likely to exceed estimates, however carefully made. Additional money had to be found for proper furnishings and arrangements made to connect the new building with the power plant, which was likely to need adaptation in order to carry the extra burden. Rockefeller would be called upon to make up the balance—which he was reluctant to do but nevertheless had always done. On the next budget, a considerable deficit for care and maintenance appeared. Gates scolded Harper:

You know how often we have said that we cannot afford to have new buildings, but we have kept on building just the same, and always with the same experience, always recurring again and again, with increased emphasis, to the declaration that we cannot afford to have new buildings. Is not now a good time for us to actually act upon this resolution? I, for one, do not want to go to Mr. Rockefeller again for moneys either for a deficit on the new building or for enlarged appropriations for the budget on account of the new building. . . . I am sure that Mr. Rockefeller will not be willing to see the deficit increased.[46]

At the budget conference in December, 1904, a very large subsidy was requested for 1905–06. The meeting was attended by Gates and Murphy and, for the University, by Harper, Ryerson, Hutchinson, and George C. Walker, whom Gates characterized as one of the most careful of the Trustees in his financial estimates. When it became apparent that receipts for 1904–05 would fall short of original calculations, the Board reduced current expenses; but all the representatives of the University said that even if the Trustees succeeded in making the cut for this year, they could not do it again. Walker indeed believed that they were deceiving themselves in regard to 1904–05 and could not make the cut stick through the year. The addition of expenditures deemed absolutely necessary, and of others deemed highly desirable for 1905–06, carried the total of estimated expenditures beyond that for 1904–05—when Rockefeller contributed $245,000 toward the deficit. To cover the expected deficit in 1905–06, the University asked him for a pledge of $314,835; but Walker argued that the institution as then organized and conducted could not be run without a deficit of $325,000 and that any attempt to cut that figure would prove futile and misleading. The only way to reduce that deficit would be to dismiss professors and to reduce expenses. On that point Walker insisted vehemently. Gates himself envisaged three feasible courses open to the Founder: he could again give $245,000 and request the Trustees to cut expenses at any necessary sacrifice and economy; he could give up to $325,000 and announce that that would be all he would contribute to the deficit under any circumstances; or he could put the figure at $245,000 pending careful investigation by Murphy of possible economies. The third was the preferred course. On receipt of Murphy's report, Rockefeller could decide to what extent beyond $245,000 he would underwrite the 1905–06 deficit.[47]

Privately, Harper had urged Gates to ask Rockefeller for a contribution to endowment of $2,000,000; but the Trustees at the conference declined to seek an immediate gift of income-bearing funds. Harper stood alone and disarmed. Gates told Rockefeller:

We took up with the gentlemen present this question and discussed with them at length the financial policies and tendencies of the institution for the past ten years, and the unspeakable importance from every point of view of demonstrating now to you and to the public and to themselves that they were able to conduct this institution within a fixed sum of money annually, and not increase it. All the gentlemen agree on that point, and I think the sentiment was entirely sincere. Certainly, no more hearty response could be asked than we received, in presenting, as we did, very earnestly this view. If you could have overheard the conversation, and words were deeds, you would have been completely reassured as to the future, if you had any question of the financial management of the institution. At the close of this review,

I asked each in turn, beginning with Mr. Hutchinson, whether he would think it wise for the Trustees at the present time to request from you one million or two million or any gift toward endowment. Each replied for himself in turn, except Dr. Harper, that he could not join in any request to you at the present time for endowment. . . . I then pressed the matter a little further and asked each of the gentlemen in turn what he personally, were he in your place, would do. Mr. Hutchinson said that he . . . would make no further contribution to the endowment until the University had demonstrated its ability to conduct itself without increasing its annual deficit. Mr. Ryerson replied in the same way. Mr. Walker replied that he would make no gift now, but would ascertain what the actual deficit was, as shown by the results of this year, and that he would then capitalize it at 4 per cent and make a gift to the endowment fund at the end of this year, covering the deficit, with the statement to the Trustees that no more deficits would be provided for. . . . Dr. Harper, as before, advised that the deficit be capitalized at the rate of $2,000,000 a year until the total be provided for. He said that he could not bear to die with this deficit uncared for.

Before the gentlemen left, it was agreed that Mr. Murphy would renew and complete the incomplete report on the subject of the University of Chicago, begun a year ago. It was agreed that Mr. Murphy should visit the University, should examine into all the items for special contributions which the University asks, but should go further than this and attempt to reconstruct, if possible, in connection with the officers, their entire budget, on the basis of every economy which he can suggest, on the one hand, and a careful scrutiny of probable income on the other. It was agreed further that Mr. Murphy should, while there, consider carefully what features of the University may be eliminated, if this shall be found necessary, and report, if the knife is to be put in, at what point the surgery shall take place and how far it ought to proceed. This will be a very serious and responsible task, from which Mr. Murphy very naturally shrinks, but it seems desirable, and is urgently requested by the Trustees themselves; and they stated that they would consider Mr. Murphy as representing not necessarily Mr. Rockefeller, but the entire Board of Trustees in this study.[48]

As was his custom, Rockefeller remained silent as to his intentions beyond the year; but perhaps Walker read his mind correctly. Walker wrote Harper:

I fear he will never commence any annual contribution of any millions to capitalize the expenses until he sees the actual figures for the annual cost of maintenance. I should not if I was in his position. The amount actually paid for this year should be a basis for next. If we can assure him then of such positive fact, he will be in a situation to decide *when* he wants to commence such capitalization, and how soon he will complete it. I believe he will commence it the moment he feels sure we are doing just as we can continue to do, and that the amount he pays for this year will be all he will have to pay next year.

We should have no temporary retrenchment this year. The sooner he knows the *final status* the sooner will he commence to capitalize the deficit and the sooner finish it all up and have it out of the way. Then and not until then will he be free in his own mind to take up new questions and to offer new money for new things, and the pleasure it will give him to voluntarily do new things, will be so great that he will do more than even your sanguine mind thinks possible.[49]

In the period just prior to the circulation of Murphy's report, two men who had intimate knowledge of the day-to-day needs of the University could see few places where surgery could be performed without drastically altering the body and spirit of the patient. Harry P. Judson, head of the Department of Political Science and dean of the Faculties of Art, Literature, and Science, specified several spots where cuts could be made but did not hold out much hope for massive savings on instruction. Except in one or two departments, the University had planned from the first to provide for graduate work and research. This implied the use of high-priced instructors, small classes, and a considerable variety of offerings. Furthermore, it had been a fundamental principle that Faculty members should have time and energy for investigation. Since every member of the Faculty without exception was expected to carry on his own specialty and to keep abreast of the latest thought, it was necessary not to require an excessive amount of teaching. The fruitfulness of the plan had been marked. Finally, it had been the policy of the University to bring instructors directly in contact with students by keeping the number in any class to a small, fixed maximum. A change could be made but only at the expense of one or all of the principles of the University. If they were discarded, Judson said, the University would ". . . sink to the level of the many institutions which, while really large colleges, are adding a small portion of advanced work in the hands of overburdened teachers under the name of a graduate school."[50] Reinforcing Judson's views, Goodspeed asserted that the Faculty was not overappointed but underappointed. Frequently, instructors were called upon to teach more courses than the statutes required; and temporary assistants often had to be brought in to teach a course for a quarter. Frequently, instructors were called upon to teach four quarters instead of three, and when a professor resigned, it was found almost invariably that the University was indebted to him for extra terms or quarters which he had been compelled to teach.

Elsewhere, the hope of economies was no brighter. The appropriation for books and equipment could be cut, but it should be increased. "One of the most urgent needs of a new University is books and more books and still more books." Although preaching was not indispensable—the University could be conducted without it—the preachers kept the Gospel in its most attractive and convincing form before students and professors alike, and emphasized the Christian character of the institution. The sum spent on this work went farther than any other equal expenditure ". . . in promoting the highest end the University seeks, *viz.* character-building, the sending out into the world of men and women of the highest moral as well as intellectual type."[51] Those were the thoughts that retrenchment brought forward. Behind financial issues stood the question: what should the University be?

Unlike Murphy's first report, his second did not begin with an appreciative vignette. The words of 1905 were often astringent and sometimes stinging. The matter which seemed most vital to him and which most immediately concerned Rockefeller, Murphy reported, was the constant increase of the budget deficits. The amount of endowment needed to wipe out the deficit was not the $2,000,000 of earlier calculations but rather $8,000,000. Moreover, the history of the three preceding years demonstrated that the demands upon the Founder had not been limited to the deficit shown in the proposed budgets, which might almost have been dispensed with entirely. Budget estimates were utterly worthless:

. . . they offer no protection whatever to Mr. Rockefeller. They are purely a matter of form, as the University authorities do not consider themselves in any way bound by them. They offer no protection to him as a limitation of the amounts to be de- manded from him at the end of the year. They merely fix a minimum which the University can demand from him as a matter of right, but do not present any obstacles to the incurring of additional obligations which he must pay unless he is willing to let the University fall into financial disrepute.[52]

Murphy's specific findings did nothing to soften the impact of these words. In regard to actual as against estimated receipts from students, Murphy noted that the issuing of extra scholarships operated ". . . as a means of concealing the decrease in the number of paying students, and covers up, to that extent, an error in the estimates."[53] Murphy saw how lower estimates for fuel and light had come about but believed that in view of the addition of new build- ings, the reduction of estimates so far below actual expenditures was a piece of unwarranted optimism. Murphy found the general financial condition un- satisfactory and noted that the working fund of $200,000 had been absorbed. The University was running to a considerable extent by paying one month's bills out of the next month's income and by overdrawing its bank account.

"I understand that a considerable portion of the cash overdraft represents checks which have been drawn but which are not expected to reach the bank until funds are there to meet them, in other words, a part of the indebtedness of the University is carried by the process known as 'kiting checks.' "[54]

None of Murphy's recommendations envisaged increased expenditure and several called for reductions. Outlying departments such as the Morgan Park Academy were of secondary importance and should be the first to feel the pressure of needed economy. An earnest effort was under way to make University Extension self-sufficient, but one of the economies consisted simply of transferring charges to another department. Eventually, the Law School ought to be a paying investment. If possible, the journals should be published jointly with other leading universities. Five-sixths of the costs resulted from publishing material which did not originate in the University. Also, the journals contained a good deal of padding. Noting that increased costs for instruction came mainly from raising salaries of instructors already in the University, Murphy suggested a new policy in regard to promotions. Salaries should not be raised in order to hold men who had become so valuable that they had calls from other universities. In every department a good deal of the teaching could be satisfactorily done by younger men: "You cannot expect to have a teaching staff composed entirely of full professors."[55] If a course could be properly taught by a $1,000 man, the University was not justified in paying $1,500 simply because the incumbent had become a $1,500 man after a lapse of years. The University should recognize the fact that its younger men would outgrow it; one of the most useful contributions it could make to the cause of higher education in the United States was that of training younger instructors for higher usefulness elsewhere. The University should be organized like the Army, where the number of men in each rank and their salaries were fixed by law. Among the younger instructors it might be well to provide a sliding scale. This plan would do away with the constant increase in the amount paid for instruction and would relieve the enormous pressure on the administrators. The plan would eliminate the discontentment that arose when one man learned another's salary had been increased and his had not. Schedules should not be static, but changes should no longer be made by informal additions to the budget—but rather by deliberate legislative act of the Trustees, with provision for increased expense. Murphy was astonished to discover that the cost of one journal exceeded appropriations, which indicated, he believed, that details of expenditure were not effectively controlled by the Trustees, without whose approval no obligations could be incurred or expenditure made.

Finally, Murphy recommended that the Founder should have a direct personal representative in Chicago. In response to Murphy's criticism of the constant and alarming increases in budget deficits, Harper had pointed out that the Trustees in New York approved each budget; but Murphy replied that they could not possibly have independent knowledge of the accuracy of the budget estimates or of the necessity of the expenditure items. The main difficulty lay, not in the fact that the approved budget estimates were excessive, but that expenditures had not been held to the estimates.

While the funds which have actually been given to the University are, of course, under the sole control of the Trustees [Murphy wrote], it is entirely proper, so long as this budget deficit is being incurred year after year, which the Trustees are looking to Mr. Rockefeller to pay, that he should have a controlling voice in determining the conditions under which it is incurred.[56]

Murphy's report introduced both a new interpretation of the past and the prospect of a new relationship between the Founder and the University. By 1905 its governors had produced several explanations of the difficulties of the University. In 1897, Goodspeed had argued that the deficits were the product of the decision, made before the University opened, to operate on a large scale. Goodspeed admitted that mistakes had been made but attributed them to inexperience. Gates had insisted that expansion after the opening was partly to blame for the deficits but had not pressed against the Trustees a charge of serious negligence. In 1903, the New York and Chicago men agreed that a building program for which they all shared responsibility was the cause of financial difficulty. These views differed in content but they indicated the same path toward the future: the officers of the University and the Trustees in Chicago should strive from day to day to bring the books of the University into balance; and the Founder, acting through his representatives, would stand by to render the special assistance that a new institution required. Rockefeller had not interfered in the daily life of the University; and its Trustees had promised not to undertake new enterprises which might prove to be embarrassing. Murphy's analysis called the premises of that collaboration into question, for the report left room for the inference that the University was in trouble because the Trustees could not or would not keep their house in order. It was one thing for old friends of the University to show impatience over conditions, another for a relative stranger to be distrustful of intentions.

Goodspeed, always sensitive to criticism of the University from New York, reacted strongly, in protest. The report was not, he thought, the work of a sympathetic reviewer but of a hostile critic. In Goodspeed's opinion, Murphy was unconsciously incapacitated for his task: he was a graduate of a small college, who could not divest himself of the suspicion and prejudice which the small colleges felt toward the large university. He had no conception of the University as a great educational institution, organized on new lines and in accordance with the latest and wisest educational ideals, and could not appreciate its function of research. To Murphy, the fact that a man, engaged in important and far-reaching investigation, taught little was evidence that he was receiving money he had not earned. Murphy had reached the conclusion that the University was an organized conspiracy to rob Rockefeller of his wealth: "It is all a scheme to plunder the founder."[57] How else, Goodspeed wanted to know, were Murphy's comments on the Trustees' attitude toward budgeting to be understood? And then the crucial point: "If Mr. Rockefeller believes these statements, he will never give another dollar to the University. And if they are true, he ought not to do so."[58]

Goodspeed was willing to agree that, if Rockefeller accepted Murphy's report, in the future the University must conform to the letter and spirit of its suggestions loyally and cheerfully. The time had come, he wrote Harper, to allow the University to develop at a slower pace, to make a radical departure from Harper's methods. "I have often opposed your plans, because I feared you were going too fast. . . ." Yet Goodspeed's characteristic anxiety over Harper's anticipation of the future was mixed with appreciation of his past achievements. Goodspeed admitted tacitly that Harper had been right: "Every passing year will justify your methods up to this time. . . ."[59]

But Goodspeed was less disturbed about the old question of Harper's pace than about the immediate matter of Murphy's allegations, which he set out to refute. He took aim at Murphy's statements about scholarships and fellowships, padding of the journals, and the release of valuable young professors. No better and quicker method of reducing the University to mediocrity could be devised. Goodspeed also attacked Murphy's claim that the budget estimates were unreliable and worthless. It was unjust, Goodspeed argued, to base an indictment calculated to do the University fatal injury upon the unfavorable showing of the three exceptional years just past. Using tabulated statistics, as Murphy had done, Goodspeed demonstrated that for the four years from 1897–98 to 1900–01, the sum of estimated receipts had come within $5,034 of actual

357

income and that actual expenditures had been less than appropriations and receipts. To Goodspeed, this indicated extraordinary reliability in budget estimates: "... in ordinary years and therefore as a rule, they had been reduced to almost an exact science...."[60] Murphy had ignored the fact, Goodspeed's argument implied, that the University no longer lacked experience.

Goodspeed did not stand alone in his distress. A Trustee who had recently joined the Board and had had no personal connection with most of the matter in the report was plainly shocked by the discrepancy between its tone and contents and his own observations. He had been attracted to the University by Harper's educational work and had been anxious to help it forward, but he had not been prepared to find such sacrifice of time by Board members and such assiduous attention to business and details as he at once saw.

I do not believe that the like of it exists in any charitable or educational institution of this Country and I doubt whether many business institutions in Chicago have so much time and close attention of so high an order bestowed upon them by their directors. I was not prepared to find such a body of men such as compose this Board giving gratuitously such an extraordinary amount of valuable time and making its interests foremost and subordinating their own engagements to it.

The tone and contents of the report were inconsistent with the self-respect of the Trustees.[61] Another member of the Board remarked on what he described as the extraordinary suggestion that a representative of Rockefeller be set over the Board to keep watch over its members and their actions.[62] None of the three Trustees whose reactions to the report are recorded said that he believed Murphy spoke for the Founder—and one Trustee felt sure that Rockefeller knew nothing of the report—but they all spoke of resigning from the Board.[63] Had they, and other Trustees, done so, the concert of interests and purposes upon which the University had been established would have been seriously damaged and might have been destroyed. Gates did in fact call the attention of John D. Rockefeller, Jr., to an unofficial, and extended, text of the report. (The report seen by the Trustees was Gates's edited version.)[64] How, then, would the Founder react to an appraisal that by direct judgment or implication put in shadow the management of the University over years?

THE STATE OF THE UNIVERSITY

But the past had become an obsolete guidepost. The major premise of University policy had always been Harper's leadership, with all it meant in energy, imagination, enthusiasm, great aspirations, great enterprises, and great risks.

Just as the Murphy report was being completed, the University discovered that it could not take Harper's presence for granted. Although in May, 1904, Harper had undergone an appendectomy and microscopic examination of excised tissue had given clear evidence of cancerous growth, Harper himself was not told of his condition until early in 1905. On February 3, feeling perfectly well, he reported to Gates: "It is as clearly a case of execution announced beforehand as it could possibly be. . . ."[65] As Harper wrote these words, Murphy was probably composing the final draft of his report, which was dated February 9. A week later, Rockefeller wrote to Harper:

You are constantly in my thoughts. The feelings which I have always cherished towards you are intensified at this time. . . . I have the greatest satisfaction and pleasure in our united efforts for the University, and I am full of hope for its future. No man could have filled your place.[66]

In that future the irritations of the past quickly evaporated, and Murphy's controversial recommendation of change in the management of the University was allowed to drop into limbo. The announcement of Harper's condition and the disappearance of the Murphy report as a threat to the united efforts of which the Founder wrote may have been coincidence. Rockefeller was certainly not bound to follow Murphy's advice or even to recognize an investigation which had been undertaken officially at the behest of the Board. Or did compassion for Harper and awareness of the radical difference which his imminent death would make in the affairs of the University fill the minds of its supporters to the exclusion of dark afterthoughts about an era which had possessed its glory as well as its anxieties and which was soon to end? No Rockefeller agent came to reside in Chicago, no Trustees resigned in protest, and no breaks occurred in the Founder's support.

In *Chimes,* Robert Herrick's novel about the University, the first President dies of angina pectoris, leaving behind him, as Harper did, an ideal only partially realized.[67] Had Harper resembled his fictional counterpart in the manner of his death as well as in the measure of his achievement, it might be supposed that the very difficulties in finance which threatened to produce a crisis of confidence also caused the collapse of Harper's health and so worked ultimately to avert that crisis. The need of the University for money put a terrible strain upon the President, who in the person of William Rainey Harper was particularly frustrated by the policy of 1903. A heart attack was the predictable end of his career and would have been the appropriate *dénouement* of the situation in which the University found itself in 1905. And yet actuality refused to abide by the classic rules of dramatic inevitability and indeed anticipated the modern canon of senseless catastrophe occurring without the intervention of Nemesis. Had Harper been killed by a fall from his bicycle, his death would have been no more an accident or a terrible absurdity than it was. Yet a quality of character, Harper's inordinate drive, may have influenced indirectly the timing of his affliction and thus the outcome of the crisis in the midst of which his condition was announced; for Harper's frustrations, the converse of his enterprise, may possibly have accelerated the growth of cancer.[68] Whatever was the connection—close, remote, or non-existent—between Harper's medical history and the history of the University before the time of that announcement, it was only by the working of the harshest dialectic that the prospect of his dying produced an easing of the tension that his living had created. The price of tranquillity was truly monstrous.

Although Harper's doctors seemed to announce the coming of a new dispensation in University affairs, the expansionism of the old regime remained and the problem of its deficits still had to be faced. The persistence of ambition was illustrated by the desire of Harper's colleagues to institute research into cancer. They may even have hoped that Harper himself could be saved. But a committee, to which Harper belonged, rejected the proposal, which called for $30,500, because the University did not have money available to support the research.[69]

As Dr. Frank Billings recalled years later, Harper's illness also led to the momentary revival of another and much more expensive medical project. In conversation with Rockefeller, Billings spoke of Harper's main regret that he was to die before he had achieved his one great and final desire, a medical school for the University. Harper's life would be prolonged and he would be happy for the remainder of his days on earth if Rockefeller would reconsider his decision against supporting a school. It was Rockefeller's belief, as Billings understood, that research into the causes of disease and the discovery of specific treatment were more important than the instruction of students. Rockefeller expressed great respect and admiration for Harper as an educator and for his accomplishments but added, ". . . my convictions are such that I cannot accede to his request for the gift to the University for the organization of a medical school."[70] The remark rings true: the building of the University was not to be guided by personal sentiment, however moving.

Harper himself did not lose heart: "I have begun to think," he wrote John

D. Rockefeller, Jr., in February, 1905, "that perhaps there is still a work to be done."[71] As he looked ahead to surgery, he thought of the University: "All the budgets have been passed and everything is in shape for the next fifteen months. This will give ample time in which to turn around in case anything should happen to me." Harper hoped in particular that the Founder and his son would see their way to capitalize the budget at the earliest possible moment. "I believe that this would give a responsibility to all of us that will mean very much. It will cinch the situation as nothing else will do it. It will put things in an absolutely strong position."[72] Would not Gates take up the case?[73] Gates continued to be concerned over the deficit and objected to a proposed expenditure that violated firmly adopted principle.[74] The receipt of a voucher for the unused residue of a grant obviously delighted him: "I venture to say that is the first time in the history of the world where money contributed to an object has been found by using economy to be unnecessary."[75] Gates showed his friendliness by deciding to send his son to the University instead of to Harvard. A man who had often scrutinized the management of the University, Gates could in the autumn of 1905 view its "interior life and work" through his son's eyes: "The spirit of the University," Gates then wrote Rockefeller, "the life of the student body, their relations to each other and to their instructors, would seem to be thoroughly ideal. . . ."[76]

In February, 1905, Harper was confident that the University would be able to pull through the year without a deficit in excess of Rockefeller's contribution. At the same time he pointed to the fact that the estimates of income for the coming year were much more conservative than ever before.[77] To offset a discrepancy between estimated and actual income, Harper solicited funds from at least two Trustees. "It is extremely desirable that we should be able to show no deficit at the end of the fiscal year." The result would have a large bearing upon the effort to capitalize the annual deficit of $245,000. The moment was critical in the history of the University, Harper said; the present exigency would not appeal to any but those intimately acquainted with the situation.[78] As contributions totaling $9,800 were forthcoming, the University closed its books for the year without a deficit beyond that provided for by Rockefeller: about twenty-five dollars were unspent.[79] The effort, Harper thought, demonstrated the Trustees' interest in and appreciation of the whole situation—which, he did not say, had so deeply disturbed Murphy. The Trustees had given tangible evidence of their unwillingness to depend upon the Founder for extra subsidies. As the autumn quarter of 1905 opened, Harper observed to

Gates: "Everybody is enthusiastic and things seem really to be booming . . . we brought the budget out last year as we said we would and we are holding it down . . . and a little more."[80]

The financial optimism of the hour went beyond satisfaction over successful economizing. After Goodspeed studied the Murphy report, he touched upon the wisdom of rounding out the organization of the University while "our President still lives, and the University has the advantage of his genius for organizing wisely educational work which it will never enjoy after his death."[81] In a Convocation address in 1901, Harper had summed up what remained to be done to complete the University: ". . . much, very much, almost everything."[82] The University made progress in four years, but much of Harper's design was still but a blueprint.

In August, after an informal discussion of University matters with the Founder, Harper linked capitalization of the deficit with the rounding out of the University. Harper had never known Rockefeller to be more genial or communicative but received the impression that anything like a business proposition was not what he was expecting. His "tremendous" confidence in Gates, however, gave a cue to Harper, who wrote Gates that he was fully convinced that Gates could persuade Rockefeller to take another step forward in the autumn if Gates would contrive a plan and put it before Rockefeller. The three items which Harper called to Gates's attention were $6,000,000 to capitalize the deficit, $5,000,000 to round out the University (including funds for a library and for the inauguration of technological and medical work), and a sustaining (endowment) fund of $5,000,000 or $6,000,000 to establish new chairs and so on. If Rockefeller would do these things, he could dismiss the University from his mind and be sure that it would go on forever. "It may not be wise, of course, to put all these before him at once, but I believe that he is prepared for large things and that you [Gates] could accomplish all this if you were so minded."[83] In October, Harper reminded Gates of ". . . that great piece of work before you to do this autumn in behalf of the University of Chicago"; perhaps Gates could come to Chicago and talk matters over. At the end of the month, Gates spent two days at the University and left Harper so encouraged that he began to write of ". . . the next gift of Mr. Rockefeller for endowment."[84] Harper was deeply disappointed when his illness prevented him from seeing Gates during a later visit. Sooner or later the opportunity for the two men to talk would come, Harper thought in the last month of 1905; but before the first month of 1906 had run its course, Harper was dead. Just

too late, John D. Rockefeller, Jr., announced the results of the annual negotiations over the extent and terms of the Founder's assistance. He would underwrite the budget deficit for 1906–07 and give $1,000,000 toward capitalization of
the deficit.* The events of Harper's last year brought the University that much
nearer to financial security. In the following eighteen months, Rockefeller gave
general endowment funds of $3,700,000—less than Harper had dreamed of at
the end of his career but far more than the University had possessed when
Harper drew up its plan.[85]

As a source of tradition, an intangible endowment, Harper's death supplemented his life. Dying, he provided a climax to his hitherto unceasing pursuit
of unity. His defects were not immediately forgotten and indeed were spoken
of with remarkable frequency; but even before his death, the impression that he
created as a fallible man began to dim as a heroic Harper emerged. More closely
perhaps than that of any other university president, the stark outline of his history did resemble the myth of the hero—of the champion struck down in
battle, before his time but to the salvation of his cause. Ten years earlier, before
coming to the University, William Vaughn Moody had said of Harper: "... he
is as yet a strangely mythical figure in my mind."[86] In October, 1905, Robert
Herrick, once the sharp-tongued detractor of an academic boss, wrote from
Florence: "Harper's end is pathetic and tragic, and also ennobling. He seems
larger, the further you get away, and his educational rawness and fatuities less
important. . . . It may be cowardly, but I can't help being glad to be away from
the end—the grip of disease on the courageous man."[87]

Nothing about Harper is more impressive than the inability of his friends
and colleagues to remain indifferent to his personality. It resembled a natural
phenomenon with which beholders must somehow come to terms. The judgments passed upon Harper fell with striking frequency into balanced phrases,
as if he were the embodiment of dialectic: "He had the mind and manners of a
captain of industry, but he had the heart and soul of a scholar and a sage."[88]
"Scholars, high-minded and serious of purpose, are many. Doers, active, confident, and successful, are more numerous still. Men are harder to come upon,
and our friend was a man."[89] "President Harper, like every great man, derived
his strength from the union of opposite qualities. . . . Among these blendings in
President Harper's nature none seems . . . more noteworthy or more mysterious

---

* John D. Rockefeller, Jr., also announced that his father would contribute to the building of a
library in Harper's memory (Rockefeller, Jr., to Andrew McLeish, January, 19, 1906).

363

—for without mystery there is no deepness of soul—than his warm personal loyalty to friends, while in the conduct of any enterprise his attitude toward individuals was as impersonal as the force of gravitation."[90] "A strong man is apt to be ruthless, and President Harper had tremendous strength of will. But he never meant to be unkind. . . . Sometimes he acted to all appearances autocratically, but at heart he was a democrat of democrats."[91] "Dr. Harper had respect for the past that often seemed to verge upon ritualism. At the same time his insight into the provisional character of men's achievements prompted an independence of the past frequently branded as iconoclasm."[92] "He united in a singular degree conservatism and progressiveness, idealism and practicality, the intellectual and the emotional, the material and the spiritual."[93]

A stranger who had seen Harper order a dinner, said Albion Small, might forever cherish the illusion that the key to his whole character was to be found in the tastes of an epicure; another stranger who had seen Harper leave the table for a night or day or several days of forced work with scarcely a thought for food or sleep might say that the man was at heart an ascetic and the pleasures of the table were merely items in a program of winning his way by a show of good fellowship. Judging solely by the amount of thought and labor Harper would expend upon the forms and ceremonies of an academic or social function, one might easily classify him as a martinet with a vision only for trifles. Or knowing Harper solely while he was studying large questions of general policy, one might gain the idea that he cared nothing whatever for details but was interested only in probing essential principles. Some men might imagine that Harper was at bottom a hard-headed man of affairs, cynically indulgent of the superstitions of others, prudently silent about his contempt for their opinions, but really a pagan and a materialist. Others would discover in him a simple and sturdy Christian faith daily overcoming the world. Few personalities, Small continued, were less the consequence of a predominating trait. Harper's personality was a perpetual transformation of energy, the principle of coherence being an inclusive moral conception.[94]

It was the paradox of Harper's life that his activity was extraordinarily varied —as he struggled with finances on the hard terms set in 1903, he completed a work of fundamental scholarship, his *Commentary on Amos and Hosea*— and yet that he retained a moral simplicity that is only inadequately described as a conception. The word smacks too much of formal thought. As Harper lay dying, he had called for a few friends, notably, Ernest D. Burton and Albion W. Small:

Harper to Burton: There are only a few people that I can talk to now, or that I think can help me. . . . What is there beyond this life?

Burton: To me it all goes back to my conviction that this is a good world. That at the heart and center of things there is a mind, and that mind benevolent. But not only do I believe that it is a good world in the sense that it is under the government of a good God, but I believe also that the progress of things is toward what is better. You know already that I feel that the poets and prophets have more to teach us than the scholars and investigators, that the man of insight is wiser than the man of learn- ing, and what the poets and prophets dream of and hope for at length comes true if only they dream and hope for good things. Progress is slow, and there are many back-steps, but things are moving on toward the better. And this being the case I must believe that there is something beyond this world better than this. Fundamental to my thought of what that is is the thought of Jesus as I understand it, the thought, namely, that he who has come into fellowship with that spirit of goodness that is at the heart of things, can never lose that fellowship, and so can never cease to be, and because that spirit of goodness is good, and because things are moving on toward the better, the fellowship beyond this life must be better even than that of this life. And furthermore, because I cannot think of impersonal existence as better than per- sonal life, I am almost compelled to think of the life to come as personal.

Harper [after Burton had explained his belief]: This is good; this is helpful. But what do you mean by fellowship with God? What about the man who has not lived in fellowship with God? I cannot say anything about the rest of you, but I have had a bad past. My record is not good. . . .

Burton [in response to Harper's question about the meaning of fellowship with God]: . . . We can put it in the terms in which Jesus generally put it. He thought of God as Father, and lived in the consciousness of intimate fellowship with that Father. . . . I count myself happiest when the sense of God's fatherhood and my relation to him as son is deep and vivid. . . . But there are times when I cannot thus think of God, when I am compelled rather to think of the universe and of the spirit of goodness and of wis- dom which is at the heart of that universe. . . .

Harper: You cannot always think of God as Father?

Burton: No, I wish I could; that is the best; but I do not always find it possible. . . .

Harper [after Burton had said more about the nature of fellowship]: That helps me.

Later, Harper asked Burton about the significance of the suffering of Jesus; and as Harper talked, Burton could easily see that Harper's mind was dwelling upon the moral shortcomings and failures of his life. It occurred to Burton to speak as he supposed most Christian ministers would have done, telling Harper that Christ had suffered the penalty of his sins upon the cross and that the debt was paid there. But Burton had felt from the beginning that Harper had asked him to answer his questions because he thought that Burton would speak from his heart and without any conventional phraseology or theological formulas. He spoke of God's forgiveness for the man who turns his back upon his sins and who seeks fellowship with God. This idea was the heart of a climactic conversation.

Small: Dr. Harper, there is one thing we want to say to you, and that is that we do not at all agree with the harsh verdict which you are evidently passing upon your past life. We are not here to say that there have been no mistakes and no faults, but that as we know you, and we believe that we do know you thoroughly, your life has been controlled centrally by the purpose to do the work that God gave you to do. We know, of course, that you have been occupied with affairs and have been soiled with the dust of the everyday work and conflict, but these things were necessary, and we are perfectly confident that the main purpose of your life has been right, and that its result has been vastly helpful.

Harper: I cannot say these things. You say them because you do not know me. Your characterization of my life is not mine. Some of the things you say are true, but personal ambition will account for a large part of what I have done. . . . I have not followed Jesus Christ as closely as I ought to have done. I have come down from the plane on which I ought to have lived. I have justified it to myself at times as necessary because I was carrying so heavy loads. But I see now that it was all wrong.

Burton: Well, suppose we take your view of it, suppose we grant what all you say.

Harper [*interrupting*]: I think we will have to take it on that basis.

Burton: Now the question is after all the experiences of life, after all its successes and failures, is it your deepest wish that your will and purpose be in harmony with or contrary to that of the heavenly Father? Whether you have another year to live or a million years to live in this world or another, do you want your life in its purpose and effect to run parallel with and to be in harmony with the purpose and will of the infinite Spirit of goodness?

The answer in Harper's mind was evident to Burton. Yet, since it was also clear that Harper was not wholly satisfied, Burton tried again:

Burton: Dr. Harper, suppose your boy Paul had been out of harmony with you, disobedient to your wishes, rebellious and ugly, and after no matter how long a time, he should come back to you and say, "Father, I have done wrong, I knew your way was right, but I have preferred to do my own way, but now I want to do your way, I know it is a good way, and I am through with rebellion and selfwill, and I want to live in harmony in your home." Would you say to him, "But you or somebody else will have to be punished for that sin before you can come back," or would you say to him, "If that is the way you feel, Paul, come back to your father's house and to your father's love"? What you would do for Paul is what God is ready to do for everyone of us.

Small [*interrupting, in a choked voice*]: That is what Jesus taught us in the parable of the prodigal son.

Harper [*after some minutes of conversation*]: I can trust Him. I believe God will be as good to me as I would be to my boy.[95]

When Burton next saw Harper, he was at peace about himself. To the world, who knew Harper by his accomplishments, it might have seemed that the parable of the talents would be a source of comfort. It was in faith, however, and not in works that Harper found his peace. Even so at the end Harper prayed: May it be that for me there shall be life beyond this life, and may there be in that life work still to do, tasks still to accomplish.

That was Harper the human being, acutely sensitive in conscience, besieged by the abiding questions of life and its suffering, impatient with easy answers, hungry for friendship, comforted by an awareness of grace, and restless to the end in the thought of work to be done. The man, that paradox of simplicity and complexity, truly lived—more fully than do most men. The contradictions of his life are the most poignant evidence of his vitality. He lived enough and wrought enough, his colleagues on the Board declared, to start a new epoch and to endow it with lasting consciousness.[96]

But to what had Harper, the academic official as well as the man, awakened the people about him? The institution over which he presided became possessed by a sense of its own uniqueness. The University has never been long content to be but a member of a class: awareness of an obligation to be great has been a part of its history. But greatness in what? The University has been rich in money, buildings, and the talents of its individual professors, but other universities have been as rich. Upon the older of them Chicago drew for inspiration and for its Faculty members. The original plan of the University was spectacular, but it fell far short of fulfilment. Harper did not succeed in awakening such admiration for his ideal university—for Harper's University per se—that his colleagues would follow all the way along the course he charted. Had they tried to do so, the University might well have consumed its material wealth—and the last of their energies—only to face retrenchment. In any case, the plans Harper made could hardly have been more significant than the way in which he worked. Men make universities, Robert Herrick observed, as once they made great temples, blindly, not conceiving the ultimate ends to which they will be

367

devoted, out of some inner necessity of their spirits.[97] There is that quality in the history of the Harper administration in spite of Harper's vision and his near obsession with the elaboration of plans. The events which made the administration what it was were not wholly subject to human domination, and much of its history is the record of a struggle to harness the forces at work in the University. What might have been a disastrous explosion failed to occur, possibly because of Harper's fatal illness. And yet even after he was stricken, Harper was driven by an inner necessity of the spirit; he created an atmosphere charged with energy, excitement, tension, and a sense of mission. He left a legacy and a legend of dynamism.

The University was strenuously academic, but was that all? Other springs fed the last conversations in Harper's room. No word was said of policy, administration, or instruction, and very little of scholarship. Yet the talk consummated the early history of the University and revealed what else in essence the University was. Men who were fully immersed in academic affairs put aside their robes and their professional preoccupations to speak intimately and without embarrassment of a life and mortality. Harper and his friends used the language of the particular religion they all shared, but they did not come together to discuss creeds. They were concerned with the predicament of a man; and in a meeting of humane minds, they sought verities sufficient to the occasion.

After Harper

"I am not an enthusiast in disposition, and the western propensity to 'boom' things rather amuses me. It is my inclination always to look at facts just as they are."[1]

Harry Pratt Judson, William Rainey Harper's chief of staff, surrogate, and successor, has not been remembered as a prophet; but Judson correctly anticipated his part in affairs when he wrote these words before coming to the University. Harper had been an ardent dreamer as well as organizer, a creative artist whose medium was institutions. As dean and President, Judson was a skilful and meticulous craftsman, the conservator of an institution. The principal fact that Judson looked at when he became President was the deficit. In his first annual report, he made the topic of finance the starting point of his remarks; and in his fourth report, he was able to say, and did say, before anything else, that the annual deficit had been extinguished.[2] On its face, this announcement was less stirring than Harper's periodic revelations of expansion to come; and yet, in substance, Judson's accomplishment was extremely important to the future. Determined attack upon the deficits led to the material enrichment of the University, most notably when in 1910 Rockfeller pledged $10,000,000, to be paid over a decade. "This gift," he announced, "completes the task which I have set before myself."[3] The Founder's representatives withdrew from the Board of Trustees; and the era of the founding, and of the heavy dependence of the Univerity upon a single patron, ended without the occurrence of a crisis or a violent rupture within the coalition that had brought the University into being. By stabilizing finances, Judson insured the preservation of the Harper tradition in undiminished brilliance. So long as the deficits had remained, regularly underwritten by Rockefeller but still present like an arrested infection, the University was susceptible to attacks of acute financial distress and vulnerable to the adverse criticism that financial insecurity inspires. Even the appearance of chronic debility after 1906 could hardly have failed to reinforce the disillusionment that had become evident during Harper's life. If the University had been crippled by serious financial difficulty following his death, his work might have been discredited, to be looked back upon as a thoroughly unamusing paradigm of Western boom and bust.

While protecting the general prospects of the University, Judson presided over the liquidation of many experiments that Harper had stubbornly defended. The lecture-study department of University Extension, the most striking manifestation of Harper's academic evangelicalism and perhaps the least conventional of his projects academically, all but disappeared. The already glimmering vision of the University encircled by preparatory schools and colleges faded away when the work at Morgan Park Academy was discontinued and the contracts of collegiate affiliation were dropped. Within the Quadrangles, the polity of the University was altered as heads of departments ceased to be appointed and departmental chairmen took their places. Without reversing the direction of the University, these changes brought it nearer the course of older universities. In program, Chicago was no longer an institution conspicuously apart. Remarking on one occasion that the University was a growing institution, Judson summed up the history of the growth as he viewed it: "The development of the University has followed conservative lines. . . ."[4] The minor and often unnoticed theme of the Harper era had become grand policy. Near the end of his administration, Judson spoke of budget-balancing as if it were a University tradition.[5]

After Judson's retirement, the thrusting enterprise that had once made the University a marvel and an exhilarating—although often sorely trying—cause became again the particular mark of leadership. The third President of the University was Ernest D. Burton and one of its principal deans was Albion W. Small—men almost elderly in years but possessing an unspoiled memory of William Rainey Harper, of his energy, and of unity achieved in his presence.

Notes

In the notes which follow, the physical location of some documents is indicated in the citation by a set of initials inclosed in parentheses. Where no location is specified, the source cited is to be found in the general Presidential files of the University of Chicago Archives. Unless otherwise indicated, collections of papers of particular persons are located in the University of Chicago Archives. Papers to be found in the archives of the office of the Rockefeller family and its associates in New York are so identified.

ARCHIVES

AORFA	Archives of the office of the Rockefeller family and its associates, 30 Rockefeller Plaza, New York City
UCA	University of Chicago Archives

COLLECTIONS OF PAPERS OF PARTICULAR PERSONS

COFHA	Correspondence of the Founder and his Associates (copies)
EDB	Papers of Ernest DeWitt Burton
FTG	Papers of Frederick Taylor Gates
FTGCR	Correspondence received by Frederick Taylor Gates
HEvH	Papers of Hermann Eduard von Holst
JUN	Papers of John Ulric Nef

MT   Papers of Marion Talbot
RH   Papers of Robert Herrick
SBC   Secretary of the Board of Trustees Correspondence. During the period covered by this book Thomas Wakefield Goodspeed served as Secretary
SBL   Letters written by the Secretary of the Board of Trustees, in the Office of the President of the University, University of Chicago
TCC   Papers of Thomas Chrowder Chamberlin
TWG   Papers of Thomas Wakefield Goodspeed: Correspondence re the history of the University

MINUTE BOOKS

MBGS   Minutes of the Boards of the Graduate School of Arts and Literature and of the Ogden Graduate School of Science
MBT   Minutes of the Board of Trustees, in the Office of the President of the University, University of Chicago
MC   Minutes of the Congregation
MFALS   Minutes of the Faculty of Arts, Literature, and Science
MJCF   Minutes of the Junior College Faculty
MS   Minutes of the Senate

PRINTED MATERIALS ISSUED BY THE UNIVERSITY

Calendar   Quarterly Calender
PR   President's Report
Record   University Record
Register   Annual Register

INTRODUCTION

(pp. xv–xvi)

1. Frederick T. Gates to Thomas W. Goodspeed, Jan. 9, 1915.

PART ONE: THE FOUNDING

IN THE BEGINNING: THE PHOENIX

(pp. 3–6)

1. *Standard* (Chicago), Jan. 15 and May 14, 1885. This *Standard* was a Baptist-sponsored newspaper published in Chicago. For the most

complete account of the old University of Chicago see Arthur A. Azlein, "The Old University of Chicago," a D.B. paper, University of Chicago, 1941.

2. *The University Cases* (Chicago: Beach, Barnard & Co., 1884), II, 137. *The University Cases* is a record of the legal proceedings in which the old University was involved.

3. *Chicago Daily News,* Jan. 9, 1885.

4. *Standard,* May 7, 1885, reporting the action of a Baptist convention on May 4, 1885.

5. *Standard,* Sept. 4, 1884.

6. Thomas W. Goodspeed, *A History of the University of Chicago, Founded by John D. Rockefeller, the First Quarter-Century* (Chicago: University of Chicago Press, 1916), pp.

31–32; Goodspeed to John D. Rockefeller, Jan. 7, 1887 (COFHA, Box I).

7. Charles T. B. Goodspeed, *Thomas Wakefield Goodspeed* (Chicago: University of Chicago Press, 1932), pp. 1–34.

8. Goodspeed to Rockefeller, Jan. 7, 1887 (COFHA, Box I).

CHAPTER I

"THESE TERRIBLE TRUTHS"

(pp. 7–17)

1. Thorstein Veblen, *The Higher Learning in America* (New York: B. W. Huebsch, 1918), p. 265.

2. R. W. Cushman, "The Christian's Stewardship," *Baptist Manual* (Philadelphia: American Baptist Publication Society, n.d. [*ca.* 1853]), *passim*.

3. For a detailed account of Rockefeller's attitudes and activities see Allan Nevins, *John D. Rockefeller: The Heroic Age of American Enterprise,* 2 vols. (New York: Charles Scribner's Sons, 1940) or Allan Nevins, *Study in Power: John D. Rockefeller, Industrialist and Philanthropist,* 2 vols. (New York: Charles Scribner's Sons, 1953).

4. A. H. Newman, *A History of the Baptist Churches in the United States* (New York: The Christian Literature Co., 1894), p. 476. See also Robert G. Torbet, *A History of the Baptists* (Philadelphia: The Judson Press, 1950), p. 339.

5. *Reports of the American Baptist Home Mission Society* (New York: American Baptist Home Mission Society, 1883–1889), LV (1887), 71–73.

6. *Ibid.,* 27–28; *ibid.,* LVI (1888), 84; and *Standard,* May 24, 1888.

7. Henry Morehouse to Augustus H. Strong, June 12, 1888 (COFHA, Box I, Folder 3).

8. Gates to Morehouse, Aug. 23, 1888 (FTG, Box I, Folder 2). See also Nevins, *Study in Power,* II, 166–68.

9. Frederick T. Gates, Draft of the Second Annual Report of the Executive Board of the American Baptist Education Society, 1890; Gates to Morehouse, Oct. 9, 1888 (FTG, Box I, Folder 2).

10. Morehouse to Gates, June 12, 1888 (FTG, Box I, Folder 1); Gates to Morehouse, June 21, 1888 (FTG, Box I, Folder 1).

11. Bessie Louise Pierce, *A History of Chicago,* III (New York: Alfred A. Knopf, 1957), 20.

12. Gates to Morehouse, June 21, 1888 (FTG, Box I, Folder 1).

13. Gates to Morehouse, July 14, 1888 (FTG, Box I, Folder 1).

14. *Ibid.*

15. Morehouse to Gates, July 19, 1888 (FTG, Box I, Folder 1).

16. Gates to P. S. Henson, July 26, 1888; Gates to Morehouse, July 29, 1888 (COFHA, Box I, Folder 3).

17. Gates to Morehouse, Aug. 23, 1888 (FTG, Box I, Folder 2).

18. Draft letter, Gates to "John Doe Esq," enclosed in Gates to Morehouse, Sept. 14, 1888 (FTG, Box I, Folder 2).

19. Gates to Morehouse, Sept. 14, 1888 (FTG, Box I, Folder 2).

20. Morehouse to Gates, Sept. 17, 1888 (FTG, Box I, Folder 2).

21. Goodspeed to his sons, Oct. 14, 1888 (COFHA, Box I, Folder 3).

22. Gates to Morehouse, Oct. 9, 1888 (FTG, Box I, Folder 2).

23. Morehouse to Gates, Oct. 12, 1888 (FTG, Box I, Folder 2).

24. Frederick T. Gates, "The Need of a Baptist University in Chicago, as Illustrated by a Study of Baptist Collegiate Education in the West," a paper read before the Baptist Ministers' Conference, Chicago, Oct. 15, 1888 (FTG, Box I, Folder 2).

25. *Ibid.*

26. Gates to Morehouse, Oct. 16, 1888 (FTG, Box I, Folder 2).

27. Goodspeed to Gates, Oct. 15, 1888 (FTG, Box I, Folder 2).

CHAPTER II

A COLLEGE FOR THE METROPOLIS OF THE WEST

(pp. 18–34)

1. Thomas W. Goodspeed, *William Rainey Harper, First President of the University of Chi-*

cago (Chicago: University of Chicago Press, 1928), pp. 30–31.

2. *Ibid.*, chaps. I–III. Harper's position in regard to the relation of scholarship to religion is explained in the editorials of a journal named successively *Hebrew Student, Old Testament Student, Old and New Testament Student,* and *Biblical World,* which Harper edited from 1882 to nearly the time of his death. For an account of Harper's connection with Chautauqua see Joseph E. Gould, *The Chautauqua Movement, An Episode in the Continuing American Revolution* (State University of New York, 1961), pp. 13 ff.

3. Morehouse to Gates, Oct. 15, 1888 (FTG, Box I, Folder 2); Harper to Goodspeed, Oct. 13, 1888 (TWG: Correspondence re history of the University).

4. For the judgment that Harper did master Rockefeller at Poughkeepsie see Milton Mayer, *Young Man in a Hurry* (Chicago: University of Chicago Alumni Association, 1957), pp. 1–3.

5. Morehouse to Gates, Oct. 26, 1888 (FTG, Box I, Folder 2); Goodspeed to Harper, Oct. 25, 1888; Harper to Rockefeller, Oct. 30, 1888 (COFHA, Box I, Folder 3).

6. Harper to Goodspeed, Nov. 5, 1888 (TWG: Correspondence re history of the University).

7. *Ibid.*

8. *Ibid.*

9. Goodspeed to his sons, Nov. 11 and 16, 1888; Goodspeed to Rockefeller, Nov. 13, 1888 (COFHA, Box I, Folder 4).

10. Harper to Goodspeed, Nov. 19, 1888; Rockefeller to Goodspeed, Nov. 16, 1888 (TWG: Correspondence re history of the University).

11. Rockefeller to Goodspeed, Nov. 16, 1888 (TWG: Correspondence re history of the University).

12. Goodspeed to Rockefeller, Nov. 22, 1888 (COFHA, Box I, Folder 4).

13. Harper to Goodspeed, Nov. 26, 1888 (TWG: Correspondence re history of the University).

14. Thomas W. Goodspeed, "Reminiscences of Thomas Wakefield Goodspeed," pp. 301–2 (Manuscript in UCA).

15. Goodspeed to Harper, Nov. 28 and Dec. 15, 1888 (COFHA, Box I, Folder 4).

16. Harper to Goodspeed, Dec. 5, 1888 (TWG: Correspondence re history of the University).

17. Goodspeed to Harper, Dec. 15, 1888.

18. *Ibid.*

19. Harper to Goodspeed, Nov. 19, 1888 (TWG: Correspondence re history of the University).

20. Augustus H. Strong to Harper, Nov. 18, 1888.

21. Harper to Gates, Nov. 23, 1888.

22. Harper to Rockefeller, Nov. 15, 1888 (COFHA, Box I, Folder 4).

23. Goodspeed to Harper, Nov. 24, 1888.

24. Harper to Goodspeed, Nov. 28, 1888 (TWG: Correspondence re history of the University).

25. *Ibid.*

26. Goodspeed to Harper, Nov. 30, 1888.

27. *Ibid.*

28. Goodspeed to Gates, Dec. 7, 1888 (FTG, Box I, Folder 3).

29. Goodspeed to Harper, Dec. 7, 1888.

30. George W. Northrup to Harper, Jan. 1, 1889 (COFHA, Box I, Folder 5).

31. Harper to Rockefeller, Nov. 15, 1888 (COFHA, Box I, Folder 4).

32. Harper to Augustus H. Strong, Jan. 4, 1889 (COFHA, Box I, Folder 5).

33. Harper to Rockefeller, Jan. 13, 1889 (COFHA, Box I, Folder 5).

34. Gates to Harper, Nov. 26, 1888.

35. Gates to Morehouse, Jan. 6, 1889 (FTG, Box I, Folder 4).

36. Rockefeller to Harper, Jan. 15, 1889.

37. Morehouse to Gates, Jan. 4, 1889 (FTG, Box I, Folder 4).

38. Gates to Harper, Jan. 5, 1889.

39. Harper to Goodspeed, Jan. 8, 1889; Goodspeed to Harper, Jan. 11, 1889 (two letters); Gates to Goodspeed, Jan. 12, 1889; Harper to Rockefeller, Jan. 18, 1889; Harper to Goodspeed, Jan. 19, 1889; and Goodspeed to Harper, Jan. 22, 1889 (COFHA, Box I, Folder 5).

40. Harper to Goodspeed, Jan. 27, 1889; Harper to Gates, Jan. 31, 1889 (FTG, Box I, Folder 4).

41. Morehouse to Harper, Jan. 4, 1889.

42. Rockefeller to Harper, Jan. 11, 1889.

43. Gates to Rockefeller, Jan. 21, 1889.

44. Gates to Harper, Jan. 21, 1889.

45. Gates to Morehouse, Feb. 2, 1889 (FTG, Box I, Folder 4).

46. *First Annual Meeting of the American Baptist Education Society . . . Boston, May 18th, 1889* (Chicago: R. R. Donnelly & Sons, 1889), p. 15.

47. Gates to the Committee of Inquiry, n.d. [probably March, 1889] (FTG, Box I, Folder 4).

48. Gates to Rockefeller, Feb. 23, 1889 (FTG, Box I, Folder 4); Harper to Goodspeed, Feb. 25, 1889 (TWG: Correspondence re history of the University).

49. Rockefeller to Gates, Feb. 26, 1889 (FTG, Box I, Folder 4).

50. Goodspeed to Harper, Feb. 27, 1889.

51. Goodspeed, *History,* p. 59.

52. Gates to Morehouse, Feb. 2, 1889 (FTG, Box I, Folder 4).

53. Gates to Harper, March 14, 1889.

54. Goodspeed to Gates, March 19, 1889 (FTGCR); Goodspeed to Harper, April 9, 1889; Goodspeed to his sons, March 17, 1889 (COFHA, Box I, Folder 6).

55. Harper to Goodspeed, April 13, 1889 (TWG: Correspondence re history of the University).

56. "Report of Committee on proposed institution of learning in Chicago."

57. *Ibid.*

58. Goodspeed to his sons, April 14, 1889 (COFHA, Box II, Folder 1).

59. Harper to Goodspeed, April 13, 1889 (TWG: Correspondence re history of the University).

60. Rockefeller to Gates, May 11, 1889 (FTG, Box I, Folder 5).

61. *Ibid.*; Rockefeller to Gates, May 15, 1889 (COFHA, Box II, Folder 1); Goodspeed, *History,* see Introduction by Frederick T. Gates, pp. 9–10.

62. Rockefeller, quoted in Gates to Morehouse, Nov. 30, 1889 (COFHA, Box II, Folder 2).

63. Harper to Goodspeed, May 7, 1889; "Resolutions adopted by the Executive Board of the American Baptist Education Society at Boston, May 17th, 1889, and by the Society, May 18th, 1889," Resolution 7 (COFHA, Box II, Folder 1).

64. *First Annual Meeting of American Baptist Education Society, . . . Boston, May 18th, 1889,* pp. 14–17, 32, 42.

65. Gates to Harper, June 6, 1889.

66. Goodspeed to Harper, May 26, 1889 (COFHA, Box II, Folder 1).

67. George D. Boardman to Gates, July 17, 1889 (FTG, Box I, Folder 5). The emphasis lies on the last word.

68. Augustus H. Strong to Gates, June 3, 1889 (FTG, Box I, Folder 5).

69. Gates to Morehouse, June 7, 1889, with editorial note added later by Gates (COFHA, Box II, Folder 2).

CHAPTER III

FINANCING A COLLEGE AND FOUNDING A UNIVERSITY

(pp. 35–52)

1. Goodspeed to Harper, June 2, 1889.

2. *Ibid.*

3. Goodspeed, *History,* pp. 73–74; Gates to Harper, July 25, 1889.

4. Goodspeed to Harper, Oct. 23, 1889.

5. Subscription book of the first canvass (UCA); Goodspeed, *History,* pp. 69–97.

6. Goodspeed to his sons, Nov. 10, 17, and 24 and Dec. 8, 1889; Goodspeed to his sons, Jan. 12, 1890; Gates to Harper, Feb. 3, 1890; Goodspeed to his sons, Feb. 9, 1890; Gates to Morehouse, April 19, 1890; Goodspeed to his sons, April 26, 1890 (COFHA, Box II, Folders 2 and 3).

7. Gates to Harper, Nov. 4, 1889.

8. Justin A. Smith to Harper, Jan. 21, 1889 (COFHA, Box I, Folder 5); Goodspeed to Harper, June 7, 1889 (COFHA, Box II, Folder 2).

9. Goodspeed to his sons, Oct. 13, 1889 (COFHA, Box II, Folder 2); Goodspeed to Harper, Oct. 23, 1889.

10. Gates to Harper, Nov. 12, 1889 (FTG, Box I, Folder 5).

11. Gates to Morehouse, Nov. 14, 1889 (FTG, Box I, Folder 5).

12. Gates to Harper, Oct. 23, 1889 (COFHA, Box II, Folder 2); Thomas W. Goodspeed, "Charles Lawrence Hutchinson," *The University of Chicago Biographical Sketches* (Chicago: University of Chicago Press, 1925), II, 27–53.

13. Gates to Rockefeller, Jan. 20, 1890 (COFHA, Box II, Folder 3).

14. Rockefeller to Marshall Field, quoted in Rockefeller to Gates, Jan. 24, 1890 (FTG, Box II, Folder 1).

15. Telegram, Gates to Rockefeller, April 25, 1890; Rockefeller to Gates, April 26, 1890 (COFHA, Box II, Folder 3).

16. Goodspeed to Harper, June 1, 1890 (COFHA, Box II, Folder 4).

17. *Inter-Ocean* (Chicago), May 29, 1890.

18. E. Nelson Blake to Harper, Jan. 1, 1891.

19. "Articles of Incorporation of the University of Chicago." The original Articles of Incorporation also appear in PR, 1892–1902, pp. 503–5.

20. *Ibid.*

21. "Report by Rev. F. T. Gates," *Standard,* XXXVII, No. 46 (July 17, 1890), 1.

22. *Ibid.*; Goodspeed, *History,* pp. 94–95.

23. Gates to Harper, June 6, 1890. For the earlier list proposed see Goodspeed to Harper, June 1, 1890.

24. Harper to Gates, June 4, 1890 (FTG, Box II, Folder 1).

25. Frederick M. Jackson, "Simeon E. Baldwin and Clerical Control of Yale," *American Historical Review,* LVII, No. 4 (July, 1952), 909–18.

26. Goodspeed to Harper, Oct. 23, 1889; Morehouse to Gates, Oct. 25, 1889; Morehouse to Harper, Oct. 28, 1889; Gates to Morehouse, Oct. 28, 1889; Gates to Harper, Nov. 12, 1889 (COFHA, Box II, Folder 2).

27. Goodspeed to Harper, June 8, 1890.

28. "Report of Conference between Messrs. F. T. Gates, T. W. Goodspeed, and H. A. Rust, with reference to The University of Chicago, February 10, 1897," p. 1 (photocopy in UCA); also Gates to Harper, June 9, 1890 (COFHA, Box II, Folder 4).

29. Gates to Harper, May 13, 1892.

30. MBT, July 9 and Sept. 18, 1890.

31. George S. Goodspeed to Goodspeed, May 29, 1890.

32. Timothy Dwight to Harper, July 18, 1890.

33. George T. Ladd to Harper, July 27, 1890.

34. Harper to Gates, July 30, 1890 (FTG, Box II, Folder 1).

35. Harper to Gates, July 26, 1890 (FTG, Box II, Folder 1).

36. Henry G. Weston to Harper, Aug. 1, 1890.

37. E. H. Johnson to Harper, July 25, 1890.

38. Justin A. Smith to Harper, July 21, 1890 (COFHA, Box II, Folder 4).

39. Gates to Harper, July 28, 1890.

40. Harper to Goodspeed, July 31, 1890 (TWG: Correspondence re history of the University).

41. Frederick T. Gates, "The Memoirs of Frederick T. Gates," *American Heritage,* VI, No. 3 (April, 1955), 75; also Rockefeller to Harper, Aug. 6, 1890 (COFHA, Box II, Folder 5).

42. Harper to Rockefeller, Aug. 9, 1890 (COFHA, Box II, Folder 5).

43. Rockefeller to the Board of Trustees, Sept. 16, 1890.

44. Gates, editorial notes appended to copies of Harper to Gates, Aug. 5, 1890, and Harper to Goodspeed, Sept. 6, 1890 (COFHA, Box II, Folder 5). The notes were written about twenty-five years after the incident described.

45. Rockefeller to Gates, Aug. 6, 1890; Rockefeller to Harper, Aug. 6, 1890 (COFHA, Box II, Folder 5).

46. Gates, editorial notes appended to a copy of Harper to Gates, Aug. 5, 1890 (COFHA, Box II, Folder 5).

47. George T. Ladd to Harper, July 27, 1890.

48. Gates to Morehouse, Aug. 20, 1890 (FTG, Box II, Folder 2).

49. MBT, Sept. 18, 1890.

50. See Nevins, *Study in Power,* II, 183, for the judgment that Rockefeller was "held up" by Harper, and willingly.

51. *Official Bulletin, No. 1,* p. 6.

52. Harper to Morehouse, Nov. 11, 1890 (FTG, Box II, Folder 2).

53. Harper to Goodspeed, Feb. 5, 1889 (TWG: Correspondence re history of the University).

54. Gates to Morehouse, Feb. 6, 1891 (FTG, Box II, Folder 3); Gates to Morehouse, Feb. 3, 1891 (FTG, Box II, Folder 3).

55. Goodspeed to Harper, Jan. 14, 1891.

56. Gates to Harper, Jan. 11, 1891.

57. Harper to Rockefeller, Jan. 8, 1891 (COFHA, Box II, Folder 7).

58. Morehouse to Harper, Feb. 2, 1891.

59. *Ibid.*

60. Harper to Morehouse, Feb. 7, 1891 (FTG, Box II, Folder 3).

61. Harper to Hutchinson, May 20, 1891; William W. Farnam to Harper, June 3, 1891; Harper to Andrew McLeish, Jan. 16, 1902.

PART II: THE PLAN, THE PEOPLE, AND THE POLITY

A UNIVERSITY AMONG UNIVERSITIES

(pp. 55–56)

1. Harper to Rockefeller, Sept. 22, 1890 (COFHA, Box II, Folder 5); Harper to Morehouse, Sept. 22, 1890 (FTG, Box II, Folder 2); also see Goodspeed, *History*, p. 168.

2. See Hugh Hawkins, *Pioneer: A History of the Johns Hopkins University, 1874–1889* (Ithaca: Cornell University Press, 1960), pp. 316–26.

CHAPTER IV

THE OLD TESTAMENT AND THE NEW UNIVERSITY

(pp. 57–64)

1. William R. Harper, "The University and Democracy," *The Trend in Higher Education* (Chicago: University of Chicago Press, 1905), pp. 11–12.

2. *Old and New Testament Student*, XVI, Nos. 3–4 (Sept.–Oct., 1892), 90.

3. *Ibid.*, IX, No. 5 (Nov., 1889), 259–60.

4. *Ibid.*, XIII, No. 4 (Oct., 1891), 198.

5. *Ibid.*, XII, No. 2 (Feb., 1891), 70.

6. *Ibid.*, XI, No. 2 (Aug., 1890), 67.

7. Harper, *The Trend in Higher Education*, pp. 27–28.

8. *Official Bulletin, No. 1*, pp. 7–8.

9. *Ibid.*, p. 8.

10. *Ibid.*

11. *Ibid.*, pp. 8–12.

12. *Ibid.*, pp. 12–15.

13. *Ibid.*, pp. 15–16.

14. *Ibid.*

15. An excerpt from Arthur E. Shipley, *The Voyage of a Vice-Chancellor*, quoted in Bessie L. Pierce (ed.), *As Others See Chicago, 1673–1933* (Chicago: University of Chicago Press, 1933), p. 462.

16. William R. Harper, "Quarterly Statement of the President," *Calendar*, II, No. 2 (Aug., 1893), 9.

17. Harper to Burton, Dec. 10, 1890 (EDB, Series II, Box VI, Folder 1).

18. Harper, "Quarterly Statement," *Calendar*, II, No. 1 (May, 1893), 9.

CHAPTER V

NEGOTIATIONS

(pp. 65–85)

1. Goodspeed to Harper, Sept. 7 and 10, 1890.

2. Goodspeed to Harper, Oct. 18, 1890.

3. Goodspeed to Harper, Oct. 5, 1890.

4. Ryerson to Harper, Jan. 21, 1891.

5. Goodspeed to Harper, March 9, 1891.

6. Goodspeed to Harper, March 11, 1891.

7. Goodspeed, "Reminiscences," pp. 300–304 (UCA).

8. Gates to Harper, April 27, 1891 (COFHA, Box II, Folder 6).

9. Gates to Harper, June 8, 1891.

10. "Report of Conference between Messrs. F. T. Gates, T. W. Goodspeed and H. A. Rust with reference to The University of Chicago, February 10, 1897" (photocopy in UCA).

11. E. Nelson Blake to Goodspeed, Aug. 15, 1891.

12. Goodspeed to Harper, Oct. 5, 1890.

13. Alonzo K. Parker to Harper, Oct. 21, 1890 (COFHA, Box II, Folder 6).

14. Gates to Goodspeed, Oct. 30, 1891 (FTG, Box II, Folder 4). See Goodspeed, *History*, pp. 169–73.

15. Harper to Gates, Nov. 6, 1891 (FTG, Box II, Folder 4).

16. Harper to Rockefeller, Oct. 31, 1891 (COFHA, Box III, Folder 3); Harper to Gates, Feb. 22, 1892 (COFHA, Box III, Folder 4); Goodspeed to Gates, Feb. 29, 1892 (FTG, Box II, Folder 5); Goodspeed to Gates, June 30, 1892 (COFHA, Box III, Folder 5); Harper to Gates, July 1, 1892 (FTG, Box II, Folder 6); Gates to Rockefeller, July 2, 1892 (COFHA, Box III, Folder 6); and Harper to Gates, July 10, 1892 (FTG, Box II, Folder 6).

17. Hutchinson to Harper, Feb. 18 and 27, 1892.

18. *Official Bulletin, No. 1,* pp. 7–8.

19. William R. Harper, "The President's Report," PR, 1892–1902, p. xviii.

20. William C. Lawton to Harper, Jan. 5, 1891.

21. Frank K. Sanders to Harper, April 11, 1893.

22. David Starr Jordan to Harper, July 28, 1891.

23. Richard T. Ely to Harper, Nov. 15, 1890.

24. Alice Freeman Palmer to Harper, n.d.

25. Judson to Harper, Oct. 23, 1891.

26. Burton to Harper, March 6, April 11, and June 18, 1891; Harper to Burton, Dec. 28, 1891; telegram, Burton to Harper, March 4, 1892; Burton to Harper, March 5 and 24, 1892. A. H. Hovey to Burton, March 2, 1892; memo (March, 1892); Harper to Burton, March 5 and 20, 1892 (EDB, Series II, Box VI, Folder 3).

27. Frank B. Tarbell to Harper, May 1, 1892; Calvin Thomas to Harper, June 9, 1892; Nathaniel Butler to Harper, May 24, 1892.

28. Isaac B. Burgess to Harper, Sept. 19, 1890.

29. Small to Harper, July 14, 1892.

30. Charles O. Whitman to Harper, Jan. 15, 1892.

31. John U. Nef to Harper, May 19, 1892.

32. Marion Talbot to Harper, draft of Aug. 13, 1892 (MT, Box I, "Correspondence").

33. George H. Palmer to J. Laurence Laughlin, quoted in Hale to Harper, Dec. 14, 1891.

34. Hale to Harper, Sept. 10 and Oct. 29, 1891; Hale to Hutchinson, Nov. 14 and 25, 1891; Hale to Harper, Dec. 26, 1891.

35. *Ibid.*

36. *Ibid.*; Hale to Hutchinson, Dec. 28, 1891; Harper to Hutchinson, Dec. 28, 1891; "Records of the Board of Trustees of the University of Chicago, abridged by Thomas W. Goodspeed," item for Dec. 29, 1891 (UCA).

37. Hutchinson to Harper, Jan. 3, 1892; Hale to Harper, Jan. 2, 1892.

38. Hale to Harper, March 28, 1892.

39. W. I. Knapp to Harper, Jan. 21, 1892. See also G. Stanley Hall, *Life and Confessions of a Psychologist* (New York: D. Appleton and Company, 1923), pp. 290–300; and W. Carson Ryan, *Studies in Graduate Education, the Johns Hopkins, Clark University, the University of Chicago* (The Carnegie Foundation for the Advancement of Teaching, Bulletin No. 30, New York, 1939), pp. 57–63.

40. *Register,* 1892–1893, pp. 10–16.

41. Harper to Gates, March 27, 1891 (FTG, Box II, Folder 3).

42. Melvil Dewey to Harper, Jan. 23, 24, and 29, 1892.

43. George E. Vincent, "The University of Chicago," *The Outlook,* LXXI (Aug. 2, 1902), 842.

44. Gates to Harper, June 8, 1891.

45. *Ibid.*

46. Harper to Gates, June 11, 1892 (FTG, Box II, Folder 4).

47. See Goodspeed, *History,* pp. 173–76.

48. Gates to Harper, June 8, 1891.

49. Gates to Rockefeller, Jan. 29, 1892 (COFHA, Box III, Folder 4).

50. *Ibid.*

51. Frederick T. Gates, "Report on the University of Chicago, February 1, 1892" (COFHA, Box III, Folder 4).

52. *Ibid.*

53. *Ibid.*, supplement to Exhibit D.

54. Gates to Rockefeller, Feb. 11, 1892 (COFHA, Box III, Folder 4).

55. Gates to Goodspeed, Feb. 23, 1892 (COFHA, Box III, Folder 4).

56. Harper to Gates, Aug. 26, 1892 (FTG, Box II, Folder 6).

57. Harper to Gates, Sept. 26, 1892 (FTG, Box II, Folder 6).

58. Gates to Harper, Sept. 3, 1892 (COFHA, Box III, Folder 6).

59. Harper to Gates, Nov. 3, 1892 (FTG, Box II, Folder 6).

60. Harper to Gates, Nov. 21, 1892 (FTG, Box II, Folder 6).

61. Harper to Gates, Nov. 3, 1892 (FTG, Box II, Folder 6); Gates to Harper, Nov. 19, 1892.

62. Goodspeed to Mrs. L. M. Woodruf, Nov. 21, 1892 (SBL, A, p. 172).

63. Rockefeller to Board of Trustees, Dec. 23, 1892 (COFHA, Box III, Folder 6).

64. Gates to Harper, Dec. 22, 1892 (COFHA, Box III, Folder 6).

65. Hall, *Life and Confessions,* p. 298.

66. Harper to Hutchinson, Feb. 19, 1894.

67. Burton to Harper, Jan. 8, 1894; Burton

to Harper, March 4, 1897; Harper to Burton, March 9, 1897.

68. Clarence L. Herrick to Harper, Jan 12, 1891; Herrick to Harper, n.d. [contains outline of biological department]; Herrick to Harper, Oct. 28, Nov. 23, and Dec. 9, 1891; Charles A. Strong to Harper, March 25, 1892 (two letters); memorandum of agreement between Herrick and Harper, May 9, 1892; Herrick to Harper, May 16, 1892; Herrick to Goodspeed, May 16, 1892; Herrick to Francis W. Shepardson, April 7, 1893; and Herrick to Harper, Nov. 14, 1898. See also Charles J. Herrick, *Clarence Luther Herrick, Pioneer Naturalist, Teacher and Psychobiologist,* Transactions of the American Philosophical Society, New Series, XLV, Part 1 (Philadelphia: American Philosophical Society, 1955), 38, 68–71; and Lincoln C. Blake, "William Rainey Harper and the Beginnings of Scientific Education at the University of Chicago," unpublished PH.D. dissertation, Committee on the History of Culture, University of Chicago (1966).

69. Edward W. Bemis to Harper, Feb. 19, 21, and 26, March 8, 11, and 13, and May 13, 1892; Bemis to Laughlin, Feb. 27, 1892.

70. *Calendar,* II, No. 1 (May, 1893), 90–92; II, No. 4 (Feb., 1894), 99.

71. Harper to Edward W. Bemis, Jan. [15], 1894 (a copy possibly made in September, 1894).

72. Richard Hofstadter and Walter P. Metzger, *The Development of Academic Freedom in the United States* (New York: Columbia University Press, 1955), p. 428.

73. MBT, March 27, 1894, as recorded by Goodspeed (UCA).

74. Harper to Edward W. Bemis, as quoted in a public statement by Bemis, in *The Kingdom,* Oct. 11, 1895 (clipping in UCA).

75. "Memorandum of agreement, E. W. Bemis & William R. Harper," n.d. [before July 1, 1895].

76. Harper, "Quarterly Statement," *Calendar,* IV, No. 2 (Nov., 1895), 13.

77. Public statement by Edward W. Bemis, in *The Kingdom,* Oct. 11, 1895 (clipping in UCA); "A Statement by Professors Small and Butler," Oct. 16, 1895, printed with a statement by Harper, Oct. 21, 1895 (UCA).

CHAPTER VI

ACADEMIC POLITY

(pp. 86–105)

1. Harper to Gates, Oct. 3, 1892 [apparently written on Sunday, Oct. 2, 1892] (COFHA, Box III, Folder 6).

2. Harper to Francis Parker, Feb. 15, 1901.

3. *Nation,* LV, No. 1421 (Sept. 22, 1892), 217.

4. *Calendar,* II, No. 1 (May, 1893), 9.

5. See Frank C. Abbott, *Government Policy and Higher Education, A Study of the Regents of the University of the State of New York, 1784–1949* (Ithaca: Cornell University Press, 1958), pp. 64–67.

6. Hale to Harper, Feb. 7, 1892.

7. Hale to Harper, Feb. 10, 1892.

8. See Waterman T. Hewett, *Cornell University, A History* (New York: University Publishing Society, 1905), I, 193 ff.

9. Laughlin to Harper, Nov. 25, 1892.

10. Laughlin to Harper, Jan. 8, 1894.

11. *Nation,* LV, No. 1421, 217.

12. "The Statutes of the University," *Register,* 1892–1893, p. 6.

13. Harry P. Judson, "The Faculties of Arts, Literature, and Science," PR, 1892–1902, p. 4.

14. *Ibid.,* pp. 3–5.

15. "The Statutes of the University," *Register,* 1895–1896, p. 7.

16. *Official Bulletin, No. 2,* revised edition (April, 1891), p. 3.

17. Harry P. Judson, "The Faculties of Arts, Literature, and Science," PR, 1897–1898, p. 32.

18. *Ibid.*

19. Frank F. Abbott, "Briefs on Propositions," *Record,* V, No. 37 (Dec. 14, 1900), 321–22.

20. Robert Herrick to Robert M. Lovett, Dec. 13, 1895 (RH, Box 26).

21. Harper to Judson, April 21, 1896.

22. Harper, red memorandum book for spring and summer, 1896, p. 112.

23. MC, Feb. 22 and April 3, 1897; Jan. 3, 1899; Dec. 15, 1902.

24. Ryerson to Harper, Feb. 23, 1896.

25. Small to Harper, Dec. 29, 1894; Laughlin to Harper, Dec. 22, 1894, and Jan. 5, 189[5].

26. Untitled, undated, typewritten carbon copy of the record of a discussion in which Harper, Thomas C. Chamberlin, Charles O. Whitman, and Henry W. Donaldson took part.

27. Harper, "Quarterly Statement," *Record,* I, No. 28 (Oct. 9, 1896), 384.

28. Harper, "Quarterly Statement," *Record,* III, No. 32 (Nov. 4, 1898), 199–200.

29. Carl D. Buck to Harper, Jan. 17, 1899; Buck to Harper, n.d. [stamped by President's Office April 6, possibly 1902]; Harper to Small, Sept. 30, 1901.

30. Harper, "Quarterly Statement," *Calendar,* IV, No. 1 (Aug., 1895), 15.

31. Harper, "Quarterly Statement," *Record,* V, No. 42, 375–78.

32. Hale to Harper, Dec. 20, 1900.

33. "The Statutes of the University," *Register,* 1892–1893, p. 6; Harper, *Record,* V, No. 42, 376–77.

34. MC, May 19 and June 30, 1899; Laughlin to Harper, June 28, 1899.

35. Robert Herrick to John Manly, Dec. 1, 1923.

36. "Notes on first faculty meeting, Oct. 1, 1892" (MT, Box XIII).

37. William R. Harper, "President's Letter of Transmission," PR, 1897–1898, p. viii.

38. Harper, "Quarterly Statement," *Calendar,* II, No. 3 (Nov., 1893), 12.

39. Harper, PR, 1892–1902, pp. xviii–xix.

40. Laughlin to Harper, Nov. 25, 1892.

41. [Henry H. Donaldson] to Harper, March 29, 1894.

42. Verse sent by W. C. Wilkinson to Small, May 24, 1912; Small to W. C. Wilkinson, May 27, 1912.

43. William R. Harper, "The College President," n.d., a typewritten paper in UCA. The misspelling of "Rainey" as "Rainy" in the name signed at the bottom of this paper indicates that the name is not Harper's autograph; presumably the name was added by someone who edited the paper. "The College President" was published, with an explanatory note, by Samuel N. Harper in *The William Rainey Harper Memorial Conference* [at Muskingum College, Oct. 21–22, 1937] (Chicago: University of Chicago Press, 1938), pp. 24–34. Some of the passages in "The College President" appear in William R. Harper, "Address on Behalf of Sister Universities," *The Jubilee of the University of Wisconsin, in Celebration of the Fiftieth Anniversary of Its First Commencement, Held at Madison, June the Fifth to June the Ninth, Nineteen Hundred and Four* (Madison: The Jubilee Committee, 1905), pp. 55–65.

44. Laughlin to Harper, Sept. 29, 1892.

45. Harper to R. S. Colwell, Sept. 25, 1897.

PART III: THE ACADEMIC WAY: THE FIRST TEN YEARS

THE STUDENT BODY

(pp. 109–12)

1. *Register,* 1892–1893, pp. 96–110.

2. *Ibid.*

3. *Maroon,* June 12, 1903, p. 1.

4. Harper to Rexford Raymond, n.d. [1901]; Harper to R. A. Hall, April 27, 1904.

5. Harper to Gates, July 22, 1899 (FTGCR).

6. George E. Vincent to Harper, June 17, 1903.

7. Harper, PR, 1892–1902, p. xxxv.

8. *Ibid.,* pp. xxx–xxxi.

9. James H. Tufts, "The Senior Colleges," PR, 1892–1902, pp. 83–84.

10. Marion Talbot, "The Women of the University," PR, 1904–1905, p. 45.

11. Harper, PR, 1892–1902, p. xxxiii.

CHAPTER VII

THE APPROACHES TO ACADEME

(pp. 113–28)

1. *Official Bulletin,* No. 2, pp. 2–3.

2. *Ibid.,* p. 9.

3. Statute 25, "The Statutes of the University," *Register,* 1892–1893, pp. 7–8.

4. W. D. McClintock, "The Unclassified Students," PR, 1897–1898, p. 100.

5. *Ibid.,* p. 105.

6. *Ibid.,* p. 100.

7. *Ibid.,* p. 103.

8. *Ibid.,* pp. 103–4, and Clarence F. Castle, "The Unclassified Students," PR, 1898–1899, p. 47. There may be some duplication of persons in the figures.

9. McClintock, PR, 1897–1898, pp. 105, 109.

10. *Ibid.*, p. 109.

11. *Ibid.*, p. 104.

12. *Ibid.*, p. 99.

13. *Ibid.*

14. *Ibid.*, p. 109.

15. *Ibid.*, p. 110.

16. *Ibid.*, p. 99.

17. *Ibid.*

18. *Ibid.*, p. 109.

19. Castle, PR, 1898–1899, p. 46.

20. *Official Bulletin, No. 2*, p. 3.

21. Judson to Harper, April 30, 1892.

22. Laughlin to Harper, n.d.

23. Alice Freeman Palmer to Harper, Nov. 15[?], 1892.

24. MS, Oct. 28, 1892.

25. MS, Jan. 27 and Feb. 6, 1893.

26. Paul Shorey to Harper, Feb. 13, 1893.

27. MFALS, April 20, 1893.

28. "The Statutes of the University," *Register,* 1892–1893, p. 7; "Statutes," *Register,* 1895–1896, p. 8.

29. MFALS, April 20, 1893.

30. *Register,* 1893–1894, pp. 174–75; *ibid.,* 1896–1897, p. 58.

31. Harper, "Quarterly Statement," *Record,* III, No. 5 (April 29, 1898), 32.

32. *Ibid.*

33. See *Register,* 1892–1893, p. 128.

34. See Edward Capps, "The Junior Colleges," PR, 1897–1898, pp. 78–82.

35. Harper, red memorandum book, March, 1893, p. 108.

36. George E. Vincent, "The Junior Colleges," PR, 1892–1902, p. 109.

37. Capps, PR, 1897–1898, p. 78.

38. Vincent, PR, 1892–1902, p. 111.

39. Small to Harper, n.d. [probably 1896].

40. Statement by Albert A. Michelson *et al.,* attached to MS, May 15, 1896, p. 3 of the Statement.

41. *Ibid.*, p. 4.

42. *Ibid.*, pp. 5–6.

43. Report of the Curriculum Committee of the Junior College Faculty, MJCF, Dec. 14, 1901, p. 7.

44. Charles O. Whitman to Harper, Dec. 1, 1898.

45. Hale to Harper, May 30, 1902.

46. Hale to Marion Talbot, Dec. 3, 1896 (MT, Box II, Folder 1).

47. Thomas C. Chamberlin to Charles W. Eliot, March 18, 1898 (TCC, Box I, Folder 15).

48. Chamberlin to Harper, Feb. 5, 1900 (TCC, Letterbooks, XII, p. 181).

49. Hale to Harper, Jan. 16, 1899.

50. Report of the Ballot Submitted by the Senate to the Ogden School of Science, a form filled out in ink and pencil (TCC, Box III, General Correspondence, 1899).

51. *Ibid.*

52. Small to Harper, n.d.

53. John Dewey, "Pedagogy as a University Discipline," Part I, *Record,* I, No. 25 (Sept. 18, 1896), 354. See also the second part of the paper in the next number of the *Record,* I, No. 26 (Sept. 25, 1896), 361–63.

54. Dewey, *Record,* I, No. 25, 354.

55. MFALS, Feb. 1, 1896.

56. *Ibid.*

57. MS, May 15, 1896.

58. MS, March 3, 1900. For segment of proposition not recorded with the official minutes see summary of Senate actions of March, 1900, in *Record,* V, No. 1 (April 6, 1900), 20.

59. MS, March 3, 1900.

60. MS, April 7, 1900.

61. MJCF, Jan. 18, 1902.

62. Small to Harper, n.d.

63. William R. Harper, "The President's Report," PR, 1898–1899, pp. xxiii–xxv.

64. George E. Vincent, "The Junior Colleges," PR, 1902–1904, p. 90.

65. John U. Nef to G. Stanley Hall, March 26, 1894; G. Stanley Hall to John U. Nef, April 3, 1894 (JUN, Box I, Folder 4).

66. John U. Nef to Harper, Feb. 16, 1894 (JUN, Box I, Folder 4).

67. Harper, "Quarterly Statement," *Calendar,* II, No. 1 (May, 1893), 11.

68. Harper, "Quarterly Statement," *Calendar,* III, No. 4 (Feb., 1895), 17.

69. Harper to Lyman H. Ford, Dec. 26, 1896.

70. Harper, red memorandum book, April 1, 1902, p. 189.

71. Harper, PR, 1892–1902, p. cxxvii.

72. *Ibid.*, p. xciv.

CHAPTER VIII

THE HIGHER TEACHING

(pp. 129–46)

1. *Register*, 1897–1898, p. 55.
2. MC, Jan. 4, 1898; *Record*, V, No. 12 (June 22, 1900), 118 ff.
3. *Ibid.*
4. Harper to Hale, Aug. 5, 1900.
5. Benjamin S. Terry, "The Senior Colleges," PR, 1897–1898, pp. 71–75.
6. *Register*, 1897–1898, p. 55.
7. *Register*, 1892–1893, p. 118.
8. Harper, "Quarterly Statement," *Calendar*, III, No. 5 (May, 1895), 13.
9. *Ibid.*, p. 14.
10. Harper, memorandum book begun in Sept., 1896, pp. 118–21.
11. *Ibid.*, p. 121.
12. Harper, "University Training for a Business Career," *The Trend in Higher Education*, p. 275.
13. Gates to Rockefeller, Feb. 1, 1892, "Report on the University of Chicago."
14. E. L. Corthell to Harper, Dec. 6, 1892.
15. See "Elmer Lawrence Corthell, *National Cyclopedia of American Biography*, IX (New York: James T. White & Company, 1907), 42.
16. Harper, "Quarterly Statement," *Calendar*, III, No. 1 (May, 1894), 16 ff.
17. E. L. Corthell to Harper, Oct. 25, 1893.
18. Goodspeed to Gates, Oct. 14, 1896 (SBL, B, pp. 809–11); Goodspeed to Gates, May 20, 1897 (SBL, C, pp. 85–86); Goodspeed to Gates, May 28, 1897 (SBL, C, pp. 93–95).
19. Gates to Harper, June 1, 1897.
20. Harper, "Quarterly Statement," *Calendar*, III, No. 1 (May, 1894), 16 ff.
21. Memorandum about Armour Institute, Jan. 6, 1902 (UCA).
22. "Suggestions concerning Technological Work in the City of Chicago."
23. "Propositions with Respect to a closer connection between the work of Armour Institute and that of the University of Chicago."
24. "Suggestions concerning Technological Work in the City of Chicago."
25. Goodspeed to Gates, April 15, 1897 (SBL, B, p. 984).
26. Wesley C. Mitchell, "J. Laurence Laugh-

lin," *Journal of Political Economy*, XLIX (Dec., 1941), 877.
27. James H. S. Bossard and J. Frederic Dewhurst, *University Education for Business: A Study of Existing Needs and Practices* (Philadelphia: University of Pennsylvania Press, 1931), p. 249. See Frances Ruml, "The Formative Period of Higher Commercial Education in American Universities," *The Collegiate School of Business, Its Status at the Close of the First Quarter of the Twentieth Century*, Leo C. Marshall, ed. (Chicago: University of Chicago Press, 1928), pp. 45–57.
28. J. Laurence Laughlin, "Higher Commercial Education," in *Lectures on Commerce*, I, Henry Rand Hatfield (ed.) (Chicago: University of Chicago Press, 1904), 9.
29. *Ibid.*
30. *Ibid.*, pp. 13–14.
31. *Ibid.*, p. 8.
32. *Ibid.*
33. *Ibid.*, pp. 21, 25.
34. MS, Feb. 3, 1894.
35. MS, Oct. 29, 1894.
36. MS, Oct. 18 and Nov. 8, 1895, and Feb. 8 and March 14, 1896.
37. Rollin D. Salisbury to Harper, March, 1898.
38. *Ibid.*
39. *Ibid.*
40. Charles Zueblin to Harper, Oct. 31, 1898.
41. *Ibid.*
42. Laughlin to Harper, Aug. 18, 1900.
43. Harper to Francis W. Shepardson, Feb. 16, 1901 (Notebook File).
44. Francis W. Shepardson to Harper, Feb. 18, 1901 (Notebook File).
45. MS, March 15, 1902.
46. *Register*, 1897–1898, p. 55.
47. *Register*, 1898–1899, p. 58.
48. *Ibid.*
49. *Register*, 1900–1901, pp. 103–4.
50. *Ibid.*, p. 103; Minutes of Senior College, Oct. 19, 1899.
51. Harper, "Quarterly Statement," *Calendar*, III, No. 1 (May, 1894), 16.
52. *Ibid.*
53. George G. Hopkins to Harper, March 13, 1893. For a short history of Rush Medical College see Ernest E. Irons, *The Story of Rush Medical College* (Chicago: Board of Trustees of

Rush Medical College, 1953), especially pp. 32–38 in regard to the early affiliation of the College with the University. For a brief account of medical policy during the Harper administration see Ilza Veith and Franklin C. McLean, *The University of Chicago Clinics and Clinical Departments, 1927–1952* (Chicago, 1952), pp. 1–6. Thomas N. Bonner, *Medicine in Chicago, 1850–1950, A Chapter in the Social and Scientific Development of a City* (Madison: American History Research Center, 1957), presents a thorough review of the local context of policy pursued by the University.

54. George S. Goodspeed to Harper, May [8?], 1892.

55. Gates to Harper, May 2, 1892.

56. Ingals to Harper, Jan. 27, March 7, 1894 (two letters), and Jan. 15, 1896.

57. Ingals to Harper, Dec. 2, 1892.

58. Ingals to Harper, Aug. 3, 1896.

59. Ingals to Harper, March 24, 1897.

60. Harper, "Quarterly Statement," *Record*, II, No. 2 (April 10, 1897), 16 ff.

61. *Ibid.*; Ingals to Harper, March 24, 1897.

62. Gates to Harper, June 19, 1898.

63. Ingals to Harper, Jan. 14, 1897.

64. Goodspeed to Ingals, Jan. 3, 1898 (SBL, C, p. 264). Letter incloses substance of MBT, Dec. 29, 1897.

65. Ingals to Harper, Nov. 4, 1897.

66. Memorandum "From the Minutes of the Board of Trustees of the Meeting held Dec. 29, 1898."

67. Harper to Ryerson, March 24, 1898.

68. Gates to Harper, Jan. 8, 1898.

69. Harper to Ryerson, March 24, 1898.

70. Gates to Goodspeed, Jan. 12, 1898.

71. Goodspeed to Gates, Jan. 15, 1898 (SBL, C, pp. 277–83).

72. Gates to Goodspeed and Harper, Jan. 19, 1898.

73. Harper, "Quarterly Statement," *Record*, II, No. 42 (Jan. 14, 1898), 322.

74. Goodspeed to Gates, Jan. 28, 1898 (SBL, C, pp. 289–96).

75. "Proposed Articles of Affiliation between the University of Chicago and Rush Medical College, arranged by Dr. Harper in Conference with Mr. J. D. Rockefeller, Jr. and F. T. Gates," April 19, 1898.

CHAPTER IX

THE HIGHER TEACHING AND THE HIGHER DEGREES

(pp. 147–63)

1. *Register*, 1892–1893, p. 10.

2. Benjamin Peirce, *Working Plan for the Foundation of a University* (Cambridge, 1856).

3. *Official Bulletin, No. 1*, pp. 14–15.

4. *Ibid.*

5. *Register*, 1896–1897, p. 43.

6. *Official Bulletin, No. 4* (April, 1892), p. 5.

7. *General Register of the Officers and Alumni, 1892–1902*, p. 88.

8. *Official Bulletin, No. 4* (April, 1892), pp. 4–5.

9. MFALS, June 13, 1893.

10. *Register*, 1892–1893, p. 113.

11. *Register*, 1893–1894, p. 160.

12. Judson, PR, 1897–1898, p. 68.

13. *Register*, 1893–1894, pp. 160–61.

14. MBGS, Jan. 17, 1894.

15. MBGS, Feb. 21, 1894.

16. MS, April 7, 1894. See also the *Register*, 1894–1895, p. 212.

17. MFALS, Feb. 21, 1894.

18. MBGS, Feb. 1, 1895.

19. *Ibid.*, Feb. 16, 1895.

20. MFALS, May 18, 1895.

21. MBGS, Feb. 16, March 7, and March 16, 1895.

22. MFALS, May 18, 1895.

23. *Ibid.*, May 29, 1895.

24. *Ibid.*, June 1, 1895.

25. Judson, PR, 1897–1898, p. 68.

26. *Ibid.*

27. MC, Oct. 3, 1898.

28. MBGS, Oct. 28, 1899.

29. "Report of the Joint Committee of the Graduate Faculties appointed to report on the Master's Degree," in MBGS, Feb. 23, 1901.

30. *Register*, 1901–1902, p. 77.

31. MBGS, July 20, 1901.

32. *Register*, 1894–1895, p. 212.

33. *Register*, 1901–1902, p. 77.

34. MS, Oct. 28, 1892.

35. Burton to Mr. Lisk, Jan. 21, 1895 (EDB, II, Box 7, Folder 5).

36. Carl D. Buck to Harper, Jan. 19, 1890.

37. Hermann Eduard von Holst to Harper, Sept. 28, 1897.

38. Albion W. Small, "The Graduate School of Arts and Literature," PR, 1904–1905, p. 12.

39. *Register*, 1892–1893, pp. 113–14; *ibid.*, 1904–1905, pp. 74–75.

40. *Register*, 1893–1894, p. 53.

41. *Ibid.*, pp. 58–60.

42. See *Official Bulletin, No. 4*, p. 5.

43. MFALS, March 2, 1893.

44. *Register*, 1892–1893, p. 113.

45. MS, April 28, 1894.

46. MBGS, May 12, 1894.

47. MS, April 28, June 9, Nov. 3, and Dec. 1, 1894, and Jan. 5, 1895.

48. Charles O. Whitman to Harper, May 31, 1894.

49. MBGS, Jan. 29 and Feb. 26, 1898.

50. MS, Jan. 7, 1899.

51. Judson, PR, 1892–1902, pp. 31–38.

52. Judson to Harper, Dec. 25, 1891.

53. Albion W. Small, "Research Ideals," *Record*, X, No. 2 (Oct., 1905), 87.

54. William G. Hale, "The Graduate School," *Record*, I, No. 34 (Nov. 20, 1896), 439–41.

55. Thomas C. Chamberlin, "The Mission of the Scientific Spirit," *Calendar*, II, No. 1 (May, 1893), 15.

56. Letters from the University of Chicago during the scholastic year 1900–1901 to the Folks at Home, written by Clarence R. Williams, D.B., June, 1901 (copy in possession of the author).

CHAPTER X

OUTSIDE THE CLASSROOM

(pp. 164–89)

1. Thorstein Veblen to Jacques Loeb, Feb. 10, 1905 (Library of Congress).

2. George E. Vincent, address at Reynolds Club cornerstone ceremony, June 18, 1901, *Record*, VI, No. 3 (June 28, 1901), 88.

3. Marion Talbot to her parents, Sept. 25, 1892, with addition on Oct. 12 (MT, Box I, Folder 2).

4. *Ibid.*

5. Marion Talbot to her father, Jan. 2 [1893] (MT, Box II, Folder 3).

6. Marion Talbot to Harper, Oct. 14, 1896.

7. Marion Talbot to her mother, Nov. 25, 1892 (MT, Box I, Folder 2).

8. Alice Freeman Palmer to Marion Talbot, Feb. 26, 1893 (MT, Box I, Folder 3).

9. Marion Talbot to her parents, Sept. 25, 1892, with addition on Oct. 12 (MT, Box I, Folder 2).

10. Harper, "Quarterly Statement," *Record*, I, No. 28 (Oct. 19, 1896), 382.

11. Harper, PR, 1892–1902, p. cxxx.

12. Harper, "Quarterly Statement," *Calendar*, II, No. 2 (Aug., 1893), 11.

13. Marion Talbot to Harper, May 14, 1896.

14. Harold H. Swift, in conversation with the author, Oct. 30, 1953.

15. William R. Harper, "The Antagonism of Fraternities to the Democratic Spirit of Scholarship," *The University Magazine*, VII, No. 6 (Dec., 1892), 441.

16. MFALS, Oct. 1, 1892.

17. MFALS, Oct. 14 and 24, 1892.

18. Laughlin to Harper, Nov. 2, 1892.

19. Manuscript Presidential Report, 1892–1893, pp. 53–54 (UCA).

20. MFALS, May 19, 1894, and Feb. 2, 1895.

21. Judson to Harper, Oct. 23, 1895.

22. MFALS, Dec. 7, 1895.

23. Addison W. Moore, "The University Houses," PR, 1898–1899, p. 161.

24. George E. Vincent to Harper, Nov. 14, 1899.

25. Harper to W. A. Crawford, Jan. 29, 1902.

26. Harper, PR, 1892–1902, pp. cxxxi–cxxxii.

27. Harper to Alexander Smith, June 29, 1903.

28. Memorandum in Marion Talbot's handwriting, n.d. (MT, Box XVIII).

29. Marion Talbot to Harper, Nov. 19, 1894, with marginal notation by Harper (MT, Box XVIII, "Women's Clubs" Folder).

30. Marion Talbot to her mother, Feb. 16, 1896 (MT); Marion Talbot to Harper, March 5, 1896; Marion Talbot to Women Officers of the University, March 19, 1896; Judson to Harper, April 29, 1896; Marion Talbot to Harper, May 14, 1896; Harper to Marion Talbot, May 18, 1896; Marion Talbot to Elizabeth K. Culver, Dec. 17, 1896.

31. Minutes of Board of Student Organizations, Publications, and Exhibitions, May 13, 1897.

32. Harper, "Quarterly Statement," *Record,* II, No. 32 (Nov. 5, 1897), 259.

33. Minutes of the Club of Women Fellows, March 22 and April 9, 1898 (MT, Box XVIII).

34. Edward Capps to Harper, Aug. 11, 1902, and Marion Talbot to Harper, Aug. 16, 1902.

35. John Kennedy to ———, Oct. 17, 1892.

36. Edward Capps to Harper, Aug. 11, 1902.

37. Harper, red memorandum book, Feb., 1897, p. 120.

38. "Lincoln House," typed manuscript with corrections in ink and pencil.

39. *The History of Spelman House* (Chicago: Alumnae Chapter of Spelman House, 1910).

40. "Statement Concerning Lincoln House," inclosed in a letter from George E. Vincent to Harper, May 27, no year [presumably the first for the house, 1897].

41. *Ibid.*

42. *Weekly,* VIII, No. 15 (Jan. 25, 1900), 159.

43. Harper, red memorandum book, Jan., 1900, p. 191.

44. James P. White, "Dr. Harper in the Early Days of the University," *Record,* X, Memorial Number (March, 1906), 44.

45. Harper, PR, 1892–1902, p. cxxix.

46. "The Statutes of the University," *Register,* 1895–1896, p. 8; *Register,* 1896–1897, pp. 48–49.

47. MFALS, Feb. 16 [1895].

48. Harper, talk on April 22, 1896, *Record,* I, No. 4 (April 24, 1896), 86.

49. *Weekly,* V, No. 6 (Nov. 5, 1896), 52–53. See also George E. Vincent to Harper, Dec. 5, 1901.

50. George E. Vincent to Harper, March 10, 1900.

51. *Weekly,* V, No. 36 (June 17, 1897), 360.

52. *Ibid.*

53. Harry P. Judson, "The Graduate Schools," PR, 1898–1899, p. 18.

54. *Register,* 1892–1893, p. 229; *Weekly,* II, No. 19 (Feb. 15, 1894), 4.

55. *Ibid.*

56. *Register,* 1894–1895, p. 383.

57. *Register,* 1896–1897, pp. 145–46.

58. Minutes of the Graduate Student Faculty, Oct. 28, 1898 [1899?] (MT, Box XIX, "Graduate Student Faculty" Folder).

59. *Maroon,* Nov. 17, 1904.

60. *Ibid.*

61. *Record,* IV, No. 44 (Feb. 2, 1900), 301; IV, No. 50 (March 16, 1900), 354–55; V, No. 4 (April 27, 1900), 41–42.

62. *Record,* V, No. 4, 42.

63. Copy of letter, A. A. Stagg to his family, Jan. 20, 1891.

64. *Record,* V, No. 4, 42.

65. Briefs presented to the Congregation on the proposition that the present increasing interest in athletics in the University is undesirable, reported in *Record,* IV, No. 50, 354 ff.

66. *Record,* V, No. 4, 42.

67. Harper, PR, 1902–1904, pp. 31–32.

68. Harper, "Quarterly Statement," *Record,* I, No. 14 (July 3, 1896), 227.

69. Harry P. Judson, "The Faculties of Arts, Literature, and Science," PR, 1898–1899, p. 51.

70. "Plan for Constitution of the Athletic Association of the University of Chicago [1896]"; A. A. Stagg to Harper, June 10, 1896, with inclosure.

71. *Record,* VI, No. 40 (Jan., 1902), 311.

72. A. A. Stagg, *Touchdown* (New York: Longmans, Green, & Co., 1927), *passim.*

73. E. E. Slosson, *Great American Universities* (New York: MacMillan Company, 1910), pp. 407–8.

74. Harper, PR, 1892–1902, p. cxii.

75. Clarence R. Williams to his family, June 17, 1901 (letters from the University of Chicago during the scholastic year 1900–1901 to the Folks at Home, written by Clarence R. Williams; copy in possession of the author).

76. See William R. Harper, "Fellowship and Its Obligation—Service," *Religion and the Higher Life* (Chicago: University of Chicago Press, 1904), pp. 36–56.

77. *Ibid.,* pp. 43–44.

78. *Ibid.,* pp. 47–49.

79. *Ibid.,* p. 50.

80. *Ibid.,* p. 53.

81. Harper, PR, 1892–1902, p. cxxxiv; and Harper, "Religion and the Higher Life," *Religion and the Higher Life,* p. 9.

82. *Ibid.,* p. 7.

83. *Ibid.,* pp. 13–18.

84. Charles R. Henderson to Harper, June 23, 1892.

85. Harper, PR, 1892–1902, p. cxxxv.

86. Harper, *Religion and the Higher Life,* pp. vii–viii.

87. Gates to Mrs. John D. Rockefeller, Dec. 22, 1892.

88. Laughlin to Gates, Dec. 18, 1892.

89. C. Howard Hopkins, *History of the Y.M.C.A. in North America* (New York: Association Press, 1951), pp. 179–80. See also "The Organization of Religious Work in the University in the Year of 1892–93" (UCA).

90. John W. Mott to Harper, Oct. 4, 1892.

91. Goodspeed to Gates, Dec. 19, 1892.

92. *Register*, 1893–1894, p. 300.

93. Charles R. Henderson, "The Religious Work of the University," PR, 1892–1902, p. 371.

94. "Constitution of the Christian Union," PR, 1892–1902, pp. 374–75.

95. Goodspeed to Gates, Dec. 19, 1892.

96. MBT, April 30, 1901.

97. Nathaniel Butler, "The Religious Agencies of the University," PR, 1904–1905, p. 99.

98. *Ibid.*

99. Charles R. Henderson, "The Religious Work of the University," PR, 1902–1904, p. 189.

100. Charles R. Henderson, "The University Settlement," PR, 1897–1898, pp. 208–16.

101. Rho F. Zueblin, "The University of Chicago Settlement League," PR, 1897–1898, pp. 217–19.

102. Harper, red memorandum book, May 30, 1893.

103. Harper, "Quarterly Statement," *Record*, IV, No. 27 (Oct. 6, 1899), 153.

104. *Register*, 1893–1894, p. 302.

105. Howard E. Wilson, *Mary McDowell, Neighbor* (Chicago: University of Chicago Press, 1928), *passim*.

106. Burton to Harper, June 4, 1898; C. R. Barnes to Harper, Feb. 21, 1901.

107. Henderson, PR, 1892–1902, p. 373.

108. *Weekly*, IX, No. 16 (Jan. 31, 1901), 792.

109. Harper, "Our Intellectual Difficulties," *Religion and the Higher Life*, pp. 103–7.

PART IV: THE GREATER CONSTITUENCY

WHEREVER MANKIND IS

(pp. 193–95)

1. Harper, "The University and Democracy," *The Trend in Higher Education*, p. 13.

2. *Ibid.*, pp. 16–20.

3. *Ibid.*, pp. 23–28.

4. *Ibid.*, pp. 28–32.

5. Harper to Andrew McLeish, April 7, 1896.

CHAPTER XI

THE MISSION OF THE UNIVERSITY

(pp. 196–209)

1. Report of remarks by Edmund J. James, *Record*, I, No. 29 (Oct. 16, 1896), 395.

2. *Record*, VIII, No. 4 (Aug., 1903), 61.

3. *Register*, 1896–1897, p. 80.

4. Harper, "Quarterly Statement," *Record*, II, No. 2 (April 10, 1897), 15–16.

5. Harper, "Quarterly Statement," *Record*, I, No. 1 (April 3, 1896), 6.

6. "The University Extension Division," *Official Bulletin, No. 6* (May, 1892), p. 2.

7. *Register*, 1896–1897, pp. 79–80.

8. *Official Bulletin, No. 6*, p. 2.

9. Timothy Farrar, *Report of the Case of the Trustees of Dartmouth College against William Woodward* (Boston: John W. Foster, West, Richardson, and Lord, 1819), p. 269.

10. Edmund J. James, "The University Extension Division," PR, 1897–1898, p. 156.

11. Richard G. Moulton, quoted in Goodspeed, *History*, p. 210.

12. *Official Bulletin, No. 1*, p. 8.

13. *Official Bulletin, No. 6*, pp. 3–22.

14. *Ibid.*, pp. 2, 5.

15. "University Extension Edition No. 3 (Abridged)," (Dec., 1892), *Calendar*, I (1892–1893), 28.

16. *Official Bulletin, No. 1*, p. 8.

17. *Ibid.*, pp. 13–14.

18. "University Extension Edition No. 4," (May, 1893), *Calendar*, I (1892–1893), 3.

19. Statement re University Extension attached to letter from Nathaniel Butler to Harper, May 16, 1893.

20. Edmund J. James, "The University of Chicago College for Teachers," *Record*, III, No. 31 (Oct. 28, 1898), 189.

21. Betty F. Heycke, "A History of the Origins of Adult Education at the University of Chicago and of Sixty-two Years at the Down-

town Center," pp. 45–48 (unpublished memorandum [1959], in the possession of the author).

22. Harper, PR, 1892–1902, p. lxvi.

23. George R. Henderson, "The Univeristy Extension Division of the University of Chicago," *The University Extension World*, I, No. 2 (Feb., 1893), 28.

24. Harper, PR, 1892–1902, pp. lxv–lxvi.

25. Harper to T. P. Kiser, Dec. 3, 1901.

26. Addison W. Moore, "Philosophy by Correspondence," *Record*, VIII, No. 4 (Aug., 1903), 96.

27. Edmund J. James, "The University Extension Division," PR, 1898–1899, p. 105.

28. *Record*, VIII, No. 3 (July, 1903), 43.

29. Harper, PR, 1892–1902, pp. lxiv–lxv.

30. Hervey F. Mallory to Harper, Nov. 22, 1904; Harper to Hervey F. Mallory, Nov. 29, 1904.

31. *Official Bulletin, No. 6*, pp. 6–7.

32. "University Extension Edition No. 4," *Calendar*, I (1892–1893), 3.

33. Walter A. Payne, "The University Extension Division: The Lecture-Study Department," PR, 1892–1902, pp. 304–5, 309.

34. Harper, "Quarterly Statement," *Record*, VII, No. 5 (Sept., 1902), 179.

35. Minutes of the Board of University Extension, Jan. 7, 1905.

36. Richard G. Moulton, "Talks with Lecturers," *The University Extension World*, I, No. 6 (June, 1893), 111.

37. Payne, PR, 1892–1902, p. 310.

38. Edwin E. Sparks to Harper, March 16, 1896.

39. John Manly to Harper, Jan. 8, 1902.

40. Paul Shorey to Harper, n.d.

41. W. H. Mace to Harper, May 9, 1893.

42. Judson to Harper, n.d. Italics his.

43. Harper, PR, 1892–1902, pp. lxv–lxvi.

44. Harper, "Quarterly Statement," *Calendar*, III, No. 1 (May, 1894), 16.

45. *Official Bulletin, No. 1*, p. 7.

46. D. C. Heath to Harper, May 23, 1893.

47. "Memorandum of agreement between Dr. W. R. Harper and C. A. Piddock for the Management of the Student Publishing Company," n.d.; "Memorandum of agreement between University of Chicago & C. A. Piddock," n.d. [both before July 1, 1892].

48. Laughlin to Board of Trustees, Jan. 25, 1895 (SBC, Box III, Folder 1).

49. Newman Miller, "The University Press," PR, 1892–1902, p. 299.

50. Harper, "Quarterly Statement," *Record*, IX, No. 6 (Oct., 1904), 208 ff.

51. Miller, PR, 1892–1902, pp. 299–301.

52. Harper, PR, 1892–1902, p. lxvi.

53. *Ibid.*, p. lxiii.

CHAPTER XII

THE PRESENCE OF THE UNIVERSITY

(pp. 210–38)

1. *Life*, XLI (Feb. 26, 1903), 182.

2. Harper, "Quarterly Statement," *Record*, I, No. 16 (July 17, 1896), 258.

3. Diary of a visit to the World Columbian Exposition, by an unidentified visitor (in the possession of the author).

4. R. M. Dudley to Harper, June 22, 1891.

5. Harper to Hutchinson, Jan. 30, 1892.

6. Harper, "Quarterly Statement," *Calendar*, IV, No. 3 (Feb., 1896), 17.

7. *Register*, 1892–1893, pp. 221–25.

8. *Official Bulletin, No. 3* (June, 1891), pp. 5–6.

9. "Articles of Affiliation," a form bound into the volume containing the minutes of the Board of Affiliations.

10. Harper, *Calendar*, IV, No. 3, 17.

11. Draft of a letter, Small to J. C. Colgate, n.d.

12. *Ibid.*

13. Harper, quoted in the *Chicago Tribune*, July 16, 1893, p. 12.

14. Harper, *Calendar*, IV, No. 3, 16–17.

15. Harper, "Quarterly Statement," *Calendar*, II, No. 1 (May, 1893), 12.

16. "Higher Education," *Report of the Commissioner of Education for the Year 1890–1891*, II (Washington: Government Printing Office, 1894), 1398–1421.

17. Charles W. Eliot, "Undesirable and Desirable Uniformity in Schools," *Education Reform Essays and Addresses* (New York: Century Company, 1909), pp. 273–300. The address

was made before the National Education Association, July 12, 1892.

18. Robert Herrick, "The University of Chicago," *Scribner's Magazine,* XVIII, No. 4 (Oct., 1895), 404.

19. Harper, "Quarterly Statement," *Calendar,* II, No. 1, 12.

20. Draft of a letter, Small to J. C. Colgate, n.d.

21. L. Brent Vaughn, "Alumni Clubs," *Record,* V, No. 20 (Aug. 17, 1900), 191.

22. *Chicago Tribune,* Dec. 7, 1899, p. 12.

23. Harper, PR, 1892–1902, p. lxvi.

24. Draft of a letter, Small to J. C. Colgate, n.d.

25. H. L. Stetson to Harper, Dec. 7, 1891.

26. J. C. Sharpe to Harper, March 23, 1892.

27. H. L. Stetson to Harper, Dec. 7, 1891.

28. Herrick, *Scribner's Magazine,* XVIII, No. 4, 404.

29. Gates to Harper, May 8, 1894.

30. Draft of a letter, Small to J. C. Colgate, n.d.

31. Harper, PR, 1898–1899, p. xxi.

32. Capps, PR, 1897–1898, p. 77.

33. Harper, PR, 1892–1902, p. lxvi–lxvii.

34. *Record,* IV, No. 36 (Dec. 8, 1899), 213.

35. Albion W. Small, "The Department of Affiliations," PR, 1897–1898, p. 195.

36. Unsigned letter to P. B. Mayfield, May 24, 1900.

37. Vincent, PR, 1892–1902, pp. 108–9.

38. "The Educational Conferences of the High Schools and Academies," *Record,* IV, No. 36, p. 213.

39. Clarke B. Williams, "How can the Faculty of the University of Chicago be brought into direct touch with the Students of the High Schools and Academies Affiliating or Coöperating with the University?" *Record,* I, No. 38 (Dec. 18, 1896), 478.

40. *Register,* 1902–1903, p. 185.

41. Harper, PR, 1892–1902, p. lxvii.

42. Small, PR, 1904–1905, pp. 13–14.

43. *Ibid.,* p. 14.

44. [Harper] to Gates, June 24, 1895 (FTGCR).

45. [Harper?] to John F. Forbes, April 29, 1903.

46. Small to Harper, n.d.

47. Small to Harper, Feb. 13 [1901?].

48. Hale to Hutchinson, May 7, 1894.

49. Harper, PR, 1892–1902, p. lxvii.

50. *Weekly,* VI, No. 43 (Aug. 18, 1898), pp. 448–49.

51. Tufts, PR, 1892–1902, p. 68.

52. Harper, PR, 1892–1902, p. lxx.

53. Albion W. Small to [Francis W. Shepardson?], n.d.

54. Shailer Mathews to Harper, March 8, 1901.

55. Harper, "The Situation of the Small College," *The Trend in Higher Education,* p. 386.

56. Gates to Harper, May 13, 1892.

57. Harper, "Quarterly Statement," *Record,* II, No. 2 (April 10, 1897), 9.

58. Harper to D. J. Bailey, Sept. 25, 1897.

59. Harper to Marion Talbot, Jan. 15, 1901.

60. H. P. Chandler to Harper, Sept. 15, 1905.

61. Laicus to Harper, July 23, 1901.

62. *Ibid.*

63. [*New York Sun*], Aug. 15, 1901; Oscar Triggs to Harper, Aug. 21, 1901.

64. Harper, PR, 1892–1902, p. xxxii.

65. *Record,* V, No. 20 (Aug. 17, 1900), 200.

66. Gates to Harper, May 13, 1892.

67. Burton to Harper, July 23, 1891.

68. Howard B. Grose, quoted in *Chicago Tribune,* Dec. 4, 1897, p. 5.

69. Hugo Munsterberg, *The Americans,* Edwin B. Holt (tr.) (New York: McClure, Phillips & Co., 1904), pp. 420–21.

70. Gates to Harper, May 13, 1892.

71. "Observations in regard to the proposed plan of official reports and publications" (ink "copy"), n.d., signed by Hermann E. von Holst (HEvH, Box 13).

72. *Ibid.*

73. Harper, PR, 1892–1902, p. xxviii.

74. Harper, "Quarterly Statement," *Record,* I, No. 14 (July 3, 1896), 228.

75. Harper, PR, 1898–1899, pp. xviii–xix.

76. Harper, "Quarterly Statement," *Calendar,* III, No. 1 (May, 1894), 18.

77. [Harper] to Judson [May 11?], 1898; Harper to Judson, Feb. 27, 1904.

78. Harper, PR, 1892–1902, p. xxvii.

79. *Nation,* LXXVIII, No. 2014 (Feb. 4, 1904), 85.

80. Harper, PR, 1892–1902, pp. xi–xii.

81. *Ibid., passim,* cxliii.

82. *Record,* VI, No. 3 (June 28, 1901), 98.

83. *Ibid.,* pp. 82–91.

84. *Ibid.,* p. 114.

85. "Seen on the Campus," *Inter-Ocean* (Chicago), April 21, 1895.

86. Herrick, *Scribner's Magazine,* XVIII, No. 4, pp. 397–417.

PART V: DEMAND AND SUPPLY

TOO FAR OR NOT FAR ENOUGH

(pp. 241–43)

1. Harper, "Certainty and Uncertainty," *Religion and the Higher Life,* p. 91.

2. Harper, Statement to the Board of Trustees, n.d.

3. Edgar Goodspeed to Burton, n.d. (EDB, II, Box 8, Folder 7); Small to Harper, April 25, 1895; Laughlin to Robert Herrick, March 24, 1896 (RH, Box 22); W. D. McClintock to Harper, Oct. 14, 1899.

4. Harper, Statement to the Board of Trustees, n.d.

5. Hale to Harper, n.d.

6. Small to Harper, Dec. 11, 1900, with an indorsement by Judson.

7. Charles O. Whitman to Harper, April 9, 1895.

8. Charles O. Whitman to Harper, Sept. 4, 1899.

9. Henry H. Donaldson to Harper, Jan. 4, 1895.

10. Harper to Ryerson, Feb. 16, 1901.

CHAPTER XIII

TRIAL BALANCE

(pp. 244–57)

1. *The Graphic* (Chicago), VIII (Feb. 4, 1893), 76.

2. Harper to George C. Walker, March 4, 1893 (Walker Scrapbook).

3. Ryerson to the Board of Trustees, [probably late] Jan., 1893, quoted in Goodspeed, *History,* p. 271; MBT, Oct. 31, 1893.

4. Harper to George C. Walker, March 4, 1893 (Walker Scrapbook).

5. Harper to Gates, April 11, 21, and 27, 1893; Gates to Harper, April 22, 1893.

6. Harper to Gates, April 11, 1893 (AORFA).

7. Gates to Harper, April 17, 1893.

8. Gates to Harper, April 22, 1893.

9. Telegram, Harper to Gates, April 20, 1893 (AORFA).

10. Gates to Harper, April 21, 1893.

11. Telegram, Harper to Gates, April 21, 1893 (AORFA).

12. Harper to Gates, April 21, 1893.

13. Gates to Harper, April 22, 1893.

14. MBT, May 9, 1893.

15. Harper to Rockefeller, May 13, 1893 (AORFA).

16. See Gates to Harper, June 16, 1893, referring to a Rockefeller pledge of May 18, 1893.

17. Harper to Gates, May 22, 1893 (AORFA).

18. *Ibid.*

19. Gates to Harper, May 24, 1893.

20. Gates to Harper, June 16, 1893.

21. Charles H. Kilborn to Harper, March 25, 1893.

22. Goodspeed to S. Calvary & Co., Aug. 4, 1893 (SBL, A, p. 277).

23. Gates to Harper, Aug. 4, 1893.

24. Harper to Gates, Aug. 3, 1893 (AORFA).

25. Harper to Gates, Aug. 10, 1893 (AORFA).

26. Goodspeed to Harper, Aug. 20, 1893.

27. *New York Daily Tribune,* Aug. 21, 1893, p. 10.

28. Harper to Gates, Aug. 22, 1893 (AORFA).

29. Gates to Harper, Aug. 23, 1893.

30. Harper to Gates, Aug. 26, 1893 (AORFA); MBT, Aug. 29, 1893; Goodspeed, *History,* p. 272.

31. Rockefeller to the Trustees of the University of Chicago, Oct. 31, 1893.

32. [Harper] to Gates, Oct. 23, 1893 (FTGCR).

33. Harper to Gates, Nov. 17, 1893 (AORFA).

34. Rockefeller to the Board of Trustees, Dec. 26, 1893.

35. Goodspeed to Rockefeller, Dec. 30, 1893 (SBL, A, p. 316).

36. Goodspeed to Laughlin, Jan. 5, 1894 (SBL, A, p. 327).

37. Goodspeed to C. B. Williams, Jan. 19, 1894 (SBL, A, p. 369).
38. Goodspeed to Mrs. Zella A. Dixson, Feb. 15, 1894 (SBL, A, p. 381).
39. Goodspeed to I. A. Hourwich, April 25, 1894 (SBL, A, p. 568).
40. MBT, April 12, 1894.
41. MBT, May 8, 1894.
42. *Register,* 1893–1894, p. 28.
43. Goodspeed to George N. Carman, Nov. 10, 1894 (SBL, A, pp. 795 ff.).
44. Goodspeed to Gates, Jan. 8, 1894 (SBL, A, p. 361).
45. Hutchinson to Harper, Dec. 27, 1893.
46. Harper, "Quarterly Statement," *Calendar,* III, No. 2 (Aug., 1894), 19–20.
47. Harper to George C. Walker, July 6, 1894 (Walker Scrapbook).
48. Rockefeller to the Board of Trustees, Dec. 24, 1894.
49. MBT, Dec. 28, 1894.
50. [Harper] to Gates, Dec. 18, 1894 (FTGCR).
51. Harper to Rockefeller, Dec. 18, 1894, inclosed with Harper to Gates, Dec. 18, 1894 (AORFA).
52. *Ibid.*
53. Rockefeller to the Board of Trustees, Oct. 30, 1895 (AORFA).
54. MBT, Nov. 5, 1895.
55. Robert Herrick to Robert M. Lovett, Dec. 28, 1895 (RH, Box 26).
56. Harper to Gates, Dec. 11, 1895.
57. Harper, "Quarterly Statement," *Calendar,* IV, No. 3 (Feb., 1896), 21.

CHAPTER XIV

New York and Chicago

(pp. 258–80)

1. Harper to Gates, Dec. 5, 1896 (FTGCR).
2. Harper to Gates, Dec. 24, 1896 (FTGCR).
3. Harper to Gates, Dec. 5, 1896 (FTGCR).
4. Harper to Gates, Feb. 6, 1897 (FTGCR).
5. Harper to Rockefeller, Nov. 12, 1895.
6. Rockefeller to Harper, Nov. 19, 1895.
7. Goodspeed to Rockefeller, Dec. 10, 1895 (SBL, B, p. 363).

8. *Ibid.*
9. Goodspeed to F. E. Hinckley, July 15, 1896 (SBL, B, p. 705).
10. Gates to Harper, Nov. 5, 9, and 16, 1896.
11. Goodspeed to Zella Dixson, Nov. 19, 1896 (SBL, B, p. 839).
12. Gates to Harper, Nov. 5, 1896.
13. Harper to Gates, Dec. 24, 1896 (FTGCR).
14. Gates to Harper, Nov. 5, 1896.
15. Rockefeller, Jr., to Harper, March 8, 1899.
16. Gates to Harper, July 18, 1899.
17. Gates to Harper, June 16, 1903.
18. Harper to Judson, Nov. 12, 1896.
19. Judson to Harper, Nov. 12, 1896.
20. "Report of Conference between Messrs. F. T. Gates, T. W. Goodspeed, and H. A. Rust, with reference to The University of Chicago, February 10, 1897," pp. 4–5 (UCA).
21. *Ibid.,* pp. 6–7.
22. *Ibid.,* p. 7.
23. *Ibid.*
24. *Ibid.,* p. 8.
25. *Ibid.,* pp. 10–11.
26. *Ibid.,* p. 11.
27. *Ibid.,* pp. 11–12.
28. *Ibid.,* pp. 12–14.
29. *Ibid.,* p. 15.
30. *Ibid.,* pp. 15–16.
31. *Ibid.,* p. 17.
32. *Ibid.*
33. *Ibid.,* p. 19.
34. *Ibid.,* p. 22.
35. *Ibid.,* pp. 31–32.
36. *Ibid.,* pp. 35–37.
37. Gates to Goodspeed, April 16, 1914.
38. "Report of Conference between Messrs. F. T. Gates, T. W. Goodspeed, and H. A. Rust, with reference to The University of Chicago, February 10, 1897," p. 29 (UCA).
39. *Ibid.,* p. 30.
40. Harper to Ryerson, Feb. 20, 1897.
41. *Ibid.*
42. Ryerson to Harper, March 7, 1897.
43. Harper to Ryerson, Feb. 20, 1897.
44. Goodspeed to Gates, May 8, 1897 (SBL, E, pp. 13–15).
45. "Report of Conference between Messrs. F. T. Gates, T. W. Goodspeed, and H. A. Rust, with reference to The University of Chicago, February 10, 1897," p. 33 (UCA).
46. Goodspeed to Harper, April 20, 1897.

47. Harper to Ryerson, Feb. 20, 1897.

48. Untitled memorandum by Gates, Section I, pp. 3, 23, 25–26 (AORFA).

49. *Ibid.*, Section II, pp. 2–3.

50. *Ibid.*, Section II, pp. 9–10.

51. *Ibid.*, Section II, pp. 10–11.

52. Gates to Harper, Sept. 25, 1897.

53. Goodspeed to G. A. Pillsbury, Oct. 9, 1897 (SBL, C, p. 218).

54. "Notes on the Conversation with Dr. Harper with Respect to the University Budget for the Year Beginning July 1st, 1898, December 11/13, 1897."

55. *Ibid.*

56. *Ibid.*

57. "Report of Interview between Rev. T. W. Goodspeed, representing the University of Chicago, and Mr. J. D. Rockefeller, Jr. and Mr. F. T. Gates, February 11, 1898" (AORFA).

58. *Ibid.*, p. 5.

59. *Ibid.*

60. *Ibid.*, p. 4.

61. *Ibid.*, p. 12.

62. *Ibid.*, p. 13.

63. Goodspeed to Gates, Feb. 21, 1898 (FTGCR).

64. "Conversation between President W. R. Harper, Mr. Martin Ryerson, Maj. H. A. Rust, Mr. J. D. Rockefeller, Jr. and Mr. F. T. Gates on the Budget of the University of Chicago for 1899–1900 and Collateral Questions, December 5, 1898," pp. 19–20, 24–28.

65. *Ibid.*, p. 22.

66. *Ibid.*, pp. 28–29.

67. Goodspeed to Gates, May 23, 1898 (SBL, C, pp. 397–98).

68. "Conversation between President W. R. Harper, Mr. Martin Ryerson, Maj. H. A. Rust, Mr. J. D. Rockefeller, Jr. and Mr. F. T. Gates on the Budget of the University of Chicago for 1899–1900 and Collateral Questions, December 5, 1898," pp. 31–33.

69. Harper to Gates, Oct. 6, 1899 (AORFA).

70. *Ibid.*

71. Harper to Gates, Nov. 11, 1899 (AORFA).

72. Harper to George C. Walker, Nov. 18, 1899.

73. Ryerson to Gates, Dec. 22, 1899 (FTGCR).

74. Ryerson to Gates, Dec. 23, 1899 (FTGCR).

75. [Harper] to Members of the Board of Trustees, Dec. 25, 1899, inclosed in a letter from Harper to Gates, Dec. 25, 1899 (AORFA).

76. Telegrams, from Ryerson, Hutchinson, and Harper to Gates, Dec. 28, 1899, and from Gates to Ryerson, Dec. 28, 1899 (AORFA).

77. Telegram from Rockefeller, Jr., and Gates to Ryerson, Jan. 2, 1900.

78. Harper to Gates, March 14, 1900 (FTGCR).

79. Harper to George C. Walker, March 12, 1900.

80. Harper to Gates, March 14, 1900 (FTGCR).

81. Harper to Ryerson, March 14, 1900.

82. Harper to George C. Walker, March 12, 1900.

83. Harper to Gates, March 22, 1900 (AORFA).

84. Harper to Gates, March 28, 1900 (AORFA).

85. Gates to Harper, March 30, 1900 (AORFA).

86. Harper to Gates, March 31, 1900 (AORFA).

87. Gates to Harper, March 31, 1900 (AORFA).

88. Gates to Harper, April 2, 1900.

89. Goodspeed, *History,* pp. 282–83.

PART VI: THE UNIVERSITY ESTABLISHED

AFTER THE BEGINNING

(pp. 283–84)

1. Harper to Rockefeller, Jr., Dec. 18, 1902.

2. "Suggestions of expenditure necessary for rounding out the work of the University upon a satisfactory basis prepared at the request of Mr. John D. Rockefeller, Jr.," 1901 (AORFA).

3. Harper, PR, 1892–1902, p. cxliii.

4. *Ibid.*

5. General Balance Sheet, June 30, 1902, PR, 1892–1902, p. 471; "Suggestions of expenditure necessary for rounding out the work of the University upon a satisfactory basis prepared at the request of Mr. John D. Rockefeller, Jr.," 1901 (AORFA).

6. *Report of the Commissioner of Education for the Year 1900–1901,* II (Washington: Government Printing Office, 1902), 1688–91. According to the *Report,* Stanford was richer than the University of Chicago; but because of uncertainties in the financial history of Stanford at that time, a comparison of the resources of the two universities may have been misleading.

7. Harper, PR, 1892–1902, p. cxliii.

CHAPTER XV

TOWARD THE HIGHER TEACHING

(pp. 285–306)

1. Harper, PR, 1892–1902, p. cxliii.
2. *Ibid.*
3. Budget, Dec. 10, 1901.
4. Goodspeed to Gates, April 15, 1897 (SBL, B, p. 985).
5. Harper, PR, 1892–1902, p. cxliii.
6. Ryerson to Harper, March 4, 1901.
7. Harper to Rockefeller, Jr., Jan. 10, 1892.
8. *Ibid.*
9. Harper to Ryerson, Feb. 20, 1902.
10. [Harper] to J. Ogden Armour, Nov. 5, 1902.
11. J. Ogden Armour to Harper, Nov. 5, 1902.
12. Abram S. Hewitt to Harper, Nov. 19, 1902.
13. J. Ogden Armour to Harper, Nov. 25, 1902.
14. Harper, PR, 1892–1902, p. xviii.
15. Rockefeller, Jr., to Ryerson, July 10, 1903.
16. Trustees Committee on Rush Medical College to Rockefeller, Jr., and Gates, June 6, 1904, in MBT, June 6, 1904.
17. *Record,* VI, No. 17 (July 26, 1901), 153–55.
18. Lewellys Barker to Harper, Feb. 10, 1900.
19. Lewellys Barker to Harper, Aug. 10, 1901.
20. Lewellys F. Barker, "Medicine and the Universities," *Record,* VII, No. 3 (July, 1902), 86–94. Originally presented as an address to the Johns Hopkins University alumni.
21. Ryerson to Harper, March 2, 1898.
22. Rockefeller, Jr., and Gates to Ryerson, Sept. 26, 1902.
23. "Statement proposed by Committee on

Rush Medical College to be sent to New York" [late 1903], p. 2.
24. Harper to Frank Billings, July 7, 1903.
25. Rockefeller, Jr., to Ryerson, July 10, 1903.
26. Rockefeller, Jr., and Gates to Ryerson, Oct. 22, 1903.
27. [Harper], "Statement made October 5, 1903," in MBT, Oct. 5, 1903.
28. Rockefeller, Jr., and Gates to Ryerson, Oct. 22, 1903.
29. Trustees' Committee on Rush Medical College to Rockefeller, Jr., and Gates, June 6, 1904, Sections 4 and 9, in MBT, June 6, 1904.
30. Rockefeller, Jr., to Andrew McLeish, July 12, 1904, in MBT, July 19, 1904.
31. Hermann H. Kohlsaat to Harper, July 5, 1900.
32. Rockefeller, Jr., to Andrew McLeish, Feb. 20 and April 25, 1902.
33. *Weekly,* II, No. 35 (June 21, 1894), 9.
34. MS, March 1, 1902.
35. Harper, "Quarterly Statement," *Record,* VI, No. 51 (April, 1902), 390.
36. Ernst Freund to Harper, Dec. 3, 1901.
37. Galusha Anderson to Harper, Feb. 17, 1902.
38. Newspaper interview with Harper, quoted in *Weekly,* II, No. 4 (Oct. 26, 1893), 6.
39. Harper, "Quarterly Statement," March 18, 1902, *Record,* VI, No. 51, 389.
40. Ernst Freund, *Record,* IX, No. 2, 41.
41. Joseph H. Beale, Jr., to Harper, March 17, 1902.
42. Joseph H. Beale, Jr., "The Place of Professional Education in the Universities," *Record,* IX, No. 2, 46.
43. Joseph H. Beale, Jr., to Harper, April 2, 1902.
44. James Barr Ames to Harper, March 31, 1902 (UC Law School Archives).
45. Joseph H. Beale, Jr., to Harper, April 2, 1902.
46. Joseph H. Beale, Jr., to Ernst Freund, April 7, 1902 (UC Law School Archives).
47. Joseph H. Beale, Jr., to Harper, April 30, 1902 (UC Law School Archives).
48. *Register,* 1902–1903, pp. 18 ff. and 102.
49. *Ibid.,* p. 103; *Register,* 1903–1904, p. 104.
50. *Register,* 1901–1902, p. 98.
51. *Register,* 1902–1903, p. 103.
52. *Register,* 1893–1894, pp. 41–42. For a carefully documented account of John Dewey's ca-

reer at the University of Chicago see Robert L. McCaul, "Dewey and the University of Chicago," *School and Society,* XXLIX, No. 2189 (March 25, 1961), pp. 152–57; No. 2190 (April 8, 1961), pp. 179–83; and No. 2191 (April 22, 1961), pp. 202–6. See Lawrence H. Cremin, *The Transformation of the School* (New York: Alfred A. Knopf, 1961), pp. 135–42; and Arthur G. Wirth, "John Dewey's Design for American Education: An Analysis of Aspects of His Work at the University of Chicago, 1894–1904," *History of Education Quarterly,* IV, No. 2 (June, 1964), 83–105. See also Katherine Camp Mayhew and Anna Camp Edwards, *The Dewey School, the Laboratory School of the University of Chicago, 1896–1903* (New York: D. Appleton-Century Co., 1936), *passim.* The authors, who had been teachers in the school, wrote with first-hand knowledge but without critical examination of the records. For an account of the school by a teacher who served after Dewey's departure see Ida B. Depencier, *The History of the Laboratory Schools, University of Chicago, 1896–1957* (photo-reproduction of typescript, University of Chicago, 1960), pp. 1–57.

53. *Register,* 1894–1895, p. 49.

54. John Dewey, "Pedagogy as a University Discipline," Part I, *Record,* I, No. 25 (Sept. 18, 1896), 354.

55. John Dewey to the Board of Trustees, n.d. [1896 or before].

56. John Dewey, "The University School," *Record,* I, No. 32 (Nov. 6, 1896), 417.

57. John Dewey, "Pedagogy as a University Discipline," Part II, *Record,* I, No. 26 (Sept. 25, 1896), 363.

58. Harper, "Quarterly Statement," *Record,* IV, No. 27 (Oct. 6, 1899), 155.

59. John Dewey to the Board of Trustees, n.d. [1896 or before].

60. George S. Goodspeed to Burton, n.d. (EDB, Series II, Box 8, Folder 7).

61. See John Dewey, *The School and Society* (6th impression, Chicago: University of Chicago Press, 1907).

62. B. A. Hinsdale, "Educational Progress during the Year" [1899–1900], *Addresses and Proceedings of the National Education Association, 1900,* p. 236. An extract of this address is found on the back of a letter from Andrew Squire to B. A. Hinsdale, June 30, 1900.

63. MBT, May 12 and 19, June 11, and Aug. 11, 1896. The Minutes are unclear as to the actual amount of the appropriation.

64. McCaul, *School and Society,* XXLIX, No. 2189, 153.

65. John Dewey, "The University Elementary School," PR, 1898–1899, p. 198.

66. *Ibid.*

67. John Dewey to Harper, March 6, 1899; John Dewey to Harper, March 8, 1899, quoting Harper.

68. Harper to E. A. Turner, Aug. 15, 1899.

69. Dewey, PR, 1898–1899, pp. 197–98.

70. *Ibid.,* p. 197.

71. Harper, PR, 1898–1899, p. xiii.

72. McCaul, *School and Society,* XXLIX (March 25, 1961), 154.

73. Dewey, *The School and Society,* dedicatory page.

74. John Dewey to Harper, Sept. 16, 1901.

75. John Dewey to Harper, May 30, 1901.

76. Dewey, *The School and Society,* pp. 15–16.

77. *Register,* 1904–1905, pp. 121–27.

78. *Register,* 1901–1902, pp. 98–99, 115–17.

79. *Register,* 1904–1905, pp. 101–2.

80. *Ibid.,* p. 101.

81. *Register,* 1903–1904, p. 110.

82. *Ibid.,* p. 114.

83. *Register,* 1896–1897, pp. 52, 69.

84. *Register,* 1903–1904, pp. 114–15.

85. Albion W. Small, "The Next Steps in College Development," *Record,* VI, No. 3 (June 28, 1901), 35.

86. Tufts, PR, 1892–1902, pp. 87–88.

87. PR, 1892–1902, p. 81; 1902–1904, p. 82; 1904–1905, pp. 23–24; 1905–1906, p. 30.

88. PR, 1897–1898, p. 87.

89. Tufts, PR, 1892–1902, p. 86.

90. *Ibid.,* pp. 86–87.

91. *Official Bulletin, No. 1,* p. 16.

CHAPTER XVI

THE ACADEMIC WAY RE-EXAMINED

(pp. 307–31)

1. *Register,* 1904–1905, p. 75.

2. Harper to Judson, Nov. 18, 1901.

3. William James, "The Ph.D. Octopus," *Memories and Studies* (New York: Longmans,

Green, and Company, 1911), p. 334. Originally published in the *Harvard Magazine*, March, 1903.

4. Laurence R. Veysey, *The Emergence of the American University* (Chicago and London: University of Chicago Press, 1965), pp. 197–203.

5. Small, PR, 1904–1905, pp. 11–13; James, *Memories*, p. 344.

6. *Register*, 1904–1905, p. 173.

7. MC, Dec. 15, 1902.

8. MC, March 16, 1903.

9. Hale to Harper, April 13, 1905.

10. Vincent, PR, 1892–1902, p. 112.

11. *Ibid.*, p. 113.

12. MC, Oct. 2, 1897.

13. "Report of the Junior College Commission," filed with MJCF, Jan. 21, 1905.

14. *Ibid.*

15. George E. Vincent to Harper, Feb. 2, 1905.

16. Judson to Harper, March 11, 1905.

17. Harper to George E. Vincent, March 16, 1905.

18. *Ibid.*

19. *Ibid.*

20. George E. Vincent to Harper, March 22, 1905.

21. George E. Vincent to Harper, Feb. 2, 1905.

22. "Report of the Junior College Commission," filed with MJCF, Jan. 21, 1905.

23. MJCF, Feb. 4, 1905.

24. H. P. Chandler to Harper, March 18, 1905.

25. Minutes of the United Faculties, May 1, 1905.

26. *Ibid.*

27. Hale to Harper, May 11, 1905.

28. MS, May 17, 1905.

29. Report of the Millikan Committee, attached to MJCF, March 18, 1905.

30. *Register*, 1892–1893, p. 128; *Register*, 1905–1906, p. 60. The indicated majors of secondary school work in 1892–1893 are weighted according to the rules of 1904–1905.

31. Hale to Harper, April 13, 1905.

32. *Ibid.*, p. 4.

33. *Ibid.*

34. Report of Millikan Committee, attached to MJCF, March 18, 1905.

35. *Register*, 1905–1906, p. 60.

36. Hale to Harper, May 11, 1905.

37. Chamberlin to Harper, May 25, 1905.

38. James H. Tufts, "The Senior Colleges," PR, 1898–1899, p. 30.

39. Tufts, PR, 1892–1902, p. 78.

40. *Ibid.*, pp. 78–79.

41. Tufts, PR, 1898–1899, p. 30.

42. Marion Talbot, "Report of the Dean of Women," PR, 1892–1902, p. 138.

43. James W. Thompson, "The House System of the University," PR, 1892–1902, p. 387.

44. *Ibid.*, pp. 387, 393.

45. James M. Taylor to Burton, April 20, 1904 (EDB, Series II, Box 9, Folder 5).

46. *Harper's Weekly*, XLVIII, No. 2474 (May 21, 1904), 786.

47. George E. Vincent to Harper, Feb. 17, 1903.

48. Hutchinson to Harper [April 4, 1900].

49. W. H. Faunce to Burton, Dec. 31, 1901 (EDB, Series II, Box 8, Folder 16).

50. Burton to Harper, Oct. 16, 1902; Burton to President [James M.] Taylor, Feb. 12, 1903 (EDB, Series II, Box 9, Folder 1).

51. Harper, "The Situation of the Small College," *The Trend in Higher Education*, pp. 350–51.

52. Harper, "Quarterly Statement," *Record*, IX, No. 9 (Jan. 1905), 289.

53. Harper to the Board of Trustees, 1905, bound with MJCF, May 20, 1905.

54. Harper, "Quarterly Statement," *Record*, X, No. 1 (July, 1905), 15.

55. Vincent, PR, 1892–1902, p. 98; Judson, PR, 1892–1902, p. 11.

56. Information received from present administration of Muskingum College.

57. Marion Talbot to Harper, Nov. 15, 1900.

58. Edwin C. Whittemore, *Colby College, 1820–1925, An Account of Its Beginnings, Progress and Service* (Waterville: Trustees of Colby College, 1927), p. 119.

59. Harper, PR, 1892–1902, p. cxi.

60. Gates to Rockefeller, Aug. 25, 1902 (AORFA).

61. *Harper's Weekly*, XLVIII, No. 2474 (May 21, 1904), 786.

62. Statement by Harper, in MBT, June 8, 1905.

63. Harper, "Quarterly Statement," *Record*, X, No. 2 (Oct., 1905), 69.

64. Burton to Harper, Feb. 12, 1903 (EDB, Series II, Box 9, Folder 1); Harper "Quarterly Statement," *Record,* IX, No. 9 (Jan., 1905), 289; Harper to the Board of Trustees, n.d., in Minutes of Board excerpts made by Goodspeed (UCA).

65. Alexander Smith, "The Junior Colleges," PR, 1905–1906, p. 42.

66. *Ibid.*

67. *Harper's Weekly,* XLVIII, No. 2474 (May 21, 1904), 786.

68. "Recommendations Concerning the Reorganization of the University Extension Work of the University of Chicago, presented to Trustees Committee on University Extension, Aug. 11, 1903."

69. *Ibid.*

70. [Harper] to Gates, Aug. 13, 1903.

71. Burton to Edward Goodman, Aug. 14, 1903 (SBC, Box VI, Folder 4); [Burton] to Gates, Aug. 13, 1903.

72. Harper to Burton, Feb. 17, 1905.

73. G. L. Chamberlin, for Harper, to Ira M. Price, July 17, 1903.

74. Harper, "Quarterly Statement," *Record,* X, No. 1 (July, 1905), 14.

75. Charles O. Whitman to Harper, March 21, 1901; Board of Trustees of Marine Biological Laboratory to Harper, Aug. 13, 1901; Harper to E. G. Gardiner, Jan. 28, 1902; E. G. Gardiner to Harper, Feb. 3, 1902.

76. Elizabeth Wallace to Harper, June 15, 1901, and Harper to Elizabeth Wallace, Aug. 17, 1901. See also Elizabeth Wallace, *The Unending Journey* (Minneapolis: University of Minnesota Press, 1952), pp. 144–45.

77. Inclosure in a letter to Alleyne Ireland, April 19, 1901. The voluminous correspondence in regard to Ireland's appointment began in 1899 and continued into the Judson administration.

78. Alleyne Ireland, *The Province of Burma,* I (Boston: Houghlin Mifflin Co., 1907), i.

79. *Journal of Proceedings and Addresses of the First and Second Annual Conferences of the American Association of Universities* (1901), p. 11.

80. *Proceedings of the First Annual Meeting of the North Central Association of Colleges and Secondary Schools* (Chicago, 1896), pp. 7–8; Calvin O. Davis, *A History of the North Central Association of Colleges and Secondary*

Schools, 1895–1945 (Ann Arbor: North Central Association of Colleges and Secondary Schools, 1945), pp. 3–79.

81. *Proceedings of the Eleventh Annual Meeting of the North Central Association of Colleges and Secondary Schools* (Columbus, 1906), p. 96.

82. Harper, PR, 1892–1902, pp. lxx–lxxi.

83. "The Carnegie College Institution," n.d.

84. Gates, *American Heritage,* VI, No. 3, 82.

85. [Harper] to George E. Vincent, Feb. 13, 1905.

CHAPTER XVII

"Work Still To Do"

(pp. 332–68)

1. Albert Shaw to Harper, March 25, 1902.

2. James H. Tufts to Goodspeed, Feb. 28, 1902.

3. Harper to James H. Tufts, March 4, 1902.

4. Andrew McLeish to Rockefeller, Jr., May 14, 1904 (AORFA).

5. John Dewey to Harper, May 10, 1904.

6. James H. Breasted to Ira M. Price, March 11, 1901; Harper to Breasted, May 22, 1901; Breasted to Harper, July 28, 1901; Harper to Breasted, Aug. 20, 1901; Breasted to Rockefeller, Jr., May 20, 1903; Harper to Rockefeller, Jr., May 29, 1903; Rockefeller, Jr., to Ryerson, July 3, 1903; MBT, July 18, 1905. See also Ira M. Price, "The Oriental Exploration Fund of the University of Chicago," *Record,* VIII, No. 7 (Nov., 1903), 195–97; James H. Breasted, "The Oriental Institute," *The University of Chicago Survey,* XII (Chicago: University of Chicago Press, 1933), 1–33; and Charles Breasted, *Pioneer to the Past, The Story of James Henry Breasted, Archeologist* (New York: Charles Scribner's Sons, 1943), pp. 87–172.

7. Harper to Gates, Oct. 8, 1902 (FTGCR).

8. George C. Walker to the Board of Trustees, Dec. 1, 1902 (Walker Scrapbook).

9. MBT, March 31, 1903.

10. Minutes of the Board of Libraries, Laboratories, and Museums, Jan. 30, 1904.

11. Report presented to Museum Commission, Nov. 4, 1905.

12. Ryerson to Harper, Feb. 23, 1896; Robert

Herrick to Robert M. Lovett, Dec. 13, 1895 (RH, Box 26).

13. W. G. Hale, G. L. Hendrickson, and Joseph P. Iddings, "Report of the Committee upon the Reorganization of the Faculties," *Record,* VI, No. 40A, 321–23.

14. Harry P. Judson and Albion W. Small, "Reorganization of the Faculties, Minority Report," *Record,* VI, No. 40A, 323.

15. *Ibid.*, pp. 323–24.

16. Small to Harper, Jan. 24, 1902.

17. Laughlin to Hermann E. von Holst, March 22, 1902 (HEvH, Box XII).

18. *Ibid.*

19. Harper, PR, 1892–1902, pp. xliv–xlv.

20. "Memorandum on the Junior College," n.d.

21. John Dewey, "Academic Freedom," *Educational Review,* XXIII, No. 1 (Jan., 1902), 9–13.

22. MBT, May 19, 1903; Rockefeller, Jr., to Ryerson, June 9, 1903, in MBT, June 23, 1903; Rockefeller, Jr., to Ryerson, Dec. 11, 1903, in MBT, Dec. 15, 1903; Wallace Heckman, Financial Report, in MBT, April 19, 1904; and Wallace Heckman, Report, Aug. 14, 1904, in MBT, Oct. 4, 1904.

23. Gates to Ryerson, Nov. 4, 1903 (AORFA).

24. Ryerson to Gates, Nov. 10, 1903 (AORFA).

25. Rockefeller, Jr., to Gates, Nov. 2, 1903.

26. Gates to Harper, Nov. 25, 1903.

27. [Gates], "Memorandum of inquiries suggested to Mr. Murphy in connection with his study of the University of Chicago, New York, Nov. 17, 1903" (AORFA).

28. [Starr J. Murphy], "The University of Chicago," 1904, pp. 1–3 (AORFA).

29. *Ibid.*, p. 39.

30. Rockefeller, Jr., to Harper, Nov. 17, 1903.

31. "Memorandum on Conference held in New York, December 3rd, 1903, between Messrs. Harper, Ryerson, Baldwin and Heckman, representing the University of Chicago, and Mr. Gates and Mr. Rockefeller, Jr., representing Mr. John D. Rockefeller," in MBT, Dec. 15, 1903, pp. 381–82.

32. Rockefeller, Jr., to Ryerson, Dec. 21, 1903.

33. "Memorandum on Conference held in New York, December 3rd, 1903," in MBT, Dec. 15, 1903.

34. Rockefeller, Jr., to Ryerson, Dec. 11, 1903.

35. [Starr J. Murphy], "The University of Chicago," 1904, Section V: Finances.

36. Harper to Graham Taylor, Feb. 11, 1904.

37. Rockefeller, Jr., to Andrew McLeish, June 17, 1904.

38. Harper to Rockefeller, Jr., Dec. 15, 1903.

39. "Report of Conference between Messrs. F. T. Gates, T. W. Goodspeed, and H. A. Rust, with reference to The University of Chicago, February 10, 1897," p. 37 (UCA).

40. Harper to Rockefeller, Jr., May 20, 1904.

41. Harper, *Religion and the Higher Life,* p. viii.

42. Wallace Heckman, Financial Report, in MBT, April 19, 1904.

43. Harper to Andrew McLeish, May 2, 1904.

44. Wallace Heckman, Report, Aug. 14, 1904, in MBT, Oct. 4, 1904.

45. Harper to Gates, June 25, 1904 (FTGCR); Gates to Harper, June 25, 1904.

46. Gates to Harper, Oct. 14, 1904.

47. Gates to Rockefeller, Dec. 13, 1904.

48. *Ibid.*

49. George C. Walker to Harper, Dec. 15, 1904.

50. Copy of statement of Judson to Starr J. Murphy.

51. Goodspeed to Starr J. Murphy, Jan. 16, 1905 (SBL, F, pp. 325–30).

52. [Starr J. Murphy], Report submitted to the Trustees, Feb. 9, 1905, p. 5.

53. *Ibid.*, p. 13.

54. *Ibid.*, p. 24.

55. *Ibid.*, p. 26.

56. *Ibid.*, p. 31.

57. Goodspeed to Harper, March 29, 1905 (SBL, F, p. 468).

58. *Ibid.*

59. Goodspeed to Harper, March 28, 1905.

60. *Ibid.*

61. Remarks of Mr. McV[eagh], "Memorandum on substance of remarks of Mr. McV[eagh], Mr. Walker and Mr. B[artlett?] in regard to Murphy Report of 1905."

62. *Ibid.*, Remarks of Mr. B[artlett?].

63. "Memorandum on substance of remarks of Mr. McV[eagh], Mr. Walker, and Mr. B[artlett?]."

64. Gates to Rockefeller, Jr., March 7, 1905 (AORFA).

65. Harper to Gates, Feb. 3, 1905 (FTGCR).

66. Rockefeller to Harper, Feb. 16, 1905.

67. Robert Herrick, *Chimes* (New York: Macmillan Company, 1926), p. 15.

68. From conversations with members of the Faculty of the University of Chicago Medical School.

69. Thomas C. Chamberlin *et al.*, "To the Trustees of the University of Chicago, Concerning President Harper's Illness," April 18, 1905 (TCC, Box 3); MBT, April 18 and 25, 1905.

70. "Memoirs of Frank Billings," p. 30 (copy of manuscript in possession of the author).

71. Harper to Rockefeller, Jr., Feb. 21, 1905.

72. *Ibid.*

73. Harper to Gates, April 22, 1905 (FTGCR).

74. Gates to Harper, March 30, 1905.

75. Gates to Wallace Heckman, May 22, 1905.

76. Gates to Rockefeller, Oct. 23, 1905 (AORFA).

77. Harper to Rockefeller, Jr., Feb. 21, 1905.

78. [Harper] to Hutchinson, June 14 [15?], 1905; [Harper] to D. G. Hamilton, June 27, 1905.

79. Harper to Rockefeller, July 31, 1905; Harper to Gates, Aug. 19, 1905 (FTGCR).

80. Harper to Gates, Oct. 5, 1905 (FTGCR).

81. Goodspeed to Harper, March 28, 1905.

82. Harper, "Convocation Address," June 18, 1901, *Record*, VI, No. 13, 118.

83. Harper to Gates, Aug. 19, 1905 (FTGCR).

84. Harper to Gates, Oct. 17, 1905 (AORFA); Harper to Ryerson, Oct. 31, 1905.

85. Harry P. Judson, "The President's Report," PR, 1906–1907, pp. 12, 132.

86. William Vaughn Moody to Robert Herrick, May 22, 1895 (RH, Box 22).

87. Robert Herrick to Robert M. Lovett, Oct. 11, 1905 (RH, Box 27).

88. Joseph H. Beale, Jr., "Memorial Address at Harvard University," *Record*, X, Memorial Number (March, 1906), 19.

89. Nicholas M. Butler, "Memorial Addresses at Columbia University," *Record*, X, 20.

90. William H. P. Faunce, "Appreciations," *Biblical World*, XXVII, No. 3 (March, 1906), 229.

91. Shailer Mathews, "William Rainey Harper: An Appreciation," *Record*, X, 70.

92. Albion W. Small, "[Harper] As University President," *The Biblical World*, XXVII, (March, 1906), 216–17.

93. "By the University Senate representing the Faculties," *Record*, X, 15.

94. Albion W. Small, "William Rainey Harper, The Man," *Record*, X, 63–64.

95. Memoranda of Conversations with President Harper in December, 1905, by Ernest D. Burton.

96. See Board of Trustees' resolution after Harper's death, in *Record*, X, 13–14.

97. Herrick, *Chimes*, p. 268.

AFTER HARPER

(pp. 369–70)

1. Judson to Harper, Nov. 15, 1891.

2. Judson, PR, 1906–1907, p. 3; Judson, PR, 1909–1910, p. 3.

3. Rockefeller to the President and Trustees of the University of Chicago, Dec. 13, 1910, quoted in Thomas W. Goodspeed, *The Story of the University of Chicago, 1890–1925* (Chicago: University of Chicago Press, 1925), pp. 179–81.

4. Judson, PR, 1917–1919, p. 13.

5. Judson, PR, 1920–1921, p. 6.

Bibliographical Notes

On the Historical Sources

The founding of the University of Chicago and the administration of William Rainey Harper generated a mythology. The bare fact of its existence is not striking because every college and university has its folklore: in many academic institutions, however forward-looking they may be, the legend of a golden age is kept alive. Yet the beginnings of the University of Chicago may well be extraordinary as a source of myth. The circumstances of its founding, the names of the persons associated with it, and its ambitious plan were bound to attract attention and fire the imagination of observers; and the excitement of life within the Quadrangles provided the members of the University with innumerable highly charged experiences to recall in later years. The whole mass of reports and reminiscences about the University, samples of which appear in my text and are cited in the notes, constitutes a reservoir of impressions in regard to the motives of persons and the nature of events important to the life of the University. The historian is not at a loss to find possible explanations of its early history. The primary problem here has been to set possibilities against the evidence contained in the documents and other materials that survive from the period before Harper's death. Such evidence is the principal source of this book.

The papers drawn upon are to be found in large part in two archives, that of the office of the Rockefeller family and its associates and the University of Chicago Archives. The documents in the latter collection are distributed between the files transferred from the Office of the President of the University, including the bulk of the correspondence of William Rainey Harper, and several specialized collections of papers, most notably those of particular professors and those associated with the work of Thomas W. Goodspeed and Frederick T. Gates. The older minute books of the several Faculties and Faculty boards are also located in the University Archives. A number of scrapbooks and Harper's memorandum books are also there, together with several collections of photographs. The minute books of the Board of Trustees and its committees, as well as official copies of letters written by Goodspeed as Secretary of the Board, are in the Office of the President of the University.

The printed matter issued by the University is voluminous, partly because the diffusion of information about its work was an extension of its educational program. The official printed matter drawn upon in this book consists largely of the *Official Bulletin,* published *seriatim,* in 1891 and 1892, before the University opened; the *Quarterly Calendar,* issued between 1892 and 1896; the *University Record,* which superseded the *Quarterly Calendar* as a gazette (containing, with much else, President Harper's quarterly statements on the condition of the University) and was issued from 1896 to 1933; the *Annual Register,* or catalogue, published annually after 1893; the *General Register of the Officers and Alumni, 1892–1902;* and the *President's Report,* with the subsidiary reports of deans and other officers, which began publication with the report for the year 1897–98 and lapsed for the years 1899–1900 and 1900–1901. The *President's Report* for the next year reviews a whole decade. The student publications are the *University Weekly,* which began publication when the University opened; the student newspaper, the *Maroon,* which appeared as a daily regularly after October 1, 1902; and the yearbook, *Cap and Gown,* first issued in 1895.

Off campus, the Baptist denominational newspaper, the *Standard,* devoted much space to the events that led up to the founding; and the *Chicago Tribune* offered a running account of events at the University. As President Harper's protest suggests, sensational and unreliable reporting by the press was the plague of the University; but much of the comment upon the University, especially in the serious magazines, is highly perceptive and offers an astringent for Harper's sometimes bland exercises in presidential rhetoric. Neither the magazines nor the newspapers paid much attention to the darker, anxious side of Harper's life; perhaps only James Keeley of the *Chicago Tribune* had intimate knowledge of Harper's distaste for his reputation as a fund-raiser. The responsible periodical writing on the University is often very illuminating in regard to the University as an institution, but it throws little of its light upon a part of Harper's mind hinted at in some of his less formal talks and unmistakably revealed in his letters and the records of private conversation.

Formal writing of the early history of the University began in the period itself with the preparation of "An Historical Sketch," written by Francis W. Shepardson, a member of the Department of History, and published in 1899 with the *President's Report* for 1897–98. Just fifty years ago, in 1916, Thomas W. Goodspeed wrote a full-scale history of the University. *A History of the University of Chicago* (Chicago: University of Chicago Press, 1916) bears the subtitle *The First Quarter-Century* but is concerned very largely with the founding of the University and with the events of the Harper administration. Goodspeed did not altogether neglect the academic life of the University, but he dwelt, not surprisingly, on matters of which he had personal knowledge as a fund-raiser and Secretary of the Board of Trustees. Goodspeed was not simply a chronicler, but when he wrote for publication he drew back from full discussion of critical issues of finance on which he had strong opinions, as indicated in his unpublished "Reminiscences of Thomas Wakefield Goodspeed" in the Archives. Thomas W. Goodspeed also wrote *The University of Chicago Biographical Sketches* (Vol. I, 1922; Vol. II, 1925); *The Story of the University of Chicago* (1925); *Ernest DeWitt Burton: A Biographical Sketch* (1926); and *William Rainey Harper* (1928), all published by the University of Chicago Press. The *Story* offers a condensed account of the early history already covered by the *History,* but the other books contain much material not found there. The two volumes of *Biographical Sketches* deal with the lives of donors and do not constitute a compendium of University biography as the title suggests.

Like Goodspeed, Frederick T. Gates was seriously interested in the history of the University and added editorial notes to the copies of documents, still unpublished as a whole, which were collected while Goodspeed was at work. Gates also wrote Goodspeed long letters (now in the University Archives), making invaluable comments on Goodspeed's several writings and their subjects. Here is a critical discussion of the history by one of its makers. Gates himself wrote an account of the events which led up to John D. Rockefeller's first pledge to the University, which appears in print as the Introduction to Good-speed's *History,* as well as memoirs which deal in part with the University. The relevant segment of these memoirs was published in "The Memoirs of Frederick T. Gates," *American Heritage,* VI, No. 3 (April, 1955), 71–76.

Goodspeed did not seek to set the history of the University of Chicago into context. Of the writings that do, several are especially relevant here. In *John D. Rockefeller, the Heroic Age of American Enterprise* (2 vols.; New York: Charles Scribner's Sons, 1940) and *Study in Power, John D. Rockefeller, Industrialist and Philanthropist* (2 vols.; New York: Charles Scribner's Sons, 1953), Allan Nevins relates the early history of the University to the life of its Founder and in particular to his activity as a philanthropist. Nevins had no reason to examine the history of the University for its own sake or to dwell upon Harper's work except insofar as it was influenced by (or influenced) John D. Rockefeller.

In *The Emergence of the American University* (Chicago: University of Chicago Press, 1965), Laurence R. Veysey places the early University, as a university, in a pattern which is at once copiously documented and analytically presented. Merle Curti and Roderick Nash, in *Philanthropy in the Shaping of American Higher Education* (New Brunswick, N.J.: Rutgers University Press, 1965), discuss the University of Chicago in connection with academic philanthropy as a whole. About half of Joseph E. Gould, *The Chautauqua Movement: An Episode in the Continuing American Revolution* (State University of New York, 1961), is devoted to Harper's activity at Chautauqua and its relation to University Extension at the University of Chicago. The Bemis case has been examined in the widest possible American context in Richard Hofstadter and Walter P. Metzger, *The Development of Academic Freedom in the United States* (New York: Columbia University Press, 1955). In *The Transformation of the School, Progressivism in American Education, 1876–1957* (New York: Alfred A. Knopf, 1961), Lawrence A. Cremin places John Dewey's work at the University of Chicago in the history of progressive education. Robert McCaul carefully reviews Dewey's relation to the University in "Dewey and the University of Chicago," *School and Society,* XXXIX, No. 2189 (March 25, 1961), 152–57; No. 2190 (April 8, 1961), 179–83; and No. 2191 (April 22, 1961), 202–6. Russell Thomas refers to Harper's views on secondary and undergraduate education, in conjunction with those of other men of his generation, in *The Search for a Common Learning: General Edu-*

cation, 1800–1960 (New York: McGraw-Hill Book Company, Inc., 1962). The history of the undergraduate curriculum at the University is reviewed by Reuben Frodin in an essay entitled "Very Simple, But Thoroughgoing," published in *The Idea and Practice of General Education: An Account of the College of The University of Chicago by Present and Former Members of the Faculty* (Chicago: University of Chicago Press, 1950), pp. 25–99. In *Studies in Early Graduate Education* (Carnegie Foundation for the Advancement of Teaching, Bulletin No. 31, New York, 1939), W. Carson Ryan provides material for a comparison of the histories of graduate study at Johns Hopkins University, Clark University, and the University of Chicago. In Milton Mayer, *Young Man in a Hurry* (Chicago: University of Chicago Alumni Association, 1957), the historical setting of the University of Chicago is vivaciously if inaccurately characterized. Mayer's view of the relationship between John D. Rockefeller and William Rainey Harper differs markedly from my own.

Particular aspects of the University are examined in several specialized, unpublished PH.D. dissertations: Kooman Boycheff, "Intercollegiate Athletics and Physical Education at the University of Chicago, 1892–1952," University of Michigan, 1954; Lincoln C. Blake, "William Rainey Harper and the Beginnings of Scientific Education at the University of Chicago," University of Chicago, 1966; William James Haggerty, "The Purposes of the University of Chicago," University of Chicago, 1943; Julius Lewis, "Henry Ives Cobb and the Chicago School," University of Chicago, 1964; and Haynes McMullen, "The Administration of the University of Chicago Libraries, 1892–1928," University of Chicago, 1949. Two other unpublished studies have been useful: Betty F. Heycke, "A History of the Origins of Adult Education at the University of Chicago and of Sixty-two Years at the Downtown Center," and Roy H. Turner, "A History of the Business School of the University of Chicago." Ida B. De Pencier, *The History of The Laboratory Schools, The University of Chicago, 1896–1957* (Chicago, 1960), has been reproduced for distribution but has not been formally published.

In addition to those already mentioned, the biographical writings which have been especially useful are: Alfred Bornemann, *J. Laurence Laughlin, Chapters in the Career of an Economist* (Washington, D.C.: American Council on Public Affairs, 1940); Charles Breasted, *Pioneer to the Past, the Story of James Henry Breasted, Archaeologist* (New York: Charles Scribner's Sons,

1943); Raymond B. Fosdick, *John D. Rockefeller, Jr., a Portrait* (New York: Harper & Brothers, 1956); Charles Ten Broeke Goodspeed, *Thomas Wakefield Goodspeed* (Chicago: University of Chicago Press, 1932); W. Fiddian Moulton, *Richard Green Moulton, a Memoir* (New York: Macmillan Company, 1926); and Andrew D. Rodgers III, *John Merle Coulter, Missionary in Science* (Princeton, N.J.: Princeton University Press, 1944).

Among memoirs, the following should be noted: Lewellys F. Barker, *Time and the Physician: The Autobiography of Lewellys F. Barker* (New York: G. P. Putnam's Sons, 1942); Edgar J. Goodspeed, *As I Remember* (New York: Harper & Brothers, 1953); Harold L. Ickes, *The Autobiography of a Curmudgeon* (New York: Reynal & Hitchcock, 1943); Robert Morss Lovett, *All Our Years* (New York: Viking Press, 1948); Shailer Mathews, *New Faith for Old: An Autobiography* (New York: Macmillan Company, 1936); John D. Rockefeller, *Random Reminiscences of Men and Events* (New York: Doubleday, Page & Company, 1909); Amos A. Stagg, *Touchdown! As Told by Coach Amos Alonzo Stagg to Wesley Winans Green* (New York: Longmans, Green & Co., 1927); Marion Talbot, *More than Lore: Reminiscences of Marion Talbot, Dean of Women, The University of Chicago, 1892–1925* (Chicago: University of Chicago Press, 1936); and Elizabeth Wallace, *The Unending Journey* (Minneapolis: University of Minnesota Press, 1952).

To this list should be appended several books which are not memoirs in form but which are based upon personal memory of the early University and upon the strong personal feelings that its life generated: Will J. Cuppy, *Maroon Tales: University of Chicago Stories* (Chicago: Forbes & Co., 1910); Robert Herrick, *Chimes* (New York: Macmillan Company, 1926), a novel; James W. Linn, *This Was Life: A Novel* (Indianapolis: Bobbs-Merrill Co., 1936); and Thorstein Veblen, *The Higher Learning in America: A Memorandum on the Conduct of Universities by Business Men* (New York: B. W. Huebsch, 1918), in which Veblen explains a now classic view of the relation of businessmen to universities and of academic administrators to the life of disinterested inquiry. Does the book itself belong to the mythology of higher education? The documents in New York and Chicago are relevant to the answer.

Index

410